RACING &
Outlook

RACING GUIDE

2004

Statistics • Results
Previews • Training centre reports

Raceform

Contributors: Neil Clark, Chris Cook, Nick Deacon, Steffan Edwards, Tony Jakobsen, Kel Mansfield, Steve Mellish, Peter Naughton, Mark Nelson, Dave Nevison, Ben Osborne, Nicholas Watts, Richard Williams.

Grateful thanks also to Rodney Pettinga and Andy Scutts.

Designed and edited by Chris Cook

Published in 2004 by Outlook Press
Raceform, Compton, Newbury, Berkshire RG20 6NL
Outlook Press is an imprint of Raceform Ltd, a
wholly owned subsidiary of MGN Ltd

A catalogue record for this book is available from the
British Library.

ISBN 1-904317-50-2

Printed by Cox & Wyman, Reading

RACING & FOOTBALL
Outlook

Contents

Outlook

Editor's introduction

THE START of a new Flat season is an ideal time to reflect on what we hope to get out of it.

Let's go back to first principles. We are punters and we want to win – which is to say, we want to make a net profit in the long run.

Anyone can back a winner. But to end up ahead in the long term requires that your betting is generally smarter than most of your fellow punters can manage.

This is a fact that is often overlooked. Many racing writers will try to sell you the idea that you're betting against the bookies, "the old enemy". The bookies encourage this convenient fiction, which is given added weight by betting ring geography – the satchelmen ranged in rows, facing the oncoming hordes of punters.

But the truth is that the bookies are merely taking a percentage of the market, secure in the knowledge that they will make a small but certain profit so long as the market is lively and the racing competitive.

It's the weight of punters' money that determines what odds the runners start at. And, since it is only possible to make a long-term profit by backing horses at bigger odds than they should be, it follows that, to pull off this remarkable trick, you need to be a better-than-average bettor.

This sounds like a big ask, but we can take some comfort from one of the enduring talking points of the last Flat season. The lionising of Hawk Wing proved beyond doubt that there is a very high mug quotient among followers of racing.

Let's not pore over his mediocre record again. Suffice it to say that he won just twice from eight starts after his juvenile year, and both those wins came in very weak races that were perfectly set up for him.

The elevation of this over-rated beast to the status of best horse in the world by the International Classifications is bemusing. Possibly there is another one born every minute; if not, there may have been some outbreak of mass delusion among handicappers.

Whatever the case, this saga serves mainly to show that many people can look at a horserace without gathering the faintest idea of what's going on – and hooray for that, because we can take their money.

So to business. This year's Flat Guide is the biggest ever, about 40 pages fatter than the 2003 edition, packed with the sort of material you'll need to get from here to November with the betting bank unbroken.

We kick off by talking to a couple of Lambourn men whose careers are firmly on the up; Jamie Osborne and Hughie Morrison discuss their prospects for the coming year in *Profiles For Punters*.

If you want to remind yourself of what happened last season, we're not short of options: you can browse our News Diary, analyse our sheaf of stats on jockeys and trainers, or study the Group 1 and key two-year-old form from 2003.

New *Time Test* man Mark Nelson weighs in with his top two-year-old speed figures.

And when it comes to finding winners for the coming year, we've got a stronger team than you'll find anywhere else. We've got seven training centre reporters around Britain and Ireland, Raceform analyst Steffan Edwards cutting through the ante-post markets, Morning Mole picking out some good prospects and Richard Williams with 30 future winners to watch for.

Throw in Dave Nevison, Graham Wheldon's draw analysis, *By The Numbers* and our usual hefty racecourse section, and you've got a flying start on the average punter. Take advantage!

Jamie Osborne

THAT GROUP 1 MOMENT: Osborne and wife Katie O'Sullivan savour Milk It Mick's triumph

HE'S GOT one of the most instantly recognisable faces in racing, but what is Jamie Osborne famous for?

Stylish and successful as a jockey, he's now starting to make his mark as a trainer. His abilities are undoubted, yet the many headlines to feature his name have only occasionally been concerned with his professional achievements.

While there's no reason to think that Osborne has ever sought controversy, still it has found him with uncanny regularity.

The first big 'Jamie story' has come to seem a fairly light-hearted matter by comparison with what has followed. In the weighing room at Ayr during the 1990

Scottish National meeting, he was punched in the face by Jenny Pitman (herself a good source of copy for racing hacks).

Her complaint, apparently, was that the jockey had been repeatedly attempting to interfere with her runners in mid-race.

The pair managed to bury the hatchet – his comment on Pitman's subsequent retirement was "All I'll say is that she's got a good left hook."

Another bit of trouble in running led to a bust-up with fellow rider Billy Morris at Newbury a couple of years later. Back in the weighing room, Morris head-butted Osborne, knocking out one of his teeth.

After his aggressor had been fined,

Osborne suggested that "I must have the sort of face people like to hit."

Next in line to give him the treatment were the Metropolitan Police. In early 1998, they called him into Charing Cross police station and arrested him in connection with doping and race-fixing.

Eventually released without charge, he nonetheless had to endure a protracted period of suspicion and finger-pointing. In a nasty little reversal of the presumption of innocence, the Jockey Club reacted to his arrest by suspending his license, only to back down and return it a week later.

Even then, the law wasn't done with him. While under arrest, Osborne was approached by former police officer Bob Harrington, who tried to elicit a bribe. For this, Harrington was eventually jailed for 18 months. Osborne's appearance as a prosecution witness at Harrington's trial meant that his name was still being associated with the race-fixing story 18 months after he'd been cleared.

While giving evidence, he dropped the bombshell that, as a 19-year-old, he'd been offered (and had refused) a £20,000 bribe to stop a couple of favourites at the Cheltenham Festival.

It was a time that allowed him to show his survival skills. When arrested, he was recovering from a horrendous wrist injury that kept him on the sidelines for almost a year. He was also mourning the death from leukaemia, days before, of his close friend and former housemate John Durkan.

On his first day back race-riding, he steered Coome Hill to victory in a televised race named in Durkan's memory.

But the traumas left their mark. Reporting that jockeyship had "lost its buzz", Osborne gave up riding for training in 1999.

And still he couldn't find a quiet life. In June 2002, an edition of the BBC's Kenyon Confronts programme proved a severe embarrassment to three trainers, one of them Osborne.

Approached by people who said they were thinking about buying a horse from him, he was filmed saying that he would be prepared to "cheat" and that he knew of an "in-house" jockey who could be used to that effect.

"I had a salesman's hat on," he explained afterwards. "These guys devised a scenario and were adamant that they would only buy

a horse if I would do what they wanted. I need clients. I was purely and simply trying to sell a horse.

"Every time I steered them away from this, they steered me back. And as soon as they got what they wanted, they left. It was a con, it was a sting.

"I don't have owners who have horses just for the sake of a bet. I don't want them, but I'm not in a position to choose – I've got £60,000-worth of horses that need owners."

Fined £4,000 by the Jockey Club for bringing the sport into disrepute, Osborne is now prepared to hold his hands up over the affair: "I couldn't complain. I was caught with me pants down."

Osborne's training career had started in a blaze of publicity and high expectations but his first year in charge of Kingsdown Stables, Upper Lambourn was "an unmitigated disaster" – from 253 runners, he managed a measly 10 winners.

Alhough his strike-rate had improved by the time Kenyon Confronts came along, the programme's allegations once more cast the young trainer's budding career into doubt.

"I felt a right tit. It came at a time when my back was against the wall a little bit. It was very bad timing from a personal point of view."

And then came Milk It Mick. What better way to leave your troubles behind than by producing a seemingly ordinary two-year-old to win your first Group 1?

Osborne's stable star began 2003 running in Class E races at unglamorous venues and ended it as the Dewhurst winner, having amassed over £200,000 in prizemoney.

After such high-profile success, Osborne allows himself a little cautious optimism.

At the time of the race-fixing probe, though confident he would be cleared, he still worried that "unfortunately mud does stick . . . I'm always going to be remembered in racing for being hit by Jenny Pitman in the weighing room at Ayr and being arrested on fraud charges."

Now he sounds more upbeat. "Memories are not long in this game. Just the same as if you're not training a lot of winners, I think people do forget things like that if you then get the winners."

After 20 years in racing, Osborne is finally getting the chance to let his talent do the talking.

CREME DE LA CREME:
Milk It Mick looks like butter wouldn't melt in his mouth after winning the Dewhurst

Milk It Mick

3yo bay colt

Millkom – Lunar Music (Komaite)

Five wins and three places from 12 runs at two. Started season in April when fifth of 18 in Class E maiden auction. Last two outings, won Group 3 Somerville Tattersall Stakes and Group 1 Dewhurst Stakes.

"He is phenomenally good and winning the Dewhurst begs the question: how did I get him beat seven times?

He always showed us plenty of ability. In the summer, I thought he'd levelled out and was going to be about Group 3 class, or maybe Listed, but then we had a change of tactics. He was always travelling well, running with the choke out, if you like. So before the Somerville race, I told Pat [Eddery] – drop him out and ride him like he's got a real turn of foot.

And then a fortnight later, Pat unfortunately chose the other horse [Balmont]. I told Darryll [Holland] we'd better try the same thing again.

To say I was shocked when he won would be an understatement. You go into those races full of hope but there's also an element of realism that told me he couldn't quite win it.

The plan, obviously, is to go for the Guineas. People have knocked the form, or tried to, but if you look at the Official Ratings, One Cool Cat's on 118 and we're on 118.

And then you look at the betting and One Cool Cat's 7-4 and we're 16-1.

And I do take that as a minor insult. I mean if One Cool Cat was here and Milk It Mick was at Ballydoyle, the prices would be reversed.

Anyway, he'll have a couple of runs before the Guineas, starting on the All-Weather at Lingfield on March 20 in the Spring Cup. He'll have a 10lb penalty, but it's not the end of the world.

The thing is, he needs fast ground. Some people will say, well, what are you doing running the Dewhurst winner on the All-Weather, but the surface will suit him.

He needs to have two runs because, as I've said, he's a horse who gets better if you can take some of the gas out of him. Where he goes for the second run depends on the ground, we've got the Greenham and the Craven and the Thirsk Classic Trial.

Thirsk is probably favourite because I'd rather avoid the best on the way.

I'd like to get to May 1st with the dream still intact. But he's well and he looks fantastic."

Osborne's 'opefuls

Danger Over
7yo bay horse
Warning – Danilova (Lyphard)
Trained in France by Pascal Bary until the end of 2002, winning a Group 3 and a couple of Listed races at up to 7f. Won Class C over 6f on first start for Osborne last year. Winless in nine runs since, but three places, including in 6f Group 3 and valuable 7f Ascot handicap off 111.

"He's entered in the Lincoln and we may well go there.

We tried him over a mile at Nottingham on his final start last season, and he was just beaten,

DANGER OVER

which confirmed what I thought, that the speed had just come off him a bit.

At his age, he's a bit more comfortable going at a mile pace. He's tough and, although he wouldn't be getting any better, if he's campaigned slightly differently . . . he goes well fresh, you can make a case for him in the Lincoln.

There are plenty of other races to go for if he doesn't get a mile. At the start of the season, he should get his favoured slower ground."

Desperate Dan
3yo bay colt
Danzero – Alzianah (Alzao)
Won a 6f median auction maiden on Lingfield's Polytrack on his debut in August. Was well beaten in a valuable sales race at Doncaster two weeks later but signed off with a respectable second of six in a Ripon novice event.

"He had a few niggly problems and was not always sound. Then he showed us a lot and we wanted to get him ready for the sales race.

I had to get a run into him first and Lingfield was the only place I could do that. He won, but then we had to rush him and it all went wrong for the Doncaster race.

I made a bit of a balls of it. But now he's on a mark of 92, which I think is very fair, and I like him a lot.

He's got a lot of speed - you won't see him over further than 6f. He would probably cope with soft ground, though, and I would avoid very firm ground."

Electrique
4yo bay gelding
Elmaamul – Majmu (Al Nasr)
Managed to win his maiden at the eighth attempt, on his final start last season. Was shaping well on his hurdles debut when falling in early February.

"He was just about to get beat when he fell at Musselburgh but he's a nice horse and we will probably go for the Triumph now.

There's probably a decent race on the Flat to be won with him, maybe one of the better handicaps at 1m2f. He loves fast ground."

Laawaris
3yo bay colt
Souvenir Copy – Seattle Cat (Seattle Song)
Won his only start at two, a 7f median auction maiden at Thirsk in June, beating eight rivals.

"This is a very nice horse. He was big and weak and needed time last year but he's got a lot of class.

He won't be easy to place at first but I really like the horse. He wants quite good, fast ground and about a mile to 1m2f."

Place Cowboy
3yo bay colt
Compton Place – Paris Joelle (Fairy King)
Second of nine on only start at two, in a 6f median auction maiden on Southwell's fibresand in June.

"I was disappointed with his defeat on the All-Weather.

We won the other division of the same race with Cartronageeraghlad, and I would have been scared to work them together at home because Place Cowboy was so much better.

I knew he was weak last year and I wanted to find a nice, winnable race for him, but I underestimated how weak he was.

He's strengthened up now and should definitely win a maiden over 6f or 7f. He'll be ready early on and may go to Doncaster, though I'm not sure about the ground for him there."

Red Wine
5yo bay gelding
Hamas – Red Bouquet (Reference Point)
With Osborne since his two-year-old season, he's won six races (two on fibresand, four on turf), the highlight being the 2002 November Handicap off 87. Fourth in the Northumberland Plate off 94 last year.

"He's had a good, long break since his last run in mid-July.

His main target this season will be the Northumberland Plate, though there are other races he could go for, like the Cesarewitch and the Chester Cup.

These are tough races to win but he's looked like he could improve with age."

Rules For Jokers
3yo bay gelding
Mujadil – Exciting (Mill Reef)
Two from nine as a two-year-old, having made his debut in the York maiden won by One Cool Cat. Landed a pair of backend 6f nurseries off 66 and 72. Well beaten off 79 in an open handicap final start.

"Last season, he was a bit inconsistent and took a bit of working out. But his family usually improve with age and he's done well over the winter, so there's the chance of some room for improvement.

NO SOUR AFTERTASTE: Red Wine (nearside) gets up in the 2002 November Handicap

A SERIOUS CONTENDER: Rules For Jokers scores at Pontefract under Frankie Dettori

There are going to be more restricted handicaps this year and I think it'll suit horses like him, running in races where there's a 14lb weight range rather than a 21lb weight range.

I'll have him ready for the start of the season. He must have it soft."

Rye
3yo bay filly
Charnwood Forest – Silver Hut (Silver Hawk)
Never dangerous when fifth of ten on her only start so far, a 7f fillies' maiden at Kempton in July.

"Unfortunately she chipped a knee after Kempton. She's quite decent and is back in strong work now.

In the right maiden, over 7f to a mile, I would expect her to go pretty close."

Sahaat
6yo bay or brown gelding
Machiavellian – Tawaaded (Nashwan)
Trained in France by John Hammond until 2003. Winless in 12 starts for Osborne, though was a 3l fourth of 11 off 94 in a Listed handicap last May.

"He's had some niggling problems, but I didn't do a good job with him last year. He's got a lot of ability but we never really got it all out of him.

He had a little break and we brought him back later in the season but he was

disappointing. So he's had another break and we will attempt to win some similar races to the ones he ran in last year, hoping to get a better season out of him.

The one good thing is that he's dropped to a mark of 84 on grass. If I can get him back right, he could win a good handicap."

Soliniki
3yo bay gelding
Danzero – Pride Of My Heart (Lion Cavern)
Won his only start at two, a 6f median auction race at Ascot in August, beating 15 rivals.

"This is a very nice horse.

He was a big, weak two-year-old and I felt we didn't see the best of him last year, so I advised the owners to keep him.

He's got a big engine – going round in the paddock at Ascot, he looked like a jumper - and he's done very well through the winter and strengthened up. I think there's a good race to be won with him.

We'll find a 6f classified race somewhere to start with and it'll be conditions races beyond that. He wants to get his toe in the ground a bit.

The hope is that he could be good enough to make the transition to better races and not be a ratings-limited horse."

Hughie Morrison

WHEN THE Ascot stewards disqualified Alcazar in the Sagaro Stakes last April, they picked on the wrong guy.

As his charge passed the post, Hughie Morrison was cheering what he believed to be his first Group winner. Moments later, the authorities were explaining why they felt the need to meddle – Alcazar's jockey had accidentally hit the runner-up on the nose inside the final furlong and, as the winning distance was only a neck, they were sure the outcome had been affected.

They may have calculated that Morrison, being something of an establishment figure and himself a former steward at Newbury, wouldn't be the sort of chap to make a fuss. Stewards so rarely disqualify these days that, to do so in such a marginal case, they must have felt pretty sure their decision wouldn't be challenged.

Imagine their dismay, then, on reading these words from the man himself in the following day's *Racing Post*: "There is no point beating about the bush. We want this dealt with as soon as possible. My gut feeling is if this is confirmed, jockeys should just throw away their whips.

"If this doesn't get turned over, every time a horse is interfered with by the whip, wherever it is on the racecourse, and it is beaten under half a length, the jockey will expect to get the race.

"If in doubt, the logical thing would surely be to let the result stand and then those who want to appeal can do so."

The episode (which ended, of course, with Alcazar being reinstated on appeal) illustrates two truths about Morrison: one, he's a seriously talented trainer and two, he's rarely short of a strongly-held opinion.

The Ascot race was Alcazar's third win out of three starts since switching yards from John Dunlop.

On arrival at the East Ilsley base, he had brought with him an intimidating list of ailments, including a broken pelvis and a damaged tendon. By the time Morrison had coaxed him through his troubles and got Alcazar back to a racecourse, the horse was six years old and without a run for well over 1,000 days.

But getting them fit without a run is apparently a breeze for this trainer. Not only did Alcazar overcome his long absence that day, but he won again next time after a further absence of over 500 days.

It's a trick for which Morrison is known. In the week he spoke to *Racing & Football Outlook*, his Box Builder scored, having not had a run for well over a year. He, too, had suffered leg trouble.

As for holding opinions, Morrison's strongly-expressed views have got him into the sports pages on a number of occasions.

When jockeys were encouraged to use team tactics at the 2002 Shergar Cup, his Jasmick was a notable sufferer and he was vocal in railing against the competition's set-up: "Our owners feel they were robbed as she would have been second if she had been ridden properly. The Rules of Racing have been broken by the organisers."

Later that year, the experience of running Marble Arch in the Fighting Fifth Hurdle prompted him to berate Newcastle's racecourse management for misleading trainers about the state of the track:

"They said they would race on fresh ground but it wasn't fresh ground – I walked the course. They said they had moved the obstacles two hurdle widths to the left to create fresh ground, but they didn't do that. What hope have we got if they blatantly lie?"

Ruby Walsh felt the rough end of Morrison's tongue earlier this year after allowing his mount to hang into East Ilsley inmate Thieves'glen at Ascot: "Jumping is a dangerous enough game without someone committing careless riding, resulting in a career-threatening injury to a very nice horse. The owners are totally disillusioned by the whole incident. We have every reason to be upset."

Best known as a trainer of jumpers, thanks to Festival winner Frenchman's Creek and Champion Hurdle runner-up Marble Arch, Morrison has in fact always aimed to be a trainer of good Flat runners. Alcazar's Group win was an important stepping stone for him last year and he enters 2004 with a candidate for each of the Guineas.

Still, there are serious obstacles in the path of any trainer attempting to break into the top level of the summer game. "We'd all like to win a Classic, though it is increasingly difficult," he says.

"The yearling market last year was ridiculous, it didn't reflect what was happening on the track. We had falling prizemoney and yet significantly increased yearling prices."

Morrison's owners operate within restricted budgets and he is therefore forced to hunt for bargains. But it's a task he's good at and his success is bringing him increased opportunities.

As he enters his eighth year with a license, his number of winners for the last four seasons reads: 6/17/28/45. He started 2003 with "about 50" horses and now has 75. It's safe to say we'll be hearing more from him.

Hughie's hotpots

Alcazar
9yo bay gelding
Alzao – Sahara Breeze (Ela-Mana-Mou)
Lightly raced, with just 15 career outings (seven wins). Joined Morrison from John Dunlop and won first time out for him on his first start in 34 months. Last year won Ascot Group 3 and second in French Group 1, both over 2m.

"He's in good form and seems as happy as ever.

We know he's a Group 1 performer at the top of his game, best on good going. Good to firm isn't quite his ground.

We'll start him off like last year, at Nottingham [on March 31]."

Baltic King
4yo bay colt
Danetime – Lindfield Belle (Fairy King)
Progressive sprinter. Beat 15 rivals for Class B rated handicap at Ascot off 98 in September.

"He's rated so high now, handicaps are nearly out of the question, so we'll be looking to run him in conditions races.

On his last run last season [Group 3 Bentinck Stakes at Newmarket], he was knocked over as he was about to come and win his race. He was extremely unlucky.

The time before that at Ascot, he wouldn't let himself down on the rained-on, watered ground.

I'd be surprised if we saw him run before the end of May – I sent him away to an equine therapy centre, the same place Tom Paddington went, for a holiday, basically.

It helps them recover from injuries, from aches and pains. Hopefully we might make a proper Group sprinter of him – though it might take some time, maybe by the autumn."

Fiddle Me Blue
3yo chestnut filly
Bluebird – Fiddle Dee Dee (Mujtahid)
Close third on debut, then won 6f Windsor maiden on only other start at two.

"She looks well, a bit heavy-topped. She's certainly got an engine.

She'll be running in 5f handicaps for three-year-old fillies and the target would be Royal Ascot."

Harelda
4yo chestnut filly
Hector Protector – Hen Harrier (Polar Falcon)
Two respectable outings in maidens at two. Reappeared in early February and very easy winner of 1m4f Southwell maiden.

"If staying sound, she could make up into a really nice filly. She'll be aimed at 1m4f handicaps and prefers a bit of cut in the ground.

If she can win off 85, then maybe she can pick up some black type somewhere."

Kylkenny
9yo bay gelding
Kylian – Fashion Floe (Balidar)
Popular, ageing handicapper. His 11 career wins include eight on Southwell's fibresand, the latest being in March last year off 85.

"Poor old Kylkenny, he's getting a bit long in the tooth now. We've started riding him again this week and he makes a great lead horse but he's very high in the handicap himself.

He's always had dodgy wind and I think it may be getting dodgier."

> *'We can dream of the 2,000 Guineas. They say sometimes the race is won by a sprinter who stays a mile'*

Little Ridge
3yo bay gelding
Charnwood Forest – Princess Natalie (Rudimentary)
Two from five at two, winning a brace of backend nurseries off 65 and 73.

"She only cost £5,000 but she could now be a bit high in the handicap. It was a bit disconcerting to win a couple of small races and go up 20lb!

She'll go for 5f and 6f handicaps and, if all goes really well, she may go for the 5f handicap at Royal Ascot."

Odiham
3yo bay gelding
Deploy – Hug Me (Shareef Dancer)
Winless in three outings as a juvenile, though ran a good second on final start in a mile maiden on Lingfield's Polytrack.

"He's potentially a nice three-year-old staying handicapper, though on current ratings he's not being given much of a chance."

Pastoral Pursuits
3yo bay colt
Bahamian Bounty – Star (Most Welcome)
Second of 20 in Windsor maiden on debut, then won remaining three starts at two years, all over 6f. Last seen winning Group 3 at Kempton, when he suffered a chipped knee.

"We did everything the vet told us – we took the chip out 48 hours after the race, and then he spent four months convalescing.

We started riding him out again on January 1st. He did lots of walking and now he's cantering.

Horses that do nothing for four months, it always affects the way they look but he's nicely muscled and it'll be disappointing if he hasn't trained on.

We can dream of the 2,000 Guineas. We thought he was going to be a 7f type

14

RUBY
ROCKET
(left)

as a two-year-old but he showed a lot of speed. They say sometimes the Guineas is won by a sprinter who stays a mile. He'll go to Newbury if he has a prep-run."

Ruby Rocket
3yo bay filly
Indian Rocket – Geht Schnell (Fairy King)
Three wins from five at two years, including Listed 6f race at Ayr. Fourth, beaten 2l, when last seen in Group 1 Cheveley Park.

"She did run well at Newmarket, and I'd like to think she's better than that. Whether she's trained on, only time will tell, but she's a lovely filly, strong and tough.

She may not develop as much as the classically-bred horses but you would love to train her progeny.

She'll go for the Guineas but I'm not convinced she'll stay. She'll definitely have a prep run first, over 7f, at Newmarket or Newbury."

Sangiovese
5yo bay gelding
Piccolo – Kaprisky (Red Sunset)
Finally got off the mark, after a number of good efforts, in a 1m handicap on Southwell's fibresand in December 2003, off 63.

"He's had terrible foot problems and at one stage had to spend about six months in his box.

But now we've got him right, he's potentially well handicapped on turf.

He'll be kept to good to soft and soft."

Tilla
4yo bay filly
Bin Ajwaad – Tosca (Be My Guest)
Two wins from seven at three years, in 1m4f and 1m6f handicaps off 60 and 65 respectively.

"She's got a serious attitude, she's a right old madam. But she's definitely got ability.

We've unlocked it to a certain extent and it's just a question of whether we can continue to unlock it.

She'll be running in 1m4f to 1m6f handicaps and might be capable of winning a proper race, rather than a 0-70."

Waverley
5yo bay gelding
Catrail – Marble Halls (Ballad Rock)
Winner of three handicaps, over 1m2f and 1m4f. Beat 19 to land Royal Ascot handicap off 91 last year. Got cast in his box in August, sustaining a leg injury that looked likely to end his career.

"Last week, I would have told you he wasn't coming back into training, but I've just come off the phone to the equine therapy centre, and the vet tells me his scan looks very good.

So it's possible we may see some more of him, though he won't be back in training until spring at the earliest."

Zeis
4yo chestnut gelding
Bahhare – Zoom Lens (Caerleon)
Beat Anani to win good Newbury maiden over a mile on only start at two, when with Henry Cecil. Disappointing on belated reappearance for Cecil and transferred to Morrison last backend. No show on first run for him, shortly after joining yard.

"He had a problem with a hind-leg fracture, after which Henry never really got him right.

He's incredibly green but he might make a nice handicapper and I'll give him a run on the All-Weather soon."

Profiles by Chris Cook

Sponsored by Stan James

Review of 2003

Outlook

News Diary 2003
by Richard Williams

January

1   Andrew Balding sends out his first runner as a licensed trainer, Duchamp, on New Year's Day. Sent off at 100-30, he unseats Tony McCoy, but the 30-year-old trainer can comfort himself with the thought that he has Classic prospects Rimrod and Casual Look snugly tucked up back at his Berkshire base.

2   William Hill and Paddy Power suspend betting on the jockeys' championship after "unusual betting patterns". Richard Hughes, Seb Sanders, Kevin Darley and Darryll Holland have all been backed. Kieren Fallon's agent reports that the reigning champion is on holiday but that he will be defending his title vigorously once again.

6   The minimum unit stake for the Tote Jackpot is raised to 50p, a 400 per cent increase. The news is received philosophically by small-stakes punters, by now well-used to being trodden on.

Wolverhampton's All-Weather fixture is called off after an early-morning inspection. Temperatures of -5C have caused lumps in the Fibresand. Gay Kelleway, who had two leading fancies at the meeting, is "gutted" and there are calls for the surface to be replaced with Polytrack. Racing goes ahead at Bloemfontein.

15   Five straight Group 1 wins do nothing historically for Rock Of Gibraltar's place in the International Classifications. The panel give him the worst rating (128) of a champion three-year-old since ratings began in 1977. High Chaparral and Sulamani deadheat for second place on 126. Oasis Dream is top two-year-old, followed by Tout Seul and Six Perfections. Marienbard comes out on top in the older horse division. Aidan O'Brien declines to comment.

19   A Sunday paper reveals that Kieren Fallon's holiday was in fact a 30-day sojourn at a health centre in Ireland to kick an alcohol problem. Fallon reckons that he will "be a much better jockey" as a result.

29   The proposed restrictions on jockeys' use of mobile phones on the racecourse could result in a legal challenge. Leader of the opposition, Philip Robinson, claims he has the support of at least 20 other jockeys, including Kieren Fallon, Richard Hughes and Pat Eddery, and has enlisted the support of a human rights lawyer.

February

6   Frankie Dettori picks Dubai for his return and is out of luck in two rides.

8   Kieren Fallon makes his return at Lingfield and is unplaced on his two rides. He nominates the St Leger as the race he would like to win most, as it's the only British Classic to have eluded him.

13   Moon Ballad, ridden by Dettori, wins a Group 3 at Nad Al Sheba. The Derby third looks in great shape when making all. His

success compensates Godolphin for an earlier reversal, when they'd been represented by six of the nine contenders for the UAE 2,000 Guineas, only to be beaten by South African-trained Victory Moon.

19   John Marsh, speaking on behalf of Cheveley Park Stud, the owners of Russian Rhythm, states that the filly will go straight for the 1,000 Guineas without a prep. She is a 9-2 shot with Ladbrokes.

22   Lingfield's Winter Derby Trial falls to Parasol, shot into a clear lead half a mile from home by Fallon. Trainer David Loder expresses confidence that Parasol will improve before the Winter Derby itself.

25   Godolphin announce plans to go into the Dubai World Cup triple-handed, with Sulamani, Moon Ballad and Grandera their representatives. The syndicate hints that Bourbonnais is their 2,000 Guineas hope.

28   Former Newmarket trainer Kamil Mahdi is banned from keeping horses for life after being convicted of causing unnecessary suffering to five of his charges. He was ordered to carry out 240 hours of community service and to pay £6,000 costs.

March

1   Jimmy Fitzgerald hands over his trainer's license to his son Tim. Retiring at the age of 67, Fitzgerald's many big-race successes included a Cheltenham Gold Cup with Forgive 'N Forget, a Hennessy with Galway Blaze and two Cesarewitches with Kayudee and Trainglot.

8   Grandera, the defending World Racing Series champion, passes his World Cup trial with flying colours under the floodlights of Nad Al Sheba. He is one of four winners for Frankie Dettori.

14   Cheltenham reverses for Coral (and the rest of the gang) see them cut Brian Boru into 3-1 for the Derby, although the Tote still go 7-1. A Coral spokesman explains that ante-post accumulators, involving big-race Cheltenham winners, look costly.

15   The bookmakers have their backs to the wall as another public gamble is landed – Parasol takes Lingfield's Winter Derby at 5-2, backed down from 5-1. Frankie Dettori performs his trademark flying dismount.

20   The first day of the Flat season proper coincides with a reduction in the Tote's take-out from win and place pool bets. This is estimated to be a £4m windfall for punters, based on 2002 figures. From now on, 13.5 per cent will be deducted, as against 16 per cent.

For the second successive year Dandoun wins the Doncaster Mile for trainer John Dunlop.

Paul Blockley makes a dream start to his second spell as a licensed trainer when Red Power lands that great institution the Brocklesby Stakes, the first turf two-year-old race of the year. Blockley, based near Southwell, has 12 horses in his care.

22   Heavily backed ante-post, Adiemus squeezes into the Lincoln but the race is won by Pablo. Successful trainer Barry Hills last took the race with Frankincense 35 years before. Adiemus finishes seventh and Jeremy Noseda, his trainer, advocates 1m2f as his preferred distance.

23   Tomahawk, Ireland's top-rated juvenile, is trimmed to 10-1 for the 2,000 Guineas after victory in a stakes race at The Curragh.

Aidan O'Brien parades his stable's best horses in the Curragh paddock after racing, including Brian Boru, High Chaparral and Hawk Wing. Last year's Derby winner does a nice piece of work for Mick Kinane and the Lockinge at Newbury is said to be on the agenda if O'Brien has his way.

27   Nayef looks the part in his preparation for the World Cup with a smooth workout at Nad Al Sheba and Richard Hills says that the five-year-old feels bigger and stronger.

29   The richest race on the planet, the Dubai World Cup, falls to Moon Ballad, ridden by Frankie Dettori in the Godolphin colours. After racing wide from a number 11 draw, the Italian soon has his mount on an even keel and they power away from America's Harlan's Holiday. Nayef comes home third, just ahead of Grandera.

Dettori's customary flying dismount is accompanied by cries of "show me the money". With a first prize of £2,250,000 and a jockey's percentage of ten per cent, we understand where he's coming from.

The Italian also lands the Godolphin Mile (first prize £375,000) with Firebreak and the Dubai Sheema Classic (£750,000) with Sulamani. The last-named produces a breath-taking display to come from last to first and the Coronation Cup is nominated as his next target.

April

7   Six Perfections is made clear favourite for the 1,000 Guineas after oozing class throughout her Prix Imprudence romp at Maisons-Laffitte. The Pascal Bary-trained filly, who passes the post hard-held by Thierry Thulliez, is down to 11-4 with Paddy Power, although the Tote go 7-2. This is the same trial that Six Perfections' aunt Miesque won prior to her 1,000 victory in 1987.

9   Alberto Giacometti is backed down to 10-1 for the Derby, and is now second favourite to stablemate Brian Boru. Third in the betting is Hold That Tiger, yet another Aidan O'Brien colt. The gamble coincides with O'Brien's open day, when assembled journalists pass through Ballydoyle security guards to view priceless thoroughbreds. The trainer's comment that "there is only a fraction between him [Brian Boru] and Alberto Giacometti" is obviously taken to heart by the media. Their mobile phones are busy.

13   The plunge horse is knocked back out to 20-1 after trailing in third behind 33-1 pacemaker Balestrini in a Leopardstown trial in which Alamshar comes a close second. The latter is now as low as 7-1 with Ladbrokes. After the meeting, Brian Boru pleases O'Brien with a 1m2f workout with literary pair The Great Gatsby and Dickens. Meanwhile, in England, Russian Rhythm has a gentle workout on Newmarket's Limekilns.

15   It's Classic trial time at Newmarket, where John Dunlop's Khulood lands the Nell Gwyn under a front-running ride from Richard Hills.

16   Day two of Newmarket's Craven meeting begins with Russian Rhythm doing nothing to enthuse Newmarket work-watchers in the hazy sunshine. Dunlop lands the Earl Of Sefton with Olden Times, while Indian Haven wins a weakish European Free Handicap.

17   Day three is a good one for coincidence-backers. Alan King announces the retirement of jumper Hurricane Lamp hours before Hurricane Alan masters Lundy's Lane in the Craven.

The equine flu outbreak in Britain has Pascal Bary musing over whether to risk sending his Six Perfections for the Guineas.

20   The saga surrounding plans to build a meat and bonemeal incinerator close to Aidan O'Brien's stable at Ballydoyle is over. The planning application has been withdrawn.

24   Sir Michael Stoute sounds a note of caution over Russian Rhythm's prospects in the 1,000 Guineas, saying: "I'm hoping the race isn't going to come too soon."

28   The BHB's racing review committee comes up with 76 recommendations to improve racing, the main thrust of the report being that the fixture list needs expanding. The report proposes a Regional Racing programme for horses rated 45 and under.

May

3   The first Saturday in May is 2,000 Guineas day. Ireland's Refuse To Bend (9-2) sees off Zafeen (33-1) and Norse Dancer (100-1). Dermot Weld, the colt's globe-trotting trainer, now has two British Classics to his name, to go with his two Melbourne Cups and a Belmont Stakes. Not to mention ten Irish Classics.

4 Russian Rhythm, despite drifting out to 12-1, lifts the 1,000 Guineas. Sir Michael Stoute comments: "I really haven't a been pleased with her preparation. She wasn't really blooming and wasn't eating as well as she can." Six Perfections, under Thierry Thulliez, finds all kinds of traffic problems from stall 1, yet comes fast and late down the middle, prompting Pascal Bary to say: "She was the best filly." The Paris-Turf calls the filly's run "a nightmare under the English sun".

8 Fergal Lynch is the fall guy at Chester. After passing the post first on Kris Kin in the Dee Stakes, he celebrates too soon and finds himself hitting the deck.

Chester's chief executive reveals that he is considering axing either the Dee Stakes or the Chester Vase after the two historic Classic trials attract four runners apiece. Robert Sangster chimes in: "There are not enough horses to go round."

11 Alamshar fails to impress when beating The Great Gatsby in Leopardstown's Derrinstown Derby Trial, whereas Dalakhani sparkles in Longchamp's Lupin.

17 It's a case of as you were for David Loder, who decides to carry on training, freed of his bond to Godolphin. He will still enjoy the backing of Sheikh Mohammed. Hong Kong-based Peter Chapple-Hyam confirms that he is coming home to train in England.

18 "Astounding" is the one-word headline of the Racing Post after Hawk Wing wins the Lockinge by 11 lengths. But the *Outlook* begs to differ – *Off The Bit* confidently predicts that the colt will never win another race.

25 Johnny Murtagh replaces Thierry Thulliez in the plate, but it's another horror show for connections of Six Perfections, who look on in agony as the filly has no run behind Yesterday in the Irish 1,000 Guineas. "What do you expect me to say?" asks Bary. How about: "I'm going to ride it myself next time"?

June

1 One of the great images of the Flat season is Christophe Soumillon on Dalakhani, waving to Dominique Boeuf on Super Celebre in the French Derby, inviting him to overtake, if he can.

6 Andrew Balding is speechless when sister Clare thrusts a microphone in his face after his Casual Look wins the Oaks at 10-1, his first Classic win in his first season as a trainer. Nothing can be extracted from father Ian, either. Not surprising, really, as Clare is too emotional to ask any questions. Is there a technical fault? wonder bemused viewers.

7 Much more noise after Kris Kin wins the Derby, landing a massive public gamble (14-1 to 6-1), inspired as much as anything by the fact that Kieren Fallon is riding. David Hood of William Hill says: "The roof has caved in." Chester's chief executive reconsiders his stand over the Dee Stakes (see May 8).

17 The Royal meeting starts with an 8l win for Three Valleys in the Coventry and is followed by a 25-1 victory for Choisir in the King's Stand, but most interest is in the Queen Anne, in which Dubai Destination makes a great comeback, ending a long barren patch for Godolphin. One horse notably fails to make the frame, seventh-placed Hawk Wing.

20 Friday sees Russian Rhythm shave the course record in the Coronation Stakes and become the first filly to do the Newmarket/Ascot double for 24 years. Mark Johnston makes it five for the meeting when Shanty Star grabs the Queen's Vase.

21 Highlight of the Royal meeting comes when Choisir doubles up in the Golden Jubilee at 13-2. Trainer Paul Perry says: "They'll be going mad back home."

23 Pat Eddery, 51, announces that he will retire at the end of the season. He was 11 times champion jockey in Britain and once in Ireland. He points out: "I can't go on forever."

29 A good day for the Aga Khan, who owns the first two home in the Irish Derby, Alamshar and Dalakhani. Not enjoying the occasion so much is Aidan O'Brien, who fields six of the last seven home.

July

1   Interpol join in the hunt for runaway bookmakers Chris and Nick Velounias, who ran the London-based Burns Bookmakers. The brothers appear to have absconded with £200,000 of unpaid debts and are spotted at St Pancras. The police believe they may be in Europe, possibly Ireland.

John Batten, who laid bets on Epsom Downs the day Benny The Dip won the Derby, but left the course during the race, is still on the missing list.

5   It's a fifth Group 1 success for Falbrav in the Eclipse. The race results in controversy, as Jamie Spencer is accused of using team tactics on Narrative, acting as pacemaker for Grandera. The jockey is found guilty of breaching Rule 153 for purposely steering a course to the inside and causing minor interference to Nayef.

Peter Savill announces a commission to investigate working conditions, but not pay, for stable staff.

6   The BHB holds discussions with racecourses to stage 272 of unbroken days of racing – apart from on Good Friday.

8   "The best two-year-old I've trained" says Mark Johnston after Attraction takes the Cherry Hinton. "She must have the most famous legs since Clodagh Rodgers," he adds, confusing all but the saddest members of the press, Rodgers being the singer who finished an unlucky fourth in the 1971 Eurovision Song Contest.

10   Oasis Dream, who'd been top-rated two-year-old in 2002, dashes Choisir's bid for further glory in the July Cup, a third battle in the space of 24 days proving just too much for the Australian. "It was a hell of a horse-race," says John Gosden, the winning trainer.

13   The BHB respond to fears of saturation racing by upping the ante – 320 days of unbroken racing (Good Friday excepted) are planned for 2004. There will be just nine blank days in this period.

26   Irish Derby winner beats Derby winner – Alamshar first, Kris Kin third is the outcome of Ascot's King George. "I don't think I've had a horse run a better race than that," says John Oxx, who trained Arc winner Sinndar. The three-year-old crop, widely denigrated this season, can count this as one in the eye for their critics, especially with Sulamani, Falbrav and Nayef in the field.

30   Pat Eddery rides his last Group 1 winner as Reel Buddy comes in at 20-1 in the Sussex Stakes at Glorious Goodwood. The veteran jockey, whose sixth Sussex this is (equalling Lester Piggott's record), takes it in his stride but even he shows a flicker of emotion when all the jockeys come out of the weighing room to applaud him.

When Knavesmire Omen wins the Goodwood Stakes, Mark Johnston breaks Henry Cecil's record of most consecutive seasonal centuries by chalking up his tenth domestic 100.

August

1   Records continue to tumble at Goodwood. David Nicholls saddles 12 out of the 21 runners in the Stewards' Sprint Stakes and narrowly misses out.

2   Nicholls takes things relatively easy on Saturday, with just the six in the Stewards' Cup, but none of them can live with the gambled-on Patavellian.

3   At his open day at Beckhampton in Wilt-

shire, Roger Charlton says that Three Valleys is "the best two-year-old I've trained."

5   David Loder announces that he has found new stables from which to train in 2004, at the Egerton Stud, next to Newmarket's July Course. The Stud hasn't been used as a racing stable since the Second World War.

6   The racing calendar for 2004 is published, revealing that the number of fixtures

is up by 70 to 1,340. Racing will take place on 47 Sundays (there were 24 in 2003), with 125 Sunday meetings. Newmarket's Guineas meeting is down to two days, while Chester's May meeting (including the Dee Stakes) will begin on Wednesday. There will be 66 days of Regional Racing.

10   John Banks, flamboyant and controversial bookmaker, dies aged 68. A fearless layer on the rails, he lost £80,000 when Persian War won the Champion Hurdle (in the days when £80,000 was a lot of money) and still sent the owner a bottle of champagne.

Other news from the ring is that Gary Wiltshire is under doctor's orders to lose seven stone.

16   Newmarket stages the inaugural running of the very silly Grey Horse Handicap, a race restricted to greys. Smart Predator, trained by John Quinn, carries the day.

In America, Sulamani is awarded the Arlington Million on the disqualification of Storming Home, which brings up Godolphin's 100th Group/Grade 1 success.

17   Six Perfections banishes her demons by taking on her elders and winning the Prix Jacques le Marois.

A Sunday newspaper reports that bloodstock magnate John Magnier and Sir Alex Ferguson have had a row over the income generated by Rock Of Gibraltar at stud. Ferguson apparently believes he is entitled to 50 per cent. Magnier is not sure he is entitled to anything. Incidentally, this story was broken by RFO when Off The Bit wrote about it in our July 15 edition.

19   York's Ebor meeting kicks off. Highlight of the first day is Falbrav's victory in the Juddmonte.

20   Islington wins the Yorkshire Oaks and Saint Alebe the Ebor Handicap.

21   Day Three glory goes to Oasis Dream, a facile winner of the Nunthorpe, prompting John Gosden to say: "He could have won by 5l or 6l, rather than 3l. Richard [Hughes] was posing at the screen."

26   More in-fighting among racing's leaders as Peter Savill blasts the Levy Board and the Tote, accusing them of not having "the best interests of racing at heart". David James, chairman of Racecourse Holdings Trust, is interviewed by the *Racing Post* and predicts an utterly chaotic future if the Office of Fair Trading finds racing in breach of competition laws. "A completely deregulated market would create a nightmare world where every separate interest could seek to sell its data, fixtures or media rights," he says.

30   Ken Hussey dies, aged 75, in the early hours of the morning. The pioneer of speed ratings, who wrote under the nom de plume Split Second for the *Raceform Handicap Book* and under his own name for RFO, had many devoted followers, partly thanks to a lifetime tipping long-priced winners. No-one matched him for showing up the nonsense of official going descriptions, using the evidence of the clock.

September

1   Jockeys protest about not being allowed to use their mobile phones on the racetrack from 30 minutes before the first race. The rules allow them to use three phones provided by the Jockey Club. All 23 jockeys on duty at Leicester walk off the track between races, with their mobiles. The jockeys at Hamilton join them, but not the riders at Folkestone.

6   High Chaparral wins the Irish Champion Stakes, beating Falbrav and Islington by a neck and a head with Alamshar, Moon Ballad and Vintage Tipple also in the race.

Darryll Holland, rider of Falbrav, submits an objection to the winner, although many viewers feel that Holland himself got his own horse beat. Luca Cumani says: "Falbrav was probably the moral winner but morals do not put the bread on the table."

12   Lucky Story, trained by Mark Johnston, wins the Champagne Stakes, despite frothing up at the start. Bruce Raymond, racing manager to owner Abdulla Buhaleeba, says: "I wouldn't worry about him sweating, as all the stock of the sire Kris S seem to do so. In America, they say that they are no

good if they don't sweat."

13 The English and Irish St Legers take place on the same Saturday and both fall to Irish-trained horses. The Doncaster version goes to Aidan O'Brien's Brian Boru, while the Curragh version goes to Dermot Weld's Vinnie Roe for the third year running.

14 The phoney war for the Arc begins on trial day at Longchamp. Dalakhani looks super-smooth when staying in third gear to win the Prix Niel and Christophe Soumillon reckons his mount had plenty left in the tank. Doyen is second, Kris Kin third. Sir Michael Stoute, trainer of the Derby winner, is "disgusted" with the tactics employed by Yann Lerner, jockey of Look Honey. Kris Kin is repeatedly locked in by Lerner, but few in the stands believe that Kris Kin could ever reverse placings with Dalakhani under any circumstances.

Racing is abandoned at Sandown as jockeys go on strike over the use of mobile phones. Philip Robinson, who is co-ordinating the actions of the riders, says: "I do think we're going to end up in court and I'd rather take it to Europe as a human rights issue. I'm up for it, too, as it's a winnable case and no court in the world would support what the Jockey Club has done."

16 Concessions are forthcoming. The Jockey Club will allow riders to use their phones to make outgoing calls and check for messages within a designated phone zone, without having to ask permission. But it doesn't impress Robinson, who says: "They will lose in the courts and I can't wait to get there."

17 Russian Rhythm puts in a sparkling piece of work on the Watered Gallop at Newmarket as she prepares for Ascot's Queen Elizabeth II. Given her poor work before the 1,000 Guineas, contrarian thinkers consider this a bad sign.

20 Will Dandy Nicholls win the Ayr Gold Cup? He clearly doesn't have faith in any one horse, because he runs seven in an attempt to win the race for the fourth year running. In fact, it is the master who gets the better of his apprentice. David Chapman, who teamed up with Nicholls so successfully when the younger man was a jockey, saddles 20-1 shot Quito to show he has lost none of his knack of turning dodge-pots into heroes.

21 Yeats bursts onto the Derby scene after winning a mile maiden at The Curragh. Aidan O'Brien leaves nobody in any doubt about his high regard for the colt in nominating a similar schedule to the 2001 dual Derby winner Galileo. "This colt is a beauty," he says.

27 Falbrav, dubbed by Luca Cumani as "the best horse anywhere in the world" wins the Queen Elizabeth II Stakes at Ascot, beating Russian Rhythm by 2l. The race is something of an afterthought for Cumani and his owners, because the trip of a mile is not considered Falbrav's optimum. The Italian trainer tempers his earlier assessment, saying: "He's probably the best horse in the world on grass between a mile and 1m2f".

Snow Ridge emerges as a Classic contender by showing a brilliant turn of foot to land the Royal Lodge Stakes, prompting Marcus Tregoning to say: "He's the best two-year-old I've trained. He'd win the Derby, wouldn't he?" Ladbrokes make him 16-1.

29 Frankie Dettori is fined £250 for using a mobile phone while walking back to the weighing room after riding his third winner at Bath. He is handed the phone by a female well-wisher as he walks back through the crowd. He emerges from the stewards' room to say: "Who grassed me up?"

October

2 Carry On Katie, trained by Jeremy Noseda, just gets the better of Majestic Desert to land the Cheveley Park Stakes. She will winter in Dubai.

3 Three Valleys shows a nice turn of foot to lift the Middle Park Stakes, chased home by another of Noseda's in Balmont.

The draw takes place for the Arc de Triomphe, putting High Chaparral next to the rail in stall 1. Dalakhani is drawn widest in 14.

4 Flat racing's oldest and perhaps

oddest couple, Sir Mark Prescott and George Duffield take their third Cambridgeshire together, courtesy of Chivalry, who short-heads Adiemus. This is Chivalry's first run of the season. It is also the 31st year that Duffield has been riding for Prescott. You wouldn't think it, though, as the couple rarely speak. "People say communication is everything," says Prescott. "I disagree. George and I don't really get on, certainly not socially."

5   A great day for the Aga Khan, Alain de Royer-Dupre and Christophe Soumillon as Dalakhani delivers the Arc on a plate. The rest are effectively nowhere, though the record books will show that Mubtaker ran a cracker in second and High Chaparral finished third. Late doubts about soft ground and a wide draw dissolve as the grey colt sweeps into the lead in the final furlong. Mares will surely queue up for him.

John Magnier and JP McManus appear to be closing in on Manchester United. The pair's investment company Cubic Expression pays £62million for 9.9 per cent of the Premiership club's shares. Will Aidan O'Brien be the next United manager? He has already trained Van Nistelrooy and Solskjaer.

8   Sir Mark Prescott is eyeing the £100,000 bonus offered by Newmarket for winning the autumn double and has four possibles in the Cesarewitch betting but Shabernak is the one that catches the eyes of work-watchers.

Derby winner Kris Kin is retired.

12   Bill Shoemaker, the legendary American jockey who rode 8,833 winners, dies aged 72. His career lasted 41 years and included four Kentucky Derby victories.

18   A ten-year-old steals the show on Champions Day at Newmarket. Persian Punch takes the Jockey Club Cup, his fourth win of the year and his 14th career success at Group-level.

There are more fairy tales, as Pat Eddery cajoles Landing Light home to lift the Cesarewitch and Jamie Osborne, who has had a few setbacks in his time, saddles Milk It Mick to win the Dewhurst.

Veteran trainer Michael Jarvis wins the Champion Stakes with Rakti.

20   European challengers for the Breeders' Cup are met with a heatwave when they arrive in California, where temperatures touch 90 degrees Fahrenheit. John Gosden points out that it is semi-desert heat and not humid heat. Which is good.

25   It's a great Breeders' Cup for the Europeans, who take three of the biggest prizes. High Chaparral dead-heats for the Turf with Johar, the pair edging out Falbrav. The French taste victory with Six Perfections and the English have their moment of glory with Islington in the Filly & Mare Turf. Islington is Kieren Fallon's first Breeders' Cup success and the filly ends a sequence of 31 British-trained losing runners in California-staged Breeders' Cup races.

30   Godolphin swoops for two top-class fillies in Carry On Katie and Cairns, winners of the Cheveley Park and Rockfel respectively. They are set to join Doyen and Refuse To Bend in the care of Saeed Bin Suroor. Mamool, another Godolphin horse, has his final gallop under Suroor's watchful eye on Australia's Sandown Park racecourse.

November

4   Jardines Lookout and Hugs Dancer join Mamool and Millstreet in the stalls for the Melbourne Cup at Flemington but it is the home-trained Makybe Diva who comes home first at 7-1. Jardines Lookout runs a screamer to be third at 40-1, while 11-2 favourite Mamool finishes last. It's Godolphin's sixth unsuccessful attempt, but they vow to return.

8   Crowds throng to Doncaster to witness Pat Eddery's last ride in Britain on board Gamut and the omens look good as the horse is back over his favourite trip of 1m4f. It is not to be, though, as Gamut tires close home and finishes third. Fellow jockeys spray Eddery with a colourful party foam and the stewards chip in too, with a caution for his use of the whip in the nursery.

26   Darryll Holland learns that he won't be riding Falbrav in the Hong Kong Cup. The

ride goes to Frankie Dettori. The horse is jointly-owned by a Milan-based businessman and it is believed that the Italian connection is the reason for the jockey switch, rather than any implied criticism of Holland's earlier rides on the horse.

27 Writing in the *Racing Post*, sometime TV presenter Julian Wilson suggests that owners are "blocking" their horses because they had missed the early prices available on betting exchanges. He wants the exchanges to delay opening their markets until 11am of the day of the race. On the face of it, this would be a remarkably philanthropic move if the exchanges were to sign up to it.

30 No joy for Tout Seul (fifth) or Islington (ninth) in the Japan Cup. Tap Dance City makes all to come home 9l clear.

December

1 A bad start to the month for Wolverhampton, where rain waterlogs the track and the meeting is called off. "You don't mind losing the occasional meeting to frost," says Nick Littmoden, "but to lose it to rain is an insult to everyone's intelligence."

8 Falbrav and Rakti have a workout on the All-Weather at Sha Tin ahead of their Hong Kong Cup engagement. Hills have chalked them up at 11-8 and 4-1 respectively.

14 Falbrav captures the final leg of the World Series under Frankie Dettori. The Italian pays a compliment to the five-year-old's acceleration and says: "He took my breath away and I've not felt a sensation like that for a long time."

Quotes of the year

"I'm looking forward to this season like I've never looked forward to a season in my life. I believe I'll be a much better jockey and I want to be a better person."
Kieren Fallon, following his 30-day stint at an Irish health centre, confronting his problems with alcohol.

"I really haven't been pleased with her preparation. She wasn't really blooming and wasn't eating as well as she can."
After Russian Rhythm's 2,000 Guineas win, Sir Michael Stoute explains why he'd recently gone all coy about her prospects. The filly drifted out to an SP of 12-1, having been less than half that price through the winter.

"It's amazing how many horses drawn low seem to hurt their legs on the morning of races."
Sally Iggulden, racing manager at Beverley, shows her cynical side.

"We were 14-1 in the morning and within eight minutes of trading had six-figure liabilities on him."
Neal Wilkins, spokesman for Victor Chandler, on the Derby-day gamble on Kris Kin.

"The defeat of Brian Boru meant that we breathed a sigh of relief, but Kris Kin soon became the No. 1 shop horse. We took a bit of a beating."
Simon Clare of Coral tells a similar story.

"Turnover has gone through the roof, but the roof has caved in!"
David Hood reports that Hills were also on the wrong side of the Derby result.

"I've never seen a horse backed like it in this race. Ladbrokes, Hills, Corals and Victor Chandler all backed it. I've done my money."
Gary Wiltshire indicates that the result was no good for on-course layers, either.

"I can't remember a horse's price coming down as much as Kris Kin's on Derby day. It is very unusual."

John Broadway, senior SP reporter.

"I wouldn't mind if there was a little evening meeting on the way home, maybe get another couple of winners."

Fallon, leaving Epsom after riding Kris Kin, had obviously enjoyed his day.

"He's a monster of a horse, like a Brahma bull, and Johnny Murtagh will feel the power. I expect him to be hard to catch."

A week before Ascot, trainer's son Shannon Perry was happy to tell us all about Australian raider Choisir. So why didn't we listen?

"I can safely say that only jockey error will get this horse beaten!"

An object lesson in why jockeys don't usually express much confidence in their mounts. This is Frankie Dettori, before riding Kheleyf in the Norfolk Stakes – the combination could finish only second, at 8-13.

"In a nutshell, small players on Betfair are ruining the market for those entitled to a decent bet. Owners still pay the bills – up to £400 a week – but they cannot get on without dishonesty or deception. Worse still, certain owners this year, having missed their price, have given instructions that the horse be blocked for another day."

Julian Wilson says the betting exchanges are giving the game away about plot horses before those involved have got their bets on – and he expects us to be worried about this. Subsequently, he declined to name the owners who'd "blocked" their runners.

"This encourages betting with unlicensed and anonymous individuals and opens the floodgates for illegal betting, which already involves the participation of money launderers and the drugs trade."

Ladbrokes chief executive Chris Bell also wanted to put forward a self-serving argument against the betting exchanges, after the Levy Board decided to allow on-course

bookies to use them for hedging.

"Every year, these firms come in, desperately trying to attract business by offering the best prices on ante-post betting and money back offers etcetera. It's just not sustainable."

Coral's Simon Clare on the collapse of Burns Bookmakers, which left punters out of pocket.

"That's my first winner since Sandy Forest Lady beat one of Aidan O'Brien's in a two-horse hurdle race at Tipperary in August 1995. I suppose you could say our careers have gone in different directions."

Trainer Myles Coughlan celebrated success with See The Lady at Fairyhouse.

"He was so composed, he looked like Muhammad Ali walking around the parade ring."

Luca Cumani on Falbrav, after his charge had won the Hong Kong Cup.

"I can't understand why he's giving up when he's so young – he must have made more money than I did!"

Lester Piggott on Pat Eddery, who retired at the age of 51.

"I think he'll be back. If I were a betting man – and if jockeys were allowed to bet – I'd have my maximum on it!"

Kieren Fallon reckons we haven't seen the last of Eddery.

"It's marvellous to see someone who has been at it for so long riding so well. I can't get rid of George. I expect when he dies, the Science Museum will want to open his body up and see why he keeps going for so long."

Sir Mark Prescott on George Duffield, who's been riding for him for over 31 years, after they'd teamed up yet again to win the Cambridgeshire with Chivalry.

"Half a loaf is better than no fish."

Mick Kinane in cryptic mode after riding High Chaparral to dead-heat for the Breeders' Cup Turf.

RACE OF THE YEAR: Johar (left) flies at the finish to dead-heat with High Chaparral (centre) for the Breeders' Cup Turf. Falbrav (rails) was third

Top Jockeys (Turf)

W	R	%	Jockey & Weight	Best Trainer	W	R	%
207	949	22	**Kieren Fallon** 8st4lb	Sir M Stoute	62	235	26
122	835	15	**Darryll Holland** 8st4lb	G Wragg	9	85	11
120	845	14	**Kevin Darley** 8st3lb	M Johnston	14	69	20
117	714	16	**Richard Hughes** 8st4lb	R Hannon	39	186	21
93	569	16	**Jamie Spencer** 8st5lb	D Loder	22	73	30
88	464	19	**Frankie Dettori** 8st5lb	D Loder	21	80	26
88	807	11	**Steve Drowne** 8st4lb	M Channon	23	176	13
79	737	11	**Seb Sanders** 8st4lb	Sir M Prescott	8	59	14
77	617	12	**George Duffield** 7st12lb	Sir M Prescott	27	98	28
75	615	12	**Pat Eddery** 8st3lb	J Dunlop	21	136	15
75	627	12	**Eddie Ahern** 8st1lb	G A Butler	34	206	17
75	710	11	**Dane O'Neill** 8st5lb	H Candy	14	53	26
74	366	20	**Richard Hills** 8st1lb	M Tregoning	19	72	26
74	661	11	**Martin Dwyer** 7st12lb	A Balding	22	213	10
72	599	12	**Tony Culhane** 8st5lb	M Channon	30	133	23
70	490	14	**Richard Quinn** 8st4lb	H Cecil	16	76	21
63	567	11	**Joe Fanning** 8st2lb	M Johnston	45	216	21
62	458	14	**Philip Robinson** 8st2lb	M Jarvis	31	183	17
62	517	12	**Willie Supple** 8st	T Easterby	10	76	13
58	646	9	**Robert Winston** 8st4lb	J J Quinn	6	24	25
57	411	14	**Michael Hills** 8st5lb	B Hills	47	283	17
52	414	13	**Keith Dalgleish** 8st5lb	M Johnston	40	202	20
52	540	10	**Ryan Moore** 7st11lb	R Hannon	15	137	11
51	588	9	**John Egan** 7st13lb	J Dunlop	8	30	27
47	550	9	**Francis Norton** 7st12lb	A Berry	12	204	6
47	584	8	**Paul Hanagan** 7st12lb	R Fahey	20	196	10
45	294	15	**Sam Hitchcott** 7st11lb	M Channon	36	182	20
42	340	12	**Jimmy Fortune** 8st6lb	J Gosden	21	104	20
40	355	11	**Royston Ffrench** 7st12lb	M Johnston	11	68	16
40	627	6	**Chris Catlin** 7st12lb	M Channon	22	213	10
38	499	8	**Dave Allan** 7st13lb	T Easterby	12	240	5
37	357	10	**Richard Mullen** 7st12lb	W Muir	14	106	13
36	242	15	**Nicky Mackay** 7st5lb	L Cumani	15	60	25
33	254	13	**Robert Miles** 7st7lb	T Mills	12	55	22
32	507	6	**Michael Fenton** 8st4lb	J Given	19	190	10
31	341	9	**Ian Mongan** 8st4lb	N Littmoden	11	152	7
30	385	8	**Adrian Nicholls** 7st12lb	D Nicholls	23	226	10
29	330	9	**Lisa Jones** 7st5lb	J Toller	7	31	23
29	360	8	**Ted Durcan** 8st3lb	M Channon	15	130	12
28	373	8	**David Kinsella** 7st9lb	H Howe	7	27	26
27	338	8	**Jamie Mackay** 7st7lb	M Bell	5	64	8
26	263	10	**Darren Williams** 8st6lb	K R Burke	16	145	11
26	301	9	**Dean Mernagh** 7st12lb	T Barron	22	135	16
25	363	7	**Simon Whitworth** 8st2lb	J W Payne	3	18	17
25	365	7	**Fergal Lynch** 8st5lb	K Ryan	10	102	10
24	245	10	**Brett Doyle** 8st3lb	Sir M Stoute	14	51	27
24	272	9	**Patrick Dobbs** 8st5lb	R Hannon	17	154	11
22	332	7	**Luke Fletcher** 8st1lb	H Morrison	5	14	36
22	338	7	**Jimmy Quinn** 7st12lb	Mrs S Lamyman	3	16	19
21	240	9	**George Baker** 8st5lb	B Millman	6	60	10
21	343	6	**Neil Callan** 8st4lb	P Harris	4	34	12

Top Jockeys (AW)

W	R	%	Jockey & Weight	Best Trainer	W	R	%
49	399	12	**Ian Mongan** 8st4lb	N Littmoden	21	120	18
40	262	15	**Tony Culhane** 8st5lb	H Morrison	5	9	56
35	155	23	**Darryll Holland** 8st4lb	C Brittain	4	9	44
35	265	13	**Robert Winston** 8st4lb	B Meehan	9	34	26
35	306	11	**Dane O'Neill** 8st5lb	B Johnson	5	18	28
32	225	14	**Eddie Ahern** 8st1lb	G A Butler	13	68	19
31	296	10	**Neil Callan** 8st4lb	T Barron	5	15	33
27	306	9	**Jimmy Quinn** 7st12lb	Mrs N Macauley	3	9	33
26	291	9	**Simon Whitworth** 8st2lb	A Newcombe	6	44	14
23	181	13	**Jean-Pierre Guillambert** 8st1lb	N Littmoden	5	66	8
23	250	9	**Michael Fenton** 8st4lb	J Given	7	46	15
22	123	18	**Seb Sanders** 8st4lb	Sir M Prescott	8	24	33
21	186	11	**Joe Fanning** 8st2lb	M Johnston	4	32	13
21	215	10	**Steve Drowne** 8st4lb	H Morrison	5	13	38
21	250	8	**Francis Norton** 7st12lb	A Berry	4	55	7
19	273	7	**Luke Fletcher** 8st1lb	M Polglase	5	62	8
19	319	6	**Chris Catlin** 7st12lb	I Williams	4	24	17
18	150	12	**Neil Chalmers** 7st12lb	A Balding	5	22	23
18	176	10	**Dean McKeown** 8st2lb	T Barron	9	35	26
17	122	14	**Paul Hanagan** 7st12lb	R Fahey	8	20	40
17	187	9	**Shane W Kelly** 8st4lb	J Noseda	5	19	26
16	125	13	**Martin Dwyer** 7st12lb	A Balding	5	34	15
14	107	13	**Keiren Fallon** 8st4lb	C Brittain	3	13	23
14	116	12	**Dominic Fox** 7st5lb	Miss A Stokell	3	8	38
14	190	7	**Lisa Jones** 7st5lb	Mrs N Macauley	3	25	12
14	201	7	**Graham Gibbons** 8st	R Hollinshead	6	42	14
13	31	42	**Frankie Dettori** 8st5lb	D Loder	4	6	67
12	97	12	**Richard Quinn** 8st4lb	J Akehurst	2	3	67
12	120	10	**Keith Dalgleish** 8st5lb	P Cundell	3	4	75
11	72	15	**Brett Doyle** 8st3lb	C Brittain	3	17	18
11	94	12	**Amir Quinn** 7st13lb	R Cowell	4	10	40
11	124	9	**Jamie Mackay** 7st7lb	J Spearing	4	15	27
11	177	6	**Darren Williams** 8st6lb	K R Burke	6	65	9
10	61	16	**Dean Mernagh** 7st12lb	T Barron	9	51	18
10	89	11	**Paul Eddery** 8st2lb	D Haydn Jones	5	42	12
10	91	11	**Paul Scallan** 8st3lb	B Smart	8	38	21
10	131	8	**Lee Enstone** 8st3lb	Miss G Kelleway	5	26	19
10	133	8	**John Egan** 7st13lb	W Haggas	2	2	100
9	27	33	**Jamie Spencer** 8st5lb	D Loder	5	7	71
9	77	12	**Brian Reilly** 7st10lb	G Margarson	2	4	50
9	87	10	**Royston Ffrench** 7st12lb	B Smart	3	28	11
9	91	10	**George Duffield** 7st12lb	Sir M Prescott	7	23	30
9	191	5	**John F McDonald** 7st5lb	D Shaw	2	11	18
8	29	28	**Philip Robinson** 8st2lb	M Jarvis	7	16	10
8	68	12	**Jason Edmunds** 8st2lb	J Balding	8	65	12
8	77	10	**Richard Thomas** 7st5lb	D Haydn Jones	3	9	33
7	52	13	**Fergal Lynch** 8st5lb	K Ryan	5	28	18
7	82	9	**Fran Ferris** 7st7lb	P S McEntee	2	11	18
7	87	8	**Ryan Moore** 7st11lb	R Hannon	3	14	21
7	90	8	**Jason Tate** 8st	J Eustace	4	53	8
7	129	5	**Liam Keniry** 8st1lb	A Reid	2	9	22

Top Apprentices

W	R		Jockey & Weight	Best Trainer	W	R	%
59	627	9	**Ryan Moore** 7st11lb	R Hannon	18	151	12
45	322	14	**Sam Hitchcott** 7st11lb	M Channon	36	189	19
43	520	8	**Lisa Jones** 7st5lb	W Musson	8	57	14
43	558	8	**David Allan** 7st13lb	T Easterby	12	255	5
41	605	7	**Luke Fletcher** 8st1lb	M Polglase	9	121	7
38	312	12	**Robert Miles** 7st7lb	T Mills	17	74	23
37	347	11	**Jean-Pierre Guillambert** 8st1lb	N Littmoden	8	117	7
36	252	14	**Nicky Mackay** 7st5lb	L Cumani	15	61	25
29	377	8	**Dominic Fox** 7st5lb	P Haslam	7	59	12
28	503	6	**John F McDonald** 7st5lb	R Hodges	5	29	17
27	296	9	**Neil Chalmers** 7st12lb	A Balding	8	52	15
26	432	6	**Liam Keniry** 8st1lb	A Balding	5	80	6
23	251	9	**Derek McGaffin** 8st4lb	I Semple	18	149	12
22	298	7	**Tony Hamilton** 7st12lb	B Ellison	9	95	9
22	360	6	**Lee Enstone** 8st3lb	P Haslam	7	94	7
21	187	11	**Brian Reilly** 7st10lb	S C Williams	5	22	23
18	280	6	**Fran Ferris** 7st7lb	J Eustace	5	23	22
17	205	8	**Amir Quinn** 7st13lb	R Cowell	7	19	37
15	164	9	**David Nolan** 8st2lb	P Blockley	6	39	15
15	306	5	**Dean Corby** 8st2lb	J Jenkins	3	11	27
14	228	6	**Hayley Turner** 7st5lb	D Cantillon	2	9	22
12	94	13	**Mark Flynn** 8st1lb	W Brisbourne	11	84	13
10	111	9	**Liam Treadwell** 8st	D Nicholls	3	21	14
9	95	9	**Richard Lake** 7st5lb	J R Best	6	66	9
9	114	8	**Paul Mulrennan** 8st1lb	M W Easterby	8	78	10
9	150	6	**Phillip Makin** 7st11lb	S Bowring	6	106	6
9	191	5	**Mark Savage** 8st2lb	J Bradley	4	123	3
9	278	3	**Richard Thomas** 7st5lb	D Haydn Jones	3	14	21
8	78	10	**Stephanie Hollinshead** 7st9lb	R Hollinshead	6	59	10
8	92	9	**Pierce Gallagher** 8st	R Hannon	5	30	17
7	81	9	**Charles Poste** 7st13lb	R Fahey	6	59	10
7	361	2	**Tom Eaves** 8st1lb	J J Quinn	2	9	22
6	60	10	**Mark Worrell** 8st1lb	Sir M Prescott	4	19	21
6	128	5	**Chris Cogan** 7st10lb	D Ivory	6	68	9
6	215	3	**Paul Bradley** 7st11lb	A Berry	5	156	3
5	75	7	**Suzanne France** 7st9lb	N Bycroft	5	73	7
4	17	24	**Chris Connett** 8st2lb	A Stewart	3	14	21
4	40	10	**Tony Beech** 8st5lb	D Loder	2	9	22
4	125	3	**Eddie Creighton** 7st7lb	M Channon	2	59	3
3	7	43	**Tom Best** 10st3lb	R J Smith	1	1	100
3	18	17	**Matthew Lewis** 8st2lb	H Morrison	2	8	25
3	27	11	**Rory Moore** 7st5lb	P Haslam	3	16	19
3	28	11	**Glen Sparkes** 7st11lb	J Bridger	3	14	21
3	35	9	**Wayne Hogg** 7st10lb	M Johnston	2	16	13
3	58	5	**Saleem Golam** 7st10lb	M Tompkins	2	16	13
3	72	4	**Kristin Stubbs** 7st5lb	Mrs L Stubbs	2	48	4
3	79	4	**Leanne Kershaw** 7st5lb	J Wainwright	1	3	33
3	97	3	**Natalia Gemelova** 7st5lb	W Storey	2	55	4
2	18	11	**Laura-Jayne Crawford** 8st4lb	T Barron	2	16	13
2	46	4	**James D O'Reilly** 8st1	J O'Reilly	2	45	4
2	50	4	**Jonathan Currie** 7st5lb	J Goldie	2	46	4

Top Trainers by Winners (Turf)

	All runs			First time out			Horses*		
Won	Ran	%	Trainer	Won	Ran	%	Won	Ran	%
138	1072	13	**Mick Channon**	12	147	8	79	147	54
132	699	19	**Mark Johnston**	20	150	13	79	150	53
113	471	24	**Sir Michael Stoute**	37	154	24	81	154	53
112	942	12	**Richard Hannon**	13	179	7	73	179	41
98	581	17	**Barry Hills**	28	142	20	70	142	49
86	565	15	**John Dunlop**	21	148	14	64	148	43
66	367	18	**John Gosden**	12	127	9	51	127	40
56	191	29	**David Loder**	20	60	33	33	60	55
56	666	8	**Dandy Nicholls**	2	80	3	36	80	45
54	792	7	**Tim Easterby**	5	124	4	37	124	30
53	235	23	**Marcus Tregoning**	16	69	23	32	69	46
52	244	21	**Roger Charlton**	8	69	12	30	69	43
51	250	20	**Luca Cumani**	7	62	11	26	62	42
50	357	14	**Amanda Perrett**	8	91	9	34	91	37
48	335	14	**Paul Cole**	7	67	10	30	67	45
47	412	11	**Ed Dunlop**	11	105	10	39	105	37
45	269	17	**James Fanshawe**	5	66	8	30	66	45
44	253	17	**Michael Jarvis**	12	66	18	27	66	41
41	290	14	**Gerard Butler**	7	60	12	28	60	47
41	415	10	**Richard Fahey**	1	69	1	26	69	38
40	188	21	**Sir Mark Prescott**	8	41	20	22	41	54
40	420	10	**Andrew Balding**	3	75	4	25	75	33
39	396	10	**Peter Harris**	5	67	7	22	67	33
38	266	14	**T David Barron**	5	38	13	21	38	55
37	379	10	**W Mark Brisbourne**	1	46	2	18	46	39
36	411	9	**Brian Meehan**	5	74	7	25	74	34
34	219	16	**Jamie Osborne**	5	35	14	17	35	49
34	279	12	**Michael Bell**	5	59	8	23	59	39
33	258	13	**Hughie Morrison**	5	48	10	19	48	40
33	331	10	**James Given**	7	89	8	19	89	21
33	373	9	**P David Evans**	1	38	3	16	38	42
33	615	5	**J Milton Bradley**	1	59	2	19	59	32
32	176	18	**Neville Callaghan**	3	27	11	19	27	70
32	204	16	**Willie Haggas**	4	55	7	19	55	35
32	267	12	**David Elsworth**	4	38	11	21	38	55
31	355	9	**Karl Burke**	1	39	3	20	39	51
29	255	11	**John Quinn**	2	31	6	11	31	35
28	317	9	**Clive Brittain**	3	34	9	15	34	44
27	154	18	**Jeremy Noseda**	3	36	8	15	36	42
27	306	9	**Ian Wood**	0	51	0	18	51	35
26	174	15	**Alec Stewart**	2	43	5	20	43	47
25	149	17	**Henry Cecil**	7	50	14	22	50	44
25	224	11	**Ian Semple**	1	29	3	12	29	41
25	259	10	**Bryan Smart**	4	45	9	17	45	38
25	629	4	**Alan Berry**	2	69	3	18	69	26
24	233	10	**Sylvester Kirk**	3	36	8	15	36	42
24	248	10	**Mark Tompkins**	3	41	7	19	41	46
24	296	8	**Kevin Ryan**	2	45	4	16	45	36
23	178	13	**Chris Wall**	1	31	3	12	31	39

*Shows how many individual horses ran last season, how many won at least once, and percentage.

Top Trainers by Prizemoney (Turf)

Total prizemoney	Trainer	Win prizemoney	Wins	Class A-C			Class D-G		
				Won	Ran	%	Won	Ran	%
£3,702,619	Sir Michael Stoute	£2,749,001	113	54	260	21	59	211	28
2,033,108	Mick Channon	1,141,308	138	41	407	10	97	665	15
2,020,138	Mark Johnston	1,399,198	132	41	279	15	91	420	22
1,591,107	Richard Hannon	995,200	112	27	307	9	85	635	13
1,388,775	Barry Hills	897,982	98	34	265	13	64	316	20
1,345,573	Marcus Tregoning	904,539	53	27	96	28	26	139	19
1,316,759	John Gosden	864,142	66	18	130	14	48	237	20
1,227,673	Aidan O'Brien	465,813	6	3	52	6	3	6	50
1,150,133	Tim Easterby	673,920	54	24	252	10	30	540	6
1,142,678	Luca Cumani	1,008,793	51	14	80	18	37	170	22
1,073,320	John Dunlop	672,198	86	21	190	11	65	375	17
1,058,667	Andrew Balding	665,987	40	18	181	10	22	239	9
1,047,067	David Elsworth	572,914	32	15	148	10	17	119	14
966,761	David Loder	603,420	56	24	106	23	32	85	38
964,371	Saeed Bin Suroor	520,708	22	15	82	18	7	14	50
928,706	Roger Charlton	683,351	52	21	97	22	31	147	21
856,694	Clive Brittain	504,890	28	10	170	6	18	147	12
845,848	Michael Jarvis	562,857	44	16	116	14	28	137	20
802,201	James Fanshawe	461,185	45	16	117	14	29	152	19
793,265	Brian Meehan	461,222	36	8	139	6	28	272	10
769,144	Jeremy Noseda	525,612	27	11	76	14	16	78	21
739,425	Paul Cole	534,594	48	12	136	9	36	199	18
717,812	Amanda Perrett	353,788	50	18	139	13	32	218	15
716,820	Gerard Butler	474,581	41	15	103	15	26	187	14
680,923	Dandy Nicholls	414,466	56	11	268	4	45	398	11
607,465	John Oxx	435,000	1	1	5	20	0	0	0
601,773	Ed Dunlop	318,238	47	10	130	8	37	282	13
533,315	Peter Harris	382,025	39	15	121	12	24	275	9
524,884	Michael Bell	355,567	34	15	103	15	19	176	11
516,621	Jamie Osborne	365,147	34	9	65	14	25	154	16
510,472	J Milton Bradley	245,929	33	6	96	6	27	519	5
485,909	James Given	295,896	33	10	87	11	23	244	9
479,382	Richard Fahey	313,117	41	6	91	7	35	324	11
476,420	Neville Callaghan	291,878	32	10	67	15	22	109	20
410,189	Sir Mark Prescott	335,087	40	9	40	23	31	148	21
386,972	Willie Haggas	263,238	32	8	65	12	24	139	17
379,644	Hughie Morrison	239,851	33	8	80	10	25	178	14
364,451	T David Barron	209,039	38	5	47	11	33	219	15
349,769	Henry Cecil	175,958	25	4	52	8	21	97	22
314,067	Geoff Wragg	150,778	13	5	70	7	8	81	10
305,981	W Mark Brisbourne	201,566	37	2	42	5	35	337	10
305,714	Alec Stewart	172,441	26	7	44	16	19	130	15
302,265	Terry Mills	123,752	19	7	76	9	12	60	20
299,026	Mark Tompkins	168,117	24	7	76	9	17	172	10
298,492	Henry Candy	158,048	21	5	17	29	16	84	19
294,103	Kevin Ryan	203,102	24	8	78	10	16	218	7
291,565	Dermot Weld	214,600	2	2	13	15	0	0	0
280,893	Ian Semple	209,507	25	5	65	8	20	159	13
278,144	Chris Wall	165,257	23	6	60	10	17	118	14
274,912	Jim Goldie	163,695	23	5	91	5	18	256	7

Top Trainers by Winners (AW)

\multicolumn{3}{Allruns}				\multicolumn{3}{First time out}			\multicolumn{3}{Horses*}	
Won	Ran	%	Trainer	Won	Ran	%	Won	Ran	%
35	304	12	**Nick Littmoden**	8	68	12	25	68	37
33	171	19	**T David Barron**	6	37	16	24	37	65
27	95	28	**Sir Mark Prescott**	6	29	21	14	29	48
25	188	13	**Gay Kelleway**	4	33	12	14	33	42
21	116	18	**Gerard Butler**	6	35	17	14	35	40
20	194	10	**Norma Macauley**	2	30	7	10	30	33
19	111	17	**Brian Meehan**	4	24	17	16	24	67
19	161	12	**Gary Moore**	3	37	8	11	37	30
17	122	14	**Kevin Ryan**	1	32	3	9	32	28
16	287	6	**Derek Shaw**	0	40	0	10	40	25
15	210	7	**Karl Burke**	3	37	8	10	37	27
14	34	41	**David Loder**	6	12	50	11	12	92
14	89	16	**James Given**	3	15	20	10	15	67
14	101	14	**Andrew Balding**	5	28	18	12	28	43
14	102	14	**Bryan Smart**	4	21	19	10	21	48
14	110	13	**John Balding**	5	23	22	8	23	35
14	146	10	**Jamie Osborne**	4	35	11	11	35	31
13	45	29	**Michael Jarvis**	3	11	27	9	11	82
13	63	21	**Hughie Morrison**	2	14	14	7	14	50
13	80	16	**Clive Brittain**	4	22	18	10	22	45
13	150	9	**Reg Hollinshead**	3	28	11	8	28	29
12	56	21	**Willie Haggas**	2	13	15	8	13	62
12	91	13	**Tony Newcombe**	1	26	4	7	26	27
12	103	12	**Andrew Reid**	1	21	5	7	21	33
12	140	9	**Peter Hiatt**	1	22	5	7	22	32
11	71	15	**Charles Cyzer**	1	14	7	7	14	50
11	79	14	**W Mark Brisbourne**	2	20	10	7	20	35
11	84	13	**James Unett**	1	16	6	7	16	44
10	37	27	**Jeremy Noseda**	2	16	13	7	16	44
10	86	12	**Derek Haydn Jones**	0	18	0	6	18	33
10	89	11	**Richard Hannon**	2	21	10	9	21	43
10	92	11	**Pat Haslam**	2	31	6	7	31	23
10	100	10	**Dean Ivory**	0	15	0	6	15	40
9	39	23	**Chris Wall**	1	13	8	5	13	38
9	51	18	**Richard Fahey**	4	14	29	5	14	36
9	59	15	**Barry Hills**	3	23	13	9	23	39
9	73	12	**Paul Blockley**	1	14	7	7	14	50
9	82	11	**John Jenkins**	2	18	11	6	18	33
9	116	8	**Dandy Nicholls**	2	26	8	5	26	19
9	163	6	**P David Evans**	1	37	3	6	37	16
8	34	24	**David Elsworth**	2	13	15	7	13	54
8	38	21	**Willie Jarvis**	1	10	10	6	10	60
8	47	17	**Chris Dwyer**	2	10	20	6	10	60
8	52	15	**Terry Mills**	2	21	10	7	21	33
8	52	15	**John Quinn**	0	13	0	6	13	46
8	61	13	**John Spearing**	2	8	25	3	8	38
8	61	13	**Ian Semple**	2	18	11	7	18	39
8	68	12	**Willie Muir**	1	18	6	3	18	17
8	73	11	**Paul Cole**	3	17	18	7	17	41

*Shows how many individual horses ran last season, how many won at least once, and percentage.

Top Trainers by Prizemoney (AW)

Total prizemoney	Trainer	Win prizemoney	Wins	Class A-C Won	Ran	%	Class D-G Won	Ran	%
£204,653	Nick Littmoden	£149,992	35	5	46	11	30	258	12
172,574	Gay Kelleway	123,978	25	5	17	29	20	171	12
149,598	T David Barron	107,139	33	2	21	10	31	150	21
124,882	Clive Brittain	92,382	13	2	22	9	11	58	19
119,856	Brian Meehan	82,892	19	1	7	14	18	104	17
114,709	David Loder	105,084	14	4	12	33	10	22	45
114,254	Gerard Butler	92,448	21	4	24	17	17	92	18
103,417	Sir Mark Prescott	88,698	27	0	1	0	27	94	29
100,204	Gary Moore	59,123	19	1	14	7	18	147	12
86,331	Karl Burke	41,645	15	0	15	0	15	195	8
77,628	Norma Macauley	58,367	20	1	11	9	19	183	10
77,152	Jamie Osborne	45,490	14	0	5	0	14	141	10
72,542	Kevin Ryan	53,206	17	2	9	22	15	113	13
71,589	Peter Hiatt	46,237	12	1	13	8	11	127	9
71,238	Jeremy Noseda	43,719	10	1	7	14	9	30	30
70,173	Paul Cole	46,250	8	2	15	13	6	58	10
69,600	Derek Shaw	48,336	16	0	3	0	16	284	6
68,997	Andrew Balding	47,022	14	0	11	0	14	90	16
67,372	Bryan Smart	45,338	14	0	6	0	14	96	15
59,726	John Balding	42,293	14	0	6	0	14	104	13
58,875	Tony Newcombe	40,369	12	1	4	25	11	87	13
58,810	Willie Haggas	43,758	12	1	8	13	11	48	23
57,998	Andrew Reid	46,492	12	1	3	33	11	100	11
57,639	Dandy Nicholls	39,571	9	2	13	15	7	103	7
56,923	P David Evans	37,799	9	1	14	7	8	149	5
55,930	Hughie Morrison	47,563	13	1	6	17	12	57	21
55,216	Michael Jarvis	41,951	13	0	4	0	13	41	32
54,980	Reg Hollinshead	35,186	13	0	1	0	13	149	9
54,116	John Best	36,983	7	2	7	29	5	92	5
50,421	Richard Hannon	31,865	10	0	10	0	10	79	13
49,374	Dean Ivory	33,687	10	0	0	0	10	100	10
49,007	James Given	40,520	14	0	2	0	14	87	16
47,231	Charles Cyzer	37,208	11	0	6	0	11	65	17
45,831	John Jenkins	34,305	9	1	5	20	8	77	10
44,944	Barry Hills	31,389	9	0	3	0	9	56	16
44,581	James Unett	30,875	11	0	0	0	11	84	13
43,641	Terry Mills	26,757	8	0	4	0	8	48	17
43,178	Pat Haslam	26,035	10	0	3	0	10	89	11
40,957	Richard Fahey	32,262	9	1	2	50	8	49	16
40,622	Sid Bowring	23,339	8	0	2	0	8	121	7
40,433	Alan Berry	23,554	7	0	4	0	7	162	4
40,001	W Mark Brisbourne	30,323	11	0	1	0	11	78	14
39,813	David Chapman	25,011	7	1	11	9	6	106	6
39,181	Mark Polglase	14,554	6	0	10	0	6	111	5
38,195	Peter Harris	28,329	7	1	6	17	6	46	13
37,380	B Rod Millman	21,996	7	0	3	0	7	62	11
36,848	Chris Wall	33,967	9	0	2	0	9	37	24
36,646	Derek Haydn Jones	25,202	10	0	1	0	10	85	12
36,608	Ian Williams	32,474	4	2	4	50	2	38	5
36,582	Ian Wood	23,464	8	0	2	0	8	112	7

Outlook

Trainer statistics

IF YOU want your opinion about a horser-ace to have some grounding in fact, you'd be well advised to get yourself clued up about racing statistics.

Whilst such numbers can certainly be deceptive and always need interpretation, they offer an easy route to greater understanding of the sport.

Most of this section is taken up with fairly traditional three-year trainer statistics, concerning ten of the winningmost trainers in Britain last year. But first, a quick word about the bar charts at the foot of this page and spread over the next three.

What we've done here is attempt a visual representation of each trainer's strike-rate as it varies through the season. We've looked at the returns for the last three seasons and taken the average of each trainer's strike-rate for each month of the turf season. Then, we've shown this as a bar chart (the taller the bar, the higher the strike-rate).

The cut-off point is five per cent. Where the trainer concerned did not manage to do better than a five per cent strike-rate in a particular month, there will be no bar for that month.

For ease of comparison, the 17 per cent line is marked off on each trainer's chart. So, for example, we can see that Sir Michael Stoute consistently exceeded a 17 per cent strike-rate, whereas Tim Easterby never got near it.

The charts allow us to see how the form of each trainer changes through the year – Mick Channon is very consistent, whereas Richard Hannon tails off after a midsummer peak, and so on.

After these charts, we have four-page stats on each trainer. Note that the 2003 stats will differ slightly from those in the tables on pages 32-33, which are calculated slightly differently (not including All-Weather racing or racing abroad).

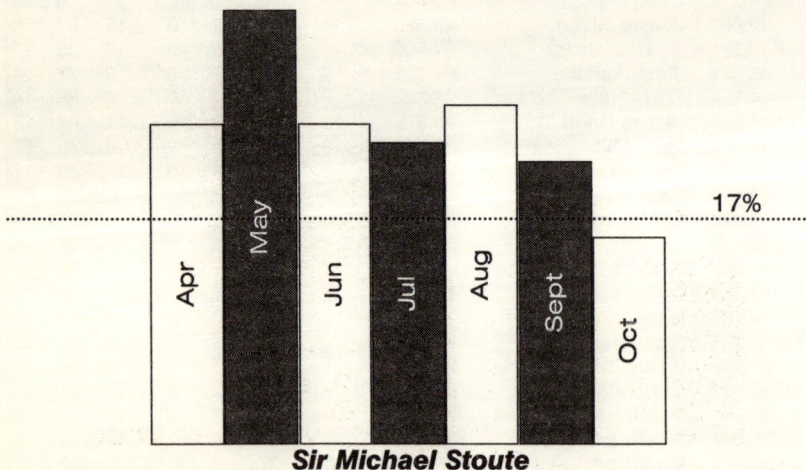

17%

Apr | May | Jun | Jul | Aug | Sept | Oct

Sir Michael Stoute

17%

Mar | Apr | May | Jun | Jul | Aug | Sept | Oct | Nov

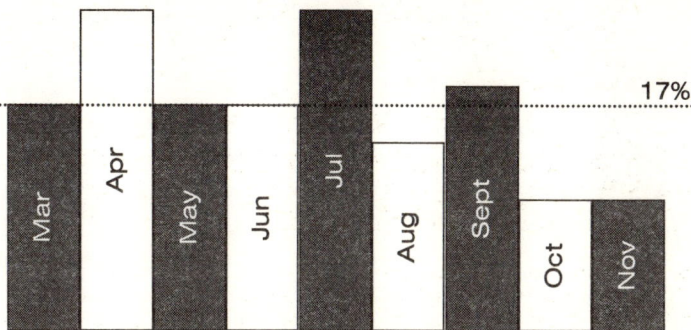

Mark Johnston

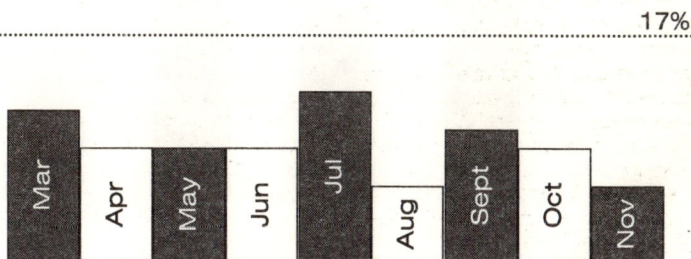

17%

Mar | Apr | May | Jun | Jul | Aug | Sept | Oct | Nov

Mick Channon

17%

Mar | Apr | May | Jun | Jul | Aug | Sept | O |

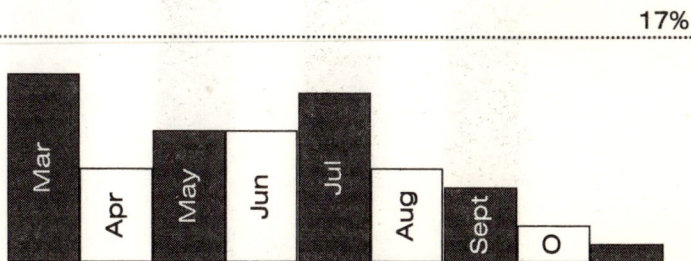

Richard Hannon

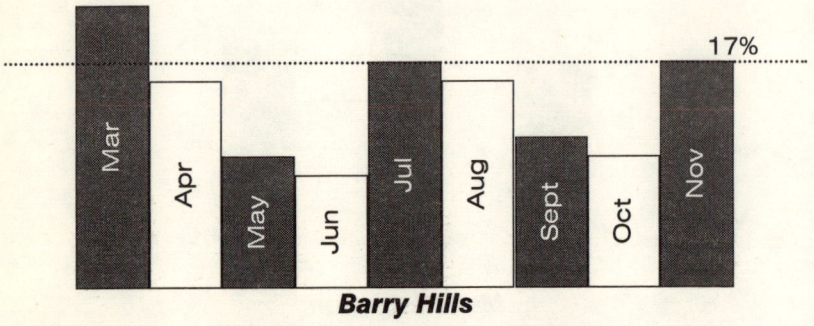

Barry Hills

17%

Mar | Apr | May | Jun | Jul | Aug | Sept | Oct | Nov

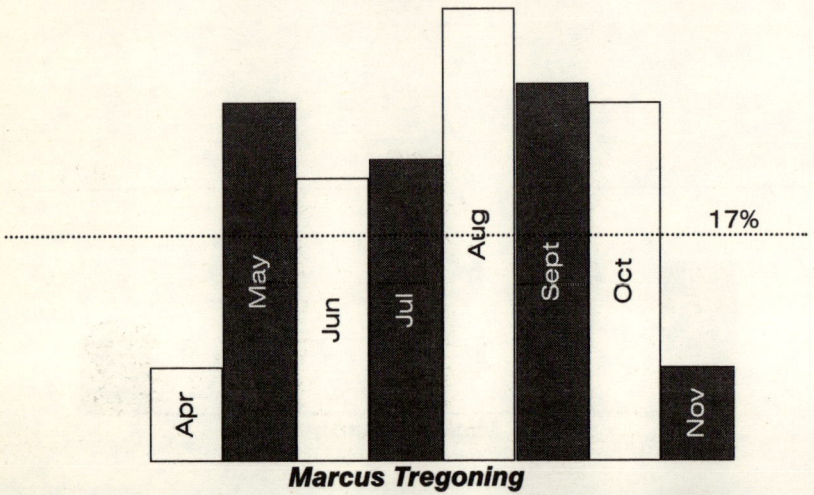

Marcus Tregoning

17%

Apr | May | Jun | Jul | Aug | Sept | Oct | Nov

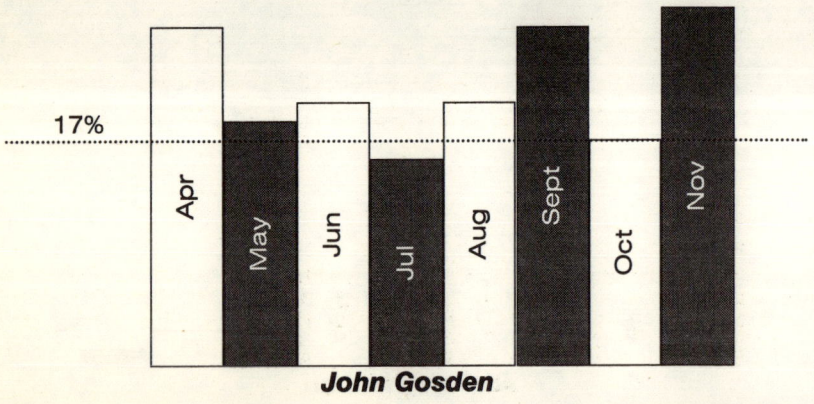

John Gosden

17%

Apr | May | Jun | Jul | Aug | Sept | Oct | Nov

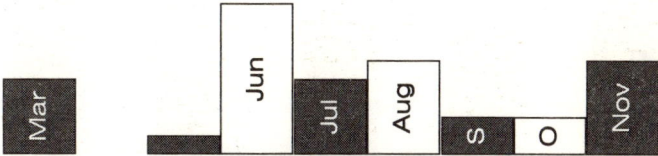

17%

Tim Easterby

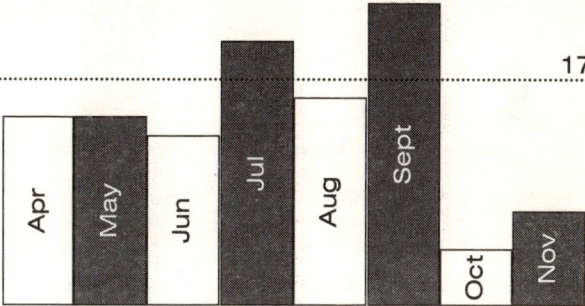

17%

Luca Cumani

17%

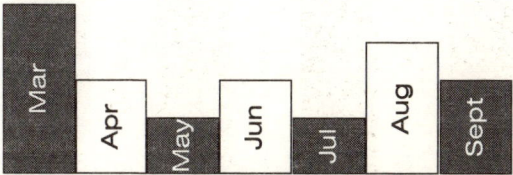

Andrew Balding

Sir Michael Stoute

CHAMPION trainer once more, thanks to a massive prize-money haul of almost £4million, Sir Michael is nonetheless a hard man for poor punters to get money out of.

The truth is, his horses are highly unlikely to be a value price because nearly every one of the yard's runners is popular with bettors.

However, it's interesting to note that his older handicappers have made profit twice in the last three years, while Willie Supple is an underrated rider for him.

By month

2003

	Overall			Two-year-olds			Three-year-olds			Older horses		
	W-R	%	£1	W-R	%	£1	W-R	%	£1	W-R	%	£1
January	0-0			0-0			0-0			0-0		
February	0-0			0-0			0-0			0-0		
March	0-0			0-0			0-0			0-0		
April	8-20	40	-2.85	0-0			7-18	38	-3.85	1-2	50	+1.00
May	31-80	38	+58.69	1-1	100	+0.83	19-55	34	+27.60	11-24	45	+30.26
June	16-72	22	-25.63	0-4		-4.00	12-41	29	-3.43	4-27	14	-18.20
July	12-75	16	-31.26	3-13	23	-8.26	6-43	13	-26.75	3-19	15	+3.75
August	25-101	24	-22.66	6-25	24	-8.69	14-54	25	-9.25	5-22	22	-4.72
September	16-71	22	+19.63	8-36	22	+1.12	5-24	20	-1.48	3-11	27	+20.00
October	8-61	13	-25.95	6-39	15	-14.45	2-17	11	-6.50	0-5		-5.00
November	0-8		-8.00	0-6		-6.00	0-1		-1.00	0-1		-1.00
December	0-0			0-0			0-0			0-0		

2002

	Overall			Two-year-olds			Three-year-olds			Older horses		
	W-R	%	£1	W-R	%	£1	W-R	%	£1	W-R	%	£1
January	0-0			0-0			0-0			0-0		
February	0-0			0-0			0-0			0-0		
March	0-0			0-0			0-0			0-0		
April	7-35	20	+8.24	0-0		+0.00	7-35	20	+8.24	0-0		+0.00
May	19-77	24	+22.24	0-1		-1.00	19-68	27	+31.24	0-8		-8.00
June	18-84	21	-19.11	1-6	16	-2.75	14-67	20	-20.61	3-11	27	+4.25
July	13-58	22	+3.12	4-12	33	+3.75	8-42	19	-3.13	1-4	25	+2.50
August	21-89	23	-19.92	4-22	18	-9.76	17-60	28	-3.17	0-7		-7.00
September	14-72	19	-22.03	10-39	25	+1.23	4-30	13	-20.27	0-3		-3.00
October	13-63	20	-5.33	10-40	25	+7.75	3-20	15	-10.08	0-3		-3.00
November	1-10	10	-7.62	0-5		-5.00	1-5	20	-2.62	0-0		+0.00
December	0-2		-2.00	0-2		-2.00	0-0		+0.00	0-0		+0.00

2001

	Overall			Two-year-olds			Three-year-olds			Older horses		
	W-R	%	£1	W-R	%	£1	W-R	%	£1	W-R	%	£1
January	0-0			0-0			0-0			0-0		
February	0-0			0-0			0-0			0-0		
March	0-0			0-0			0-0			0-0		
April	1-19	5	-16.90	0-0		+0.00	1-16	6	-13.90	0-3		-3.00
May	10-56	17	+10.99	0-0		+0.00	8-44	18	+17.19	2-12	16	-6.20
June	15-64	23	+9.82	1-3	33	-1.64	12-52	23	+0.96	2-9	22	+10.50
July	16-66	24	-5.08	3-9	33	-3.80	11-50	22	-3.29	2-7	28	+2.00
August	19-90	21	-17.32	3-25	12	-11.50	13-57	22	-11.57	3-8	37	+5.75
September	9-57	15	-12.77	4-23	17	-11.60	4-29	13	-3.17	1-5	20	+2.00
October	5-41	12	-11.17	4-19	21	+6.50	1-20	5	-15.67	0-2		-2.00
November	0-8		-8.00	0-7		-7.00	0-1		-1.00	0-0		+0.00
December	0-0			0-0			0-0			0-0		

All runners

2003	Wins	Runs	%	2nd	3rd	rest	Win prize	Total prize	£1 Stake
2yo	24	124	(19%)	21	12	19	237,922.08	353,334.28	-39.45
3yo	65	253	(25%)	41	38	21	1,934,014.71	2,477,145.58	-24.66
4yo+	27	111	(24%)	12	21	9	643,699.22	1,049,521.95	+26.09
TOTAL	116	488	(23%)	74	71	49	2,815,636.01	3,880,001.81	-38.02

2002	Wins	Runs	%	2nd	3rd	rest	Win prize	Total prize	£1 Stake
2yo	29	127	(22%)	22	19	18	221,774.35	404,548.30	-7.78
3yo	73	327	(22%)	48	46	40	793,731.64	1,281,815.17	-20.42
4yo+	4	36	(11%)	2	4	9	563,047.85	791,416.74	-14.25
TOTAL	106	490	(21%)	72	69	67	1,578,553.84	2,477,780.21	-42.45

2001	Wins	Runs	%	2nd	3rd	rest	Win prize	Total prize	£1 Stake
2yo	15	86	(17%)	19	13	7	109,800.62	174,899.12	-29.03
3yo	50	269	(18%)	44	32	32	640,738.61	1,267,695.50	-30.44
4yo+	10	46	(21%)	5	9	8	511,950.99	779,549.66	+9.05
TOTAL	75	401	(18%)	68	54	47	1,262,490.22	2,222,144.28	-50.42

By race type

2003

	Overall			Two-year-olds			Three-year-olds			Older horses		
	W-R	%	£1	W-R	%	£1	W-R	%	£1	W-R	%	£1
Handicap	24-127	18	+22.53	0-2		-2.00	13-74	17	-5.30	11-51	21	+29.83
Group 1,2,3	10-71	14	-4.30	1-8	12	-4.00	7-34	20	+17.97	2-29	6	-18.27
Maiden	54-195	27	-46.15	15-94	15	-38.62	38-99	38	-8.53	1-2	50	+1.00
1st time out	11-83	13	-27.86	6-61	9	-27.83	5-21	23	+0.98	0-1		-1.00

2002

	Overall			Two-year-olds			Three-year-olds			Older horses		
	W-R	%	£1	W-R	%	£1	W-R	%	£1	W-R	%	£1
Handicap	12-107	11	-56.38	1-4	25	+0.50	11-98	11	-51.88	0-5		-5.00
Group 1,2,3	10-71	14	-33.22	2-11	18	-7.39	5-35	14	-18.83	3-25	12	-7.00
Maiden	68-242	28	+45.47	23-91	25	+9.13	45-151	29	+36.33	0-0		+0.00
1st time out	21-107	19	+25.47	13-61	21	+8.25	8-46	17	+17.22	0-0		+0.00

2001

	Overall			Two-year-olds			Three-year-olds			Older horses		
	W-R	%	£1	W-R	%	£1	W-R	%	£1	W-R	%	£1
Handicap	13-77	16	+8.91	0-1		-1.00	11-66	16	+0.91	2-10	20	+9.00
Group 1,2,3	11-65	16	-3.97	1-6	16	-1.20	5-34	14	-5.27	5-25	20	+2.50
Maiden	39-195	20	-39.61	10-62	16	-22.03	29-133	21	-17.58	0-0		+0.00
1st time out	11-84	13	-28.18	6-50	12	-34.43	5-34	14	+6.25	0-0		+0.00

By jockey

2003

	Overall			Two-year-olds			Three-year-olds			Older horses		
	W-R	%	£1	W-R	%	£1	W-R	%	£1	W-R	%	£1
K Fallon	64-243	26	-21.88	15-59	25	-13.39	30-124	24	-20.35	19-60	31	+11.84
B Doyle	15-57	26	-9.50	2-19	10	-15.39	11-32	34	+4.39	2-6	33	+1.50
R Hills	5-20	25	-6.97	2-6	33	+3.00	3-9	33	-4.97	0-5		-5.00
W Supple	4-13	30	+4.29	0-0		+0.00	3-11	27	-4.71	1-2	50	+9.00
J P Murtagh	4-16	25	-8.64	0-0		+0.00	3-8	37	-2.89	1-8	12	-5.75
R Hughes	4-26	15	-11.68	1-11	9	-9.43	2-11	18	-3.25	1-4	25	+1.00
J P Spencer	3-9	33	+16.50	2-5	40	+9.50	0-3		-3.00	1-1	100	+10.00
Pat Eddery	3-22	13	-8.75	1-9	11	-5.25	1-4	25	+3.00	1-9	11	-6.50
F Lynch	3-24	12	+2.08	0-3		-3.00	3-17	17	+9.08	0-4		-4.00
F Norton	2-4	50	+1.25	0-1		-1.00	2-3	66	+2.25	0-0		+0.00

By jockey ctd

2002

	Overall			Two-year-olds			Three-year-olds			Older horses		
	W-R	%	£1	W-R	%	£1	W-R	%	£1	W-R	%	£1
K Fallon	36-151	23	-30.25	11-44	25	-9.93	23-90	25	-13.56	2-17	11	-6.75
F Lynch	22-72	30	-0.63	9-22	40	+12.90	13-49	26	-12.53	0-1		-1.00
Pat Eddery	11-43	25	-5.34	1-7	14	-4.00	10-34	29	+0.67	0-2		-2.00
J Fortune	7-30	23	+33.00	2-10	20	-0.25	5-20	25	+33.25	0-0		
J P Murtagh	7-36	19	-1.88	1-7	14	-0.50	5-22	22	-1.89	1-7	14	+0.50
R Hughes	7-43	16	-10.22	2-11	18	+4.25	5-32	15	-14.47	0-0		
R Hills	6-30	20	-7.47	3-9	33	+6.75	3-16	18	-9.22	0-5		-5.00
J P Spencer	2-7	28	-1.00	0-2		-2.00	2-5	40	+1.00	0-0		
S W Kelly	2-19	10	-6.50	0-2		-2.00	2-16	12	-3.50	0-1		-1.00
K Dalgleish	1-1	100	+4.00	0-0			1-1	100	+4.00	0-0		

2001

	Overall			Two-year-olds			Three-year-olds			Older horses		
	W-R	%	£1	W-R	%	£1	W-R	%	£1	W-R	%	£1
K Fallon	46-225	20	-33.78	7-49	14	-30.10	30-141	21	-19.23	9-35	25	+15.55
F Lynch	8-49	16	-16.94	2-9	22	+8.50	6-38	15	-23.44	0-2		-2.00
R Hills	7-23	30	+3.57	5-9	55	+6.07	1-9	11	-2.00	1-5	20	-0.50
W Supple	3-10	30	+21.75	0-0			3-10	30	+21.75	0-0		
G Hind	3-15	20	+3.00	0-2		-2.00	3-13	23	+5.00	0-0		
J P Spencer	2-5	40	+2.23	1-2	50	+3.50	1-2	50	-0.27	0-1		-1.00
K Darley	1-1	100	+10.00	0-0			1-1	100	+10.00	0-0		
D McKeown	1-1	100	+2.75	0-0			1-1	100	+2.75	0-0		
J Mackay	1-4	25		0-0			1-4	25		0-0		
Pat Eddery	1-4	25	+1.50	0-0			1-4	25	+1.50	0-0		

By class

2003

	Overall			Two-year-olds			Three-year-olds			Older horses		
	W-R	%	£1	W-R	%	£1	W-R	%	£1	W-R	%	£1
A	22-128	17	-17.43	3-14	21	-0.50	10-66	15	-5.72	9-48	18	-11.21
B	11-60	18	+4.65	0-3		-3.00	4-24	16	-12.40	7-33	21	+20.05
C	21-72	29	+20.54	2-6	33	+1.90	9-42	21	-1.61	10-24	41	+20.25
D	60-214	28	-37.88	19-98	19	-34.85	40-113	35	-3.03	1-3	33	
E	1-7	14	-3.00	0-3		-3.00	1-4	25		0-0		
F	0-1		-1.00	0-0			0-1		-1.00	0-0		
G	0-0			0-0			0-0			0-0		

2002

	Overall			Two-year-olds			Three-year-olds			Older horses		
	W-R	%	£1	W-R	%	£1	W-R	%	£1	W-R	%	£1
A	13-100	13	-49.18	3-15	20	-4.39	8-57	14	-30.79	2-28	7	-14.00
B	6-37	16	-12.91	1-5	20	-3.27	4-27	14	-8.38	1-5	20	-1.25
C	12-64	18	-23.68	1-9	11	-6.75	11-54	20	-15.93	0-1		-1.00
D	71-270	26	+45.07	23-96	23	+4.63	48-174	27	+40.43	0-0		
E	2-8	25	+1.25	0-1		-1.00	2-7	28	+2.25	0-0		
F	1-5	20	-1.00	1-1	100	+3.00	0-4		-4.00	0-0		
G	0-0			0-0			0-0			0-0		

2001

	Overall			Two-year-olds			Three-year-olds			Older horses		
	W-R	%	£1	W-R	%	£1	W-R	%	£1	W-R	%	£1
A	15-95	15	-12.17	2-11	18	-1.70	6-52	11	-12.27	7-32	21	+1.80
B	3-29	10		0-2		-2.00	2-18	11	+5.00	1-9	11	-3.00
C	7-37	18	+1.00	1-6	16	-1.50	4-28	14	-9.75	2-3	66	+12.25
D	47-223	21	-40.58	12-66	18	-22.83	35-157	22	-17.75	0-0		
E	3-12	25	+6.33	0-1		-1.00	3-11	27	+7.33	0-0		
F	0-1		-1.00	0-0			0-1		-1.00	0-0		
G	0-0			0-0			0-0			0-0		

Sponsored by Stan James

KRIS KIN (third left): wins the Derby for Stoute

By course

2003

	Overall			Two-year-olds			Three-year-olds			Older horses		
	W-R	%	£1	W-R	%	£1	W-R	%	£1	W-R	%	£1
Ascot	8-50	16	-27.28	1-4	25		5-25	20	-10.08	2-21	9	-17.20
Ayr	2-5	40	+5.13	0-1		-1.00	1-3	33	-1.88	1-1	100	+8.00
Bath	1-4	25	-2.33	0-0			1-4	25	-2.33	0-0		
Beverley	1-6	16	-4.33	0-1		-1.00	1-5	20	-3.33	0-0		
Brighton	3-5	60	+2.03	0-1		-1.00	3-4	75	+3.03	0-0		
Carlisle	1-2	50	-0.17	0-0			1-2	50	-0.17	0-0		
Catterick	0-2		-2.00	0-1		-1.00	0-1		-1.00	0-0		
Chepstow	1-4	25	-1.63	0-0			1-4	25	-1.63	0-0		
Chester	4-13	30	+18.00	0-2		-2.00	2-6	33	+17.50	2-5	40	+2.50
Curragh	0-4		-4.00	0-0			0-2		-2.00	0-2		-2.00
Doncaster	3-21	14	-10.10	1-10	10	-8.60	2-7	28	+2.50	0-4		-4.00
Epsom	2-9	22	+0.25	0-0			1-6	16	+1.00	1-3	33	-0.75
Folkestone	0-4			0-1		-1.00	0-3		-3.00			
Goodwood	7-25	28	+1.55	1-2	50	-0.80	2-14	14	-8.45	4-9	44	+10.80
Hamilton	3-4	75	+3.50	0-0			2-3	66	+2.25	1-1	100	+1.25
Haydock	2-7	28	-2.40	0-0			2-4	50	+0.60	0-3		-3.00
Kempton	3-9	33	-3.85	1-5	20	-3.33	2-2	100	+1.48	0-2		-2.00
Leicester	3-19	15	+1.50	2-13	15	+2.50	0-3		-3.00	1-3	33	+2.00
Le'pardstown	1-2	50	+0.10	0-0			1-1	100	+1.10	0-1		-1.00
Lingfield	3-13	23	-6.76	1-5	20	-2.90	2-8	25	-3.86	0-0		
Musselburgh	1-2	50	-0.78	0-0			1-1	100	+0.22	0-1		-1.00
Newbury	4-20	20	+12.17	0-5		-5.00	2-9	22	-5.33	2-6	33	+22.50
Newcastle	1-5	20	+2.50	1-2	50	+5.50	0-1		-1.00	0-2		-2.00
Newmarket	10-83	12	-23.58	2-27	7	-18.00	5-43	11	-12.33	3-13	23	+6.75
Nottingham	2-10	20	+1.57	1-6	16	-4.43	1-4	25	+6.00	0-0		
Pontefract	5-9	55	+10.83	2-3	66	+2.41	3-6	50	+8.42	0-0		
Redcar	1-5	20	+6.00	0-1		-1.00	0-3		-3.00	1-1	100	+10.00
Ripon	4-8	50	-0.80	1-1	100	+1.50	3-7	42	-2.31	0-0		
Salisbury	3-11	27	-3.43	1-4	25	-1.63	1-5	20	-2.80	1-2	50	+1.00
Sandown	4-29	13	-15.31	1-6	16	+0.50	3-15	20	-7.81	0-8		-8.00
Southwell	0-1		-1.00	0-0			0-1		-1.00	0-0		
Thirsk	0-5		-5.00	0-0			0-4		-4.00	0-1		-1.00
Warwick	3-8	37	+0.04	0-3		-3.00	3-5	60	+3.04	0-0		
Windsor	12-26	46	+8.80	3-9	33	-4.09	7-14	50	+9.31	2-3	66	+3.58
Wolver	1-2	50		0-0			1-2	50		0-0		
Yarmouth	9-20	45	+13.60	5-9	55	+9.92	3-10	30	+1.68	1-1	100	+2.00
York	8-36	22	-6.84	0-2		-2.00	3-16	18	-2.50	5-18	27	-2.34

Mark Johnston

'ALWAYS TRYING' is the motto, and this yard is indeed always a reliable source of winners.

Last season, Johnston recorded his tenth consecutive century of domestic winners, surpassing the record set by Henry Cecil. The best way to make money following his runners may be to get the timing right – his horses have run well, at good prices, in April in two of the last three seasons, and seem to peak again in July at the time of the big Ascot and Goodwood meetings.

By month

2003

	Overall			Two-year-olds			Three-year-olds			Older horses		
	W-R	%	£1	W-R	%	£1	W-R	%	£1	W-R	%	£1
January	3-16	18	+0.41	0-0			2-12	16	-0.09	1-4	25	+0.50
February	3-16	18	-9.10	0-0			3-15	20	-8.10	0-1		-1.00
March	1-22	4	-10.00	0-0			0-14		-14.00	1-8	12	+4.00
April	12-57	21	+27.12	2-7	28	-1.83	8-34	23	+30.85	2-16	12	-1.90
May	25-135	18	-13.41	9-22	40	-0.35	14-87	16	-1.05	2-26	7	-12.00
June	29-137	21	-15.61	13-34	38	+12.11	13-59	22	+1.24	3-44	6	-28.96
July	28-113	24	+45.97	8-27	29	-7.49	15-59	25	+32.46	5-27	18	+21.00
August	16-102	15	-13.37	6-33	18	-8.55	9-49	18	+13.35	1-20	5	-18.17
September	14-84	16	-13.41	10-45	22	-5.01	3-28	10	+0.50	1-11	9	-8.90
October	7-53	13	+4.13	6-38	15	+6.13	0-10		-10.00	1-5	20	+8.00
November	2-24	8	-7.00	1-17	5	-9.00	0-5		-5.00	1-2	50	+7.00
December	0-3		-3.00	0-3		-3.00	0-0			0-0		

2002

	Overall			Two-year-olds			Three-year-olds			Older horses		
	W-R	%	£1	W-R	%	£1	W-R	%	£1	W-R	%	£1
January	4-28	14	-17.89	0-0			3-20	15	-12.89	1-8	12	-5.00
February	3-15	20	-2.30	0-0			3-12	25	+0.70	0-3		-3.00
March	8-21	38	+8.43	0-0			6-16	37	+9.14	2-5	40	-0.70
April	9-43	20	-10.86	0-1		-1.00	6-30	20	-15.36	3-12	25	+5.50
May	19-109	17	-9.05	8-21	38	+12.82	8-66	12	-6.75	3-22	13	-15.13
June	19-121	15	+6.47	4-22	18	+11.63	12-66	18	-9.55	3-33	9	+4.40
July	25-110	22	-0.96	7-30	23	+3.97	11-56	19	-16.68	7-24	29	+11.75
August	16-103	15	-19.01	3-32	9	-16.50	9-49	18	-10.14	4-22	18	+7.63
September	18-81	22	+5.39	4-38	10	-18.59	9-26	34	+18.25	5-17	29	+5.73
October	8-65	12	-22.28	1-28	3	-22.00	4-24	16	+0.62	3-13	23	-0.90
November	4-43	9	-7.50	2-25	8	-18.50	1-9	11	-1.00	1-9	11	+12.00
December	2-15	13	-6.25	2-12	16	-3.25	0-2		-2.00	0-1		-1.00

2001

	Overall			Two-year-olds			Three-year-olds			Older horses		
	W-R	%	£1	W-R	%	£1	W-R	%	£1	W-R	%	£1
January	2-13	15	-5.27	0-0			0-5		-5.00	2-8	25	-0.27
February	0-23		-23.00	0-0			0-11		-11.00	0-12		-12.00
March	0-10		-10.00	0-0			0-2		-2.00	0-8		-8.00
April	11-43	25	+16.25	0-6		-6.00	8-19	42	+18.75	3-18	16	+3.50
May	14-92	15	+29.17	0-13		-13.00	8-39	20	+2.30	6-40	15	+39.88
June	14-98	14	-9.40	4-15	26	+3.50	3-45	6	-21.80	7-38	18	+8.90
July	19-106	17	+35.02	8-36	22	+22.77	7-41	17	+22.00	4-29	13	-9.75
August	16-123	13	-40.05	8-42	19	+2.24	4-54	7	-35.42	4-27	14	-6.87
September	18-110	16	-3.30	10-53	18	-15.90	6-36	16	+11.60	2-21	9	-4.00
October	12-102	11	-15.67	5-51	9	-16.50	4-30	13	+6.20	3-21	14	-5.38
November	7-42	16	-1.91	2-20	10	-16.60	2-14	14	+0.44	3-8	37	+14.25
December	2-14	14	-2.67	1-5	20	-0.67	1-8	12	-1.00	0-1		-1.00

All runners

2003	Wins	Runs	%	2nd	3rd	rest	Win prize	Total prize	£1 Stake
2yo	55	226	24	35	20	20	602,277.18	731,823.16	-17.01
3yo	67	372	18	57	34	23	544,026.44	806,894.87	+40.17
4yo+	18	164	10	15	19	21	315,131.50	588,372.10	-30.42
TOTAL	140	762	18	107	73	64	1,461,435.12	2,127,090.13	-7.26

2002	Wins	Runs	%	2nd	3rd	rest	Win prize	Total prize	£1 Stake
2yo	31	209	14	31	33	22	194,065.40	316,360.93	-51.42
3yo	72	376	19	49	42	37	775,035.38	1,027,849.67	-45.64
4yo+	32	169	18	20	21	9	700,537.41	998,577.82	+21.27
TOTAL	135	754	17	100	96	68	1,669,638.19	2,342,788.42	-75.79

2001	Wins	Runs	%	2nd	3rd	rest	Win prize	Total prize	£1 Stake
2yo	38	241	15	35	26	24	448,669.00	563,476.57	-40.17
3yo	43	304	14	36	32	25	416,217.23	605,994.18	-14.93
4yo+	34	231	14	19	20	20	492,788.54	660,439.40	+19.26
TOTAL	115	776	14	90	78	69	1,357,674.77	1,829,910.15	-35.84

By race type

2003

	Overall			Two-year-olds			Three-year-olds			Older horses		
	W-R	%	£1	W-R	%	£1	W-R	%	£1	W-R	%	£1
Handicap	56-372	15	+46.82	2-31	6	-19.75	43-233	18	+74.07	11-108	10	-7.50
Group 1,2,3	9-45	20	-14.25	6-18	33	-1.35	1-7	14	-2.50	2-20	10	-10.40
Maiden	46-233	19	-44.65	32-132	24	+0.26	14-98	14	-41.91	0-3		-3.00
1st time out	14-96	14	-24.28	12-68	17	-9.12	1-25	4	-14.00	1-3	33	-1.17

2002

	Overall			Two-year-olds			Three-year-olds			Older horses		
	W-R	%	£1	W-R	%	£1	W-R	%	£1	W-R	%	£1
Handicap	44-338	13	-64.38	1-32	3	-30.33	31-205	15	-23.92	12-101	11	-10.12
Group 1,2,3	13-57	22	+12.05	0-10		-10.00	6-19	31	-1.08	7-28	25	+23.13
Maiden	38-227	16	-63.96	20-127	15	-26.83	18-99	18	-36.13	0-1		-1.00
1st time out	12-96	12	-35.11	6-63	9	-26.34	6-30	20	-5.77	0-3		-3.00

2001

	Overall			Two-year-olds			Three-year-olds			Older horses		
	W-R	%	£1	W-R	%	£1	W-R	%	£1	W-R	%	£1
Handicap	47-404	11	-15.76	3-44	6	-26.17	24-183	13	+0.43	20-177	11	+9.98
Group 1,2,3	3-43	6	-14.00	1-10	10	-2.00	1-16	6	-4.00	1-17	5	-8.00
Maiden	32-205	15	-25.08	22-138	15	-12.61	9-65	13	-16.47	1-2	50	+4.00
1st time out	12-87	13	-13.13	7-58	12	-6.50	3-20	15	-7.50	2-9	22	+0.88

By jockey

2003

	Overall			Two-year-olds			Three-year-olds			Older horses		
	W-R	%	£1	W-R	%	£1	W-R	%	£1	W-R	%	£1
J Fanning	49-249	19	+35.05	14-83	16	-26.36	28-130	21	+39.36	7-36	19	+22.04
K Dalgleish	41-213	19	+9.29	20-65	30	+17.29	17-97	17	+25.57	4-51	7	-33.57
K Darley	14-70	20	-8.18	6-15	40	+10.20	6-33	18	-10.48	2-22	9	-7.90
R Ffrench	13-75	17	+18.08	2-20	10	-11.25	10-48	20	+23.33	1-7	14	+6.00
D Holland	8-44	18	-21.04	6-13	46	-0.66	1-17	5	-14.38	1-14	7	-6.00
G Duffield	3-15	20	-1.92	1-3	33	-1.92	1-8	12	-5.00	1-4	25	+5.00
S Chin	2-3	66	-0.39	2-2	100	+0.61	0-1		-1.00	0-0		
L Dettori	2-5	40	+3.33	2-4	50	+4.33	0-1		-1.00	0-0		
J F Egan	2-9	22	-1.50	0-0			2-7	28	+0.50	0-2		-2.00
W Hogg	2-16	12	+4.00	0-0			1-10	10	+1.00	1-6	16	+3.00

By jockey ctd

2002

	Overall			Two-year-olds			Three-year-olds			Older horses		
	W-R	%	£1	W-R	%	£1	W-R	%	£1	W-R	%	£1
K Darley	47-230	20	-45.54	13-76	17	-32.92	25-106	23	-2.22	9-48	18	-10.40
K Dalgleish	35-222	15	-14.94	10-64	15	+21.46	19-109	17	-13.65	6-49	12	-22.75
J Fanning	24-153	15	-64.20	6-37	16	-14.47	13-90	14	-41.46	5-26	19	-8.27
R Hills	5-12	41	+31.70	0-0			4-9	44	+19.30	1-3	33	+12.40
D Holland	4-12	33	+11.50	0-1		-1.00	3-6	50	+10.00	1-5	20	+2.50
R Ffrench	3-41	7	-23.75	1-16	6	-14.00	2-19	10	-3.75	0-6		-6.00
W Hogg	2-13	15	-3.00	0-0			1-8	12	-3.00	1-5	20	
D Corby	1-1	100	+4.50	0-0			0-0			1-1	100	+4.50
K Fallon	1-1	100	+0.50	0-0			1-1	100	+0.50	0-0		
J Quinn	1-1	100	+4.50	0-0			1-1	100	+4.50	0-0		

2001

	Overall			Two-year-olds			Three-year-olds			Older horses		
	W-R	%	£1	W-R	%	£1	W-R	%	£1	W-R	%	£1
K Darley	49-240	20	+56.53	20-98	20	+26.22	16-81	19	+19.91	13-61	21	+10.40
K Dalgleish	26-170	15	+47.51	4-48	8	-31.17	13-74	17	+43.55	9-48	18	+35.12
J Fanning	22-187	11	-92.92	6-60	10	-35.26	12-81	14	-25.38	4-46	8	-32.27
D Holland	5-40	12	-9.63	2-7	28	-2.63	0-16		-16.00	3-17	17	+9.00
R Hills	4-14	28	+6.50	2-3	66	+3.50	1-6	16	+1.00	1-5	20	+2.00
M Roberts	4-15	26	+4.67	2-3	66	+5.67	1-5	20	+3.00	1-7	14	-4.00
J P Murtagh	1-4	25	+5.00	0-1		-1.00	0-0			1-3	33	+6.00
Dean McKeown	1-5	20	+4.00	1-3	33	+6.00	0-2		-2.00	0-0		
J P Spencer	1-7	14	-4.00	0-2		-2.00	0-0			1-5	20	-2.00
M Hills	1-14	7	+20.00	0-1		-1.00	0-6		-6.00	1-7	14	+27.00

By class

2003

	Overall			Two-year-olds			Three-year-olds			Older horses		
	W-R	%	£1	W-R	%	£1	W-R	%	£1	W-R	%	£1
A	16-86	18	-18.70	10-29	34	+8.10	2-18	11	-8.50	4-39	10	-18.30
B	8-82	9	-22.50	1-9	11	-7.00	5-43	11	-3.50	2-30	6	-12.00
C	17-114	14	-14.44	3-13	23	-1.34	12-61	19	+17.37	2-40	5	-30.46
D	58-290	20	+8.19	25-120	20	-8.11	27-141	19	-0.54	6-29	20	+16.83
E	29-132	21	+43.44	9-42	21	-16.64	16-75	21	+35.58	4-15	26	+24.50
F	8-40	20	+0.77	3-6	50	+1.02	5-27	18	+6.75	0-7		-7.00
G	3-14	21	-2.29	3-4	75	+7.71	0-7		-7.00	0-3		-3.00

2002

	Overall			Two-year-olds			Three-year-olds			Older horses		
	W-R	%	£1	W-R	%	£1	W-R	%	£1	W-R	%	£1
A	22-92	23	+44.76	3-22	13	+8.21	9-31	29	+7.93	10-39	25	+28.62
B	14-83	16	-7.59	0-5		-5.00	7-37	18	-3.39	7-41	17	+0.79
C	18-112	16	-18.23	1-17	5	-13.50	11-57	19	+3.04	6-38	15	-7.77
D	47-281	16	-69.37	19-117	16	-19.16	28-148	18	-34.21	0-16		-16.00
E	21-127	16	-20.49	7-38	18	-13.22	11-76	14	-23.77	3-13	23	+16.50
F	8-40	20	-8.63	1-7	14	-5.75	3-19	15		4-14	28	-2.87
G	4-13	30	+5.25	0-2		-2.00	3-7	42	+5.75	1-4	25	+1.50

2001

	Overall			Two-year-olds			Three-year-olds			Older horses		
	W-R	%	£1	W-R	%	£1	W-R	%	£1	W-R	%	£1
A	12-89	13	-19.79	4-22	18	+1.50	3-40	7	-16.67	5-27	18	-4.63
B	22-119	18	+65.28	4-17	23	+9.88	10-39	25	+29.53	8-63	12	+25.88
C	24-137	17	+37.79	3-19	15	-8.50	11-54	20	+29.79	10-64	15	+16.50
D	34-243	13	-72.69	18-108	16	-31.04	12-97	12	-23.05	4-38	10	-18.60
E	12-117	10	-28.19	6-55	10	-2.67	1-41	2	-38.75	5-21	23	+13.23
F	9-54	16	-7.93	2-14	14	-5.00	5-25	20	+7.20	2-15	13	-10.12
G	1-8	12	-6.33	1-5	20	-3.33	0-2		-2.00	0-1		-1.00

ATTRACTION:
wins Newmarket's
Cherry Hinton for
Johnston

By course

2003

	Overall			Two-year-olds			Three-year-olds			Older horses		
	W-R	%	£1	W-R	%	£1	W-R	%	£1	W-R	%	£1
Ascot	9-45	20	+0.22	3-9	33	+0.73	5-18	27	+11.50	1-18	5	-12.00
Ayr	12-41	29	+20.91	9-21	42	+10.91	1-14	7	+1.00	2-6	33	+9.00
Bath	1-4	25	+8.00	0-1		-1.00	1-3	33	+9.00	0-0		
Beverley	13-39	33	+38.13	4-9	44	+0.05	9-28	32	+40.08	0-2		-2.00
Brighton	2-7	28	+0.38	1-1	100	+1.38	0-4		-4.00	1-2	50	+3.00
Carlisle	3-14	21	-3.75	0-3		-3.00	3-8	37	+2.25	0-3		-3.00
Catterick	9-27	33	+13.82	4-8	50	-1.91	3-15	20	-4.27	2-4	50	+20.00
Chepstow	1-3	33	-1.20	1-1	100	+0.80	0-0			0-2		-2.00
Chester	1-9	11	-4.00	0-0			1-6	16	-1.00	0-3		-3.00
Curragh	1-4	25	-1.75	1-3	33	-0.75	0-0			0-1		-1.00
Doncaster	9-45	20	+9.94	3-16	18	-5.43	4-15	26	+18.83	2-14	14	-3.46
Epsom	4-14	28	+8.00	2-2	100	+7.50	1-8	12	-3.00	1-4	25	+3.50
Folkestone	0-1		-1.00	0-0			0-1		-1.00	0-0		
Goodwood	3-37	8	-14.80	1-7	14	-4.80	0-17		-17.00	2-13	15	+7.00
Hamilton	11-53	20	+22.34	5-21	23	+13.00	5-20	25	+19.50	1-12	8	-10.17
Haydock	8-35	22	-0.87	2-8	25	+2.00	5-18	27	+4.03	1-9	11	-6.90
Kempton	0-3		-3.00	0-0			0-2		-2.00	0-1		-1.00
Leicester	7-25	28	+9.66	3-10	30	+3.83	4-11	36	+9.83	0-4		-4.00
Lingfield	1-19	5	-17.09	1-2	50	-0.09	0-15		-15.00	0-2		-2.00
Musselburgh	3-22	13	-8.98	0-7		-7.00	2-7	28	-2.98	1-8	12	+1.00
Newbury	0-13		-13.00	0-3		-3.00	0-4		-4.00	0-6		-6.00
Newcastle	0-20		-20.00	0-8		-8.00	0-9		-9.00	0-3		-3.00
Newmarket	4-34	11	-1.43	1-7	14	-5.43	3-17	17	+14.00	0-10		-10.00
Nottingham	3-20	15	-6.13	2-8	25	-1.63	1-10	10	-2.50	0-2		-2.00
Pontefract	6-32	18	+16.91	2-15	13	-11.42	2-14	14	+5.33	2-3	66	+23.00
Redcar	4-26	15	-2.38	3-11	27	+10.00	1-13	7	-10.38	0-2		-2.00
Ripon	4-29	13	-18.78	1-7	14	-5.39	3-17	17	-8.39	0-5		-5.00
Salisbury	0-6		-6.00	0-0			0-5		-5.00	0-1		-1.00
Sandown	7-20	35	+4.99	3-6	50	+3.64	3-5	60	+8.25	1-9	11	-6.90
Southwell	2-19	10	-12.59	0-4		-4.00	1-13	7	-11.09	1-2	50	+2.50
Thirsk	3-23	13	-3.00	2-8	25	-3.00	1-12	8	+3.00	0-3		-3.00
Warwick	0-7		-7.00	0-2		-2.00	0-5		-5.00	0-0		
Windsor	1-8	12	-4.50	0-2		-2.00	1-4	25	-0.50	0-2		-2.00
Wolver	4-25	16	-8.10	0-6		-6.00	4-17	23	-0.10	0-2		-2.00
Yarmouth	0-4		-4.00	0-0			0-4		-4.00	0-0		
York	4-29	13	+2.75	1-10	10	+5.00	3-13	23	+3.75	0-6		-6.00

Mick Channon

MORE WINNERS came from this yard than anywhere else last season, so we should follow this man, right?

Wrong. One of the reasons there are so many Channon winners in these stats is that he regularly sends out many more runners than anyone else. His strike-rate last season was about half of Sir Michael Stoute's, making it desperately difficult to turn a profit by following him.

Try catching him early on – his runners hit a net profit in April last year and March the year before.

By month

2003

	Overall			Two-year-olds			Three-year-olds			Older horses		
	W-R	%	£1	W-R	%	£1	W-R	%	£1	W-R	%	£1
January	3-20	15	-5.00	0-0			2-7	28	+4.50	1-13	7	-9.50
February	0-6		-6.00	0-0			0-2		-2.00	0-4		-4.00
March	1-24	4	-22.20	1-2	50	-0.20	0-13		-13.00	0-9		-9.00
April	15-83	18	+15.51	5-15	33	+1.73	6-35	17	+25.16	4-33	12	-11.38
May	19-148	12	-40.22	7-35	20	-12.45	7-59	11	-28.57	5-54	9	+0.80
June	12-136	8	-32.45	3-35	8	-22.63	5-49	10	+15.55	4-52	7	-25.38
July	27-190	14	+5.37	14-70	20	+13.24	9-62	14	-9.63	4-58	6	+1.75
August	21-187	11	-80.85	8-85	9	-47.63	8-51	15	-14.97	5-51	9	-18.25
September	21-155	13	+4.45	7-80	8	-26.92	5-36	13	-5.79	9-39	23	+37.17
October	21-151	13	-12.72	6-78	7	-47.33	7-36	19	+26.00	8-37	21	+8.61
November	4-41	9	-15.90	2-17	11	+0.50	2-12	16	-4.40	0-12		-12.00
December	2-7	28	+1.75	1-3	33	-0.25	1-4	25	+2.00	0-0		

2002

	Overall			Two-year-olds			Three-year-olds			Older horses		
	W-R	%	£1	W-R	%	£1	W-R	%	£1	W-R	%	£1
January	1-5	20	-0.50	0-0			0-0			1-5	20	-0.50
February	0-9		-9.00	0-0			0-4		-4.00	0-5		-5.00
March	6-28	21	+20.20	1-3	33	-0.80	2-15	13	+2.50	3-10	30	+18.50
April	9-87	10	-25.83	4-17	23	-2.75	3-49	6	-41.08	2-21	9	+18.00
May	18-140	12	-7.84	6-36	16	-16.59	7-67	10	+7.25	5-37	13	+1.50
June	16-134	11	-23.31	7-46	15	-16.31	4-41	9		5-47	10	-7.00
July	23-143	16	-21.13	11-58	18	-13.99	4-48	8	-25.90	8-37	21	+18.75
August	16-166	9	-58.98	6-70	8	-51.53	2-57	3	-23.00	8-39	20	+15.55
September	22-141	15	+33.79	9-63	14	-1.27	10-48	20	+37.56	3-30	10	-2.50
October	9-117	7	-33.50	5-61	8	-23.50	1-31	3	-23.00	3-25	12	+13.00
November	2-27	7	+5.00	1-11	9	-5.00	0-10		-10.00	1-6	16	+20.00
December	3-16	18	-2.50	2-10	20	-2.50	0-3		-3.00	1-3	33	+3.00

2001

	Overall			Two-year-olds			Three-year-olds			Older horses		
	W-R	%	£1	W-R	%	£1	W-R	%	£1	W-R	%	£1
January	2-5	40	+4.00	0-0			1-3	33	+1.00	1-2	50	+3.00
February	0-1		-1.00	0-0			0-1		-1.00	0-0		
March	1-11	9	-7.75	0-2		-2.00	1-6	16	-2.75	0-3		-3.00
April	1-48	2	-45.90	0-7		-7.00	1-32	3	-29.90	0-9		-9.00
May	7-115	6	-81.34	4-34	11	-19.34	3-57	5	-38.00	0-24		-24.00
June	16-138	11	-75.01	10-47	21	-6.23	6-65	9	-42.78	0-26		-26.00
July	11-110	10	-65.26	6-42	14	-20.26	4-50	8	-40.00	1-18	5	-5.00
August	10-147	6	-86.38	6-73	8	-39.38	2-48	4	-36.50	2-26	7	-10.50
September	6-118	5	-77.59	5-65	7	-30.09	1-35	2	-29.50	0-18		-18.00
October	10-84	11	-15.84	7-52	13	-12.84	1-19	5	-10.00	2-13	15	+7.00
November	3-29	10	-2.00	3-16	18	+11.00	0-5		-5.00	0-8		-8.00
December	0-2		-2.00	0-1		-1.00	0-0			0-1		-1.00

All runners

2003	Wins	Runs	%	2nd	3rd	rest	Win prize	Total prize	£1 Stake
2yo	54	420	12	57	70	39	442,294.77	770,230.84	-141.93
3yo	52	366	14	33	38	35	481,057.75	770,039.39	-5.14
4yo+	40	362	11	37	46	36	391,978.05	649,220.13	-41.17
TOTAL	146	1148	12	127	154	110	1,315,330.57	2,189,490.36	-188.24

2002	Wins	Runs	%	2nd	3rd	rest	Win prize	Total prize	£1 Stake
2yo	52	375	13	57	56	51	368,590.67	617,943.12	-134.23
3yo	33	373	8	47	49	47	193,105.59	409,904.87	-82.67
4yo+	40	265	15	24	29	22	442,304.94	659,819.82	+93.30
TOTAL	125	1013	12	128	134	120	1,004,001.20	1,687,667.81	-123.60

2001	Wins	Runs	%	2nd	3rd	rest	Win prize	Total prize	£1 Stake
2yo	41	339	12	43	35	38	359,472.05	583,291.17	-127.14
3yo	20	321	6	26	42	39	87,168.70	269,407.91	-234.43
4yo+	6	148	4	18	9	17	33,371.00	128,124.55	-94.50
TOTAL	67	808	8	87	86	94	480,011.75	980,823.63	-456.07

By race type

2003

	Overall			Two-year-olds			Three-year-olds			Older horses		
	W-R	%	£1	W-R	%	£1	W-R	%	£1	W-R	%	£1
Handicap	67-579	11	-15.36	8-81	9	-28.34	31-219	14	+15.87	28-279	10	-2.89
Group 1,2,3	4-55	7	-22.00	1-25	4	-12.00	1-14	7	-5.00	2-16	12	-5.00
Maiden	39-275	14	-65.57	26-189	13	-56.34	12-78	15	-2.89	1-8	12	-6.33
1st time out	9-110	8	-69.15	9-87	10	-46.15	0-22		-22.00	0-1		-1.00

2002

	Overall			Two-year-olds			Three-year-olds			Older horses		
	W-R	%	£1	W-R	%	£1	W-R	%	£1	W-R	%	£1
Handicap	50-493	10	-26.05	10-91	10	-16.13	12-189	6	-58.27	28-213	13	+48.35
Group 1,2,3	5-41	12	-21.19	2-18	11	-7.27	1-7	14	-5.67	2-16	12	-8.25
Maiden	37-250	14	-64.38	27-154	17	-61.82	10-92	10	+1.44	0-4		-4.00
1st time out	11-105	10	-51.13	8-71	11	-40.47	3-32	9	-8.67	0-2		-2.00

2001

	Overall			Two-year-olds			Three-year-olds			Older horses		
	W-R	%	£1	W-R	%	£1	W-R	%	£1	W-R	%	£1
Handicap	14-342	4	-235.75	4-70	5	-38.00	4-155	2	-134.25	6-117	5	-63.50
Group 1,2,3	3-47	6	-29.59	3-17	17	+0.41	0-21		-21.00	0-9		-9.00
Maiden	27-225	12	-115.61	21-162	12	-71.33	6-62	9	-43.28	0-1		-1.00
1st time out	5-81	6	-62.25	4-64	6	-49.25	1-14	7	-10.00	0-3		-3.00

By jockey

2003

	Overall			Two-year-olds			Three-year-olds			Older horses		
	W-R	%	£1	W-R	%	£1	W-R	%	£1	W-R	%	£1
S Hitchcott	36-189	19	+78.04	6-45	13	-25.59	18-63	28	+71.38	12-81	14	+32.25
A Culhane	34-152	22	+35.33	15-75	20	+5.83	10-34	29	+25.51	9-43	20	+3.98
C Catlin	24-220	10	-59.16	12-97	12	-8.92	5-61	8	-46.59	7-62	11	-3.66
S Drowne	22-184	11	-79.57	11-75	14	-35.87	8-83	9	-43.45	3-26	11	-0.25
T E Durcan	15-133	11	-26.38	8-69	11	-27.13	3-35	8	+15.00	4-29	13	-14.25
D Corby	3-87	3	-64.25	0-18		-18.00	1-29	3	-25.00	2-40	5	-21.25
E Creighton	2-59	3	-37.00	0-5		-5.00	1-21	4	-4.00	1-33	3	-28.00
M J Kinane	1-1	100	+1.25	1-1	100	+1.25	0-0			0-0		
J F McDonald	1-2	50	+4.50	0-0			1-2	50	+4.50	0-0		
R L Moore	1-2	50	+19.00	0-0			0-1		-1.00	1-1	100	+20.00

By jockey ctd

2002

	Overall			Two-year-olds			Three-year-olds			Older horses		
	W-R	%	£1	W-R	%	£1	W-R	%	£1	W-R	%	£1
S Drowne	40-325	12	-29.71	20-139	14	-42.88	14-130	10	+24.67	6-56	10	-11.50
C Catlin	26-256	10	-67.90	10-101	9	-53.93	6-99	6	-39.22	10-56	17	+25.25
A Culhane	21-91	23	+27.67	10-42	23	+1.04	4-33	12	-4.00	7-16	43	+30.63
D Corby	20-162	12	+23.18	6-30	20	+6.43	2-45	4	-37.17	12-87	13	+53.92
T E Durcan	6-41	14	-6.81	2-10	20	-4.56	2-15	13	-8.25	2-16	12	+6.00
J Carroll	3-10	30	+2.48	1-4	25	-2.09	1-4	25	-2.43	1-2	50	+7.00
J F McDonald	3-17	17	-2.27	1-6	16	-1.00	2-3	66	+6.73	0-8		-8.00
W Ryan	2-5	40	+16.00	0-1		-1.00	2-4	50	+17.00	0-0		
L Dettori	2-11	18	+3.00	0-5		-5.00	0-1		-1.00	2-5	40	+9.00
M Tebbutt	1-8	12	-5.25	1-3	33	-0.25	0-4		-4.00	0-1		-1.00

2001

	Overall			Two-year-olds			Three-year-olds			Older horses		
	W-R	%	£1	W-R	%	£1	W-R	%	£1	W-R	%	£1
S Drowne	34-330	10	-158.72	22-155	14	-44.57	10-120	8	-77.15	2-55	3	-37.00
C Williams	13-143	9	-77.00	9-37	24	+5.17	4-73	5	-49.17	0-33		-33.00
T Quinn	3-37	8	-28.73	1-12	8	-9.90	2-22	9	-15.83	0-3		-3.00
C Catlin	2-13	15	+10.00	1-8	12	+5.00	0-3		-3.00	1-2	50	+8.00
T E Durcan	2-14	14	+3.00	2-8	25	+9.00	0-4		-4.00	0-2		-2.00
J Fortune	2-17	11	-9.50	2-10	20	-2.50	0-5		-5.00	0-2		-2.00
D Holland	1-1	100	+4.50	0-0			1-1	100	+4.50	0-0		
C Rutter	1-3	33	+6.00	1-2	50	+7.00	0-0			0-1		-1.00
A Culhane	1-3	33	-1.78	0-1		-1.00	1-2	50	-0.78	0-0		
Miss L Bates	1-4	25	+1.00	0-0			0-0			1-4	25	+1.00

By class

2003

	Overall			Two-year-olds			Three-year-olds			Older horses		
	W-R	%	£1	W-R	%	£1	W-R	%	£1	W-R	%	£1
A	8-106	7	-49.15	3-46	6	-14.00	3-35	8	-17.90	2-25	8	-17.25
B	16-119	13	+19.17	3-23	13	-6.83	5-33	15	+9.50	8-63	12	+16.50
C	16-188	8	-46.38	2-40	5	-32.25	6-60	10	-7.38	8-88	9	-6.75
D	53-401	13	-99.63	27-197	13	-75.60	17-138	12	-16.25	9-66	13	-7.78
E	27-196	13	+10.55	10-68	14	+1.37	10-63	15	+19.68	7-65	10	-10.50
F	17-94	18	-16.05	4-25	16	-11.38	9-32	28	+3.70	4-37	10	-8.39
G	6-32	18	-5.75	3-14	21	-1.25	2-4	50	+4.50	1-14	7	-9.00

2002

	Overall			Two-year-olds			Three-year-olds			Older horses		
	W-R	%	£1	W-R	%	£1	W-R	%	£1	W-R	%	£1
A	7-83	8	-35.44	1-32	3	-30.27	2-23	8	-19.42	4-28	14	+14.25
B	8-107	7	-4.50	1-21	4	-9.00	0-31		-31.00	7-55	12	+35.50
C	19-189	10	-44.19	7-46	15	-12.07	2-66	3	-53.00	10-77	12	+20.88
D	48-365	13	+7.21	23-164	14	-45.12	17-151	11	+47.26	8-50	16	+5.07
E	28-172	16	-15.50	11-65	16	-29.44	9-70	12	-2.67	8-37	21	+16.60
F	9-65	13	-30.44	4-23	17	-10.59	3-28	10	-19.85	2-14	14	
G	4-27	14	-9.75	4-20	20	-2.75	0-4		-4.00	0-3		-3.00

2001

	Overall			Two-year-olds			Three-year-olds			Older horses		
	W-R	%	£1	W-R	%	£1	W-R	%	£1	W-R	%	£1
A	6-94	6	-66.22	6-27	22	+0.78	0-48		-48.00	0-19		-19.00
B	1-73	1	-67.00	1-17	5	-11.00	0-27		-27.00	0-29		-29.00
C	9-116	7	-55.53	4-23	17	+9.50	4-54	7	-39.03	1-39	2	-26.00
D	27-302	8	-171.40	15-151	9	-91.13	9-112	8	-69.28	3-39	7	-11.00
E	12-141	8	-85.71	8-71	11	-34.21	3-53	5	-42.00	1-17	5	-9.50
F	9-60	15	-15.22	4-32	12	-10.09	4-24	16	-6.12	1-4	25	+1.00
G	3-18	16	+9.00	3-15	20	+12.00	0-3		-3.00	0-0		

ZAFEEN: winning at Royal Ascot for Channon

By course

2003

	Overall			Two-year-olds			Three-year-olds			Older horses		
	W-R	%	£1	W-R	%	£1	W-R	%	£1	W-R	%	£1
Ascot	8-50	16	-27.28	1-4	25		5-25	20	-10.08	2-21	9	-17.20
Ayr	2-5	40	+5.13	0-1		-1.00	1-3	33	-1.88	1-1	100	+8.00
Bath	1-4	25	-2.33	0-0			1-4	25	-2.33	0-0		
Beverley	1-6	16	-4.33	0-1		-1.00	1-5	20	-3.33	0-0		
Brighton	3-5	60	+2.03	0-1		-1.00	3-4	75	+3.03	0-0		
Carlisle	1-2	50	-0.17	0-0			1-2	50	-0.17	0-0		
Catterick	0-2		-2.00	0-1		-1.00	0-1		-1.00	0-0		
Chepstow	1-4	25	-1.63	0-0			1-4	25	-1.63	0-0		
Chester	4-13	30	+18.00	0-2		-2.00	2-6	33	+17.50	2-5	40	+2.50
Curragh	0-4		-4.00	0-0			0-2		-2.00	0-2		-2.00
Doncaster	3-21	14	-10.10	1-10	10	-8.60	2-7	28	+2.50	0-4		-4.00
Epsom	2-9	22	+0.25	0-0			1-6	16	+1.00	1-3	33	-0.75
Folkestone	0-4		-4.00	0-1		-1.00	0-3		-3.00	0-0		
Goodwood	7-25	28	+1.55	1-2	50	-0.80	2-14	14	-8.45	4-9	44	+10.80
Hamilton	3-4	75	+3.50	0-0			2-3	66	+2.25	1-1	100	+1.25
Haydock	2-7	28	-2.40	0-0			2-4	50	+0.60	0-3		-3.00
Kempton	3-9	33	-3.85	1-5	20	-3.33	2-2	100	+1.48	0-2		-2.00
Leicester	3-19	15	+1.50	2-13	15	+2.50	0-3		-3.00	1-3	33	+2.00
Le'pardstown	1-2	50	+0.10	0-0			1-1	100	+1.10	0-1		-1.00
Lingfield	3-13	23	-6.76	1-5	20	-2.90	2-8	25	-3.86	0-0		
Musselburgh	1-2	50	-0.78	0-0			1-1	100	+0.22	0-1		-1.00
Newbury	4-20	20	+12.17	0-5		-5.00	2-9	22	-5.33	2-6	33	+22.50
Newcastle	1-5	20	+2.50	1-2	50	+5.50	0-1		-1.00	0-2		-2.00
Newmarket	10-83	12	-23.58	2-27	7	-18.00	5-43	11	-12.33	3-13	23	+6.75
Nottingham	2-10	20	+1.57	1-6	16	-4.43	1-4	25	+6.00	0-0		
Pontefract	5-9	55	+10.83	2-3	66	+2.41	3-6	50	+8.42	0-0		
Redcar	1-5	20	+6.00	0-1		-1.00	0-3		-3.00	1-1	100	+10.00
Ripon	4-8	50	-0.80	1-1	100	+1.50	3-7	42	-2.31	0-0		
Salisbury	3-11	27	-3.43	1-4	25	-1.63	1-5	20	-2.80	1-2	50	+1.00
Sandown	4-29	13	-15.31	1-6	16	+0.50	3-15	20	-7.81	0-8		-8.00
Southwell	0-1		-1.00	0-0			0-1		-1.00	0-0		
Thirsk	0-5		-5.00	0-0			0-4		-4.00	0-1		-1.00
Warwick	3-8	37	+0.04	0-3		-3.00	3-5	60	+3.04	0-0		
Windsor	12-26	46	+8.80	3-9	33	-4.09	7-14	50	+9.31	2-3	66	+3.58
Wolver	1-2	50		0-0			1-2	50		0-0		
Yarmouth	9-20	45	+13.60	5-9	55	+9.92	3-10	30	+1.68	1-1	100	+2.00
York	8-36	22	-6.84	0-2		-2.00	3-16	18	-2.50	5-18	27	-2.34

Richard Hannon

SECOND ONLY to his sounda-like Lambourn neighbour in terms of runners sent out, Richard Hannon's strike-rate is similarly low.

And in similar vein, it seems that you really can't expect to keep your head above the punting water by regularly backing his runners.

Famous for his success with two-year-olds, it's interesting to note how his percentage of juvenile winners slides as the year progresses. His Newmarket runners turned a profit last year.

By month

2003

	Overall			Two-year-olds			Three-year-olds			Older horses		
	W-R	%	£1	W-R	%	£1	W-R	%	£1	W-R	%	£1
January	0-12		-12.00	0-0			0-12		-12.00	0-0		
February	0-0			0-0			0-0			0-0		
March	7-31	22	+5.82	3-3	100	+6.07	4-20	20	+7.75	0-8		-8.00
April	9-87	10	-41.94	4-20	20	-9.30	3-50	6	-32.25	2-17	11	-0.38
May	16-147	10	-69.85	10-46	21	-0.38	5-87	5	-61.47	1-14	7	-8.00
June	18-146	12	-11.68	10-64	15	-23.93	6-72	8	+15.50	2-10	20	-3.25
July	26-178	14	+1.28	16-96	16	-7.98	8-68	11	-4.25	2-14	14	+13.50
August	23-137	16	-4.69	14-86	16	-33.28	9-43	20	+36.58	0-8		-8.00
September	12-133	9	-65.85	10-91	10	-35.60	2-37	5	-25.25	0-5		-5.00
October	11-127	8	-46.41	9-88	10	-18.51	2-32	6	-20.90	0-7		-7.00
November	2-39	5	-27.75	1-25	4	-17.00	0-13		-13.00	1-1	100	+2.25
December	1-6	16	-2.25	1-3	33	+0.75	0-2		-2.00	0-1		-£1.00

2002

	Overall			Two-year-olds			Three-year-olds			Older horses		
	W-R	%	£1	W-R	%	£1	W-R	%	£1	W-R	%	£1
January	1-17	5	-14.38	0-0			1-14	7	-11.38	0-3		-3.00
February	0-4		-4.00	0-0			0-2		-2.00	0-2		-2.00
March	1-14	7	-10.50	0-1		-1.00	1-12	8	-8.50	0-1		-1.00
April	13-94	13	-20.25	4-15	26	+1.75	7-57	12	-9.75	2-22	9	-12.25
May	23-152	15	-36.21	12-45	26	-0.19	9-83	10	-23.40	2-24	8	-12.63
June	25-166	15	-38.65	16-71	22	-4.98	7-72	9	-23.17	2-23	8	-10.50
July	25-188	13	-43.93	14-94	14	-10.14	7-62	11	-24.92	4-32	12	-8.87
August	11-177	6	-121.20	5-90	5	-62.50	3-57	5	-41.50	3-30	10	-17.20
September	13-123	10	-41.35	9-73	12	-22.85	3-37	8	-10.50	1-13	7	-8.00
October	9-115	7	-32.54	7-75	9	-4.79	1-29	3	-23.25	1-11	9	-4.50
November	1-29	3	-12.00	1-19	5	-2.00	0-9		-9.00	0-1		-1.00
December	4-28	14	-12.45	1-16	6	-12.75	0-5		-5.00	3-7	42	+5.30

2001

	Overall			Two-year-olds			Three-year-olds			Older horses		
	W-R	%	£1	W-R	%	£1	W-R	%	£1	W-R	%	£1
January	3-16	18	-6.57	0-0			2-8	25	+0.38	1-8	12	-6.95
February	1-12	8	-8.50	0-0			1-6	16	-2.50	0-6		-6.00
March	0-9		-9.00	0-0			0-3		-3.00	0-6		-6.00
April	1-43	2	-30.00	0-5		-5.00	1-24	4	-11.00	0-14		-14.00
May	18-178	10	-79.71	9-42	21	+3.58	8-88	9	-44.29	1-48	2	-39.00
June	17-186	9	-69.96	6-65	9	-32.83	9-82	10	-20.13	2-39	5	-17.00
July	24-184	13	-73.94	8-77	10	-45.15	12-75	16	-12.63	4-32	12	-16.17
August	18-188	9	-79.28	7-90	7	-62.21	8-71	11	-11.45	3-27	11	-5.63
September	13-169	7	-50.02	11-84	13	-2.16	1-60	1	-56.86	1-25	4	+9.00
October	7-120	5	-79.00	6-66	9	-36.00	1-40	2	-29.00	0-14		-14.00
November	4-49	8	-24.84	3-27	11	-7.17	0-17		-17.00	1-5	20	-0.67
December	4-22	18	+12.00	3-13	23	+11.00	1-8	12	+2.00	0-1		-1.00

All runners

2003	Wins	Runs	%	2nd	3rd	rest	Win prize	Total prize	£1 Stake
2yo	78	522	14	75	52	73	558,392.70	944,748.08	-139.14
3yo	39	436	8	37	42	32	308,849.05	547,540.88	-111.29
4yo+	8	85	9	8	7	6	258,783.47	332,417.80	-24.88
TOTAL	125	1043	11	120	101	111	1,126,025.22	1,824,706.76	-275.31

2002	Wins	Runs	%	2nd	3rd	rest	Win prize	Total prize	£1 Stake
2yo	69	499	13	77	71	53	637,488.57	1,046,494.30	-119.44
3yo	39	439	8	49	46	34	258,552.87	551,365.46	-192.36
4yo+	18	169	10	21	14	12	196,968.64	353,258.54	-75.65
TOTAL	126	1107	11	147	131	99	1,093,010.08	1,951,118.30	-387.45

2001	Wins	Runs	%	2nd	3rd	rest	Win prize	Total prize	£1 Stake
2yo	53	469	11	53	44	53	393,101.29	660,815.10	-175.94
3yo	44	482	9	43	51	36	301,681.10	566,390.15	-205.48
4yo+	13	225	5	13	16	23	158,175.76	238,970.31	-117.41
TOTAL	110	1176	9	109	111	112	852,958.15	1,466,175.56	-498.83

By race type

2003

	Overall			Two-year-olds			Three-year-olds			Older horses		
	W-R	%	£1	W-R	%	£1	W-R	%	£1	W-R	%	£1
Handicap	31-393	7	-147.59	10-102	9	-40.13	19-243	7	-69.22	2-48	4	-38.25
Group 1,2,3	7-57	12	-7.68	2-23	8	-13.38	2-25	8	-10.67	3-9	33	+16.37
Maiden	50-321	15	-84.70	41-259	15	-71.95	9-59	15	-9.75	0-3		-3.00
1st time out	12-119	10	-59.87	12-113	10	-53.87	0-4		-4.00	0-2		-2.00

2002

	Overall			Two-year-olds			Three-year-olds			Older horses		
	W-R	%	£1	W-R	%	£1	W-R	%	£1	W-R	%	£1
Handicap	32-463	6	-186.87	8-93	8	-1.92	16-269	5	-129.00	8-101	7	-55.95
Group 1,2,3	6-66	9	-31.75	3-27	11	-7.75	1-14	7	-8.00	2-25	8	-16.00
Maiden	42-323	13	-121.18	33-249	13	-81.11	9-72	12	-38.07	0-2		-2.00
1st time out	18-108	16	+4.60	17-99	17	+4.60	0-7		-7.00	1-2	50	+7.00

2001

	Overall			Two-year-olds			Three-year-olds			Older horses		
	W-R	%	£1	W-R	%	£1	W-R	%	£1	W-R	%	£1
Handicap	34-502	6	-226.74	8-97	8	-37.17	21-262	8	-119.08	5-143	3	-70.50
Group 1,2,3	3-60	5	-23.00	2-19	10	+5.00	1-25	4	-12.00	0-16		-16.00
Maiden	41-350	11	-152.31	29-247	11	-105.53	12-101	11	-44.78	0-2		-2.00
1st time out	6-112	5	-59.50	6-101	5	-48.50	0-11		-11.00	0-0		

By jockey

2003

	Overall			Two-year-olds			Three-year-olds			Older horses		
	W-R	%	£1	W-R	%	£1	W-R	%	£1	W-R	%	£1
R Hughes	42-204	20	-15.66	29-110	26	+16.86	10-74	13	-24.14	3-20	15	-8.38
R L Moore	18-151	11	-10.85	8-67	11	-22.85	10-72	13	+24.00	0-12		-12.00
P Dobbs	18-170	10	-74.28	13-94	13	-36.53	4-67	5	-43.75	1-9	11	+6.00
Dane O'Neill	16-217	7	-138.86	13-128	10	-63.61	2-79	2	-68.50	1-10	10	-6.75
Pat Eddery	8-67	11	-9.80	6-30	20	+1.70	1-23	4	-18.50	1-14	7	+7.00
R Smith	6-80	7	-9.13	2-27	7	-20.63	4-45	8	+19.50	0-8		-8.00
P Gallagher	5-30	16	+21.50	1-9	11	-4.50	3-16	18	+24.50	1-5	20	+1.50
D Holland	3-18	16	-9.40	0-7		-7.00	3-11	27	-2.40	0-0		
K Fallon	2-7	28	+16.00	1-3	33	+3.00	1-4	25	+13.00	0-0		
J Fortune	2-13	15	-0.25	0-2		-2.00	1-8	12	+2.00	1-3	33	-0.25

By jockey ctd

2002

	Overall			Two-year-olds			Three-year-olds			Older horses		
	W-R	%	£1	W-R	%	£1	W-R	%	£1	W-R	%	£1
Dane O'Neill	34-264	12	-102.46	22-143	15	-48.13	6-83	7	-41.37	6-38	15	-12.95
R Hughes	32-227	14	-80.75	22-107	20	-0.21	10-92	10	-52.54	0-28		-28.00
Pat Eddery	10-70	14	-14.93	4-27	14	-3.30	1-24	4	-16.50	5-19	26	+4.88
R Smith	7-86	8	-36.25	3-37	8	-13.25	4-38	10	-12.00	0-11		-11.00
D Holland	6-44	13	-15.50	2-14	14	-4.00	4-28	14	-9.50	0-2		-2.00
P Dobbs	6-74	8	-37.72	2-33	6	-22.50	3-34	8	-13.27	1-7	14	-1.95
R L Moore	5-81	6	-23.75	3-26	11	+12.25	2-32	6	-13.00	0-23		-23.00
P Fitzsimons	4-34	11	-8.18	3-19	15	-2.18	0-7		-7.00	1-8	12	+1.00
E Ahern	3-12	25	+13.50	2-8	25	+4.50	1-4	25	+9.00	0-0		
K Fallon	3-17	17	+8.25	0-4		-4.00	3-12	25	+13.25	0-1		-1.00

2001

	Overall			Two-year-olds			Three-year-olds			Older horses		
	W-R	%	£1	W-R	%	£1	W-R	%	£1	W-R	%	£1
Dane O'Neill	38-350	10	-165.82	23-162	14	-59.44	12-134	8	-62.25	3-54	5	-44.13
R Hughes	18-133	13	-11.29	7-42	16	-7.63	9-60	15	+18.50	2-31	6	-22.17
P Dobbs	16-168	9	-59.86	6-63	9	-16.00	8-79	10	-41.92	2-26	7	-7.50
Pat Eddery	9-64	14	-19.54	2-29	6	-26.14	5-27	18	+1.26	2-8	25	+5.33
R Smith	8-73	10	+16.55	2-13	15		3-25	12	+3.50	3-35	8	+13.05
L Newman	6-115	5	-77.51	2-41	4	-25.38	3-48	6	-35.13	1-26	3	-17.00
P Fitzsimons	4-47	8	-27.53	2-22	9	-11.33	2-16	12	-7.20	0-9		-9.00
J Fortune	3-29	10	-4.75	2-8	25	+9.25	1-12	8	-5.00	0-9		-9.00
T Williams	1-1	100	+0.73	1-1	100	+0.73	0-0			0-0		
D Holland	1-5	20	-1.25	0-2		-2.00	1-1	100	+2.75	0-2		-2.00

By class

2003

	Overall			Two-year-olds			Three-year-olds			Older horses		
	W-R	%	£1	W-R	%	£1	W-R	%	£1	W-R	%	£1
A	10-113	8	-43.88	7-49	14	-15.38	2-51	3	-36.50	1-13	7	+8.00
B	6-84	7	-46.47	3-37	8	-12.00	2-34	5	-27.47	1-13	7	-7.00
C	11-121	9	-66.84	8-41	19	-16.09	3-59	5	-29.75	0-21		-21.00
D	56-447	12	-130.19	38-264	14	-87.04	18-165	10	-25.15	0-18		-18.00
E	30-196	15	+34.43	18-99	18	-0.33	10-84	11	+26.25	2-13	15	+8.50
F	8-58	13	-9.68	3-24	12	-2.93	3-29	10	-9.00	2-5	40	+2.25
G	1-12	8	-9.38	1-4	25	-1.38	0-8		-8.00	0-0		

2002

	Overall			Two-year-olds			Three-year-olds			Older horses		
	W-R	%	£1	W-R	%	£1	W-R	%	£1	W-R	%	£1
A	11-122	9	-63.33	3-45	6	-26.25	3-36	8	-18.50	5-41	12	-18.58
B	12-92	13	-19.45	9-46	19	+8.17	1-26	3	-21.50	2-20	10	-6.12
C	20-163	12	-59.86	7-48	14	-17.32	10-88	11	-31.54	3-27	11	-11.00
D	47-452	10	-214.47	30-235	12	-98.15	17-185	9	-84.32	0-32		-32.00
E	22-207	10	-53.20	12-94	12	+0.25	6-76	7	-35.50	4-37	10	-17.95
F	8-52	15	+15.00	3-20	15	+3.00	2-24	8	+3.00	3-8	37	+9.00
G	1-11	9	-1.00	1-5	20	+5.00	0-3		-3.00	0-3		-3.00

2001

	Overall			Two-year-olds			Three-year-olds			Older horses		
	W-R	%	£1	W-R	%	£1	W-R	%	£1	W-R	%	£1
A	10-119	8	-43.25	3-28	10	+2.50	4-59	6	-28.63	3-32	9	-17.13
B	9-116	7	-31.75	3-31	9	-8.25	4-44	9	-20.50	2-41	4	-3.00
C	15-178	8	-91.28	4-42	9	-25.50	4-73	5	-48.50	7-63	11	-17.28
D	40-435	9	-205.65	22-223	9	-100.13	17-173	9	-75.53	1-39	2	-30.00
E	22-220	10	-93.55	12-106	11	-46.05	10-80	12	-13.50	0-34		-34.00
F	13-79	16	-13.34	8-29	27	+2.49	5-39	12	-4.82	0-11		-11.00
G	1-19	5	-10.00	1-6	16	+3.00	0-10		-10.00	0-3		-3.00

REEL BUDDY: Sussex Stakes winner for Richard Hannon and Pat Eddery

By course

2003

	Overall			Two-year-olds			Three-year-olds			Older horses		
	W-R	%	£1	W-R	%	£1	W-R	%	£1	W-R	%	£1
Ascot	7-56	12	-3.88	5-29	17	-1.88	2-22	9	+3.00	0-5		-5.00
Ayr	2-4	50	+4.00	2-4	50	+4.00	0-0			0-0		
Bath	2-20	10	-15.10	1-13	7	-11.60	1-5	20	-1.50	0-2		-2.00
Beverley	0-3		-3.00	0-3		-3.00	0-0			0-0		
Brighton	5-28	17	-1.70	3-13	23	-3.20	2-12	16	+4.50	0-3		-3.00
Chepstow	3-36	8	-27.05	1-11	9	-8.80	2-21	9	-14.25	0-4		-4.00
Chester	2-11	18	-5.10	2-8	25	-2.10	0-3		-3.00	0-0		
Curragh	3-10	30	-1.30	0-3		-3.00	1-5	20	-0.67	2-2	100	+2.37
Doncaster	4-35	11	-14.00	1-20	5	-15.00	3-11	27	+5.00	0-4		-4.00
Epsom	0-20		-20.00	0-9		-9.00	0-8		-8.00	0-3		-3.00
Folkestone	3-14	21	-1.70	3-7	42	+5.30	0-6		-6.00	0-1		-1.00
Goodwood	7-82	8	-39.31	5-40	12	-22.81	1-31	3	-26.50	1-11	9	+10.00
Gowran Park	0-1		-1.00	0-0			0-1		-1.00	0-0		
Haydock	3-22	13	+10.50	1-14	7	-9.00	2-8	25	+19.50	0-0		
Kempton	5-57	8	-37.95	5-21	23	-1.95	0-29		-29.00	0-7		-7.00
Leicester	7-29	24	+8.10	2-12	16	-6.50	5-16	31	+15.60	0-1		-1.00
Leopardstown	0-1		-1.00	0-1		-1.00	0-0			0-0		
Lingfield	12-100	12	-23.92	6-43	13	-7.75	5-52	9	-26.17	1-5	20	+10.00
Newbury	8-93	8	-27.75	4-48	8	-22.25	2-35	5	-8.00	2-10	20	+2.50
Newmarket	20-108	18	+18.83	15-60	25	+23.83	5-44	11	-1.00	0-4		-4.00
Nottingham	1-24	4	-15.00	1-15	6	-6.00	0-8		-8.00	0-1		-1.00
Pontefract	0-4		-4.00	0-3		-3.00	0-1		-1.00	0-0		
Redcar	1-5	20	+12.00	1-4	25	+13.00	0-1		-1.00	0-0		
Ripon	1-6	16	+5.00	1-5	20	+6.00	0-1		-1.00	0-0		
Salisbury	9-76	11	-29.77	5-38	13	-16.47	3-34	8	-13.30	1-4	25	
Sandown	7-52	13	-0.13	5-22	22	-5.13	2-21	9	+14.00	0-9		-9.00
Thirsk	0-1		-1.00	0-0			0-1		-1.00	0-0		
Warwick	1-19	5	-10.50	1-11	9	-2.50	0-8		-8.00	0-0		
Windsor	8-95	8	-46.85	5-49	10	-38.35	3-38	7	-0.50	0-8		-8.00
Wolver	2-14	14	+1.25	1-6	16	+6.00	0-7		-7.00	1-1	100	+2.25
Yarmouth	0-5		-5.00	0-3		-3.00	0-2		-2.00	0-0		
York	2-12	16	+1.00	2-7	28	+6.00	0-5		-5.00	0-0		

Barry Hills

AT THE end of another highly effective season, during which his runners nonetheless attracted little in the way of publicity, Barry Hills was close to returning a level-stakes profit on all his starters.

With just a 3 per cent loss on turnover, this is a yard whose runners are close to being consistently underbet.

It's no surprise that he likes to win at Doncaster, yet he returned a profit there last season, while his backend runners have also been worth following.

By month

2003

	Overall			Two-year-olds			Three-year-olds			Older horses		
	W-R	%	£1	W-R	%	£1	W-R	%	£1	W-R	%	£1
January	4-15	26	-0.64	0-0			3-9	33	-2.14	1-6	16	+1.50
February	1-8	12	-3.00	0-0			0-4		-4.00	1-4	25	+1.50
March	8-22	36	+5.18	0-1		-1.00	5-16	31	-1.57	3-5	60	+7.75
April	10-45	22	-5.07	2-3	66	+3.79	7-33	21	-5.86	1-9	11	-3.00
May	11-81	13	-18.33	2-14	14	-9.25	8-50	16	+2.42	1-17	5	-11.50
June	7-74	9	-36.53	0-14		-14.00	6-50	12	-16.53	1-10	10	-6.00
July	19-105	18	+13.83	11-34	32	+33.00	5-55	9	-32.17	3-16	18	+13.00
August	13-89	14	-26.59	9-43	20	-2.17	4-36	11	-14.42	0-10		-10.00
September	17-94	18	+16.46	9-54	16	-1.17	6-28	21	+22.63	2-12	16	-5.00
October	12-77	15	+24.00	4-43	9	-25.00	5-25	20	+37.50	3-9	33	+11.50
November	5-33	15	+14.50	2-18	11	+7.00	3-13	23	+9.50	0-2		-2.00
December	0-2		-2.00	0-1		-1.00	0-1		-1.00	0-0		

2002

	Overall			Two-year-olds			Three-year-olds			Older horses		
	W-R	%	£1	W-R	%	£1	W-R	%	£1	W-R	%	£1
January	0-9		-9.00	0-0			0-5		-5.00	0-4		-4.00
February	1-5	20	-3.00	0-0			1-4	25	-2.00	0-1		-1.00
March	3-28	10	-8.63	0-0			2-21	9	-12.63	1-7	14	+4.00
April	6-61	9	-24.65	0-6		-6.00	4-44	9	-21.15	2-11	18	+2.50
May	8-93	8	-51.75	0-11		-11.00	8-62	12	-20.75	0-20		-20.00
June	6-80	7	-56.39	3-19	15	-7.50	2-44	4	-39.39	1-17	5	-9.50
July	22-137	16	-10.05	9-52	17	-9.74	10-61	16	-4.82	3-24	12	+4.50
August	16-98	16	-35.00	13-44	29	+6.25	1-39	2	-33.00	2-15	13	-8.25
September	11-98	11	-6.56	3-46	6	-39.31	5-37	13	+18.75	3-15	20	+14.00
October	10-98	10	-38.80	6-44	13	-14.52	2-39	5	-19.50	2-15	13	-4.78
November	6-33	18	+20.15	3-19	15	+4.65	3-12	25	+17.50	0-2		-2.00
December	2-11	18	-3.25	2-6	33	+1.75	0-3		-3.00	0-2		-2.00

2001

	Overall			Two-year-olds			Three-year-olds			Older horses		
	W-R	%	£1	W-R	%	£1	W-R	%	£1	W-R	%	£1
January	3-24	12	-10.83	0-0			3-14	21	-0.83	0-10		-10.00
February	2-11	18	-0.89	0-0			1-7	14	-5.89	1-4	25	+5.00
March	2-14	14	+0.73	0-1		-1.00	1-7	14	-5.27	1-6	16	+7.00
April	9-47	19	+4.46	1-1	100	+3.00	7-34	20	+6.46	1-12	8	-6.00
May	13-93	14	-38.48	1-13	7	-10.90	6-55	10	-30.53	6-25	24	+2.95
June	14-97	14	-15.93	2-11	18	-1.50	8-69	11	-34.93	4-17	23	+20.50
July	17-93	18	-36.47	7-27	25	-0.73	8-50	16	-23.73	2-16	12	-12.02
August	21-132	15	-32.80	10-47	21	+5.37	11-61	18	-14.18	0-24		-24.00
September	11-101	10	-16.37	7-45	15	+21.13	2-40	5	-30.50	2-16	12	-7.00
October	10-88	11	+13.43	5-45	11	-0.80	3-24	12	+24.63	2-19	10	-10.40
November	6-33	18	+9.05	5-24	20	+5.05	1-7	14	+6.00	0-2		-2.00
December	0-4		-4.00	0-2		-2.00	0-1		-1.00	0-1		-1.00

All runners

2003	Wins	Runs	%	2nd	3rd	rest	Win prize	Total prize	£1 Stake
2yo	39	225	17	33	24	28	255,538.95	439,907.90	-9.81
3yo	52	320	16	28	42	25	410,311.35	653,862.77	-5.63
4yo+	16	100	16	11	10	9	265,566.88	367,524.24	-2.75
TOTAL	107	645	16	72	76	62	931,417.18	1,461,294.91	-18.19

2002	Wins	Runs	%	2nd	3rd	rest	Win prize	Total prize	£1 Stake
2yo	39	247	15	44	29	22	266,014.40	439,187.55	-75.4
3yo	38	371	10	48	44	40	314,627.41	601,032.08	-124.97
4yo+	14	133	10	14	12	10	491,430.35	744,880.22	-26.54
TOTAL	91	751	12	106	85	72	1,072,072.16	1,785,099.85	-226.92

2001	Wins	Runs	%	2nd	3rd	rest	Win prize	Total prize	£1 Stake
2yo	38	216	17	29	33	18	248,128.39	358,612.80	+17.62
3yo	51	369	13	56	47	43	549,441.72	1,043,718.28	-109.77
4yo+	19	152	12	12	12	12	246,573.76	373,201.02	-35.97
TOTAL	108	737	14	97	92	73	1,044,143.87	1,775,532.10	-128.12

By race type

2003

	Overall			Two-year-olds			Three-year-olds			Older horses		
	W-R	%	£1	W-R	%	£1	W-R	%	£1	W-R	%	£1
Handicap	24-251	9	-96.76	5-30	16	-3.51	8-140	5	-86.25	11-81	13	-7.00
Group 1,2,3	3-48	6	-9.50	0-15		-15.00	2-29	6	+4.00	1-4	25	+1.50
Maiden	58-260	22	+62.78	26-149	17	+6.12	31-109	28	+56.41	1-2	50	+0.25
1st time out	13-98	13	+6.25	10-83	12	-1.75	3-15	20	+8.00	0-0		

2002

	Overall			Two-year-olds			Three-year-olds			Older horses		
	W-R	%	£1	W-R	%	£1	W-R	%	£1	W-R	%	£1
Handicap	25-318	7	-117.26	4-29	13	-16.86	14-186	7	-60.15	7-103	6	-40.25
Group 1,2,3	6-47	12	-17.15	2-13	15	-3.00	1-18	5	-15.25	3-16	18	+1.10
Maiden	45-290	15	-88.14	27-162	16	-49.05	17-127	13	-55.08	1-1	100	+16.00
1st time out	3-91	3	-74.75	3-78	3	-61.75	0-13		-13.00	0-0		

2001

	Overall			Two-year-olds			Three-year-olds			Older horses		
	W-R	%	£1	W-R	%	£1	W-R	%	£1	W-R	%	£1
Handicap	33-297	11	-72.50	5-37	13	-8.25	13-146	8	-59.00	15-114	13	-5.25
Group 1,2,3	8-59	13	+2.88	0-5		-5.00	7-37	18	+22.63	1-17	5	-14.75
Maiden	54-282	19	-77.04	25-133	18	-7.10	28-146	19	-68.14	1-3	33	-1.80
1st time out	10-88	11	+26.75	8-69	11	+23.75	2-17	11	+5.00	0-2		-2.00

By jockey

2003

	Overall			Two-year-olds			Three-year-olds			Older horses		
	W-R	%	£1	W-R	%	£1	W-R	%	£1	W-R	%	£1
M Hills	48-297	16	-31.22	24-119	20	+10.86	17-131	12	-37.33	7-47	14	-4.75
R Hills	9-42	21	+3.42	6-20	30	+9.25	3-18	16	-1.83	0-4		-4.00
A Culhane	8-34	23	+30.94	1-7	14	-1.50	6-20	30	+34.44	1-7	14	-2.00
R Hughes	8-44	18	-7.56	1-10	10	-7.00	5-27	18	-6.06	2-7	28	+5.50
W Supple	6-24	25	+20.13	1-5	20	+0.50	5-19	26	+19.63	0-0		
Pat Eddery	5-22	22	-0.22	0-3		-3.00	3-11	27	+0.78	2-8	25	+2.00
K Darley	3-9	33	+9.33	1-4	25	-2.67	2-5	40	+12.00	0-0		
D McKeown	3-16	18	-2.25	1-6	16	-2.00	1-8	12	-4.25	1-2	50	+4.00
P Hanagan	2-4	50	+1.16	1-3	33	+0.25	1-1	100	+0.91	0-0		
G Duffield	2-8	25	-1.67	0-1		-1.00	2-5	40	+1.33	0-2		-2.00

By jockey ctd

2002

	Overall			Two-year-olds			Three-year-olds			Older horses		
	W-R	%	£1	W-R	%	£1	W-R	%	£1	W-R	%	£1
M Hills	43-301	14	-54.68	18-119	15	-32.21	14-119	11	-32.42	11-63	17	+9.97
R Hills	9-58	15	-15.38	4-27	14	-16.38	5-27	18	+5.00	0-4		-4.00
R Hughes	7-60	11	-24.65	2-12	16	-4.75	5-38	13	-9.90	0-10		-10.00
A Culhane	6-17	35	+34.28	2-2	100	+6.53	3-13	23	+12.75	1-2	50	+15.00
Pat Eddery	5-23	21	+16.50	3-5	60	+19.75	1-14	7	-10.25	1-4	25	+7.00
D Holland	5-54	9	-38.99	4-22	18	-9.74	1-23	4	-20.25	0-9		-9.00
K Darley	3-12	25	+0.10	0-2		-2.00	3-9	33	+3.10	0-1		-1.00
D McKeown	3-19	15	+13.75	1-4	25	-1.25	2-12	16	+18.00	0-3		-3.00
W Supple	2-22	9	-16.50	1-9	11	-5.50	1-13	7	-11.00	0-0		
J D Smith	2-34	5	-23.00	1-11	9	-2.00	1-18	5	-16.00	0-5		-5.00

2001

	Overall			Two-year-olds			Three-year-olds			Older horses		
	W-R	%	£1	W-R	%	£1	W-R	%	£1	W-R	%	£1
M Hills	33-236	13	-14.08	15-89	16	+40.60	14-102	13	-37.43	4-45	8	-17.25
R Hughes	19-94	20	-1.73	7-21	33	+12.00	7-53	13	-24.48	5-20	25	+10.75
D Holland	12-39	30	+53.66	3-16	18	-7.95	8-19	42	+62.61	1-4	25	-1.00
J D Smith	8-56	14	-18.28	2-16	12	-9.05	5-33	15	-4.33	1-7	14	-4.90
R Hills	8-56	14	-13.58	3-17	17	-9.48	2-26	7	-15.33	3-13	23	+11.23
K Fallon	3-8	37	-1.21	1-2	50	+1.25	2-5	40	-1.46	0-1		-1.00
W Supple	3-19	15	-12.39	2-6	33	-1.00	1-10	10	-8.39	0-3		-3.00
G Duffield	3-21	14	-12.18	0-3		-3.00	2-13	15	-5.38	1-5	20	-3.80
J Reid	3-28	10	-18.65	0-4		-4.00	3-21	14	-11.65	0-3		-3.00
Pat Eddery	2-14	14	-2.00	1-5	20	+0.50	0-5		-5.00	1-4	25	+2.50

By class

2003

	Overall			Two-year-olds			Three-year-olds			Older horses		
	W-R	%	£1	W-R	%	£1	W-R	%	£1	W-R	%	£1
A	15-86	17	+25.33	4-26	15	-12.67	9-53	16	+32.50	2-7	28	+5.50
B	6-78	7	-35.50	1-7	14	-1.00	1-30	3	-26.50	4-41	9	-8.00
C	13-104	12	-48.13	4-18	22	-8.84	5-57	8	-33.29	4-29	13	-6.00
D	62-307	20	+66.83	26-158	16	+13.58	33-142	23	+44.99	3-7	42	+8.25
E	10-44	22	-5.72	4-12	33	+3.12	4-23	17	-8.34	2-9	22	-0.50
F	1-19	5	-14.00	0-2		-2.00	0-12		-12.00	1-5	20	
G	0-2		-2.00	0-1		-1.00	0-0			0-1		-1.00

2002

	Overall			Two-year-olds			Three-year-olds			Older horses		
	W-R	%	£1	W-R	%	£1	W-R	%	£1	W-R	%	£1
A	10-91	10	-26.04	3-30	10	-3.00	4-42	9	-19.75	3-19	15	-3.29
B	5-78	6	-23.50	0-11		-11.00	1-22	4	-11.00	4-45	8	-1.50
C	14-115	12	-44.39	6-20	30	-1.99	5-58	8	-23.40	3-37	8	-19.00
D	50-358	13	-105.65	25-163	15	-52.83	22-177	12	-61.08	3-18	16	+8.25
E	9-70	12	-12.85	5-22	22	-5.60	4-43	9	-2.25	0-5		-5.00
F	1-29	3	-12.00	0-0			1-25	4	-8.00	0-4		-4.00
G	1-5	20	-0.50	0-1		-1.00	1-3	33	+1.50	0-1		-1.00

2001

	Overall			Two-year-olds			Three-year-olds			Older horses		
	W-R	%	£1	W-R	%	£1	W-R	%	£1	W-R	%	£1
A	10-85	11	+11.63	2-13	15	-2.00	8-52	15	+33.63	0-20		-20.00
B	9-94	9	-33.00	2-20	10	+1.00	2-34	5	-21.75	5-40	12	-12.25
C	15-116	12	+11.60	4-25	16	+28.88	6-58	10	-24.00	5-33	15	+6.73
D	63-330	19	-55.77	27-128	21	+8.80	31-176	17	-66.77	5-26	19	+2.20
E	6-69	8	-38.05	3-24	12	-13.05	2-27	7	-16.00	1-18	5	-9.00
F	2-27	7	-23.27	0-4		-4.00	1-16	6	-14.37	1-7	14	-4.90
G	2-9	22	+3.50	0-0			1-3	33	+2.50	1-6	16	+1.00

PABLO (centre): landing the Lincoln for Hills

By course

2003

	Overall			Two-year-olds			Three-year-olds			Older horses		
	W-R	%	£1	W-R	%	£1	W-R	%	£1	W-R	%	£1
Ascot	1-23	4	-17.50	1-6	16	-0.50	0-9		-9.00	0-8		-8.00
Ayr	3-14	21	+4.00	0-6		-6.00	3-8	37	+10.00	0-0		
Bath	5-15	33	+8.83	2-3	66	+6.83	1-9	11	-2.50	2-3	66	+4.50
Beverley	0-6		-6.00	0-0			0-6		-6.00	0-0		
Brighton	1-7	14	-3.25	0-1		-1.00	1-6	16	-2.25	0-0		
Catterick	1-7	14	-2.50	0-1		-1.00	1-6	16	-1.50	0-0		
Chepstow	0-2		-2.00	0-0			0-2		-2.00	0-0		
Chester	6-28	21	-5.51	4-8	50	+0.99	2-17	11	-3.50	0-3		-3.00
Curragh	0-5		-5.00	0-1		-1.00	0-3		-3.00	0-1		-1.00
Doncaster	9-55	16	+23.13	2-25	8	-4.00	6-22	27	+29.13	1-8	12	-2.00
Epsom	1-5	20	+0.50	0-0			1-4	25	+1.50	0-1		-1.00
Folkestone	1-5	20	-2.25	1-3	33	-0.25	0-2		-2.00	0-0		
Goodwood	2-30	6	-23.75	1-7	14	-4.00	1-15	6	-11.75	0-8		-8.00
Hamilton	2-3	66	+2.41	0-0			2-3	66	+2.41	0-0		
Haydock	5-31	16	+33.63	1-6	16	+7.00	3-15	20	+26.63	1-10	10	
Kempton	3-19	15	-3.75	2-9	22	+1.75	1-7	14	-2.50	0-3		-3.00
Leicester	1-8	12	-2.50	1-5	20	+0.50	0-3		-3.00	0-0		
Lingfield	5-36	13	-26.21	0-5		-5.00	5-30	16	-20.21	0-1		-1.00
Newbury	8-59	13	-16.50	7-34	20	+1.50	1-19	5	-12.00	0-6		-6.00
Newcastle	3-8	37	-0.17	0-2		-2.00	2-4	50	+1.58	1-2	50	+0.25
Newmarket	13-81	16	+47.75	8-37	21	+30.58	3-34	8	+14.67	2-10	20	+2.50
Nottingham	2-19	10	-2.00	0-8		-8.00	1-10	10	+3.00	1-1	100	+3.00
Pontefract	5-14	35	-3.69	1-3	33	-1.71	4-9	44	+0.03	0-2		-2.00
Redcar	3-12	25	-1.21	1-5	20	+0.50	1-5	20	-3.71	1-2	50	+2.00
Ripon	7-16	43	+23.33	1-4	25		5-11	45	+18.33	1-1	100	+5.00
Salisbury	1-17	5	-10.50	1-9	11	-2.50	0-8		-8.00	0-0		
Sandown	1-13	7	-10.25	1-3	33	-0.25	0-8		-8.00	0-2		-2.00
Southwell	0-8		-8.00	0-2		-2.00	0-2		-2.00	0-4		-4.00
Thirsk	1-4	25	-0.75	0-0			1-4	25	-0.75	0-0		
Warwick	2-11	18	-4.28	0-4		-4.00	1-5	20	-3.78	1-2	50	+3.50
Windsor	4-17	23	-0.75	2-10	20	-4.00	2-5	40	+5.25	0-2		-2.00
Wolver	4-21	19	+4.50	0-1		-1.00	2-11	18	+2.00	2-9	22	+3.50
Yarmouth	2-9	22	-4.70	1-4	25	-1.50	1-5	20	-3.20	0-0		
York	5-37	13	-3.25	1-13	7	-9.75	1-13	7	-9.50	3-11	27	+16.00

Marcus Tregoning

SECOND ONLY to Sir Michael Stoute in terms of strike-rate among trainers who won over £1million in prizemoney last term, Tregoning is clearly a man to have on your side.

Not one to overface his charges, he's been hitting some very impressive win-percentages in the better races in recent years. You'd have made a level-stakes profit on his Class A runners in each of the last three years, and a profit on all runners in two of those seasons.

He hits form in May/June.

By month

2003

	Overall			Two-year-olds			Three-year-olds			Older horses		
	W-R	%	£1	W-R	%	£1	W-R	%	£1	W-R	%	£1
January	0-1		-1.00	0-0			0-0			0-1		-1.00
February	1-4	25	+7.00	0-0			0-2		-2.00	1-2	50	+9.00
March	0-2		-2.00	0-0			0-0			0-2		-2.00
April	1-13	7	+4.00	0-0			1-10	10	+7.00	0-3		-3.00
May	7-24	29	+17.28	1-2	50	+0.88	5-17	29	+12.40	1-5	20	+4.00
June	5-23	21	-6.14	0-2		-2.00	3-12	25	-2.50	2-9	22	-1.64
July	8-44	18	-14.08	2-8	25	-0.50	5-24	20	-4.58	1-12	8	-9.00
August	9-43	20	-1.92	1-5	20	+1.50	6-22	27	-0.08	2-16	12	-3.33
September	12-39	30	+35.90	4-15	26	+0.38	5-14	35	+11.41	3-10	30	+24.11
October	10-45	22	-1.76	4-22	18	+3.91	5-16	31	-1.92	1-7	14	-3.75
November	3-17	17	-2.17	2-12	16	-1.50	1-5	20	-0.67	0-0		
December	0-5		-5.00	0-2		-2.00	0-3		-3.00	0-0		

2002

	Overall			Two-year-olds			Three-year-olds			Older horses		
	W-R	%	£1	W-R	%	£1	W-R	%	£1	W-R	%	£1
January	0-0			0-0			0-0			0-0		
February	0-0			0-0			0-0			0-0		
March	0-0			0-0			0-0			0-0		
April	1-4	25	+1.50	0-0			1-3	33	+2.50	0-1		-1.00
May	7-25	28	-4.64	0-1		-1.00	6-20	30	-2.89	1-4	25	-0.75
June	8-36	22	+7.83	2-7	28	-3.17	5-22	22	+15.00	1-7	14	-4.00
July	6-36	16	-10.92	0-9		-9.00	6-23	26	+2.08	0-4		-4.00
August	4-23	17	-11.53	0-7		-7.00	2-12	16	-5.40	2-4	50	+0.88
September	3-5	60	+4.12	1-1	100	+0.62	1-3	33	+0.75	1-1	100	+2.75
October	3-14	21	+4.50	1-6	16	+5.00	2-5	40	+2.50	0-3		-3.00
November	0-8		-8.00	0-5		-5.00	0-3		-3.00	0-0		
December	0-5		-5.00	0-3		-3.00	0-2		-2.00	0-0		

2001

	Overall			Two-year-olds			Three-year-olds			Older horses		
	W-R	%	£1	W-R	%	£1	W-R	%	£1	W-R	%	£1
January	2-3	66	+11.57	0-0			0-0			2-3	66	+11.57
February	0-0			0-0			0-0			0-0		
March	0-2		-2.00	0-0			0-0			0-2		-2.00
April	1-14	7	-5.00	0-0			0-9		-9.00	1-5	20	+4.00
May	4-27	14	+3.50	0-0			3-17	17	+9.00	1-10	10	-5.50
June	5-33	15	+9.38	3-11	27	+22.00	1-16	6	-9.00	1-6	16	-3.63
July	9-28	32	+3.96	1-8	12	-4.75	4-14	28	+1.00	4-6	66	+7.71
August	17-38	44	+31.93	5-13	38	+14.73	10-23	43	+2.64	2-2	100	+14.57
September	7-43	16	-25.76	2-20	10	-13.50	4-19	21	-9.98	1-4	25	-2.27
October	8-27	29	+8.53	5-17	29	+7.15	2-7	28	+1.50	1-3	33	-0.13
November	0-4		-4.00	0-2		-2.00	0-1		-1.00	0-1		-1.00
December	0-0			0-0			0-0			0-0		

Sponsored by Stan James

All runners

2003	Wins	Runs	%	2nd	3rd	rest	Win prize	Total prize	£1 Stake
2yo	14	68	20	10	4	9	133,276.91	177,205.76	+0.66
3yo	31	125	24	28	10	9	389,259.05	582,821.75	+16.06
4yo+	11	67	16	9	8	11	405,704.60	627,249.95	+13.40
TOTAL	56	260	21	47	22	29	928,240.56	1,387,277.46	+30.12

2002	Wins	Runs	%	2nd	3rd	rest	Win prize	Total prize	£1 Stake
2yo	4	39	10	2	4	5	19,136.00	29,159.00	-22.56
3yo	23	93	24	16	18	8	316,753.00	547,078.66	+9.55
4yo+	5	24	20	2	3	5	318,352.75	533,096.93	-9.13
TOTAL	32	156	20	20	25	18	654,241.75	1,109,334.59	-22.14

2001	Wins	Runs	%	2nd	3rd	rest	Win prize	Total prize	£1 Stake
2yo	16	71	22	11	12	8	115,880.22	211,057.62	+23.63
3yo	24	106	22	11	11	11	466,725.15	524,791.65	-14.85
4yo+	13	42	30	14	5	1	137,158.34	239,751.64	+23.33
TOTAL	53	219	24	36	28	20	719,763.71	975,600.91	+32.11

By race type

2003

	Overall			Two-year-olds			Three-year-olds			Older horses		
	W-R	%	£1	W-R	%	£1	W-R	%	£1	W-R	%	£1
Handicap	11-53	20	+34.00	0-3		-3.00	8-29	27	+16.50	3-21	14	+20.50
Group 1,2,3	7-39	17	-9.09	1-6	16	-3.13	2-11	18	-4.25	4-22	18	-1.72
Maiden	23-121	19	-8.52	10-52	19	+1.63	12-60	20	-12.15	1-9	11	+2.00
1st time out	11-53	20	+10.13	7-31	22	+11.63	4-17	23	+3.50	0-5		-5.00

2002

	Overall			Two-year-olds			Three-year-olds			Older horses		
	W-R	%	£1	W-R	%	£1	W-R	%	£1	W-R	%	£1
Handicap	5-31	16	-5.00	1-2	50	+9.00	2-18	11	-10.00	2-11	18	-4.00
Group 1,2,3	4-25	16	+2.38	0-2		-2.00	2-16	12	+6.50	2-7	28	-2.13
Maiden	14-80	17	-39.02	3-33	9	-27.56	10-43	23	-10.46	1-4	25	-1.00
1st time out	3-37	8	-25.27	0-20		-20.00	3-16	18	-4.27	0-1		-1.00

2001

	Overall			Two-year-olds			Three-year-olds			Older horses		
	W-R	%	£1	W-R	%	£1	W-R	%	£1	W-R	%	£1
Handicap	6-43	13	+1.50	1-6	16	+5.00	2-27	7	-16.50	3-10	30	+13.00
Group 1,2,3	6-28	21	+9.48	1-6	16	+7.00	4-11	36	-1.52	1-11	9	+4.00
Maiden	24-105	22	+7.27	10-50	20	+7.88	11-51	21	-8.51	3-4	75	+7.90
1st time out	8-36	22	+28.00	4-23	17	+13.50	3-10	30	+8.50	1-3	33	+6.00

By jockey

2003

	Overall			Two-year-olds			Three-year-olds			Older horses		
	W-R	%	£1	W-R	%	£1	W-R	%	£1	W-R	%	£1
R Hills	20-75	26	+21.64	5-19	26	-1.47	8-27	29	+22.71	7-29	24	+0.40
Martin Dwyer	19-75	25	+8.10	5-20	25	+0.63	13-44	29	+7.48	1-11	9	
W Supple	7-33	21	+2.30	2-9	22	+1.50	4-15	26	+6.80	1-9	11	-6.00
A Daly	5-40	12	-2.17	0-10		-10.00	4-21	19	-9.17	1-9	11	+17.00
R Hughes	2-3	66	+15.00	1-1	100	+14.00	1-2	50	+1.00	0-0		
W Ryan	1-3	33	+8.00	0-0			0-0			1-3	33	+8.00
Pat Eddery	1-3	33	+2.00	1-2	50	+3.00	0-0			0-1		-1.00
P Dobbs	1-5	20	-1.75	0-0			1-4	25	-0.75	0-1		-1.00
P Fitzsimons	0-1		-1.00	0-1		-1.00	0-0			0-0		
K Fallon	0-1		-1.00	0-0			0-0			0-1		-1.00

By jockey ctd

	Overall			Two-year-olds			Three-year-olds			Older horses		
	W-R	%	£1	W-R	%	£1	W-R	%	£1	W-R	%	£1
R Hills	15-54	27	-2.90	1-10	10	-8.39	11-32	34	+9.61	3-12	25	-4.12
W Supple	7-26	26	-2.67	0-5		-5.00	6-16	37	+4.08	1-5	20	-1.75
Martin Dwyer	5-47	10	-9.65	1-18	5	-15.90	4-28	14	+7.25	0-1		-1.00
A Daly	4-18	22	+2.35	1-4	25	+7.00	2-11	18	-5.40	1-3	33	+0.75
P Dobbs	1-1	100	+0.73	1-1	100	+0.73	0-0			0-0		
J F Egan	0-1		-1.00	0-0			0-1		-1.00	0-0		
M Hills	0-1		-1.00	0-0			0-1		-1.00	0-0		
Dane O'Neill	0-1		-1.00	0-0			0-1		-1.00	0-0		
J Fortune	0-1		-1.00	0-1		-1.00	0-0			0-0		
T E Durcan	0-1		-1.00	0-0			0-1		-1.00	0-0		

2001

	Overall			Two-year-olds			Three-year-olds			Older horses		
	W-R	%	£1	W-R	%	£1	W-R	%	£1	W-R	%	£1
R Hills	20-75	26	-3.20	4-20	20	-1.50	9-33	27	-4.12	7-22	31	+2.42
Martin Dwyer	13-69	18	+32.05	6-29	20	+23.98	5-38	13	-6.50	2-2	100	+14.57
A Daly	9-21	42	+22.75	3-7	42	+2.75	3-7	42	+4.00	3-7	42	+16.00
W Supple	7-31	22	-15.89	0-5		-5.00	6-19	31	-5.22	1-7	14	-5.67
D Holland	1-1	100	+0.40	1-1	100	+0.40	0-0			0-0		
G Duffield	1-1	100	+3.00	1-1	100	+3.00	0-0			0-0		
Craig Williams	1-3	33	+5.00	1-1	100	+7.00	0-1		-1.00	0-1		-1.00
L Dettori	1-6	16		0-1		-1.00	1-4	25	+2.00	0-1		-1.00
A Clark	0-1		-1.00	0-1		-1.00	0-0			0-0		
G Carter	0-1		-1.00	0-1		-1.00	0-0			0-0		

By class

2003

	Overall			Two-year-olds			Three-year-olds			Older horses		
	W-R	%	£1	W-R	%	£1	W-R	%	£1	W-R	%	£1
A	13-68	19	+2.49	1-7	14	-4.13	6-28	21	+13.08	6-33	18	-6.47
B	4-11	36	+4.30	1-2	50	+1.25	3-7	42	+5.05	0-2		-2.00
C	11-19	57	+30.52	2-3	66	+5.91	7-10	70	+20.25	2-6	33	+4.36
D	24-137	17	-18.59	9-52	17	-4.87	13-68	19	-14.22	2-17	11	+0.50
E	2-21	9	+11.50	1-3	33	+3.50	0-10		-10.00	1-8	12	+18.00
F	1-2	50	+0.10	0-1		-1.00	1-1	100	+1.10	0-0		
G	1-2	50	-0.20	0-0			1-1	100	+0.80	0-1		-1.00

2002

	Overall			Two-year-olds			Three-year-olds			Older horses		
	W-R	%	£1	W-R	%	£1	W-R	%	£1	W-R	%	£1
A	12-39	30	+25.78	0-2		-2.00	10-30	33	+29.91	2-7	28	-2.13
B	0-6		-6.00	0-0			0-4		-4.00	0-2		-2.00
C	2-13	15	-6.25	0-2		-2.00	1-5	20	-1.50	1-6	16	-2.75
D	18-93	19	-30.67	4-33	12	-16.56	12-52	23	-12.86	2-8	25	-1.25
E	0-3		-3.00	0-2		-2.00	0-1		-1.00	0-0		
F	0-1		-1.00	0-0			0-1		-1.00	0-0		
G	0-0			0-0			0-0			0-0		

2001

	Overall			Two-year-olds			Three-year-olds			Older horses		
	W-R	%	£1	W-R	%	£1	W-R	%	£1	W-R	%	£1
A	14-51	27	+23.46	3-9	33	+11.50	6-21	28	+6.48	5-21	23	+5.48
B	1-13	7	-10.63	0-3		-3.00	0-6		-6.00	1-4	25	-1.62
C	8-23	34	+9.61	3-3	100	+13.25	3-12	25	-2.21	2-8	25	-1.43
D	25-119	21	-22.71	8-52	15	-17.50	13-61	21	-16.11	4-6	66	+10.90
E	3-11	27	+27.50	1-3	33	+18.00	1-5	20	-0.50	1-3	33	+10.00
F	2-2	100	+4.88	1-1	100	+1.38	1-1	100	+3.50	0-0		
G	0-0			0-0			0-0			0-0		

SNOW RIDGE (furthest right): swoops to take the Royal Lodge for Tregoning

By course

2003

	Overall			Two-year-olds			Three-year-olds			Older horses		
	W-R	%	£1	W-R	%	£1	W-R	%	£1	W-R	%	£1
Ascot	8-21	38	+10.66	2-4	50	+0.78	5-10	50	+10.88	1-7	14	-1.00
Ayr	0-1		-1.00	0-0			0-0			0-1		-1.00
Bath	4-9	44	+5.40	1-3	33	+1.00	3-5	60	+5.40	0-1		-1.00
Beverley	2-5	40	+18.50	1-1	100	+5.50	1-3	33	+14.00	0-1		-1.00
Chepstow	0-1		-1.00	0-0			0-1		-1.00	0-0		
Chester	1-2	50	+8.00	0-0			1-1	100	+9.00	0-1		-1.00
Doncaster	2-9	22	-4.64	1-5	20	-2.00	0-3		-3.00	1-1	100	+0.36
Epsom	0-4		-4.00	0-1		-1.00	0-2		-2.00	0-1		-1.00
Folkestone	0-1		-1.00	0-0			0-0			0-1		-1.00
Goodwood	7-25	28	+14.30	1-6	16	-3.50	4-11	36	+5.80	2-8	25	+12.00
Hamilton	0-2		-2.00	0-1		-1.00	0-0			0-1		-1.00
Haydock	1-7	14	+2.00	0-0			1-6	16	+3.00	0-1		-1.00
Kempton	2-11	18	-2.39	1-6	16	+1.00	0-4		-4.00	1-1	100	+0.62
Leicester	2-4	50	+12.53	1-1	100	+14.00	1-2	50	-0.47	0-1		-1.00
Lingfield	3-23	13	-5.87	0-7		-7.00	2-11	18	-4.87	1-5	20	+6.00
Newbury	8-27	29	+0.54	4-9	44	+4.38	2-12	16	-2.50	2-6	33	-1.33
Newcastle	0-6		-6.00	0-1		-1.00	0-5		-5.00	0-0		
Newmarket	3-29	10	-20.33	0-9		-9.00	2-11	18	-5.58	1-9	11	-5.75
Nottingham	3-8	37	+30.00	1-3	33	+4.50	1-4	25	+0.50	1-1	100	+25.00
Pontefract	0-4		-4.00	0-0			0-2		-2.00	0-2		-2.00
Redcar	0-2		-2.00	0-0			0-1		-1.00	0-1		-1.00
Ripon	1-6	16	-0.50	0-1		-1.00	1-4	25	+1.50	0-1		-1.00
Salisbury	3-14	21	-3.34	0-2		-2.00	2-9	22	-4.84	1-3	33	+3.50
Sandown	4-17	23	-3.00	1-4	25	+1.00	3-6	50	+3.00	0-7		-7.00
Southwell	0-1		-1.00	0-1		-1.00	0-0			0-0		
Warwick	1-3	33	+5.00	0-0			1-2	50	+6.00	0-1		-1.00
Windsor	1-4	25	-0.75	0-0			1-4	25	-0.75	0-0		
Wolver	0-1		-1.00	0-1		-1.00	0-0			0-0		
Yarmouth	0-2		-2.00	0-0			0-1		-1.00	0-1		-1.00
York	0-11		-11.00	0-2		-2.00	0-5		-5.00	0-4		-4.00

John Gosden

OTHER THAN Tregoning, Gosden is the only one of our featured top trainers who's returned a level-stakes profit on all runners at any time in the last three years.

That was 2002 – last year was rather less successful but Gosden maintained a healthy strike-rate and it will always be worth taking a look at his entries when weighing up a race.

Judging by strike-rate and profit figures, he has his runners in good shape around the end of summer/beginning of autumn.

By month

2003

	Overall			Two-year-olds			Three-year-olds			Older horses		
	W-R	%	£1	W-R	%	£1	W-R	%	£1	W-R	%	£1
January	0-0			0-0			0-0			0-0		
February	0-0			0-0			0-0			0-0		
March	1-1	100	+10.00	0-0			1-1	100	+10.00	0-0		
April	2-24	8	-15.25	0-0			1-20	5	-17.25	1-4	25	+2.00
May	7-57	12	-13.95	1-7	14	+6.00	5-41	12	-13.95	1-9	11	-6.00
June	14-72	19	-26.39	3-9	33	+0.88	10-52	19	-18.78	1-11	9	-8.50
July	9-45	20	+10.38	1-10	10	-7.50	6-25	24	-1.00	2-10	20	+18.88
August	11-62	17	-30.63	1-16	6	-13.63	10-41	24	-12.01	0-5		-5.00
September	18-69	26	+15.89	12-38	31	-1.86	5-26	19	-3.25	1-5	20	+21.00
October	7-50	14	-30.54	6-27	22	-10.54	1-21	4	-18.00	0-2		-2.00
November	4-18	22	-1.50	3-8	37	+5.88	1-10	10	-7.38	0-0		
December	0-0			0-0			0-0			0-0		

2002

	Overall			Two-year-olds			Three-year-olds			Older horses		
	W-R	%	£1	W-R	%	£1	W-R	%	£1	W-R	%	£1
January	0-0			0-0			0-0			0-0		
February	0-0			0-0			0-0			0-0		
March	0-0			0-0			0-0			0-0		
April	11-34	32	+14.80	0-0			11-33	33	+15.80	0-1		-1.00
May	10-46	21	+27.95	1-6	16	+28.00	8-37	21	-9.45	1-3	33	+9.40
June	7-47	14	-5.29	1-7	14	-4.38	3-35	8	-27.83	3-5	60	+26.91
July	4-35	11	-22.88	2-7	28	-0.88	1-24	4	-22.00	1-4	25	
August	18-64	28	+18.63	4-21	19	+1.58	12-37	32	+15.43	2-6	33	+1.62
September	17-63	26	+17.69	9-20	45	+14.44	5-31	16	+2.25	3-12	25	+1.00
October	13-68	19	-5.17	10-42	23	-8.17	2-21	9	+4.50	1-5	20	-1.50
November	5-17	29	+13.50	4-15	26	+11.50	1-2	50	+2.00	0-0		
December	0-4		-4.00	0-4		-4.00	0-0			0-0		

2001

	Overall			Two-year-olds			Three-year-olds			Older horses		
	W-R	%	£1	W-R	%	£1	W-R	%	£1	W-R	%	£1
January	0-1		-1.00	0-0			0-0			0-1		-1.00
February	0-2		-2.00	0-0			0-0			0-2		-2.00
March	0-0			0-0			0-0			0-0		
April	2-8	25	-2.75	0-0			2-8	25	-2.75	0-0		
May	9-44	20	-12.98	1-4	25	-1.25	7-33	21	-6.52	1-7	14	-5.20
June	15-67	22	+22.70	2-13	15	-0.33	10-43	23	+5.03	3-11	27	+18.00
July	8-50	16	-27.45	2-13	15	-7.89	6-33	18	-15.56	0-4		-4.00
August	3-43	6	-19.63	0-17		-17.00	3-23	13	+0.37	0-3		-3.00
September	7-51	13	-24.17	4-25	16	-12.67	3-18	16	-3.50	0-8		-8.00
October	9-57	15	+16.65	7-39	17	+17.65	1-14	7	-4.00	1-4	25	+3.00
November	2-11	18	+5.00	1-5	20		1-6	16	+5.00	0-0		
December	0-2		-2.00	0-0			0-2		-2.00	0-0		

All runners

2003	Wins	Runs	%	2nd	3rd	rest	Win prize	Total prize	£1 Stake
2yo	27	115	23	13	12	11	268,580.45	315,228.45	-20.77
3yo	40	237	16	48	35	26	526,247.18	901,241.14	-81.61
4yo+	6	46	13	9	2	7	108,059.60	177,703.04	+20.38
TOTAL	73	398	18	70	49	44	902,887.23	1,394,172.63	-82.00

2002	Wins	Runs	%	2nd	3rd	rest	Win prize	Total prize	£1 Stake
2yo	31	122	25	12	15	14	342,490.60	407,550.27	+38.11
3yo	43	220	19	33	28	22	260,175.50	527,205.88	-19.30
4yo+	11	36	30	3	1	4	270,232.85	396,328.60	+36.42
TOTAL	85	378	22	48	44	40	872,898.95	1,331,084.75	+55.23

2001	Wins	Runs	%	2nd	3rd	rest	Win prize	Total prize	£1 Stake
2yo	17	116	14	17	13	12	73,200.00	128,944.17	-21.49
3yo	33	180	18	21	24	22	265,331.49	501,011.55	-23.93
4yo+	5	40	12	4	7	4	59,656.00	141,270.38	-2.20
TOTAL	55	336	16	42	44	38	398,187.49	771,226.10	-47.62

By race type

2003

	Overall			Two-year-olds			Three-year-olds			Older horses		
	W-R	%	£1	W-R	%	£1	W-R	%	£1	W-R	%	£1
Handicap	11-73	15	-12.50	3-7	42	-0.50	8-53	15	+1.00	0-13		-13.00
Group 1,2,3	3-33	9	-0.06	0-5		-5.00	2-18	11	-11.06	1-10	10	+16.00
Maiden	44-218	20	-68.73	19-90	21	-17.64	25-124	20	-47.08	0-4		-4.00
1st time out	8-83	9	-22.84	4-46	8	-19.67	3-36	8	-28.18	1-1	100	+25.00

2002

	Overall			Two-year-olds			Three-year-olds			Older horses		
	W-R	%	£1	W-R	%	£1	W-R	%	£1	W-R	%	£1
Handicap	13-68	19	-0.07	2-7	28	+3.00	9-53	16	-11.58	2-8	25	+8.50
Group 1,2,3	4-37	10	-2.50	3-12	25	+5.50	0-14		-14.00	1-11	9	+6.00
Maiden	55-214	25	+57.29	22-89	24	+33.34	30-121	24	+7.93	3-4	75	+16.02
1st time out	15-94	15	+13.25	6-53	11	+7.75	8-40	20	+0.50	1-1	100	+5.00

2001

	Overall			Two-year-olds			Three-year-olds			Older horses		
	W-R	%	£1	W-R	%	£1	W-R	%	£1	W-R	%	£1
Handicap	6-73	8	-8.25	0-7		-7.00	5-49	10	-5.25	1-17	5	+4.00
Group 1,2,3	1-37	2	-27.00	0-9		-9.00	1-20	5	-10.00	0-8		-8.00
Maiden	34-177	19	-10.43	15-89	16	+2.78	18-84	21	-13.71	1-4	25	+0.50
1st time out	10-76	13	-11.23	7-53	13	+6.15	3-21	14	-15.38	0-2		-2.00

By jockey

2003

	Overall			Two-year-olds			Three-year-olds			Older horses		
	W-R	%	£1	W-R	%	£1	W-R	%	£1	W-R	%	£1
J Fortune	22-109	20	-27.90	5-21	23	+4.38	13-75	17	-33.65	4-13	30	+1.38
L Dettori	14-41	34	+2.44	11-25	44	+10.06	3-13	23	-4.62	0-3		-3.00
R Hughes	8-64	12	-37.97	3-21	14	-9.67	5-36	13	-21.31	0-7		-7.00
R Havlin	7-55	12	+4.69	1-12	8	-6.00	5-35	14	-7.31	1-8	12	+18.00
R Hills	6-18	33	+27.75	1-2	50	+2.00	4-10	40	+5.75	1-6	16	+20.00
F Norton	5-24	20	-1.60	0-3		-3.00	5-20	25	+2.40	0-1		-1.00
W Supple	4-16	25	-6.13	2-4	50	+0.38	2-10	20	-4.50	0-2		-2.00
Dane O'Neill	2-13	15	-9.09	2-7	28	-3.09	0-5		-5.00	0-1		-1.00
K Darley	2-16	12	-10.75	1-8	12	-5.63	1-8	12	-5.13	0-0		
C Catlin	1-1	100	+12.00	0-0			1-1	100	+12.00	0-0		

By jockey ctd

2002

	Overall			Two-year-olds			Three-year-olds			Older horses		
	W-R	%	£1	W-R	%	£1	W-R	%	£1	W-R	%	£1
J Fortune	34-134	25	+20.91	15-53	28	+9.43	19-74	25	+18.48	0-7		-7.00
R Hughes	12-44	27	+25.23	3-9	33	+7.63	6-28	21	-4.80	3-7	42	+22.40
R Hills	10-33	30	+0.92	3-5	60	+5.43	4-17	23	-3.12	3-11	27	-1.38
L Dettori	7-25	28	+6.08	3-9	33	+2.25	3-15	20	+1.33	1-1	100	+2.50
R Havlin	6-49	12	+1.28	3-13	23	+25.16	3-35	8	-22.88	0-1		-1.00
K Fallon	3-8	37	+5.21	2-5	40	+1.71	0-2		-2.00	1-1	100	+5.50
W Supple	3-11	27	-1.59	0-5		-5.00	1-4	25	-1.00	2-2	100	+4.41
Dane O'Neill	2-5	40	+8.50	0-1		-1.00	2-4	50	+9.50	0-0		
P Robinson	2-6	33	+10.50	0-0			2-5	40	+11.50	0-1		-1.00
J Carroll	2-8	25	-1.56	0-0			2-7	28	-0.56	0-1		-1.00

2001

	Overall			Two-year-olds			Three-year-olds			Older horses		
	W-R	%	£1	W-R	%	£1	W-R	%	£1	W-R	%	£1
J Fortune	17-110	15	-49.52	8-40	20	-6.39	7-52	13	-30.44	2-18	11	-12.70
L Dettori	7-37	18	-3.85	3-15	20	+1.90	4-20	20	-3.75	0-2		-2.00
R Hughes	6-25	24	-5.25	0-8		-8.00	6-15	40	+4.75	0-2		-2.00
R Hills	6-27	22	+3.81	1-9	11	+2.00	5-15	33	+4.81	0-3		-3.00
R Havlin	5-51	9	-18.88	2-11	18	+7.50	2-33	6	-23.88	1-7	14	-2.50
G Duffield	2-3	66	+4.00	1-1	100	+0.50	1-2	50	+3.50	0-0		
K Fallon	2-6	33	+17.50	0-2		-2.00	1-2	50	+0.50	1-2	50	+19.00
J P Spencer	2-7	28	+15.00	0-4		-4.00	2-3	66	+19.00	0-0		
F Norton	2-10	20	+16.00	0-4		-4.00	2-5	40	+21.00	0-1		-1.00
K Darley	2-14	14	-2.80	0-5		-5.00	2-8	25	+3.20	0-1		-1.00

By class

2003

	Overall			Two-year-olds			Three-year-olds			Older horses		
	W-R	%	£1	W-R	%	£1	W-R	%	£1	W-R	%	£1
A	8-65	12	-12.93	1-10	10	-7.25	4-34	11	-16.56	3-21	14	+10.88
B	5-25	20	+25.50	1-2	50	+3.00	2-14	14	-0.50	2-9	22	+23.00
C	5-41	12	-21.97	0-1		-1.00	4-32	12	-15.47	1-8	12	-5.50
D	43-229	18	-72.30	18-92	19	-25.48	25-132	18	-41.83	0-5		-5.00
E	7-20	35	+2.92	3-3	100	+3.58	4-16	25	+0.34	0-1		-1.00
F	3-10	30	+1.15	2-4	50	+5.75	1-6	16	-4.60	0-0		
G	1-1	100	+0.13	1-1	100	+0.13	0-0			0-0		

2002

	Overall			Two-year-olds			Three-year-olds			Older horses		
	W-R	%	£1	W-R	%	£1	W-R	%	£1	W-R	%	£1
A	8-63	12	+8.00	3-15	20	+2.50	2-30	6	-4.00	3-18	16	+9.50
B	5-25	20	+0.12	0-0			2-17	11	-10.38	3-8	37	+10.50
C	9-39	23	-3.09	2-6	33	+0.83	5-27	18	-4.32	2-6	33	+0.41
D	60-236	25	+60.56	25-98	25	+36.44	32-134	23	+8.11	3-4	75	+16.02
E	1-9	11	-7.43	0-1		-1.00	1-8	12	-6.43	0-0		
F	0-1		-1.00	0-0			0-1		-1.00	0-0		
G	2-2	100	+1.06	1-1	100	+0.33	1-1	100	+0.73	0-0		

2001

	Overall			Two-year-olds			Three-year-olds			Older horses		
	W-R	%	£1	W-R	%	£1	W-R	%	£1	W-R	%	£1
A	4-57	7	-33.75	0-9		-9.00	3-32	9	-12.25	1-16	6	-12.50
B	4-31	12	+11.87	0-5		-5.00	3-21	14	+0.88	1-5	20	+16.00
C	8-33	24	+6.54	1-8	12	-6.67	5-18	27	+11.40	2-7	28	+1.80
D	34-189	17	-15.93	13-85	15	+3.28	20-92	21	-11.71	1-12	8	-7.50
E	2-17	11	-11.50	1-7	14	-5.00	1-10	10	-6.50	0-0		
F	1-5	20	-3.50	1-1	100	+0.50	0-4		-4.00	0-0		
G	2-3	66	-0.35	1-1	100	+0.40	1-2	50	-0.75	0-0		

OASIS DREAM: flew home for Gosden in the Nunthorpe

By course

2003

	Overall			Two-year-olds			Three-year-olds			Older horses		
	W-R	%	£1	W-R	%	£1	W-R	%	£1	W-R	%	£1
Ascot	2-26	7	-16.50	1-6	16	-1.00	1-14	7	-9.50	0-6		-6.00
Ayr	1-9	11	-6.50	1-5	20	-2.50	0-3		-3.00	0-1		-1.00
Bath	2-9	22	-3.90	0-0			2-9	22	-3.90	0-0		
Brighton	0-1		-1.00	0-0			0-1		-1.00	0-0		
Catterick	1-1	100	+0.80	1-1	100	+0.80	0-0			0-0		
Chepstow	1-8	12	-6.00	1-2	50		0-3		-3.00	0-3		-3.00
Chester	3-8	37	+12.37	0-0			3-8	37	+12.37	0-0		
Curragh	0-4		-4.00	0-1		-1.00	0-2		-2.00	0-1		-1.00
Doncaster	2-15	13	+13.38	1-6	16	-3.63	0-4		-4.00	1-5	20	+21.00
Epsom	0-7		-7.00	0-0			0-6		-6.00	0-1		-1.00
Goodwood	5-27	18	-5.79	1-6	16	-1.67	4-16	25	+0.88	0-5		-5.00
Hamilton	1-1	100	+1.38	1-1	100	+1.38	0-0			0-0		
Haydock	5-20	25	+16.37	1-5	20	-3.17	3-13	23	-4.47	1-2	50	+24.00
Kempton	1-20	5	-18.43	1-5	20	-3.43	0-14		-14.00	0-1		-1.00
Leicester	1-10	10	-8.47	1-4	25	-2.47	0-6		-6.00	0-0		
Leopardstown	1-3	33	-0.50	1-1	100	+1.50	0-1		-1.00	0-1		-1.00
Lingfield	3-22	13	-2.87	1-7	14	-3.50	2-15	13	+0.63	0-0		
Musselburgh	0-1		-1.00	0-0			0-1		-1.00	0-0		
Newbury	4-49	8	-37.25	1-16	6	-14.20	3-28	10	-18.05	0-5		-5.00
Newcastle	0-1		-1.00	0-0			0-1		-1.00	0-0		
Newmarket	7-40	17	-10.25	4-18	22	+0.63	2-18	11	-9.75	1-4	25	-1.12
Nottingham	3-14	21	-9.22	2-6	33	-2.62	1-6	16	-4.60	0-2		-2.00
Pontefract	2-4	50	+4.00	1-2	50	+3.50	0-1		-1.00	1-1	100	+1.50
Redcar	2-6	33	-2.63	0-0			2-5	40	-1.63	0-1		-1.00
Ripon	2-7	28	+0.44	0-0			1-6	16	-4.56	1-1	100	+5.00
Salisbury	6-20	30	+7.50	2-8	25	+7.75	4-11	36	+0.75	0-1		-1.00
Sandown	4-21	19	-7.05	1-7	14	-3.00	3-12	25	-2.05	0-2		-2.00
Southwell	1-2	50	+4.00	1-1	100	+5.00	0-1		-1.00	0-0		
Thirsk	1-3	33	-0.75	0-0			1-3	33	-0.75	0-0		
Windsor	7-21	33	+7.07	1-1	100	+2.75	5-18	27	+3.32	1-2	50	+1.00
Wolver	2-4	50	+9.37	1-1	100	+1.38	1-3	33	+8.00	0-0		
Yarmouth	2-9	22	-5.02	1-4	25	-2.27	1-4	25	-1.75	0-1		-1.00
York	1-5	20	-3.56	0-1		-1.00	1-4	25	-2.56	0-0		

Tim Easterby

A POOR tally of winners was recorded last season, dropping significantly on what had been achieved in preceding years.

Easterby also posted the lowest strike-rate of anyone in the top half of our 'trainers by winners'

table on page 32 and it will be necessary to see some strong indication that the stable has recovered its form before following them.

Having said which, his runners have generated slight profits at Group level.

By month

2003

	Overall			Two-year-olds			Three-year-olds			Older horses		
	W-R	%	£1	W-R	%	£1	W-R	%	£1	W-R	%	£1
January	1-8	12	-1.00	0-0			0-3		-3.00	1-5	20	+2.00
February	0-4		-4.00	0-0			0-2		-2.00	0-2		-2.00
March	3-21	14	+22.00	0-2		-2.00	2-13	15	+25.00	1-6	16	-1.00
April	5-60	8	-19.50	0-7		-7.00	2-35	5	-22.50	3-18	16	+10.00
May	5-145	3	-101.50	1-31	3	-27.50	3-66	4	-32.00	1-48	2	-42.00
June	19-161	11	-66.52	5-34	14	+5.05	6-71	8	-48.19	8-56	14	-23.38
July	9-133	6	-65.25	0-33		-33.00	6-57	10	-11.25	3-43	6	-21.00
August	10-125	8	-81.07	2-37	5	-31.38	4-50	8	-31.67	4-38	10	-18.02
September	4-100	4	-62.00	0-34		-34.00	3-30	10	+3.50	1-36	2	-31.50
October	2-56	3	-50.33	0-19		-19.00	2-22	9	-16.33	0-15		-15.00
November	1-20	5	-15.50	1-7	14	-2.50	0-9		-9.00	0-4		-4.00
December	0-0			0-0			0-0			0-0		

2002

	Overall			Two-year-olds			Three-year-olds			Older horses		
	W-R	%	£1	W-R	%	£1	W-R	%	£1	W-R	%	£1
January	0-0			0-0			0-0			0-0		
February	1-1	100	+10.00	0-0			1-1	100	+10.00	0-0		
March	1-22	4	-5.00	0-1		-1.00	1-15	6	+2.00	0-6		-6.00
April	4-72	5	-39.88	1-17	5	-5.00	3-42	7	-21.87	0-13		-13.00
May	9-114	7	-71.00	3-26	11	-17.25	3-54	5	-34.00	3-34	8	-19.75
June	23-165	13	-13.33	6-52	11	-31.85	6-71	8	-23.68	11-42	26	+42.20
July	17-151	11	-62.69	7-53	13	-19.44	8-55	14	-16.25	2-43	4	-27.00
August	9-115	7	-46.13	6-55	10	-14.50	3-38	7	-9.63	0-22		-22.00
September	8-94	8	-15.45	5-45	11	+11.75	2-23	8	-13.20	1-26	3	-14.00
October	6-61	9	-10.00	3-27	11	-3.50	2-18	11	-1.50	1-16	6	-5.00
November	3-24	12	-6.50	1-11	9	-7.00	0-4		-4.00	2-9	22	+4.50
December	0-7		-7.00	0-1		-1.00	0-0			0-6		-6.00

2001

	Overall			Two-year-olds			Three-year-olds			Older horses		
	W-R	%	£1	W-R	%	£1	W-R	%	£1	W-R	%	£1
January	0-8		-8.00	0-0			0-5		-5.00	0-3		-3.00
February	0-8		-8.00	0-0			0-3		-3.00	0-5		-5.00
March	1-13	7	-5.50	0-1		-1.00	0-7		-7.00	1-5	20	+2.50
April	0-40		-40.00	0-7		-7.00	0-19		-19.00	0-14		-14.00
May	9-133	6	-29.13	3-35	8	-13.13	5-68	7	-1.00	1-30	3	-15.00
June	17-136	12	-32.89	5-44	11	-21.89	8-59	13	-8.50	4-33	12	-2.50
July	12-138	8	-59.15	5-49	10	-9.50	6-68	8	-32.50	1-21	4	-17.15
August	18-134	13	+20.94	11-66	16	+9.19	3-48	6	-13.75	4-20	20	+25.50
September	10-116	8	-56.30	4-64	6	-37.50	2-32	6	-23.50	4-20	20	+4.70
October	4-60	6	-31.80	1-28	3	-22.00	2-18	11	+0.95	1-14	7	-10.75
November	2-14	14	+4.00	0-1		-1.00	0-6		-6.00	2-7	28	+11.00
December	0-4		-4.00	0-2		-2.00	0-0			0-2		-2.00

All runners

2003	Wins	Runs	%	2nd	3rd	rest	Win prize	Total prize	£1 Stake
2yo	9	204	4	17	27	35	43,115.95	150,748.21	-151.33
3yo	28	358	7	41	37	32	370,341.21	531,897.17	-147.44
4yo+	22	271	8	23	23	28	294,957.11	550,307.10	-145.90
TOTAL	59	833	7	81	87	95	708,414.27	1,232,952.48	-444.67

2002	Wins	Runs	%	2nd	3rd	rest	Win prize	Total prize	£1 Stake
2yo	32	288	11	28	42	36	443,583.75	561,400.93	-88.79
3yo	29	321	9	26	33	24	435,954.80	629,336.25	-112.13
4yo+	20	217	9	27	23	17	154,706.67	270,735.07	-66.05
TOTAL	81	826	9	81	98	77	1,034,245.22	1,461,472.25	-266.97

2001	Wins	Runs	%	2nd	3rd	rest	Win prize	Total prize	£1 Stake
2yo	29	297	9	25	21	38	237,830.20	335,350.95	-105.82
3yo	26	333	7	36	21	39	117,678.50	210,611.38	-118.30
4yo+	18	174	10	17	16	13	176,348.75	238,281.68	-25.70
TOTAL	73	804	9	78	58	90	531,857.45	784,244.01	-249.82

By race type

2003

	Overall			Two-year-olds			Three-year-olds			Older horses		
	W-R	%	£1	W-R	%	£1	W-R	%	£1	W-R	%	£1
Handicap	36-530	6	-292.42	1-40	2	-37.38	18-254	7	-126.02	17-236	7	-129.03
Group 1,2,3	3-16	18	+4.25	0-1		-1.00	1-4	25	+9.00	2-11	18	-3.75
Maiden	12-201	5	-105.43	6-129	4	-86.45	5-69	7	-19.83	1-3	33	+0.85
1st time out	3-64	4	-0.50	2-48	4	-18.50	1-13	7	+21.00	0-3		-3.00

2002

	Overall			Two-year-olds			Three-year-olds			Older horses		
	W-R	%	£1	W-R	%	£1	W-R	%	£1	W-R	%	£1
Handicap	46-472	9	-132.22	6-55	10	-8.67	21-223	9	-73.50	19-194	9	-50.05
Group 1,2,3	1-6	16	+2.00	0-2		-2.00	1-4	25	+4.00	0-0		
Maiden	22-216	10	-81.35	17-158	10	-51.73	5-56	8	-27.63	0-2		-2.00
1st time out	4-68	5	-13.50	3-60	5	-16.50	1-7	14	+4.00	0-1		-1.00

2001

	Overall			Two-year-olds			Three-year-olds			Older horses		
	W-R	%	£1	W-R	%	£1	W-R	%	£1	W-R	%	£1
Handicap	39-436	8	-109.00	7-68	10	-11.50	19-229	8	-80.05	13-139	9	-17.45
Group 1,2,3	1-18	5	-3.00	0-6		-6.00	0-3		-3.00	1-9	11	+6.00
Maiden	18-227	7	-103.07	16-161	9	-54.57	2-61	3	-43.50	0-5		-5.00
1st time out	1-75	1	-54.00	1-64	1	-43.00	0-7		-7.00	0-4		-4.00

By jockey

2003

	Overall			Two-year-olds			Three-year-olds			Older horses		
	W-R	%	£1	W-R	%	£1	W-R	%	£1	W-R	%	£1
K Darley	13-111	11	-49.23	4-26	15	-14.13	4-36	11	-12.85	5-49	10	-22.25
D Allan	12-255	4	-158.92	1-69	1	-66.00	11-123	8	-29.92	0-63		-63.00
W Supple	10-76	13	-30.80	1-18	5	-12.50	3-28	10	-13.42	6-30	20	-4.88
R Winston	5-53	9	-11.00	0-11		-11.00	1-25	4	-18.00	4-17	23	+18.00
J F Egan	3-20	15	+3.25	0-2		-2.00	3-15	20	+8.25	0-3		-3.00
K Dalgleish	3-20	15	-5.00	1-6	16	-1.50	0-6		-6.00	2-8	25	+2.50
K Fallon	2-13	15	-2.50	0-2		-2.00	0-2		-2.00	2-9	22	+1.50
P Doe	2-13	15	+25.00	1-5	20	+21.00	1-5	20	+7.00	0-3		-3.00
S Sanders	2-15	13	-4.00	0-0			2-8	25	+3.00	0-7		-7.00
T E Durcan	2-22	9	-1.00	0-3		-3.00	2-13	15	+8.00	0-6		-6.00

By jockey ctd

2002

	Overall			Two-year-olds			Three-year-olds			Older horses		
	W-R	%	£1	W-R	%	£1	W-R	%	£1	W-R	%	£1
R Winston	20-219	9	-59.33	12-86	13	+12.87	6-84	7	-39.70	2-49	4	-32.50
W Supple	11-76	14	-9.76	2-27	7	-16.20	8-41	19	+3.44	1-8	12	+3.00
T Quinn	8-34	23	+36.50	1-10	10	-5.00	1-8	12	-2.50	6-16	37	+44.00
D Allan	8-103	7	-54.63	2-48	4	-38.00	4-32	12	-10.13	2-23	8	-6.50
T E Durcan	6-55	10	-18.50	4-15	26	+10.50	0-16		-16.00	2-24	8	-13.00
P Hanagan	5-15	33	+13.73	2-5	40	+1.73	2-4	50	+11.00	1-6	16	+1.00
K Fallon	4-11	36	+0.38	2-4	50	+2.43	1-3	33	-0.25	1-4	25	-1.80
K Darley	3-31	9	-13.75	0-6		-6.00	1-10	10	-2.00	2-15	13	-5.75
E Ahern	2-6	33	+7.50	1-3	33	+2.50	1-1	100	+7.00	0-2		-2.00
Dale Gibson	2-17	11	+12.00	1-9	11	-6.00	1-5	20	+21.00	0-3		-3.00

2001

	Overall			Two-year-olds			Three-year-olds			Older horses		
	W-R	%	£1	W-R	%	£1	W-R	%	£1	W-R	%	£1
K Darley	14-95	14	-15.89	4-29	13	-17.64	4-38	10	-16.50	6-28	21	+18.25
W Supple	9-90	10	+12.25	6-35	17	+20.25	2-38	5	-8.00	1-17	5	
M Roberts	6-36	16	+3.50	4-15	26	+18.00	0-13		-13.00	2-8	25	-1.50
T E Durcan	6-66	9	-10.80	0-16		-16.00	4-36	11	+6.20	2-14	14	-1.00
R Winston	5-40	12	+4.45	3-17	17	-5.25	1-17	5	+9.00	1-6	16	+0.70
J Fanning	4-15	26	+4.50	1-6	16	+4.00	3-7	42	+2.50	0-2		-2.00
T Williams	4-33	12	-12.50	4-18	22	+2.50	0-14		-14.00	0-1		-1.00
J P Spencer	4-33	12	+14.38	2-9	22	-1.13	1-9	11	-3.50	1-15	6	+19.00
K Dalgleish	3-15	20	+7.75	1-6	16	+4.00	2-7	28	+5.75	0-2		-2.00
J Carroll	3-52	5	-29.71	2-28	7	-9.56	0-15		-15.00	1-9	11	-5.15

By class

2003

	Overall			Two-year-olds			Three-year-olds			Older horses		
	W-R	%	£1	W-R	%	£1	W-R	%	£1	W-R	%	£1
A	4-33	12	-8.88	0-1		-1.00	2-16	12	+3.00	2-16	12	-10.88
B	3-82	3	-68.25	0-8		-8.00	1-27	3	-22.00	2-47	4	-38.25
C	17-139	12	-46.38	0-13		-13.00	8-53	15	+13.75	9-73	12	-7.13
D	16-256	6	-154.31	6-72	8	-51.63	5-111	4	-58.18	5-73	6	-44.50
E	14-231	6	-155.77	1-74	1	-72.20	10-103	9	-41.92	3-54	5	-41.65
F	3-78	3	-46.09	1-30	3	-4.00	2-44	4	-38.09	0-4		-4.00
G	1-10	10	-5.50	1-5	20	-0.50	0-3		-3.00	0-2		-2.00

2002

	Overall			Two-year-olds			Three-year-olds			Older horses		
	W-R	%	£1	W-R	%	£1	W-R	%	£1	W-R	%	£1
A	2-23	8	-12.63	1-9	11	-6.63	1-13	7	-5.00	0-1		-1.00
B	7-77	9	-3.50	5-21	23	+23.50	1-28	3	-2.00	1-28	3	-25.00
C	17-130	13	-12.04	3-24	12	-5.67	7-39	17	-0.62	7-67	10	-5.75
D	28-241	11	-107.56	13-85	15	-33.80	8-92	8	-58.76	7-64	10	-15.00
E	21-245	8	-66.25	8-107	7	-42.20	9-98	9	-10.75	4-40	10	-13.30
F	5-96	5	-59.00	2-35	5	-17.00	2-46	4	-38.00	1-15	6	-4.00
G	1-14	7	-6.00	0-7		-7.00	1-5	20	+3.00	0-2		-2.00

2001

	Overall			Two-year-olds			Three-year-olds			Older horses		
	W-R	%	£1	W-R	%	£1	W-R	%	£1	W-R	%	£1
A	3-33	9	-4.50	2-13	15	+0.50	0-5		-5.00	1-15	6	
B	3-48	6	-4.50	2-19	10	-9.50	0-15		-15.00	1-14	7	+20.00
C	8-105	7	-59.75	4-27	14	-0.75	0-48		-48.00	4-30	13	-11.00
D	28-292	9	-61.11	13-121	10	-27.31	10-113	8	-22.05	5-58	8	-11.75
E	20-201	9	-58.93	6-80	7	-48.13	10-86	11	+1.00	4-35	11	-11.80
F	10-109	9	-51.54	2-31	6	-14.64	5-57	8	-26.75	3-21	14	-10.15
G	1-16	6	-9.50	0-6		-6.00	1-9	11	-2.50	0-1		-1.00

SOMNUS (nearest): a shock winner of the Haydock Sprint Cup for Easterby

By course

2003

	Overall			Two-year-olds			Three-year-olds			Older horses		
	W-R	%	£1	W-R	%	£1	W-R	%	£1	W-R	%	£1
Ascot	1-22	(4%)	-16.00	0-0			0-6		-6.00	1-16	(6%)	-10.00
Ayr	0-20		-20.00	0-3		-3.00	0-7		-7.00	0-10		-10.00
Beverley	5-85	(5%)	-66.17	2-25	(8%)	-19.00	2-44	(4%)	-33.67	1-16	(6%)	-13.50
Carlisle	0-22		-22.00	0-2		-2.00	0-14		-14.00	0-6		-6.00
Catterick	4-41	(9%)	+13.91	0-15		-15.00	4-16	(25%)	+38.91	0-10		-10.00
Chester	1-27	(3%)	-16.00	0-5		-5.00	0-11		-11.00	1-11	(9%)	
Curragh	1-4	(25%)	+0.50	0-1		-1.00	0-1		-1.00	1-2	(50%)	+2.50
Doncaster	2-37	(5%)	-29.70	1-9	(11%)	-7.20	0-13		-13.00	1-15	(6%)	-9.50
Epsom	0-1		-1.00	0-0			0-0			0-1		-1.00
Goodwood	0-8		-8.00	0-0			0-1		-1.00	0-7		-7.00
Hamilton	2-17	(11%)	-10.50	0-5		-5.00	1-5	(20%)	-2.50	1-7	(14%)	-3.00
Haydock	8-67	(11%)	-1.85	1-17	(5%)	-11.50	5-26	(19%)	+18.15	2-24	(8%)	-8.50
Kempton	0-1		-1.00	0-0			0-1		-1.00	0-0		
Leicester	0-8		-8.00	0-1		-1.00	0-4		-4.00	0-3		-3.00
Lingfield	2-7	(28%)	+5.00	0-0			0-4		-4.00	2-3	(66%)	+9.00
Musselburgh	2-14	(14%)	-4.50	0-6		-6.00	2-4	(50%)	+5.50	0-4		-4.00
Newbury	1-4	(25%)	+2.00	0-1		-1.00	1-1	(100%)	+5.00	0-2		-2.00
Newcastle	6-61	(9%)	-21.50	1-18	(5%)	-15.25	4-24	(16%)	+5.75	1-19	(5%)	-12.00
Newmarket	4-32	(12%)	+2.87	0-4		-4.00	1-12	(8%)	+5.00	3-16	(18%)	+1.88
Nottingham	0-23		-23.00	0-4		-4.00	0-13		-13.00	0-6		-6.00
Pontefract	5-42	(11%)	-9.50	0-13		-13.00	3-22	(13%)	-4.50	2-7	(28%)	+8.00
Redcar	2-65	(3%)	-57.33	0-17		-17.00	1-33	(3%)	-31.33	1-15	(6%)	-9.00
Ripon	3-63	(4%)	-52.63	1-22	(4%)	-19.38	2-30	(6%)	-22.25	0-11		-11.00
Sandown	1-2	(50%)	+4.50	0-0			0-0			1-2	(50%)	+4.50
Southwell	2-25	(8%)	+5.50	2-7	(28%)	+23.50	0-14		-14.00	0-4		-4.00
Thirsk	3-62	(4%)	-51.28	0-15		-15.00	1-26	(3%)	-21.50	2-21	(9%)	-14.78
Wolver	0-8		-8.00	0-1		-1.00	0-5		-5.00	0-2		-2.00
Yarmouth	0-1		-1.00	0-0			0-1		-1.00	0-0		
York	4-64	(6%)	-50.00	1-13	(7%)	-9.50	1-20	(5%)	-15.00	2-31	(6%)	-25.50

Luca Cumani

IF ONE can have such a thing as a Red Letter Year, then that would sum up 2003 for Luca Cumani.

In addition to the globetrotting, Group 1-gathering exploits of Falbrav, he won more races than he had in the previous two seasons put together, at a strike-rate of about double the one he'd been operating at before.

On the face of it, the most likely scenario for 2004 is a slight regression, but our stats indicate he's likely to hit good form in September.

By month

2003

	Overall			Two-year-olds			Three-year-olds			Older horses		
	W-R	%	£1	W-R	%	£1	W-R	%	£1	W-R	%	£1
January	0-0			0-0			0-0			0-0		
February	0-0			0-0			0-0			0-0		
March	0-0			0-0			0-0			0-0		
April	6-21	28	+14.55	0-0			4-17	23	+12.05	2-4	50	+2.50
May	11-47	23	-11.08	0-0			8-35	22	-6.91	3-12	25	-4.18
June	6-32	18	-14.48	0-1		-1.00	5-22	22	-8.98	1-9	11	-4.50
July	6-39	15	-8.72	0-6		-6.00	3-19	15	-5.63	3-14	21	+2.91
August	9-32	28	+13.12	0-3		-3.00	5-17	29	+7.12	4-12	33	+9.00
September	11-37	29	+6.25	1-7	14	-1.00	5-18	27	-2.75	5-12	41	+10.00
October	3-38	7	-22.68	0-16		-16.00	1-13	7	-5.50	2-9	22	-1.17
November	3-18	16	+2.03	3-13	23	+7.03	0-3		-3.00	0-2		-2.00
December	2-5	40	+0.83	0-3		-3.00	1-1	100	+3.00	1-1	100	+0.83

2002

	Overall			Two-year-olds			Three-year-olds			Older horses		
	W-R	%	£1	W-R	%	£1	W-R	%	£1	W-R	%	£1
January	0-0			0-0			0-0			0-0		
February	0-0			0-0			0-0			0-0		
March	0-1		-1.00	0-0			0-1		-1.00	0-0		
April	2-14	14	-7.00	0-0			2-9	22	-2.00	0-5		-5.00
May	3-32	9	-21.65	0-1		-1.00	3-27	11	-16.65	0-4		-4.00
June	3-29	10	-19.00	0-1		-1.00	2-20	10	-13.25	1-8	12	-4.75
July	4-32	12	-10.27	2-3	66	+11.00	1-21	4	-15.00	1-8	12	-6.27
August	4-31	12	-11.70	1-11	9	-6.50	2-12	16	-4.70	1-8	12	-0.50
September	5-20	25	+10.12	2-5	40	+0.61	1-9	11	+2.00	2-6	33	+7.50
October	4-27	14	+14.00	0-12		-12.00	4-11	36	+30.00	0-4		-4.00
November	0-17		-17.00	0-7		-7.00	0-8		-8.00	0-2		-2.00
December	0-6		-6.00	0-3		-3.00	0-2		-2.00	0-1		-1.00

2001

	Overall			Two-year-olds			Three-year-olds			Older horses		
	W-R	%	£1	W-R	%	£1	W-R	%	£1	W-R	%	£1
January	0-0			0-0			0-0			0-0		
February	0-0			0-0			0-0			0-0		
March	0-0			0-0			0-0			0-0		
April	0-17		-17.00	0-0			0-16		-16.00	0-1		-1.00
May	2-27	7	-8.00	0-0			1-22	4	-18.00	1-5	20	+10.00
June	3-25	12	-17.34	0-0			3-17	17	-9.34	0-8		-8.00
July	10-33	30	+27.84	2-6	33	+8.62	5-20	25	+11.63	3-7	42	+7.60
August	4-41	9	-31.27	2-14	14	-10.02	2-22	9	-16.25	0-5		-5.00
September	4-39	10	-14.45	1-15	6	-13.20	3-18	16	+4.75	0-6		-6.00
October	0-28		-28.00	0-15		-15.00	0-9		-9.00	0-4		-4.00
November	2-15	13	-8.50	0-6		-6.00	1-6	16	-2.00	1-3	33	-0.50
December	0-0			0-0			0-0			0-0		

Sponsored by Stan James

All runners

2003	Wins	Runs	%	2nd	3rd	rest	Win prize	Total prize	£1 Stake
2yo	4	49	8	6	7	5	12,236.50	28,780.50	-22.97
3yo	32	145	22	13	18	12	186,102.80	231,912.30	-10.60
4yo+	21	75	28	11	8	6	810,833.15	1,018,287.40	+13.39
TOTAL	57	269	21	30	33	23	1,009,172.45	1,278,980.20	-20.18

2002	Wins	Runs	%	2nd	3rd	rest	Win prize	Total prize	£1 Stake
2yo	5	43	11	3	5	7	24,878.75	36,359.95	-18.89
3yo	15	120	12	19	18	9	217,229.70	266,532.52	-30.60
4yo+	5	46	10	7	7	10	140,948.50	239,090.05	-20.02
TOTAL	25	209	11	29	30	26	383,056.95	541,982.52	-69.51

2001	Wins	Runs	%	2nd	3rd	rest	Win prize	Total prize	£1 Stake
2yo	5	56	8	7	5	6	152,920.75	166,118.88	-35.61
3yo	15	130	11	17	7	12	138,806.90	219,632.39	-54.21
4yo+	5	39	12	5	4	4	56,788.75	106,918.75	-6.90
TOTAL	25	225	11	29	16	22	348,516.40	492,670.02	-96.72

By race type

2003

	Overall			Two-year-olds			Three-year-olds			Older horses		
	W-R	%	£1	W-R	%	£1	W-R	%	£1	W-R	%	£1
Handicap	28-117	23	+13.07	1-7	14	-1.00	16-64	25	+5.82	11-46	23	+8.25
Group 1,2,3	3-11	27	+4.00	0-0			0-1		-1.00	3-10	30	+5.00
Maiden	15-104	14	-42.39	3-38	7	-17.97	9-60	15	-26.40	3-6	50	+1.98
1st time out	2-41	4	-21.50	0-16		-16.00	2-19	10	+0.50	0-6		-6.00

2002

	Overall			Two-year-olds			Three-year-olds			Older horses		
	W-R	%	£1	W-R	%	£1	W-R	%	£1	W-R	%	£1
Handicap	11-79	13	-6.52	2-7	28	+1.50	7-52	13	+1.25	2-20	10	-9.27
Group 1,2,3	3-16	18	+1.00	0-2		-2.00	1-3	33	+2.00	2-11	18	+1.00
Maiden	9-83	10	-41.24	3-32	9	-16.39	6-51	11	-24.85	0-0		
1st time out	2-33	6	-19.39	2-16	12	-2.39	0-17		-17.00	0-0		

2001

	Overall			Two-year-olds			Three-year-olds			Older horses		
	W-R	%	£1	W-R	%	£1	W-R	%	£1	W-R	%	£1
Handicap	7-76	9	-37.15	0-2		-2.00	4-56	7	-31.75	3-18	16	-3.40
Group 1,2,3	2-17	11	-12.95	2-2	100	+2.05	0-5		-5.00	0-10		-10.00
Maiden	10-97	10	-45.37	3-47	6	-30.66	6-48	12	-27.71	1-2	50	+13.00
1st time out	1-33	3	-20.00	1-20	5	-7.00	0-13		-13.00	0-0		

By jockey

2003

	Overall			Two-year-olds			Three-year-olds			Older horses		
	W-R	%	£1	W-R	%	£1	W-R	%	£1	W-R	%	£1
N Mackay	15-61	24	+19.79	0-8		-8.00	10-42	23	+10.29	5-11	45	+17.50
K Darley	8-28	28	-4.69	0-3		-3.00	5-14	35	+1.49	3-11	27	-3.18
D Holland	8-31	25	+3.83	0-4		-4.00	0-8		-8.00	8-19	42	+15.83
K Fallon	7-14	50	+8.76	0-1		-1.00	7-11	63	+11.76	0-2		-2.00
E Ahern	3-6	50	+10.83	1-3	33	+8.00	1-2	50	+2.00	1-1	100	+0.83
L Dettori	3-11	27	-4.80	1-1	100	+0.53	2-5	40	-0.33	0-5		-5.00
J P Spencer	3-19	15	+2.75	0-2		-2.00	2-10	20	+7.75	1-7	14	-3.00
S W Kelly	3-34	8	-23.72	1-11	9	-5.00	1-20	5	-17.63	1-3	33	-1.09
T Quinn	1-1	100	+0.07	0-0			1-1	100	+0.07	0-0		
Mrs S Cumani	1-1	100	+6.00	0-0			0-0			1-1	100	+6.00

By jockey ctd

2002

	Overall			Two-year-olds			Three-year-olds			Older horses		
	W-R	%	£1	W-R	%	£1	W-R	%	£1	W-R	%	£1
J P Spencer	16-116	13	-45.26	3-23	13	-12.89	9-62	14	-24.10	4-31	12	-8.27
S W Kelly	5-48	10	-8.00	2-17	11	-3.00	3-26	11		0-5		-5.00
J Carroll	2-5	40	+15.00	0-1		-1.00	2-4	50	+16.00	0-0		
J Mackay	1-2	50	+3.50	0-0			1-2	50	+3.50	0-0		
R Hughes	1-2	50	+1.25	0-0			0-0			1-2	50	+1.25
W Supple	0-1		-1.00	0-0			0-1		-1.00	0-0		
W Ryan	0-1		-1.00	0-0			0-1		-1.00	0-0		
C Poste	0-1		-1.00	0-0			0-0			0-1		-1.00
K Fallon	0-1		-1.00	0-0			0-0			0-1		-1.00
K Darley	0-1		-1.00	0-0			0-1		-1.00	0-0		

2001

	Overall			Two-year-olds			Three-year-olds			Older horses		
	W-R	%	£1	W-R	%	£1	W-R	%	£1	W-R	%	£1
J P Spencer	22-155	14	-35.59	5-39	12	-18.61	12-84	14	-17.08	5-32	15	+0.10
S W Kelly	2-42	4	-35.75	0-9		-9.00	2-29	6	-22.75	0-4		-4.00
J Mackay	1-5	20	-2.38	0-0			1-4	25	-1.38	0-1		-1.00
G Sparkes	0-1		-1.00	0-0			0-1		-1.00	0-0		
R Hughes	0-1		-1.00	0-0			0-1		-1.00	0-0		
Mr G Arizkorreta	0-1		-1.00	0-0			0-1		-1.00	0-0		
K Fallon	0-1		-1.00	0-0			0-0			0-1		-1.00
R Winston	0-1		-1.00	0-1		-1.00	0-0			0-0		
J Reid	0-1		-1.00	0-1		-1.00	0-0			0-0		
Miss F Cumani	0-1		-1.00	0-0			0-1		-1.00	0-0		

By class

2003

	Overall			Two-year-olds			Three-year-olds			Older horses		
	W-R	%	£1	W-R	%	£1	W-R	%	£1	W-R	%	£1
A	3-21	14	-6.00	0-0			0-7		-7.00	3-14	21	+1.00
B	3-22	13	-9.43	0-2		-2.00	2-8	25	+2.07	1-12	8	-9.50
C	8-39	20	-5.80	0-1		-1.00	3-19	15	-10.13	5-19	26	+5.33
D	23-124	18	-19.86	3-35	8	-14.97	14-73	19	-9.21	6-16	37	+4.31
E	14-48	29	+19.96	1-10	10	-4.00	7-27	25	+8.71	6-11	54	+15.25
F	6-14	42	+1.96	0-1		-1.00	6-11	54	+4.96	0-2		-2.00
G	0-0			0-0			0-0			0-0		

2002

	Overall			Two-year-olds			Three-year-olds			Older horses		
	W-R	%	£1	W-R	%	£1	W-R	%	£1	W-R	%	£1
A	3-32	9	-16.75	0-3		-3.00	0-9		-9.00	3-20	15	-4.75
B	0-10		-10.00	0-1		-1.00	0-3		-3.00	0-6		-6.00
C	3-18	16	-0.25	0-1		-1.00	3-11	27	+6.75	0-6		-6.00
D	13-112	11	-49.74	4-30	13	-17.89	8-76	10	-34.85	1-6	16	+3.00
E	5-29	17	+10.23	1-7	14	+5.00	3-17	17	+8.50	1-5	20	-3.27
F	0-5		-5.00	0-1		-1.00	0-2		-2.00	0-2		-2.00
G	0-1		-1.00	0-0			0-1		-1.00	0-0		

2001

	Overall			Two-year-olds			Three-year-olds			Older horses		
	W-R	%	£1	W-R	%	£1	W-R	%	£1	W-R	%	£1
A	5-34	14	-16.95	2-3	66	+1.05	2-16	12	-5.50	1-15	6	-12.50
B	3-18	16	+0.25	0-2		-2.00	2-10	20	+1.25	1-6	16	+1.00
C	2-25	8	-1.00	0-2		-2.00	2-16	12	+8.00	0-7		-7.00
D	9-99	9	-48.98	2-38	5	-23.27	6-55	10	-34.71	1-6	16	+9.00
E	5-36	13	-22.54	1-9	11	-7.39	3-24	12	-14.25	1-3	33	-0.90
F	1-13	7	-7.50	0-2		-2.00	0-9		-9.00	1-2	50	+3.50
G	0-0			0-0			0-0			0-0		

FALBRAV (left): devastating winner of the QEII Stakes for Cumani

By course

2003

	Overall			Two-year-olds			Three-year-olds			Olderhorses		
	W-R	%	£1	W-R	%	£1	W-R	%	£1	W-R	%	£1
Ascot	1-9	11	-6.50	0-1		-1.00	0-1		-1.00	1-7	14	-4.50
Ayr	5-7	71	+11.61	0-0			3-5	60	+7.53	2-2	100	+4.07
Bath	2-3	66	+9.00	0-0			0-1		-1.00	2-2	100	+10.00
Beverley	4-6	66	+17.00	0-0			3-4	75	+15.00	1-2	50	+2.00
Brighton	1-7	14	+0.50	0-2		-2.00	1-5	20	+2.50	0-0		
Carlisle	2-2	100	+2.12	0-0			1-1	100	+0.62	1-1	100	+1.50
Catterick	0-1		-1.00	0-1		-1.00	0-0			0-0		
Chepstow	1-2	50	-0.93	0-0			1-2	50	-0.93	0-0		
Doncaster	0-9		-9.00	0-5		-5.00	0-2		-2.00	0-2		-2.00
Epsom	0-1		-1.00	0-0			0-0			0-1		-1.00
Folkestone	0-3		-3.00	0-2		-2.00	0-1		-1.00	0-0		
Goodwood	0-4		-4.00	0-0			0-2		-2.00	0-2		-2.00
Hamilton	1-8	12	-4.75	0-2		-2.00	0-3		-3.00	1-3	33	+0.25
Haydock	4-10	40	+7.48	0-2		-2.00	1-4	25	-2.27	3-4	75	+11.75
Kempton	1-7	14	-4.00	0-0			1-5	20	-2.00	0-2		-2.00
Leicester	2-9	22	+1.00	0-3		-3.00	0-4		-4.00	2-2	100	+8.00
Leopardstown	0-1		-1.00	0-0			0-0			0-1		-1.00
Lingfield	6-19	31	+4.62	3-11	27	+4.03	2-5	40	+1.75	1-3	33	-1.17
Musselburgh	1-3	33	+0.25	0-0			1-2	50	+1.25	0-1		-1.00
Newbury	1-11	9	-8.00	0-2		-2.00	1-9	11	-6.00	0-0		
Newcastle	1-4	25	-1.00	0-1		-1.00	1-2	50	+1.00	0-1		-1.00
Newmarket	2-32	6	-12.67	0-4		-4.00	1-15	6		1-13	7	-8.68
Nottingham	2-15	13	-8.76	0-4		-4.00	2-11	18	-4.76	0-0		
Pontefract	4-8	50	+3.03	0-0			2-6	33	-0.63	2-2	100	+3.66
Redcar	3-10	30	+10.25	1-3	33	+8.00	1-5	20	-1.25	1-2	50	+3.50
Ripon	0-7		-7.00	0-0			0-7		-7.00	0-0		
Salisbury	2-6	33	+1.17	0-0			2-5	40	+2.17	0-1		-1.00
Sandown	2-5	40	+9.50	0-0			1-3	33	+2.50	1-2	50	+7.00
Warwick	3-6	50	+8.50	0-0			2-5	40	+7.00	1-1	100	+1.50
Windsor	1-14	7	-6.00	0-1		-1.00	1-11	9	-3.00	0-2		-2.00
Wolver	1-1	100	+0.67	0-0			1-1	100	+0.67	0-0		
Yarmouth	3-18	16	-10.76	0-4		-4.00	3-9	33	-1.75	0-5		-5.00
York	1-21	4	-17.50	0-1		-1.00	0-9		-9.00	1-11	9	-7.50

Andrew Balding

IN HIS wildest dreams, Andrew Balding surely couldn't have hoped for a better first season with a training license.

With a very healthy winners tally, over £1 million in win and place prizemoney and a first Classic success to boot, it was a resounding success.

By comparing his 2003 figures with the 2002 and 2001 returns of the same stable when run by his father Ian, you can see that he'll be upholding the family tradition in some style and is clearly a trainer to keep onside.

By month

2003

	Overall			Two-year-olds			Three-year-olds			Older horses		
	W-R	%	£1	W-R	%	£1	W-R	%	£1	W-R	%	£1
January	4-17	23	+16.10	0-0			0-1		-1.00	4-16	25	+17.10
February	3-17	17	+2.00	0-0			1-4	25	+7.00	2-13	15	-5.00
March	5-35	14	-7.75	0-0			0-15		-15.00	5-20	25	+7.25
April	6-57	10	-31.42	1-5	20	-1.25	3-26	11	-8.67	2-26	7	-21.50
May	5-58	8	-33.25	2-7	28	+5.00	0-31		-31.00	3-20	15	-7.25
June	8-76	10	-20.35	2-16	12	-8.00	4-33	12	-15.35	2-27	7	+3.00
July	6-68	8	-17.65	1-17	5	-14.90	3-24	12	+3.50	2-27	7	-6.25
August	8-62	12	+7.53	2-17	11	-11.50	0-15		-15.00	6-30	20	+34.03
September	7-66	10	+12.62	2-21	9	-13.63	0-16		-16.00	5-29	17	+42.25
October	1-38	2	-29.00	0-18		-18.00	1-9	11		0-11		-11.00
November	1-19	5	-11.00	1-11	9	-3.00	0-2		-2.00	0-6		-6.00
December	0-11		-11.00	0-7		-7.00	0-2		-2.00	0-2		-2.00

2002

	Overall			Two-year-olds			Three-year-olds			Older horses		
	W-R	%	£1	W-R	%	£1	W-R	%	£1	W-R	%	£1
January	5-16	31	+6.60	0-0			2-6	33	+0.60	3-10	30	+6.00
February	3-14	21	-5.25	0-0			2-5	40	+0.50	1-9	11	-5.75
March	0-9		-9.00	0-0			0-4		-4.00	0-5		-5.00
April	5-47	10	-28.65	0-2		-2.00	0-23		-23.00	5-22	22	-3.65
May	9-74	12	+29.10	2-11	18	+12.00	4-38	10	-0.90	3-25	12	+18.00
June	12-72	16	+10.28	2-17	11	-9.25	6-29	20	+12.53	4-26	15	+7.00
July	7-60	11	-26.84	3-16	18	-1.09	3-21	14	-7.25	1-23	4	-18.50
August	11-70	15	-2.50	7-32	21	+11.25	4-29	13	-4.75	0-9		-9.00
September	7-61	11	-13.80	6-27	22	+7.20	1-21	4	-8.00	0-13		-13.00
October	4-68	5	-20.00	1-32	3	-19.00	2-27	7	-12.00	1-9	11	+6.00
November	1-15	6	+2.00	1-6	16	+11.00	0-6		-6.00	0-3		-3.00
December	3-11	27	+11.50	1-3	33	+0.50	1-6	16	+2.00	1-2	50	+9.00

2001

	Overall			Two-year-olds			Three-year-olds			Older horses		
	W-R	%	£1	W-R	%	£1	W-R	%	£1	W-R	%	£1
January	1-4	25	+17.00	0-0			0-2		-2.00	1-2	50	+19.00
February	2-7	28	+1.00	0-0			1-2	50	+3.50	1-5	20	-2.50
March	0-13		-13.00	0-0			0-3		-3.00	0-10		-10.00
April	3-30	10	-5.00	0-0			1-15	6	-11.50	2-15	13	+6.50
May	5-68	7	-14.00	1-9	11	-4.50	2-28	7		2-31	6	-9.50
June	6-80	7	-50.56	2-24	8	-14.56	1-23	4	-18.00	3-33	9	-18.00
July	5-71	7	-31.97	1-21	4	-19.47	3-23	13	+10.00	1-27	3	-22.50
August	5-56	8	-15.37	1-21	4	-19.27	3-18	16	+7.90	1-17	5	-4.00
September	5-76	6	-54.42	2-24	8	-15.92	3-24	12	-10.50	0-28		-28.00
October	4-47	8	+1.70	1-20	5	-3.80	0-11		-11.00	3-16	18	+16.50
November	0-10		-10.00	0-3		-3.00	0-0			0-7		-7.00
December	0-4		-4.00	0-1		-1.00	0-0			0-3		-3.00

All runners

2003	Wins	Runs	%	2nd	3rd	rest	Win prize	Total prize	£1 Stake
2yo	11	119	9	15	12	11	56,607.75	171,411.31	-72.28
3yo	12	178	6	13	18	22	340,883.15	497,351.67	-95.52
4yo+	31	227	13	28	27	24	305,556.58	513,904.80	+44.63
TOTAL	54	524	10	56	57	57	703,047.48	1,182,667.78	-123.17

2002	Wins	Runs	%	2nd	3rd	rest	Win prize	Total prize	£1 Stake
2yo	23	146	15	13	22	17	128,191.24	253,533.04	+10.61
3yo	25	215	11	27	22	19	186,903.89	291,922.41	-50.27
4yo+	19	156	12	19	20	13	146,650.55	249,950.07	-11.90
TOTAL	67	517	12	59	64	49	461,745.68	795,405.52	-51.56

2001	Wins	Runs	%	2nd	3rd	rest	Win prize	Total prize	£1 Stake
2yo	8	123	6	13	11	6	64,337.89	109,371.12	-81.51
3yo	14	149	9	16	13	11	78,831.60	132,538.15	-34.60
4yo+	14	194	7	17	19	16	223,785.70	371,138.45	-62.50
TOTAL	36	466	7	46	43	33	366,955.19	613,047.72	-178.61

By race type

2003

	Overall			Two-year-olds			Three-year-olds			Older horses		
	W-R	%	£1	W-R	%	£1	W-R	%	£1	W-R	%	£1
Handicap	23-275	8	-80.50	1-12	8	-7.00	2-95	2	-79.00	20-168	11	+5.50
Group 1,2,3	2-25	8	-1.00	0-6		-6.00	2-9	22	+15.00	0-10		-10.00
Maiden	15-134	11	-70.54	8-81	9	-49.03	6-45	13	-17.27	1-8	12	-4.25
1st time out	8-102	7	-38.40	2-38	5	-27.50	2-36	5	-17.50	4-28	14	+6.60

2002

	Overall			Two-year-olds			Three-year-olds			Older horses		
	W-R	%	£1	W-R	%	£1	W-R	%	£1	W-R	%	£1
Handicap	34-277	12	+4.60	8-29	27	+48.25	15-137	10	-23.75	11-111	9	-19.90
Group 1,2,3	0-14		-14.00	0-9		-9.00	0-0			0-5		-5.00
Maiden	23-159	14	-27.16	11-83	13	-19.64	8-63	12	-23.77	4-13	30	+16.25
1st time out	3-54	5	-34.00	1-39	2	-31.00	1-14	7	-6.00	1-1	100	+3.00

2001

	Overall			Two-year-olds			Three-year-olds			Older horses		
	W-R	%	£1	W-R	%	£1	W-R	%	£1	W-R	%	£1
Handicap	20-252	7	-82.90	1-12	8	+4.20	9-85	10	-20.60	10-155	6	-66.50
Group 1,2,3	3-12	25	+15.83	1-2	50	+2.33	0-2		-2.00	2-8	25	+15.50
Maiden	8-129	6	-73.99	5-84	5	-64.49	3-43	6	-7.50	0-2		-2.00
1st time out	2-51	3	-29.50	1-41	2	-36.50	1-8	12	+9.00	0-2		-2.00

By jockey

2003

	Overall			Two-year-olds			Three-year-olds			Older horses		
	W-R	%	£1	W-R	%	£1	W-R	%	£1	W-R	%	£1
Martin Dwyer	27-247	10	-47.16	7-69	10	-37.53	8-98	8	-35.17	12-80	15	+25.53
N Chalmers	8-52	15	+30.60	0-5		-5.00	0-14		-14.00	8-33	24	+49.60
L P Keniry	5-80	6	-33.75	1-12	8	-7.00	0-24		-24.00	4-44	9	-2.75
K Darley	4-24	16	-12.14	3-10	30	+0.25	1-3	33	-1.39	0-11		-11.00
K Fallon	2-10	20	-2.25	0-1		-1.00	1-1	100	+2.75	1-8	12	-4.00
D J Whyte	1-1	100	+7.00	0-0			0-0			1-1	100	+7.00
F Johansson	1-1	100	+5.50	0-0			0-0			1-1	100	+5.50
Sara Metcalfe	1-1	100	+5.00	0-0			0-0			1-1	100	+5.00
Miss M Sowerby	1-2	50	+6.00	0-0			0-0			1-2	50	+6.00
G Duffield	1-4	25	-2.71	0-2		-2.00	1-2	50	-0.71	0-0		

By jockey ctd

2002

	Overall			Two-year-olds			Three-year-olds			Older horses		
	W-R	%	£1	W-R	%	£1	W-R	%	£1	W-R	%	£1
Martin Dwyer	36-232	15	+10.38	14-81	17	+2.61	15-106	14	-9.98	7-45	15	+17.75
L P Keniry	13-85	15	+31.75	4-22	18	+3.75	5-41	12	+12.00	4-22	18	+16.00
N Chalmers	3-28	10	-10.50	0-4		-4.00	0-4		-4.00	3-20	15	-2.50
K Fallon	3-31	9	-17.90	1-5	20	+3.00	0-6		-6.00	2-20	10	-14.90
W Ryan	2-17	11	-8.25	1-2	50	+4.00	1-12	8	-9.25	0-3		-3.00
W Supple	1-1	100	+2.25	1-1	100	+2.25	0-0			0-0		
A P McCoy	1-1	100	+2.00	0-0			1-1	100	+2.00	0-0		
M Fenton	1-2	50	+4.50	0-0			1-2	50	+4.50	0-0		
J Fanning	1-2	50	+13.00	1-2	50	+13.00	0-0			0-0		
D Kinsella	1-4	25	+11.00	1-2	50	+13.00	0-1		-1.00	0-1		-1.00

2001

	Overall			Two-year-olds			Three-year-olds			Older horses		
	W-R	%	£1	W-R	%	£1	W-R	%	£1	W-R	%	£1
Martin Dwyer	8-117	6	-39.63	3-36	8	-22.13	3-34	8	-6.50	2-47	4	-11.00
K Fallon	7-71	9	-23.56	2-17	11	-11.06	2-22	9	-8.50	3-32	9	-4.00
K Darley	5-23	21	+21.00	0-4		-4.00	2-9	22	+11.50	3-10	30	+13.50
J P Spencer	3-9	33	+20.50	0-0			2-5	40	+13.50	1-4	25	+7.00
Michael Doyle	2-24	8	-2.30	1-8	12	+8.20	1-7	14	-1.50	0-9		-9.00
W Ryan	2-26	7	-6.50	0-9		-9.00	0-6		-6.00	2-11	18	+8.50
A Clark	2-38	5	-29.27	1-17	5	-15.27	1-15	6	-8.00	0-6		-6.00
P Whelan	1-1	100	+1.50	0-0			0-0			1-1	100	+1.50
J Carroll	1-3	33		0-0			1-1	100	+2.00	0-2		-2.00
L Dettori	1-5	20	+1.50	0-0			0-1		-1.00	1-4	25	+2.50

By class

2003

	Overall			Two-year-olds			Three-year-olds			Older horses		
	W-R	%	£1	W-R	%	£1	W-R	%	£1	W-R	%	£1
A	7-47	14	+40.28	0-7		-7.00	3-17	17	+10.75	4-23	17	+36.53
B	6-74	8	-26.25	1-8	12	-4.25	1-16	6	-7.00	4-50	8	-15.00
C	5-71	7	-35.00	1-5	20		0-26		-26.00	4-40	10	-9.00
D	20-193	10	-78.58	7-69	10	-39.03	6-70	8	-30.05	7-54	12	-9.50
E	11-93	11	-8.96	2-23	8	-15.00	2-26	7	-20.21	7-44	15	+26.25
F	5-35	14	-3.65	0-4		-4.00	0-17		-17.00	5-14	35	+17.35
G	0-8		-8.00	0-2		-2.00	0-5		-5.00	0-1		-1.00

2002

	Overall			Two-year-olds			Three-year-olds			Older horses		
	W-R	%	£1	W-R	%	£1	W-R	%	£1	W-R	%	£1
A	3-28	10	-19.00	2-12	16	-6.00	0-2		-2.00	1-14	7	-11.00
B	6-55	10	+18.00	0-8		-8.00	4-28	14	+22.00	2-19	10	+4.00
C	9-65	13	+16.60	3-11	27	+12.00	3-28	10	+0.50	3-26	11	+4.10
D	26-185	14	-28.26	7-68	10	-16.64	12-83	14	-34.12	7-34	20	+22.50
E	20-126	15	-6.90	11-38	28	+38.25	4-53	7	-35.65	5-35	14	-9.50
F	3-49	6	-23.00	0-7		-7.00	2-20	10		1-22	4	-16.00
G	0-9		-9.00	0-2		-2.00	0-1		-1.00	0-6		-6.00

2001

	Overall			Two-year-olds			Three-year-olds			Older horses		
	W-R	%	£1	W-R	%	£1	W-R	%	£1	W-R	%	£1
A	5-33	15	+10.33	1-5	20	-0.67	1-9	11	+2.00	3-19	15	+9.00
B	4-69	5	-24.56	1-10	10	-8.56	1-12	8	+5.00	2-47	4	-21.00
C	7-76	9	-1.40	1-13	7	+3.20	1-15	6	-2.10	5-48	10	-2.50
D	9-156	5	-89.75	3-60	5	-43.75	6-64	9	-14.00	0-32		-32.00
E	7-98	7	-51.27	1-29	3	-27.27	4-34	11	-14.00	2-35	5	-10.00
F	3-30	10	-20.47	1-6	16	-4.47	1-15	6	-11.50	1-9	11	-4.50
G	1-4	25	-1.50	0-0			0-0			1-4	25	-1.50

CASUAL LOOK: gives Andrew Balding his first Classic in his first season as a trainer

By course

2003

	Overall			Two-year-olds			Three-year-olds			Older horses		
	W-R	%	£1	W-R	%	£1	W-R	%	£1	W-R	%	£1
Ascot	4-35	11	-7.75	1-5	20	-1.25	1-9	11		2-21	9	-6.50
Ayr	1-4	25	+1.00	1-2	50	+3.00	0-0			0-2		-2.00
Bath	5-21	23	+9.63	4-6	66	+11.63	0-10		-10.00	1-5	20	+8.00
Beverley	3-7	42	+2.62	1-2	50	+1.50	2-3	66	+3.12	0-2		-2.00
Brighton	0-5		-5.00	0-2		-2.00	0-1		-1.00	0-2		-2.00
Carlisle	1-4	25	-2.71	0-0			1-4	25	-2.71	0-0		
Catterick	0-2		-2.00	0-2		-2.00	0-0			0-0		
Chepstow	0-7		-7.00	0-3		-3.00	0-3		-3.00	0-1		-1.00
Chester	0-4		-4.00	0-0			0-1		-1.00	0-3		-3.00
Curragh	0-2		-2.00	0-1		-1.00	0-1		-1.00	0-0		
Doncaster	2-22	9	+3.00	0-4		-4.00	0-5		-5.00	2-13	15	+12.00
Epsom	5-24	20	+12.10	1-4	25	-1.90	2-7	28	+7.75	2-13	15	+6.25
Folkestone	1-3	33	+14.00	0-1		-1.00	0-1		-1.00	1-1	100	+16.00
Goodwood	1-36	2	-23.00	0-8		-8.00	1-15	6	-2.00	0-13		-13.00
Hamilton	0-1		-1.00	0-0			0-0			0-1		-1.00
Haydock	0-8		-8.00	0-2		-2.00	0-3		-3.00	0-3		-3.00
Kempton	1-22	4	-15.00	0-3		-3.00	0-12		-12.00	1-7	14	
Leicester	1-14	7	-11.25	0-3		-3.00	0-6		-6.00	1-5	20	-2.25
Lingfield	14-97	14	-1.15	1-22	4	-14.00	2-24	8	-2.00	11-51	21	+14.85
Newbury	3-32	9	-13.25	0-7		-7.00	1-10	10	-2.50	2-15	13	-3.75
Newcastle	0-4		-4.00	0-1		-1.00	0-0			0-3		-3.00
Newmarket	0-31		-31.00	0-8		-8.00	0-9		-9.00	0-14		-14.00
Nottingham	0-8		-8.00	0-2		-2.00	0-4		-4.00	0-2		-2.00
Pontefract	1-6	16	-4.47	0-4		-4.00	0-0			1-2	50	-0.47
Redcar	0-2		-2.00	0-1		-1.00	0-1		-1.00	0-0		
Ripon	0-2		-2.00	0-1		-1.00	0-0			0-1		-1.00
Salisbury	3-22	13	+18.00	0-6		-6.00	1-9	11	-2.00	2-7	28	+26.00
Sandown	1-20	5	-16.75	0-2		-2.00	0-9		-9.00	1-9	11	-5.75
Southwell	1-6	16	-2.25	0-1		-1.00	0-2		-2.00	1-3	33	+0.75
Thirsk	2-5	40	+1.75	2-2	100	+4.75	0-2		-2.00	0-1		-1.00
Tipperary	0-1		-1.00	0-0			0-0			0-1		-1.00
Warwick	0-6		-6.00	0-2		-2.00	0-3		-3.00	0-1		-1.00
Windsor	2-42	4	-36.67	0-9		-9.00	1-17	5	-15.17	1-16	6	-12.50
Wolver	0-8		-8.00	0-1		-1.00	0-3		-3.00	0-4		-4.00
Yarmouth	1-3	33	+14.00	0-1		-1.00	0-1		-1.00	1-1	100	+16.00
York	1-8	12	+26.00	0-1		-1.00	0-3		-3.00	1-4	25	+30.00

Outlook

Group 1 Review
by Nicholas Watts

For two-year-old Group 1s, see 'Two-year-olds of 2003', page 88

1   **Dubai World Cup (Dirt), (1m2f) Nad Al Sheba March 29 (Standard)**

1 **Moon Ballad** 9-0   L Dettori
2 **Harlan's Holiday** 9-0   J Velazquez
3 **Nayef** 9-0   R Hills
11-4, 11-2, 11-8f. 5l, 1l. 11 ran. 2m 0.5
Godolphin (S Bin Suroor, Newmarket)

Moon Ballad produced a sensational performance on the day, but this race is increasingly becoming a benefit for the local runners, and its relevance from a form perspective must be doubted. The winner (now retired to stud, having never scored at Group 1 level in Britain) was never to win another race, while Nayef wasn't at his best.

2   **Sagitta 2,000 Guineas Stakes (1m) Newmarket May 3 (Good)**

1 **Refuse To Bend** 9-0   P J Smullen
2 **Zafeen** 9-0   S Drowne
3 **Norse Dancer** 9-0   P Robinson
9-2, 33-1, 100-1. ¾l, hd. 20 ran. 1m 38.0 (b5.94)
Moyglare Stud Farms Ltd (D Weld, Ireland)

A sub-standard Guineas, with Refuse To Bend not advertising the value of the form in his subsequent outings, winning only a Group 3 at Leopardstown in August. Zafeen ran with credit in the face of traffic problems, while Norse Dancer began a trend that lasted through the season, of flattering to deceive.

3   **Sagitta 1,000 Guineas Stakes (1m) Newmarket May 4 (Good to Firm)**

1 **Russian Rhythm** 9-0   K Fallon
2 **Six Perfections** 9-0   T Thulliez
3 **Intercontinental** 9-0   C Soumillon
12-1, 7-4f, 5-1. 1½l, 1¼l. 19 ran. 1m 38.4 (b5.49)
Cheveley Park Stud (Sir M Stoute, Newmarket)

Despite rumours that she wasn't working well, Michael Stoute's Russian Rhythm never looked like being caught once sent to the front a furlong out. However, Six Perfections, ridden by Thierry Thulliez, had to go all round the houses to launch her challenge, and that detour ultimately cost her victory. Subsequent performances of both winner and runner-up suggest this was an above-average renewal.

4   **Juddmonte Lockinge Stakes (1m) Newbury May 17 (Good to Firm)**

1 **Hawk Wing** 9-0   M J Kinane
2 **Where Or When** 9-0   K Darley
3 **Olden Times** 9-0   K Fallon
2-1f, 7-2, 10-1. 11l, 8l. 6 ran. 1m 36.8 (b6.02)
S Magnier (A P O'Brien, Ireland)

One of the most talked-about races of the season, as the enigma that is Hawk Wing galloped his rivals into submission. Conditions may well have served to exaggerate his margin of superiority, but future Group 1 winner **Reel Buddy** was one of those left toiling, along with other Group 1 winners in Where Or When, Olden Times and **Domedriver**, so it wasn't too shabby a performance. We would only see Hawk Wing on a racecourse once more *(12)*.

5   **Entenmann's Irish 2,000 Guineas (1m) Curragh May 24 (Soft)**

1 **Indian Haven** 9-0   J F Egan
2 **France** 9-0   J A Heffernan
3 **Tout Seul** 9-0   S Carson
8-1, 14-1, 5-1. 1l, 2½l. 16 ran. 1m 41.5 (b3.05)
J M & E E Ranson (P d'Arcy, Newmarket)

Indian Haven provided Paul d'Arcy with his first Group 1 success, and compensated for a luckless run when only 14th in the English equivalent *(2)* with a comfortable win. This, however, was very much the high point of his season. The runner-up, France, was by no means one of Aidan O'Brien's best three-year-old's, while Tout Seul (a Group 1 winner at two and fourth in the Newmarket Guineas) was repeatedly found wanting in subsequent runs – he finished his season with a fifth place in a Listed race in Japan. **Zafeen** (14th) was most disappointing, though this was almost certainly due to a dislike for the surface.

6   **Tattersalls Gold Cup (1m2f110yds) Curragh May 25 (Soft)**

1 **Black Sam Bellamy** 9-0   M J Kinane
2 **Highdown** 9-0   J P Spencer
3 **Narrative** 9-0   R Hills
6-1, 5-1, 14-1. 8l, 1¹/₂l. 8 ran. 2m 14.8 (b11.23)
M Tabor (A P O'Brien, Ireland)

A weak Group 1 but an improved showing from the regally-bred Black Sam Bellamy (by Sadler's Wells out of an Arc winner, and a full-brother to Derby winner Galileo). He had progressed throughout his three-year-old season, eventually winning a Group 1 in Italy, but even so it was surprising to see him take this by 8l. Tougher contests later in the season would reveal the extent of his improvement.

7   **Entenmann's Irish 1,000 Guineas (1m) Curragh May 25 (Soft)**

1 **Yesterday** 9-0   M J Kinane
2 **Six Perfections** 9-0   J P Murtagh
3 **Dimitrova** 9-0   P J Smullen
11-2, 3-10, 16-1. shd, ³/₄l. 8 ran. 1m 40.8 (b3.75)
S Magnier (A P O'Brien, Ireland)

A change of jockey, but no change of luck for Six Perfections, who just failed to peg back the alert Mick Kinane and Yesterday. The winning pair kicked on while Six Perfections was stuck in a pocket and it turned out to be a decisive move. Again, a moral victory was all Pascal Bary (trainer of the runner-up) could claim.

8   **Vodafone Coronation Cup (1m4f110yds) Epsom June 6 (Good)**

1 **Warrsan** 9-0   P Robinson
2 **Highest** 9-0   L Dettori
3 **Black Sam Bellamy** 9-0   M J Kinane
9-2, 6-1, 4-1f. ¹/₂l, shd. 9 ran. 2m 35.7 (b10.67)
Saeed Manana (C Brittain, Newmarket)

Probably not the best renewal of this race.

Warrsan is a typical Clive Brittain horse, campaigned aggressively and running often. He came up trumps here and, being related to the ex-Brittain Luso and Needle Gun, could well improve again. Favourite Black Sam Bellamy, who looked so good when winning at the Curragh last time, was disappointing in third – he didn't win again during the season, though he was sixth in the Arc *(32)*.

9   **Vodafone Oaks (1m4f10yds) Epsom June 6 (Good)**

1 **Casual Look** 9-0   Martin Dwyer
2 **Yesterday** 9-0   M J Kinane
3 **Summitville** 9-0   M Fenton
10-1, 10-3f, 25-1. nk, ¹/₂l. 15 ran. 2m 38.1 (b8.28)
W S Farish III (A Balding, Kingsclere)

A messy race, but that won't have bothered Andrew Balding, who was training his first Classic winner in his debut season. Casual Look was almost certainly lucky, however, as Yesterday endured a nightmare passage in the latter half of the race and was only beaten a neck. The proximity of the exposed Summitville in third proves this was far from a vintage Oaks.

10   **Vodafone Derby Stakes (1m4f10yds) Epsom June 7 (Good)**

1 **Kris Kin** 9-0   K Fallon
2 **The Great Gatsby** 9-0   Pat Eddery
3 **Alamshar** 9-0   J P Murtagh
6-1, 20-1, 4-1. 1l, shd. 20 ran. 2m 33.4 (b13.00)
Saeed Suhail (Sir M Stoute, Newmarket)

This won't be remembered as a great Derby, notwithstanding the notable presence of a running-on Alamshar in third. Kris Kin, a supplementary entry after causing a 20-1 upset in Chester's Dee Stakes, took the measure of The Great Gatsby inside the final furlong to win comfortably – but he never won again in three subsequent starts. Now retired, it's hard to see him making a great impact at stud. **Norse Dancer** finished fourth after passing most of the field in the straight, prompting criticism of Richard Quinn's riding. Subsequent races proved, however, that this is by no means an easy horse to ride. **Refuse To Bend** and **Brian Boru** were thereabouts turning for home but both faded tamely away.

11   **St James's Palace Stakes (1m) Ascot June 17 (Good to Firm)**

1 **Zafeen** 9-0   D Holland

2 **Kalaman** 9-0   J Murtagh
3 **Martillo** 9-0   W Mongil
8-1, 5-2f, 12-1. 1l, 3l. 11 ran. 1m 39.9 (b7.37)
Jaber Abdullah (M Channon, West Ilsley)

Steve Drowne lost the ride on Zafeen and could only look on as Darryll Holland guided Mick Channon's colt to victory. But it could have been a different story if Kalanisi's half-brother Kalaman had endured a better passage – he was almost stopped at one stage inside the final two furlongs. The race was as good as over once he had managed to extricate himself and he can be considered an unlucky loser.

12 **Queen Anne Stakes (1m) Ascot June 17 (Good to Firm)**

1 **Dubai Destination** 9-0   L Dettori
2 **Right Approach** 9-0   K Fallon
3 **Where Or When** 9-0   K Darley
9-2, 20-1, 8-1. ³/₄l, 3¹/₂l. 10 ran. 1m 38.6 (b8.72)
Godolphin (S Bin Suroor, Newmarket)

Dubai Destination had the distinction of beating Rock Of Gibraltar as a two-year-old, and bounced back to that kind of form here to win a race afforded Group 1 status for the first time. Unfortunately, though, this proved to be only a brief flash of brilliance, as he was stuffed in both subsequent outings. This was Hawk Wing's last hurrah. He had the full support of the *Racing Post*, who splashed him on the front page on the morning of this race, bearing a pair of eagle's wings and under the headline "Now watch him fly". Sent off the 8-13 favourite (and the most heavily-traded runner in the history of betting exchanges), he let everyone down, finding nothing when asked and finishing a wimpish seventh. His connections (no doubt thinking of his stud career and keen to find some explanation for the defeat) reported that he finished lame and that he may have coughed. He never ran again. At the other end of the 'gameness' spectrum, **Tillerman** ran above himself to be second, but was disqualified five months later when a banned substance was found in his sample.

13 **Prince Of Wales's Stakes (1m2f) Ascot June 18 (Good to Firm)**

1 **Nayef** 9-0   R Hills
2 **Rakti** 9-0   P Robinson
3 **Islington** 8-11   K Fallon
5-1, 50-1, 7-1. 2¹/₂l, 1l. 10 ran. 2m 5.3 (b10.70)
Hamdan Al Maktoum (M Tregoning, Lambourn)

In what turned into a gruelling campaign for Nayef, he gained a sole and deserved Group 1 success over Rakti and Islington. Little was known at the time about the merit of second-placed Rakti, and he was allowed to go off at 50-1. He nearly made a mockery of those odds, however, and is clearly a smart performer. Islington ran her usual honest race without ever threatening to win.

14 **Gold Cup (2m4f) Ascot June 19 (Good to Firm)**

1 **Mr Dinos** 9-0   K Fallon
2 **Persian Punch** 9-2   Martin Dwyer
3 **Pole Star** 9-2   Pat Eddery
3-1, 20-1, 12-1. 6l, ³/₄l. 12 ran. 4m 20.2 (b11.85)
C Shiacolas (P Cole, Whatcombe)

A thoroughly convincing performance by Mr Dinos, who looks set to be a force in the staying division for some years to come. A healthy margin separated him from old warrior Persian Punch. The latter again ran his heart out and is now a dual runner-up in this race. He looks set to race on in 2004, seeking to crown his career with that elusive Group 1 win.

15 **Coronation Stakes (Fillies) (1m) Ascot June 20 (Good to Firm)**

1 **Russian Rhythm** 9-0   K Fallon
2 **Soviet Song** 9-0   O Urbina
3 **Mail The Desert** 9-0   S Drowne
4-7f, 9-2, 14-1. 1¹/₂l, 3l. 9 ran. 1m 38.5 (b8.77)
Cheveley Park Stud (Sir M Stoute, Newmarket)

No 1,000 Guineas winner had gone on to land this since 1979, but Russian Rhythm laid that curse in style, shaving a fraction of a second off the course record. She was pursued all the way by Soviet Song, who ran a tremendous race for second and could have been attempting the impossible in trying to beat this exceptional filly.

16 **Golden Jubilee Stakes (6f) Ascot June 21 (Firm)**

1 **Choisir** 9-4   J Murtagh
2 **Airwave** 8-8   Dane O'Neill
3 **Baron's Pit** 8-11   J Fortune
13-2, 11-8f, 50-1. ¹/₂l, 1l. 17 ran. 1m 12.2 (b8.59)
T W Wallace & Partners (P Perry, Australia)

Australian-trained Choisir was an unknown in Europe before the start of Royal Ascot week but had caused a 25-1 shock in the Group 2 King's Stand Stakes on opening day. Here, he stunned onlookers by winning his second race in five days, beating the filly Airwave by half a length. Racing in the centre of the track, this huge colt tacked over to the stands' rail once clear to win in most impressive fashion. Baron's Pit had not won since taking the Norfolk at this meeting the year before but was flying at the death here.

17 Budweiser Irish Derby (1m4f) Curragh June 29 (Good to Soft)

1 **Alamshar** 9-0	J P Murtagh
2 **Dalakhani** 9-0	C Soumillon
3 **Roosevelt** 9-0	C O'Donoghue

4-1, 4-7f, 150-1. ½l, 3½l. 9 ran. 2m 28.2 (b10.13)
HH Aga Khan (J Oxx, Ireland)

A tactical error by Christophe Soumillon resulted in Dalakhani getting beat for the only time in his nine-race career. The young Frenchman sat too close behind **High Country**, setting the pace for Aidan O'Brien's five other runners. When the leader dropped out, Dalakhani was left in front too early with more than quarter of a mile to cover, and proved to be a sitting duck. O'Brien's Roosevelt rewarded adventurous each-way punters by edging **Brian Boru** and **The Great Gatsby** out of the frame.

18 Coral-Eclipse Stakes (1m2f7yds) Sandown July 5 (Good to Firm)

1 **Falbrav** 9-7	D Holland
2 **Nayef** 9-7	R Hills
3 **Kaieteur** 9-7	E Ahern

8-1, 6-4f, 100-1. ¾l, 1¼l. 15 ran. 2m 5.6 (b8.54)
Scuderia Rencati Srl (L Cumani, Newmarket)

This race gave British punters their first glimpse of the brilliant Falbrav at his very best. He reversed Prince Of Wales form (13) with Nayef in no uncertain manner, winning what was quite a rough race by a comfortable margin. The presence of 100-1 shot Kaieteur in third might seem disconcerting, but he had been running on strongly one place behind Falbrav in the Ascot race and was again closest at the finish. Brian Meehan's charge went on to be second in Chicago's Arlington Million.

19 Darley July Cup (6f) Newmarket July 10 (Good to Firm)

1 **Oasis Dream** 8-13	R Hughes
2 **Choisir** 9-5	J Murtagh
3 **Airwave** 8-10	K Fallon

9-2, 9-4f, 11-4. 1½l, nk. 16 ran. 1m 9.9 (b5.96)
K Abdulla (J Gosden, Manton)

Finally an English-trained horse managed to lower the colours of Aussie upstart Choisir. Oasis Dream locked horns with Choisir from a fair way out but, hard as the other tried, Richard Hughes's mount held too many aces at the finish, winning fairly comfortably. Choisir's Ascot exertions (16) may well have been kicking in, but he still confirmed the form with Airwave and was beaten by a top-notch rival. Airwave's style of running (she's usually held up for a strong finish) means it is very hard for her to succeed at this level.

20 Darley Irish Oaks (1m4f) Curragh July 13 (Good to Soft)

1 **Vintage Tipple** 9-0	L Dettori
2 **L'Ancresse** 9-0	J A Heffernan
3 **Casual Look** 9-0	M Dwyer

12-1, 33-1, 7-1. 1½l, hd. 11 ran. 2m 28.3 (b10.03)
Patrick J O'Donovan (P Mullins, Ireland)

A surprising but popular result, veteran Irish trainer Paddy Mullins scooping his first Classic at the age of 84. Casual Look did nothing wrong in finishing third, but again showed what a moderate renewal of the Epsom Oaks she won (9). L'Ancresse astounded many with her bold showing in second place, but her Breeders' Cup exploits (35) would later show she had been under-rated.

21 King George VI & Queen Elizabeth Diamond Stakes (1m4f) Ascot July 26 (Good)

1 **Alamshar** 8-9	J Murtagh
2 **Sulamani** 9-7	L Dettori
3 **Kris Kin** 8-9	K Fallon

13-2, 9-2, 7-2. 3½l, 2l. 12 ran. 2m 33.3 (b8.26)
HH Aga Khan (J Oxx, Ireland)

A stunning performance from Alamshar, who was given a peach of a ride by Johnny Murtagh. Up with the pace and out of trouble throughout, Alamshar could be called the winner some way from home and, when Murtagh pressed the button, the response was emphatic. Sulamani plugged on for second, while Derby winner Kris Kin raced lazily throughout and never looked likely to repeat his Epsom heroics. Darryll Holland tried to make a virtue of **Falbrav**'s unfavourable draw in stall one, taking him to the wide outside of the track and only rejoining the main bunch with half a mile to run. It's a tactic that has been known to work on rain-softened ground here but the surface was fair all round for this and he gained no advantage. On the contrary, he ran much further than any other horse in the race, so it's hard to understand why so many glib pundits were quick to label him a non-stayer after he faded into fifth, two places ahead of 3-1 jolly **Nayef**.

22 Sussex Stakes (1m) Goodwood July 30 (Good to Soft)

1 **Reel Buddy** 9-7	Pat Eddery
2 **Statue Of Liberty** 8-13	M J Kinane
3 **Norse Dancer** 8-13	T Quinn

20-1, 6-1, 8-1. hd, shd. 9 ran. 1m 40.0 (b0.08)
Speedlith Group (R Hannon, Marlborough)

A strange race, with most of the runners still in with a shout 100 yards from the line. The talented (but surely not Group 1 class) Reel Buddy eventually prevailed, by a head and a short-head from Statue Of Liberty and the frustrating Norse Dancer. This very moderate renewal will be remembered chiefly for the fact that the soon-to-retire Pat Eddery partnered the winner.

23 Vodafone Nassau Stakes (Fillies & Mares), (1m1f192yds) Goodwood August 2 (Good)

1 **Russian Rhythm** 8-6	K Fallon
2 **Ana Marie** 9-1	R Hughes
3 **Zee Zee Top** 9-1	J Murtagh

4-5f, 14-1, 11-1. nk, 5l. 8 ran. 2m 4.8 (b7.99)
Cheveley Park Stud (Sir M Stoute, Newmarket)

Connections of Russian Rhythm were confident she would get 1m2f, having finished the Coronation Stakes *(15)* full of running, and they were right. She became only the second post-War 1,000 Guineas winner to add this prize, but needed every yard of the trip to overhaul Ana Marie, on ground that was unhelpfully loose. Ana Marie lost nothing in defeat but this was the closest she got to winning in her last seven outings of the season.

24 Juddmonte International Stakes (1m2f88yds) York August 19 (Good to Firm)

1 **Falbrav** 9-5	D Holland
2 **Magistretti** 8-11	K Fallon
3 **Nayef** 9-5	R Hills

5-2, 16-1, 3-1. 2l, 1¾l. 8 ran. 2m 6.8 (b13.09)

Scuderia Rencati Srl (L Cumani, Newmarket)

A majestic performance by Falbrav. Both horse and jockey oozed confidence and the winning margin of 2l doesn't tell the whole story – it could easily have been 5l. Magistretti did well for the Classic generation and proved that this course and distance suits him well (he had won the Dante here earlier in the season). Nayef, who won this in 2002, had been in some tough battles and it was starting to show.

25 Aston Upthorpe Yorkshire Oaks (1m3f198yds) York August 20 (Good to Firm)

1 **Islington** 9-4	K Fallon
2 **Ocean Silk** 8-8	J Fortune
3 **Summitville** 8-8	M Fenton

8-11f, 18-1, 25-1. 1l, 3l. 8 ran. 2m 27.4 (b14.46)
Exors of Lord Weinstock (Sir M Stoute, Newmarket)

This trip is really further than Islington cares to go but, despite tying up close home, she had the class to hold on. Ocean Silk again had to settle for second place, the same position she'd occupied in Royal Ascot's Ribblesdale. Oaks winner **Casual Look** was disappointing in seventh.

26 Victor Chandler Nunthorpe Stakes (5f3yds) York August 21 (Good to Firm)

1 **Oasis Dream** 9-9	R Hughes
2 **The Tatling** 9-11	D Holland
3 **Acclamation** 9-11	K Darley

4-9f, 9-1, 9-1. 2½l, 1¼l. 8 ran. 56.2 (b3.82)
K Abdulla (J Gosden, Manton)

A cakewalk for the lightning-quick Oasis Dream, who led from the stalls and never saw another rival. Milton Bradley's The Tatling improved out of all recognition during the season and came out best of the rest, but this was about as one-sided a contest as you will ever see at this level.

27 Stanley Leisure Sprint Cup (6f) Haydock September 6 (Heavy)

1 **Somnus** 8-11	T E Durcan
2 **Oasis Dream** 8-11	R Hughes
3 **Airwave** 8-9	Miss D O'Neill

12-1, 8-11f, 10-3. 1¼l, ¾l. 10 ran. 1m 13.5 (b1.51)
Legard Sidebottom & Sykes (T Easterby, Malton)

Two weeks after his Nunthorpe glory *(26)*, Oasis Dream had his reputation tarnished by the mud. Heavy rain produced going that neutralised the colt's immense speed and, although he struck the front two furlongs out, he was floundering inside the final furlong and unable to resist the late thrust of Somnus (who had previously looked no better than Listed class). Airwave again finished in the frame, but her limitations were starting to show.

28 Ireland The Food Island Champion Stakes (1m2f) Leopardstown September 6 (Firm)

1 **High Chaparral** 9-4   M Kinane
2 **Falbrav** 9-2   D Holland
3 **Islington** 9-1   K Fallon
4-1, 11-4, 16-1. nk, hd. 7 ran. 2m 3.3 (b10.96)
M Tabor (A P O'Brien, Ireland)

A controversial race in which many considered Falbrav an unlucky loser. He was repeatedly denied room in the home straight and, having eventually dived up the rails in search of room, only just failed to peg back High Chaparral. Islington, running over her optimum trip, ran a cracker, but **Alamshar** (fourth) never looked like winning and can be considered disappointing.

29 Irish Field St Leger (1m6f) Curragh September 13 (Good to Firm)

1 **Vinnie Roe** 9-9   P J Smullen
2 **Gamut** 9-9   K Fallon
3 **Powerscourt** 8-12   M J Kinane
2-1, 8-1, 11-4. 1l, shd. 6 ran. 2m 58.9 (b4.28)
Seamus Sheridan (D Weld, Ireland)

Vinnie Roe confirmed his position as the best Irish stayer around with his third win in a row in this contest. He had some tough opposition to get past, including Aidan O'Brien's Powerscourt and last year's English St Leger winner **Bollin Eric**. It was left to Gamut to do the chasing, however, and he could be useful in 2004. Bollin Eric was a disappointing fourth.

30 Seabiscuit St Leger (1m6f132yds) Doncaster September 13 (Good)

1 **Brian Boru** 9-0   J P Spencer
2 **High Accolade** 9-0   Martin Dwyer
3 **Phoenix Reach** 9-0   D Holland
5-4f, 8-1, 8-1. 1¼l, 1½l. 12 ran. 3m 4.6 (b23.70)
S Magnier (A P O'Brien, Ireland)

Brian Boru, a major let-down in the Derby *(10)*, made amends here with a fluent win under a typically confident Jamie Spencer ride. He was settled out the back in the early stages but, once he was produced, the result was never in danger. On this evidence, Brian Boru could well be a Cup horse in future. The quirky High Accolade ran well, considering his long campaign, and showed he stayed, while Phoenix Reach augmented Andrew Balding's fledgling Classic record.

31 Queen Elizabeth II Stakes (1m) Ascot September 27 (Good to Firm)

1 **Falbrav** 9-1   D Holland
2 **Russian Rhythm** 8-8   K Fallon
3 **Tillerman** 9-1   R Hughes
6-4f, 3-1, 22-1. 2l, 1¼l. 8 ran. 1m 39.0 (b8.29)
Scuderia Rencati Srl (L Cumani, Newmarket)

Falbrav showed here that he could mix it with the best over 1m, simply showing too much speed for Russian Rhythm, who was tasting defeat for the first time this season. Once sent to the front, the winner always had too many guns for his rivals and, considering he gave Russian Rhythm 7lb, the performance can only be described as awesome. Tillerman again ran a cracker in third and is always worth a look when racing at Ascot.

32 Prix de l'Arc de Triomphe Lucien Barriere (1m4f) Longchamp October 5 (Soft)

1 **Dalakhani** 8-11   C Soumillon
2 **Mubtaker** 9-5   R Hills
3 **High Chaparral** 9-5   M Kinane
9-4, 25-1, 13-8f. ¾l, 5l. 13 ran. 2m 32.3 (a3.70)
HH Aga Khan (A de Royer-Dupre, France)

Marcus Tregoning's late-developing Mubtaker would have beaten High Chaparral by a stunning 5l and won the Arc were it not for Dalakhani, who collared the brave runner-up inside the final furlong and did enough to hold him off. Christophe Soumillon made up for his Curragh error *(17)* by holding onto his mount for longer this time and, once he had closed to Mubtaker's quarters, there was an inevitability about the result. Mubtaker looks sure to be back here again in October 2004, while a stud career awaits Dalakhani.

33 Emirates Airline Champion Stakes (1m2f) Newmarket October 18 (Good to Firm)

1 **Rakti** 9-2   P Robinson

2 **Carnival Dancer** 9-2 D Holland
3 **Indian Creek** 9-2 Dane O'Neill
11-1, 33-1, 25-1. 2l, 1½l. 12 ran. 2m 3.3
(b8.36)
Gary A Tanaka (M Jarvis, Newmarket)

This Group 1 comes late in the season, and often benefits a horse who has had a light campaign. Step forward Rakti, who hadn't raced since Royal Ascot but who was expertly prepared by Michael Jarvis to score comfortably. What he achieved in beating Carnival Dancer and Indian Creek is open to question, but he should enjoy a profitable campaign in 2004, particularly abroad. **Nayef** bowed out of the racing scene with a disappointingly below-par effort in eighth.

34 Netjets Breeders' Cup Mile (1m) Santa Anita October 25 (Standard)
1 **Six Perfections** 8-7 J D Bailey
2 **Touch Of The Blues** 9-0
K J Desormeaux
3 **Century City** 9-0 J Valdivia, Jr
11-2, 12-1, 40-1. ¾l, nk. 12 ran. 1m 33.9
Flaxman Holdings, Ltd (P Bary, France)

After a luckless first half to the season, Six Perfections deservedly set the record straight. Many thought her outside draw would ruin her chance but Jerry Bailey gave her an outstanding ride, edging her into a winning position when the dash for home began. This supplemented her August success in Deauville's Prix Jacques le Marois and established her as a filly of the highest class. For **Refuse To Bend** (11th), this was a whimpering way to end the season – after the Guineas (2), he managed a single victory, at Group 3 level. One place ahead of him here was **Oasis Dream**, for whom the Breeders' Cup Sprint would surely have been a much more sensible target.

35 Breeders' Cup Filly & Mare Turf (1m2f) Santa Anita October 25 (Firm)
1 **Islington** 8-11 K Fallon
2 **L'Ancresse** 8-6 E S Prado
3 **Yesterday** 8-6 M J Kinane
3-1, 50-1, 15-1. nk, 2½l. 12 ran. 1m 59.1
Estate of Lord Weinstock (Sir M Stoute, Newmarket)

Islington capped a fine season with a hard-earned neck victory, in a race that proved a triumph for European raiders, with Aidan O'Brien's L'Ancresse and Yesterday filling second and third places respectively. L'Ancresse improved again from her Irish Oaks effort (20), while Yesterday (on the go all season) acquitted herself well.

36 John Deere Breeders' Cup Turf (1m4f) Santa Anita October 25 (Firm)
1 **High Chaparral** 9-0 M J Kinane
1 **Johar** 9-0 A O Solis
3 **Falbrav** 9-0 D Holland
5-1, 15-1, 4-1. dd-ht, hd. 9 ran. 2m 24.2
M Tabor & S Magnier (A P O'Brien, Ireland); The Thoroughbred Corp (R Mandella, USA)

One of the great races of all time, producing the first dead-heat in Breeders' Cup history. Falbrav looked like clinging on all the way to the line, only to be edged out by the persistent High Chaparral and American raider Johar, who came from way back and flew down the centre of the track. High Chaparral showed his Arc run did not represent any downturn in form. He became the first horse to win back-to-back renewals of this race and only the fifth horse to win any Breeders' Cup race twice (of the other four, only the French Miesque was not US-trained).

37 Breeders' Cup Classic (1m2f) Santa Anita October 25 (Standard)
1 **Pleasantly Perfect** 9-0 A O Solis
2 **Medaglia d'Oro** 9-0 J D Bailey
3 **Dynever** 8-9 C S Nakatani
15-1, 11-4, 16-1. 1½l, ¾l. 10 ran. 1m 59.9
Diamond A Racing Corp (R Mandella, USA)

Congaree set off at a million miles per hour and really set the race up for a finisher – in this case, it turned out to be Pleasantly Perfect. He was sensibly restrained in rear, keeping out of the pace race, and came with a sweeping challenge down the home straight, prevailing comfortably. Medaglia d'Oro was another to pay the penalty for forcing the pace, although he battled on manfully for second, while Congaree weakened into fourth, one place and 5l ahead of Aidan O'Brien's **Hold That Tiger**. Pleasantly Perfect confirmed the form with Congaree at Santa Anita in a Grade 2 at the end of January and is 3-1 favourite for the Dubai World Cup as we go to press.

Sponsored by Stan James

Group 1 Index

All horses placed or commented on in our Group 1 review section, with race numbers

Outlook

Two-year-olds of 2003
by Nicholas Watts

1 Isobelle Morris Memorial Marble Hill Stakes (Listed), (5f) Curragh May 24 (Soft)

1 **Newton** 9-0		M J Kinane
2 **Moon Unit** 8-11		P Shanahan
3 **Steel Light** 9-0		P J Smullen

10-3, 12-1, 11-8f. ¹/₂l, ³/₄l. 7 ran. 1m 0.9 (b1.78)
S Magnier (A P O'Brien, Ireland)

Newton responded well to his rider's urgings when driven along two out, in a race run on unsuitably soft ground. Time showed later in the season that he isn't in the top echelon of Ballydoyle youngsters, when he was thrashed by both Three Valleys and Grey Swallow. Mick Channon's **Holborn** was fourth after appearing not to act on the ground, while favourite Steel Light didn't get the clearest of runs.

2 Swordlestown Stud Sprint Stakes (Fillies Listed), (6f) Naas June 2 (Good)

1 **Miss Childrey** 8-11		J A Heffernan
2 **Little Whisper** 8-11		P Shanahan
3 **Letsimpress** 8-11		F M Berry

5-2f, 9-1, 12-1. ¹/₂l, 2¹/₂l. 9 ran. 1m 13.9 (a1.23)
Miss Alison Jones (F Ennis)

This race was undoubtedly the high point of Miss Childrey's season, as she was repeatedly found out by better horses later in the season. However, she showed admirable tenacity to hold on for a pillar-to-post win from Little Whisper, who also did nothing for the strength of the form in his subsequent exploits.

3 Vodafone Woodcote Stakes (Listed), (6f) Epsom June 7 (Good)

1 **Parkview Love** 8-11		K Darley
2 **Cedarberg** 8-11		L Dettori
3 **Cape Fear** 9-0		P J Smullen

11-2, 15-2, 8-1. nk, 1³/₄l. 10 ran. 1m 9.1 (b3.17)
C Nicholson (M Johnston, Middleham)

In typical Mark Johnston fashion, Parkview Love bounced out of the stalls, took an early lead and repelled allcomers. It was a supremely game effort from a fairly talented colt, who was to be well beaten by stable companion Lucky Story later in the season (26). Cape Fear, who was to win the St Leger Yearling Stakes in September (53), was back in third.

4 The Rochestown Stakes, (6f) Leopardstown June 11 (Good)

1 **King Hesperus** 9-0		M J Kinane
2 **Jemmy's Brother** 9-0		T P O'Shea
3 **Wathab** 9-0		D P McDonogh

5-2, 10-1, 5-4f. 2¹/₂l, ¹/₂l. 6 ran. 1m 16.7 (a0.51)
Michael Tabor (A P O'Brien, Ireland)

King Hesperus lost a race in the Stewards' room on his first start at Gowran Park, but made no mistake here with a comfortable win. Although he's probably not one of Ballydoyle's top two-year-olds, this was a decent performance, with the consistent Wathab only managing third. King Hesperus only raced once more during this season, when third in a Group 3 at Newmarket (16).

5 Coventry Stakes (Group 3), (6f) Ascot June 17 (Good to Firm)

1 **Three Valleys** 8-12		R Hughes
2 **Botanical** 8-12		L Dettori
3 **Privy Seal** 8-12		J Fortune

7-1, 7-2, 20-1. 8l, nk. 13 ran. 1m 13.6 (b7.20)
K Abdulla (R Charlton, Beckhampton)

The first really scintillating performance by a two-year-old colt this season. Three Valleys destroyed his rivals to win by a barely imaginable 8l and nothing else in the race really emerged with credit. Aidan O'Brien's **Newton** was well beaten in this first squaring-up between English and Irish juveniles. Perhaps unsurprisingly, Three Valleys didn't repeat this demolition job in his subsequent races at two.

6 Queen Mary Stakes (Group 3 Fillies), (5f) Ascot June 18 (Good to Firm)

1 **Attraction** 8-10		K Darley
2 **Catstar** 8-10		L Dettori
3 **Majestic Desert** 8-10		D Holland

13-8f, 7-2, 10-1. 3l, 5l. 14 ran. 1m 0.5 (b4.59)
Duke of Roxburghe (M Johnston, Middleham)

Attraction is only modestly bred, being by Efisio out of a once-raced (unsuccessful) Pursuit Of Love mare. Still, she shows lightning pace and never looked like being reeled in here, justifying favouritism. Bookies gave her a 25-1 quote for the 1,000 Guineas afterwards, but it must be debatable as to whether she'd stay. The form looks solid, with Cheveley Park runner-up Majestic Desert well held in third.

7 Chesham Stakes (Listed), (7f) Ascot
June 18 (Good to Firm)

1 **Pearl Of Love** 9-0   D Holland
2 **Tycoon** 8-12   M J Kinane
3 **Milk It Mick** 8-12   Martin Dwyer
11-10f, 4-1, 8-1. 1¹/₂l, 1¹/₄l. 13 ran. 1m 28.5 (b6.07)
M Doyle (M Johnston, Middleham)

Pearl Of Love sweated up before the race, but
that proved no barrier to a comfortable
success. He looked potentially Group-class in
winning this, and was to prove so later in the
season, winning the Group 1 Gran Criterium
at San Siro in October on his final start. This
was the first time on a big stage for Milk It Mick.
Jamie Osborne's charge, stepping outside
Class E company for the first time, ran well
enough without suggesting he had a Group
race in him.

8 Norfolk Stakes (Group 3), (5f) Ascot
June 19 (Good to Firm)

1 **Russian Valour** 8-12   K Darley
2 **Kheleyf** 8-12   L Dettori
3 **Nevisian Lad** 8-12   K Fallon
4-1, 8-13f, 20-1. 1³/₄l, ³/₄l. 8 ran. 1m 1.4 (b3.68)
A Latter & Partners (M Johnston, Middleham)

Russian Valour burst the hype surrounding
David Loder's second-placed Kheleyf. Mark
Johnston's horses are very difficult to pass when
on-song, and the runner-up had no answers.
The form looks solid, with subsequent Group
2 winner Nevisian Lad back in third. This was
the winner's last outing of the season.

9 Albany Stakes (Listed Fillies), (6f)
Ascot June 20 (Good to Firm)

1 **Silca's Gift** 8-11   S Drowne
2 **Tolzey** 8-9   L Dettori
3 **Malaica** 8-11   T Gillet
5-1, 10-3f, 8-1. 3l, 5l. 12 ran. 1m 15.7 (b5.16)
Aldridge Racing Limited (M Channon, West Ilsley)

Having been held up in rear, Silca's Gift came
with an irresistible late surge to win going away,
giving Mick Channon a one-two in the race.
This looked a weak contest, though, and
subsequent performances by Silca's Gift's
showed it to be so.

10 Windsor Castle Stakes (Conditions), (5f)
Ascot June 21 (Firm)

1   Holborn 8-13
S Drowne
2 **Vienna's Boy** 8-11   Dane O'Neill
3 **Howick Falls** 8-13   L Dettori
5-2f, 16-1, 11-2. 1³/₄l, 1¹/₄l. 17 ran. 1m 0.1 (b4.97)
Sheikh Mohammed (M Channon, West Ilsley)

Holborn, well beaten by Newton on soft
ground in Ireland earlier in the season *(1)*, made
amends on a much faster surface here. He
looked in trouble when scrubbed along early,
but found plenty and would be suited by further. Vienna's Boy did well considering he had

a middle draw, while **Peak To Creek** was well
beaten but made up for it later in the season.

11 Goffs Challenge, (6f63yds) Curragh
June 27 (Good to Soft)

1   Carrizo Creek 9-0
K Fallon
2 **Danesmead** 9-0   M J Kinane
3 **Kalani Girl** 8-9   R Havlin
10-3, 7-1, 16-1. 1¹/₂l, 1¹/₄l. 17 ran. 1m 17.1 (b3.11)
J S Threadwell (B Meehan, Upper Lambourn)

It's a big step from winning at Brighton to
winning at the Curragh, but Carrizo Creek managed it, coming from off the pace and going
away under a typically aggressive Fallon
drive. Both Danesmead and Kalani Girl ran fine
races, considering they were disadvantaged
by their high draws and good to soft ground.

12 Anheuser Busch Railway Stakes (Group 2),
(6f) Curragh June 29 (Good to Soft)

1 **Antonius Pius** 9-0   M J Kinane
2 **Spanish Ace** 9-0   J P Murtagh
3 **Il Pirata** 9-0   K J Manning
4-7f, 7-1, 12-1. ¹/₂l, 1¹/₂l. 7 ran. 1m 13.5 (b2.59)
Michael Tabor (A P O'Brien, Ireland)

The half-length winning margin doesn't really
tell the story, as Antonius Pius did win fairly comfortably, responding to hands and heels
driving only. The form doesn't read that well,
though, with exposed Spanish Ace in second,
and the winner only beating one home in the
Dewhurst *(88)* on his only subsequent outing.

13 Dragon Stakes (Listed), (5f6yds)
Sandown July 4 (Good)

1 **Fortunately** 8-7   K Fallon
2 **Prince Of Denmark** 8-12   R Hughes
3 **Vienna's Boy** 8-12   Dane O'Neill
16-1, 7-2, 5-2f. 1¹/₂l, 1¹/₂l. 7 ran. 1m 2.8 (b1.60)
J R Salter (P D Evans, Abergavenny)

A tribute to trainer David Evans, as his filly
Fortunately made the graduation from sellers
to Listed class under an inspired Kieren Fallon. Prince Of Denmark looked the likely winner a furlong out, but the winner nipped up his
inside (Fallon doesn't need a second invita-
tion). Both winner and runner-up will struggle
to make an impact next season.

14 Chippenham Lodge Stud Cherry Hinton
Stakes (Group 2 Fillies), (6f)
Newmarket July 8 (Good)

1 **Attraction** 8-12   K Darley
2 **Pearl Grey** 8-9   L Dettori
3 **Birthday Suit** 8-9   K Fallon
4-7f, 11-2, 7-1. 5l, 1l. 8 ran. 1m 11.1 (b4.80)
Duke of Roxburghe (M Johnston, Middleham)

Another impressive show from the season's
leading filly. The opposition may not have been
up to much, but she could do no more than
win easily. Bookies slashed her to 10-1 for the
1,000 Guineas after the race, which is an over-

reaction, as there is no guarantee that she will stay, or train on. This was her last race of the season, as she suffered a series of leg problems afterwards, but Deirdre Johnston reports her to be recovering well and on course for the Guineas *(see Borderer, page 144)*.

15 TNT July Stakes (Group 2), (6f) Newmarket July 9 (Good to Firm)

1 **Nevisian Lad** 8-10		K Fallon
2 **Cape Fear** 8-10		E Ahern
3 **Byron** 8-10		L Dettori

4-1, 20-1, 5-1. 1l, shd. 8 ran. 1m 12.4 (b3.51)
H E Sheikh Rashid Bin Mohammed (M Bell, Newmarket)

Michael Bell's Nevisian Lad reversed Windsor Castle form *(10)* with **Holborn** in emphatic manner, and he had plenty to spare on passing the post a length ahead of Cape Fear, who reversed earlier Woodcote form *(3)* with **Parkview Love**. Holborn was disappointing, with no apparent excuse.

16 Weatherbys Superlative Stakes (Group 3), (7f) Newmarket July 10 (Good to Firm)

1	**Kings Point** 8-11	
R Hughes		
2 **Chester Le Street** 8-11		D Holland
3 **King Hesperus** 9-0		M J Kinane

6-1, 3-1j, 5-1. hd, 1¹/₄l. 9 ran. 1m 24.4 (b6.02)
J R May (R Hannon, Marlborough)

The consistent Kings Point got his moment of Group glory, unusually managing to get his head past a Mark Johnston frontrunner in Chester Le Street, who was beaten only in the last strides. Kings Point will not be easy to place after his juvenile year, however, as he doesn't look good enough to take on the best – foreign races will provide his best opportunities.

17 Dubai Duty Free Anglesey Stakes (Group 3), (6f63yds) Curragh July 13 (Good to Soft)

1 **One Cool Cat** 9-0		M J Kinane
2 **Leicester Square** 9-0		L Dettori
3 **Mokabra** 9-0		K Fallon

1-3f, 4-1, 10-1. 1¹/₄l, 1¹/₂l. 6 ran. 1m 17.8 (b2.41)
S Magnier (A P O'Brien, Ireland)

One Cool Cat served notice of what he could do with a smooth performance under a cool ride by Mick Kinane. Held up in the early stages, he made ground effortlessly through the race and, when asked for his effort, the response was immediate. Leicester Square did nothing wrong but was in a different league to the winner, who will be a formidable challenger for the 2,000 Guineas.

18 Silver Flash Stakes (Listed), (6f) Leopardstown July 16 (Good)

1	**Maroochydore** 8-11	
M J Kinane		
2 **Acciacatura** 8-11		K J Manning

3 **Summer Sunset** 8-11 P J Smullen

4-1, 11-2, 10-1. 1¹/₄l, 2¹/₂l. 10 ran. 1m 13.7 (b2.49)
E Irwin (D Wachman, Ireland)

Richard Hannon's Even-money favourite **Voile** disappointed in fourth, but that shouldn't detract from what was a good performance by Maroochydore. Ridden a furlong out, she scampered clear to win a shade cosily. She disappointed in the Group 1 Moyglare Stud Stakes *(48)* on her only subsequent start.

19 Shadwell Stud Rose Bowl Stakes (Listed), (6f8yds) Newbury July 18 (Good to Firm)

1 **Venables** 8-11		R Hughes
2 **America America** 8-9		S Sanders
3 **Flip Flop And Fly** 8-11		J F Egan

7-2, 16-1, 8-1. ³/₄l. 6 ran. 1m 13.5 (b3.52)
Team Havana (R Hannon, Marlborough)

Venables had to put in some hard toil before he eventually got on top, but might have won with more in hand than the official margin. Defeats later in the season revealed his limitations, and **Milk it Mick** back in fourth had yet to make the dramatic improvement that brought him so much late-season glory.

20 Weatherbys Super Sprint, (5f34yds) Newbury July 19 (Good to Firm)

1	**If Paradise** 8-7	
Dane O'Neill		
2 **Cop Hill Lad** 8-11		S Drowne
3 **Danesmead** 8-10		K Darley

14-1, 13-2, 12-1. 1³/₄l, nk. 22 ran. 1m 1.1 (b2.30)
J Wood (R Hannon, Marlborough)

A race where those drawn high are traditionally best was turned on its head by If Paradise, who came from stall one. He showed amazing speed and led from the stalls right to the line. Cop Hill Lad did well in his private battle for second with Danesmead, who again demonstrated his need for a longer trip by staying on late. If Paradise could be a useful sprinter for the 2004 season.

21 Star Stakes (Fillies Listed), (7f16yds) Sandown July 24 (Good to Firm)

1 **Lucky Pipit** 8-9		M Hills
2 **America America** 8-12		S Sanders
3 **Leopard Hunt** 8-9		J Fortune

7-4f, 11-2, 7-2. 5l, nk. 11 ran. 1m 28.5 (b4.59)
Maktoum Al Maktoum (B Hills, Lambourn)

An eyecatching display by Lucky Pipit, who went from the front and could be called the winner some way from home. America America doesn't seem to have a trip and again made headway much too late in the day. The winner appeals as a potential Group winner for future seasons.

22 Princess Margaret Stakes (Group 3 Fillies), (6f) Ascot July 26 (Good)

1	**River Belle** 8-9	

K Fallon
2 **Rosehearty** 8-9   L Dettori
3 **Voile** 8-9   Dane O'Neill
4-1j, 13-2, 9-2. 1^1/₄l, 1l. 9 ran. 1m 15.6 (b5.27)
Christopher Shankland (A Jarvis, Aston Upthorpe).

The leaders went off at breakneck speed, which meant those coming from behind were favoured. River Belle had been scrubbed along out the back during the early part of the race, but came through strongly to win going away. **Fortunately** and **Catch The Wind** set the pace – they ended up filling the last two places. It would be unwise to get carried away with the form.

23 Tyros Stakes (Listed), (7f) Leopardstown July 26 (Good to Firm)
1 **Privy Seal** 9-0   J Fortune
2 **Wathab** 9-0   D P McDonogh
3 **Mahogany** 9-0   M J Kinane
6-4j, 10-1, 6-4j. 1l, 1^1/₂l. 5 ran. 1m 30.0 (b2.92)
Sheikh Mohammed (J Gosden, Manton).

Privy Seal, well beaten in third behind Three Valleys at Ascot last time (5), came good here, although it wasn't the best of races. He took a while to get to grips with the front-running Wathab, but was well on top by the end. The presence of the exposed runner-up indicates this wasn't the strongest event, while Mahogany is well down the Ballydoyle pecking order.

24 Prix Robert Papin (Group 2), (5f110yds) Maisons-Laffitte July 27 (Soft)
1 **Much Faster** 8-13   T Thulliez
2 **Colossus** 9-2   M Kinane
3 **Leila** 8-13   V Vion
2.3-1cf, 2.6-1, 2.3-1cf. 3l, 1^1/₂l. 8 ran. 1m 7.3 (a4.70)
Ecurie Jean-Louis Bouchar (P Bary).

The winner proved aptly-named and, after racing alone down the stands side, led two furlongs out and drew clear to win by an easy 3l. Having already scored in Listed and Group 3 company, Much Faster, a daughter of first-season sire Fasliyev, is certainly decent and could be very good indeed.

25 Four Star Sales Richmond Stakes (Group 2), (6f) Goodwood July 29 (Good)
1 **Carrizo Creek** 8-11   K Fallon
2 **Old Deuteronomy** 8-11   J P Spencer
3 **Cedarberg** 8-11   L Dettori
5-1, 3-1, 8-1. ^{1}/₂l, hd. 7 ran. 1m 12.3 (a1.03)
J S Threadwell (B Meehan, Upper Lambourn).

Carrizo Creek carried on the good work of his previous Irish win by holding on tenaciously on loose ground from Old Deuteronomy. There was nothing wrong with the performance, but you could throw a blanket over the first six home, so it would probably be unwise to get carried away with the form. **Venables** was disappointing in fourth.

26 Veuve Clicquot Vintage Stakes (Group 2), (7f) Goodwood July 30 (Good to Soft)
1 **Lucky Story** 8-11   K Dalgleish
2 **The Mighty Tiger** 8-11   M J Kinane
3 **Devil Moon** 8-11   J P Spencer
6-5f, 4-1, 100-1. 1^1/₄l, 3l. 9 ran. 1m 28.0 (b1.44)
Abdulla Buhaleeba (M Johnston, Middleham).

A striking performance from Lucky Story, who is up there with the best of a very strong bunch of Mark Johnston-trained juveniles. Once hitting the front a furlong out, he appeared to idle and pricked his ears, indicating he had plenty left. **Kings Point** and **Nevisian Lad** both had their limitations exposed in sixth and ninth respectively.

27 Betfair Molecomb Stakes (Group 3), (5f) Goodwood July 31 (Good)
1   **Majestic Missile** 8-12
M Hills
2 **Nights Cross** 8-12   S Drowne
3 **Dallaah** 8-9   P Robinson
9-4f, 14-1, 5-2. 1^3/₄l, 1^3/₄l. 9 ran. 58.8 (b0.92)
Flying Tiger Partnership (W Haggas, Newmarket).

Not the greatest of renewals, but that shouldn't detract from a decent performance by the winner, who showed lightning pace and put the race to bed in a matter of strides once unleashed. The time was good and Majestic Missile looks a force to be reckoned with for sprinting this season. **Fortunately** appeared to be out of her depth, while **If Paradise** was disappointing in sixth.

28 Prix de Cabourg (Group 3), (6f) Deauville August 2 (Good to Soft)
1 **Denebola** 8-8   T Thulliez
2 **Bonaire** 8-8   O Peslier
3 **Via Milano** 8-8   D Boeuf
9-1, 10.2-1, 4-1. ^{1}/₂l, ^{3}/₄l. 8 ran. 1m 11.2 (a2.70)
Fam Niarchos (P Bary).

If breeding is anything to go by, then Denebola is there already, being by all-conquering sire Storm Cat out of Coup De Genie, a full sister to Machiavellian. Having been held up, she squeezed through a gap a furlong out and won comfortably – a good performance on only her second start. Fourth-placed **Whipper** went on to land a Group 1 later in the season (49).

29 Irish Stallion Farms EBF Premier Nursery Handicap, (7f) Galway August 2 (Good to Soft)
1 **Steel Light** 9-7   P J Smullen
2 **Marjell** 7-12   P B Beggy (10)
3 **Tiros** 8-5   W J Lee (7)
11-4f, 10-1, 7-1. nk, 1l. 11 ran. 1m 31.4 (b3.43)
Moyglare Stud Farm (D Weld, Ireland).

A good weight-carrying performance by the winner, conceding upwards of 9lb to all his rivals. Marjell rallied to great effect in the final furlong and almost got there, while the running of the well-fancied Alexander Goldrun is best ignored, as her stall failed to open properly with the others.

30 NSPCC Shergar Cup Auction Juvenile, (7f) Ascot August 9 (Good to Firm)

1 **Kinnaird** 8-12   K Fallon
2 **Chinsola** 9-6   Andreas Suborics
3 **Think Tank** 8-12   F Johansson
7-2, 2-1f, 3-1. 1¼l, ½l. 10 ran. 1m 29.3 (b5.31)
S A B Dinsmore (P Haslam, Middleham).

Shergar Cup races should always be treated with caution from a form perspective, with jockeys competing from around the world and team tactics playing a part. Kinnaird, enjoying a great season, did the business again in the hands of Kieren Fallon, swooping past Chinsola approaching the final furlong. She is useful in her own grade.

31 Sweet Solera Stakes (Fillies Listed), (7f) Newmarket August 9 (Good to Firm)

1 **Bay Tree** 8-8   M Hills
2 **Qasirah** 8-8   P Robinson
3 **Nataliya** 8-8   S Sanders
10-3, 5-2f, 4-1. 1¼l, shd. 8 ran. 1m 25.2 (b5.24)
Wafic Said (B Hills, Lambourn).

A good performance from Bay Tree, who got the better of a protracted duel with Nataliya approaching the final furlong before fending off the rallying favourite Qasirah. The winner is almost certainly a useful filly and comes from a family with which Barry Hills has enjoyed plenty of success.

32 Independent Waterford Wedgwood Phoenix Stakes Group 1, (6f) Curragh August 10 (Good)

1 **One Cool Cat** 9-0   M J Kinane
2 **Old Deuteronomy** 9-0   J A Heffernan
3 **Three Valleys** 9-0   R Hughes
11-8, 12-1, 4-6f. 1l, 3l. 7 ran. 1m 11.4 (b4.69)
S Magnier (A P O'Brien, Ireland).

A match on paper between One Cool Cat and the stunning Ascot winner Three Valleys, but the head-to-head failed to materialise. The latter ran well below par, leaving the way clear for One Cool Cat to saunter home. Three Valleys was subsequently scoped and reported to be "full of mucus".

33 Robert H Griffin Debutante Stakes Group 3, (7f) Curragh August 10 (Good)

1 **Necklace** 8-11   M J Kinane
2 **Caldy Dancer** 8-11   J P Spencer
3 **Red Feather** 8-11   N G McCullagh
7-4f, 12-1, 10-1. 1l, 2½l. 13 ran. 1m 25.0 (b3.99)
Michael Tabor (A P O'Brien, Ireland).

Necklace, a well-supported favourite, stayed on well, benefiting from running over an extra furlong. Caldy Dancer devalues the form slightly in second, but the winner could be

better than the bare form suggests, and could be an Oaks filly. Red Feather improved again and is another on the up.

34 Stan James Online Washington Singer Stakes (Listed), (7f) Newbury August 15 (Good to Firm)

1 **Haafhd** 8-11   R Hills
2 **Orcadian** 8-11   J Tate
3 **Milk It Mick** 9-2   K Fallon
9-4f, 9-2, 14-1. 5l, ¼l. 8 ran. 1m 23.0 (b7.89)
Hamdan Al Maktoum (B Hills, Lambourn).

Haafhd broke the course record and looks a top three-year-old in the making. He was pushed along to lead with two furlongs to go and then stretched clear, putting daylight between him and his rivals. Milk It Mick again plugged on for third, not yet looking like a Group winner waiting to happen.

35 Stan James St Hugh's Stakes (Fillies Listed), (5f) Newbury August 16 (Good to Firm)

1 **Needles And Pins** 8-8   K Fallon
2 **Nyramba** 8-8   J Fortune
3 **Dolce Piccata** 8-8   R Winston
7-1, 9-2, 40-1. 2l, 1l. 10 ran. 1m 0.9 (b0.62)
DGH Partnership (M Bell, Newmarket).

Tentative set off at a suicidal pace and paid the penalty. Needles And Pins was pushed along early but came through readily to win cosily from Nyramba, who would have benefited from more cut in the ground. The winner looks speedy, and could be a useful sprinter for next season.

36 Acomb Stakes (Listed), (6f217yds) York August 19 (Good to Firm)

1 **Rule Of Law** 8-13   J P Spencer
2 **Celtic Cat** 8-13   M J Kinane
3 **Capped For Victory** 8-10   K Fallon
15-8f, 7-2, 7-2. nk, nk. 7 ran. 1m 23.4 (b6.83)
Sheikh Mohammed (D Loder, Newmarket).

A race which normally throws up some useful horses, and this renewal looked no different, as Rule Of Law and Celtic Cat both emerged with credit. The winner just held on from the fast-finishing Aidan O'Brien colt, and both look set to do well over middle-distances next season. **Top Seed** stayed on well in fourth and needs further.

37 Scottish Equitable Gimcrack Stakes (Group 2), (6f3yds) York August 20 (Good to Firm)

1 **Balmont** 8-11   Pat Eddery
2 **Fokine** 8-11   M Hills
3 **Grand Reward** 8-11   M J Kinane
7-2, 9-1, 7-4f. hd, nk. 9 ran. 1m 11.1 (b4.56)
Sanford R Robertson (J Noseda, Newmarket).

A great finish to the race, with just a head and a neck separating the first three. Pat Eddery gave the winner a vintage ride, making all and keeping just enough in reserve to repel Barry Hills's Fokine, who was bouncing back from a poor effort last time in the Richmond Stakes *(25)*.

38 **Costcutter Roses Stakes (Listed), (5f3yds) York August 20 (Good to Firm)**
1 **Howick Falls** 8-11   L Dettori
2 **If Paradise** 9-0   Dane O'Neill
3 **Fast Heart** 8-11   Pat Eddery
7-2, 7-1, 16-1. 3¹/₂l, 1l. 9 ran. 58.5 (b1.55)
Sheikh Mohammed (D Loder, Newmarket).

With favourite **Convince** disappointing, this may not have taken much winning, but Howick Falls did it well, leading two furlongs out and coming clear to beat If Paradise, who ran much better than he had at Goodwood last time out *(27)*. The winner clearly has plenty of speed.

39 **newitts.com Convivial Maiden Stakes, (6f3yds) York August 20 (Good to Firm)**
1 **Glaramara** 9-0   Pat Eddery
2 **Unshooda** 8-9   R Hills
3 **Great Exhibition** 9-0   L Dettori
33-1, 9-2, 3-1. ¹/₂l, 1¹/₄l. 11 ran. 1m 12.4 (b3.21)
C M Martin (A Bailey, Tarporley).

A real turn-up here, and probably with little meaning for the future. The winner was very slowly away, but gradually worked his way into contention and picked up well in the final furlong to nail Unshooda, who went on to win a maiden next time out. Market-leader **Finders Keepers** ran very badly.

40 **Peugeot Lowther Stakes (Fillies Group 2), (6f3yds) York August 21 (Good to Firm)**
1 **Carry On Katie** 8-11   L Dettori
2 **Badminton** 8-11   D Holland
3 **Dunloskin** 8-11   P Robinson
3-1, 8-1, 7-2. 2l, 1l. 9 ran. 1m 10.7 (b4.96)
Mohammed Rashid (J Noseda, Newmarket).

Carry On Katie gave her supporters a scare or two by pulling very hard on the way to post. She did the same in the race but it didn't seem to stop her, as she won comfortably from Clive Brittain's Badminton. **Silca's Gift** was sent off favourite on the strength of her Royal Ascot win *(9)*, but never looked likely to score at any stage.

41 **Tattersalls Breeders Stakes, (6f) Curragh August 23 (Good to Firm)**
1 **Majestic Desert** 8-7   M J Kinane
2 **Totally Yours** 8-7   R Mullen
3 **Dollivius** 8-7   Catherine Gannon
5-4f, 12-1, 20-1. hd, 4l. 24 ran. 1m 11.1 (b4.99)
Jaber Abdullah (M Channon, West Ilsley).

Majestic Desert paid a handsome compliment to Attraction in winning this – previously she had been beaten 8l in the Queen Mary *(6)* by Mark Johnston's flying filly. Totally Yours rallied well after being headed, and the pair drew

clear of the third, so the form looks good.

42 **Galileo EBF Futurity Stakes (Group 2), (7f) Curragh August 23 (Good to Firm)**
1 **Pearl Of Love** 9-0   D Holland
2 **Tumblebrutus** 9-0   P Cosgrave
3 **The Mighty Tiger** 9-0   M J Kinane
5-4f, 16-1, 9-4. 3¹/₂l, nk. 8 ran. 1m 22.5 (b6.49)
M Doyle (M Johnston, Middleham).

A very smart performance by Pearl Of Love, who never saw another horse once the gates opened. Good yardsticks in The Mighty Tiger, **Wathab**, **Newton** and **Mahogany** were well beaten off, and the Peintre Celebre colt looks out of the top drawer.

43 **Malaysia Airlines Non Stop Prestige Stakes (Group 3 Fillies), (7f) Goodwood August 24 (Good to Firm)**
1 **Gracefully** 8-9   J F Egan
2 **Ithaca** 8-9   T Quinn
3 **Dubaian Duel** 8-9   J P Spencer
7-1, 5-6f, 16-1. 2l, ¹/₂l. 6 ran. 1m 27.3 (b2.13)
Thurloe Thoroughbreds VI (S Kirk, Upper Lambourn).

Three victories in a row for Gracefully, although this was by no means a strong race. Connections were talking about a possible 1,000 Guineas raid with her, but that seems premature. **Caldy Dancer** was a long way below his Irish form in fifth.

44 **Ripon Champion Two Yrs Old Trophy 2003 (Listed), (6f) Ripon August 25 (Good to Firm)**
1 **Auditorium** 8-11   K Fallon
2 **Peak To Creek** 8-11   S W Kelly
3 **Mac Love** 8-11   A Culhane
6-4f, 5-2, 10-1. 1¹/₂l, 2l. 4 ran. 1m 15.6 (b0.88)
Cheveley Park Stud (Sir M Stoute, Newmarket).

A small field, but a cracking race and a smart winner in Auditorium, who came from last to first to win eased down. Peak To Creek was well held in second, but his exploits in the second half of the season mean this was a well above-average performance.

45 **Irish Stallion Farms EBF Premier Nursery Handicap, (1m) Tralee August 29 (Firm)**
1 **Chestnut Gallinule** 9-3   D P McDonogh
2 **Castledale** 9-4   M J Kinane
3 **Tipper Road** 7-12   Catherine Gannon (5)
7-1, 9-2, 16-1. nk, 1l. 12 ran. 1m 39.9 (b5.88)
James McEvoy (K Prendergast, Ireland).

Castledale appeared to have this race in the bag, but ran out of stamina over a trip which is a furlong further than normal for him. The winner was thus able to pounce late on, in what turned out to be his final start of the season.

46 Iveco Daily Solario Stakes (Group 3), (7f16yds) Sandown August 30 (Good to Soft)

1 **Barbajuan** 8-11   D Holland
2 **Milk It Mick** 8-11   K Fallon
3 **Matloob** 8-11   P Robinson
12-1, 9-2, 9-4j. ¹/₄l, 1¹/₄l. 8 ran. 1m 32.0 (b1.05)
Team Havana (N Callaghan, Newmarket).

A tactical triumph for Darryll Holland, who hugged the rail throughout while his adversaries all came a few horse-widths wider. Barbajuan had been relatively exposed, so the form is nothing to get excited about, although the seemingly limited Milk It Mick flew home for second. Soon, he would surprise us all.

47 Go And Go Round Tower Stakes (Listed), (6f) Curragh August 31 (Good to Firm)

1 **Wathab** 9-0   D P McDonogh
2 **Simple Exchange** 9-0   P J Smullen
3 **Troubadour** 9-0   M J Kinane
4-1, 7-2, 4-7f. ¹/₄l, 3l. 5 ran. 1m 11.2 (b4.89)
Haif Mohammed Al-Ghatani (K Prendergast, Ireland).

Wathab had had plenty of racing (one win in nine starts before this race), but had taken it well and never saw another horse here, having been bounced out in front. Simple Exchange stayed on well at the death without troubling the winner.

48 Moyglare Stud Stakes (Fillies Group 1), (7f) Curragh August 31 (Good to Firm)

1   **Necklace** 8-11
M J Kinane
2 **Red Feather** 8-11   N G McCullagh
3 **Menhoubah** 8-11   J Fortune
5-4f, 14-1, 10-1. 1l, shd. 11 ran. 1m 23.1 (b5.89)
Michael Tabor (A P O'Brien, Ireland).

Red Feather got closer to Necklace this time than over the same course and distance earlier in the month (33), but still couldn't overhaul Aidan O'Brien's smart filly. The winner quickened up readily in the final furlong, had plenty left in the locker and looked, on this show, an Oaks contender.

49 Prix Morny Casinos Barriere (Group 1), (6f) Deauville August 31 (Good)

1 **Whipper** 9-0   S Maillot
2 **Much Faster** 8-10   T Thulliez
3 **Denebola** 8-10   C P Lemaire
25.8-1, 9-10f, 9.1-1. 2l, shd. 8 ran. 1m 14.0 (a5.50)
E Zaccour (R Collet, France).

Tricky to assess, with conditions resembling a quagmire (despite the official "Good") and many of the principals disappointing. Denebola, **Old Deuteronomy**, **Carrizo Creek** and **Colossus** all fall into that category, so the form may be best ignored. Whipper, always prominent, simply handled the conditions best.

50 Coral Sirenia Stakes (Group 3), (6f) Kempton September 6 (Good to Firm)

1 **Pastoral Pursuits** 8-11   S Drowne
2 **Diosypros Blue** 8-11   T Quinn
3 **Cartography** 8-11   P Robinson
11-10f, 9-1, 4-1. 2l, nk. 9 ran. 1m 11.0 (b7.21)
The Pursuits Partnership (H Morrison, East Ilsley).

Having been really impressive at Windsor last time, Pastoral Pursuits took the step up in grade in his stride in what was his last start of the season. **Holborn**, exposed but very consistent, again ran well in fourth.

51 Irish Stallion Farms EBF Premier Nursery Handicap, (7f) Leopardstown September 6 (Good to Firm)

1 **Alexander Goldrun** 8-12   K J Manning
2 **Castledale** 9-1   M J Kinane
3 **Amourallis** 8-3   M A Cleere (10)
6-1, 5-1, 12-1. hd, hd. 11 ran. 1m 29.1 (b3.82)
N O'Callaghan (J Bolger, Ireland).

Alexander Goldrun put the trauma of her stall problem on her last start (29) behind her with a gritty success. She was headed inside the final furlong but fought back tenaciously to pop her head in front on the line. A versatile sort, she has now won at 5f and 7f.

52 EBF Carrie Red Fillies' Nursery Handicap, (6f110yds) Doncaster September 10 (Good)

1 **Ticker Tape** 8-1   G Duffield
2 **Mrs Moh** 8-0   Dale Gibson
3 **La Vie Est Belle** 8-4   A McCarthy
4 **Vonadaisy** 7-12   P Hanagan
11-2f, 33-1, 25-1, 10-1. nk, 1¹/₄l, 1l. 21 ran. 1m 21.5 (b2.73)
Chris Deuters (J A Osborne, Upper Lambourn).

A definite draw bias to this race, with the first four drawn 19, 17, 21 and 15. Ticker Tape made the most of it to just hold on from rank-outsider Mrs Moh. The winner ran with credit in all her subsequent races, but was beaten at Listed class and clearly has her limitations. **Asia Winds** and **Varnay**, fifth and sixth from stalls two and four respectively, were the only runners from single-figure draws to make the first ten.

53 £200,000 St Leger Yearling Stakes, (6f) Doncaster September 10 (Good)

1 **Cape Fear** 8-11   K Fallon
2 **Psychiatrist** 9-0   J P Spencer
3 **Axis** 8-11   D Mernagh
4-1f, 9-2, 25-1. ³/₄l, 1l. 22 ran. 1m 14.3 (b4.42)
Kennet Valley Thoroughbred II (B Meehan, Upper Lambourn).

Despite having had a long season, Cape Fear justified favouritism to win and did it well in the end, having looked to be in an unpromising position two furlongs out. He had held his form well through the season and this was a deserved success. **If Paradise**, the Super Sprint winner *(20)*, was well down the pack this time.

54 Prix d'Arenberg (Group 3), (5f110yds) Maisons-Laffitte September 10 (Soft)

1 **Villadolide** 8-8	T Gillet
2 **Needles And Pins** 8-8	D Holland
3 **Peak To Creek** 8-11	T Jarnet

5.3-1, 11-2, 4.2-1. shd, 1l. 4 ran. 1m 6.0 (a3.50). Mme A Head (C Head-Maarek, France).

Needles And Pins just failed to supplement her recent Newbury win on this step up to Group company. Villadolide regained the lead inside the final furlong and just held on. Peak To Creek needs further.

55 Betdaq May Hill Stakes (Group 2), (1m) Doncaster September 11 (Good)

1 **Kinnaird** 8-10	K Darley
2 **Hathrah** 8-10	R Hills
3 **Lucky Pipit** 8-10	M Hills

9-1, 10-3, 9-2. $1^3/4$l, $2^1/2$l. 10 ran. 1m 40.7 (b7.18) S A B Dinsmore (P Haslam, Middleham).

Kinnaird continued her improvement, bridging the class gap by winning this Group 2 comfortably. She kept going right to the line and seems sure to be suited by further next year. Lucky Pipit, winner of a Listed event earlier in the season *(21)*, is going the right way.

56 Ralph Raper Prince Of Wales Nursery, (1m) Doncaster September 11 (Good)

1 **Breathing Sun** 8-5	Pat Eddery
2 **Overdrawn** 9-10	T Quinn
3 **Less Of A Mystery** 8-8	J Fanning
4 **Queenstown** 9-7	K Fallon

9-1, 11-2, 13-2, 8-1. $3/4$l, $1/4$l, nk. 16 ran. 1m 43.7 (b4.14) Howard Spooner (W Musson, Newmarket).

Held up in the early stages, the improving Breathing Sun carved through the field to win going away. He will get further next season and is one to note. Overdrawn was hampered by an 8lb penalty for his success in a York nursery, but ran as well as could be expected.

57 Prix La Rochette (Group 3), (7f) Longchamp September 11 (Good)

1 **Diamond Green** 8-11	C Soumillon
2 **Charming Prince** 8-11	O Peslier
3 **Ershaad** 8-11	T Gillet

1-2f, 4-1, 8.6-1. $2^1/2$l, hd. 7 ran. 1m 22.5 (a3.50). Fam Lagardere (A Fabre, France).

Diamond Green easily maintained his 100 per cent record for the season with a fluent success. Ershaad paid the penalty for chasing the winner throughout and lost second close home.

58 Champagne Stakes (Group 2), (7f) Doncaster September 12 (Good)

1 **Lucky Story** 9-0	D Holland
2 **Auditorium** 8-10	K Fallon
3 **Haafhd** 8-10	R Hills

2-1, 8-1, 10-11f. nk, 2l. 6 ran. 2m 27.9 (a55.10) Abdulla Buhaleeba (M Johnston, Middleham).

Despite sweating freely, Lucky Story scored a tenacious victory, having looked as though he would be swallowed up at one stage. He has the guts to go with his talent. Haafhd was below his best in third.

59 DBS St Leger Yearling Stakes, (6f) Doncaster September 12 (Good)

1 **Jazz Scene** 8-11	A Culhane
2 **Mrs Moh** 8-6	Dale Gibson
3 **Morse** 8-11	L Dettori

10-1, 4-1f, 8-1. nk, $3/4$l. 20 ran. 1m 15.2 (b3.51) R E Sangster (M Channon, West Ilsley).

Favourably drawn, Jazz Scene came through late and would be better over further. The consistent Mrs Moh again had to settle for minor honours. This wasn't a great contest.

60 Renault Van Range Stardom Stakes (Listed), (1m) Goodwood September 12 (Good)

1 **Fantastic View** 8-11	P Dobbs
2 **Mutahayya** 8-11	W Supple
3 **Top Seed** 8-11	T E Durcan

5-1, 5-1, 16-1. $3/4$l, nk. 8 ran. 1m 38.4 (b1.67) Malih L Al Basti (R Hannon, Marlborough).

The form of this looks solid, as there was 5l back to fourth-placed **Baileys Dancer**. Fantastic View travelled well and then held on grimly in a three-way battle for the line; he could well be Group-class next term.

61 Polypipe Flying Childers Stakes (Group 2), (5f) Doncaster September 13 (Good)

1 **Howick Falls** 8-12	L Dettori
2 **China Eyes** 8-9	M Hills
3 **Nights Cross** 8-12	A Culhane

7-4f, 7-2, 12-1. $3/4$l, 2l. 13 ran. 1m 1.6 (b3.87) Sheikh Mohammed (D Loder, Newmarket).

Howick Falls doesn't get a yard beyond 5f but is pretty smart at the minimum trip, although he had to be ridden vigorously to get on top after a slow start. The lightly-raced China Eyes ran well after a setback, while Nights Cross has been consistent all season.

62 St. Bernard Blenheim Stakes, (6f) Curragh September 14 (Good to Firm)

1 **Colossus** 9-0 M J Kinane	
2 **Castledale** 9-0	R Hughes
3 **Kurlicue** 8-11	D P McDonogh

2-5f, 9-2, 10-1. shd, $3^1/2$l. 5 ran. 1m 11.9 (b4.19) S Magnier (A P O'Brien, Ireland).

A moral victory for David Wachman's Castledale, who lost the race in the stewards' room after drifting across Colossus. The latter was disappointing and isn't among the best at Ballydoyle.

63 **Dunnes Stores National Stakes (Group 1), (7f) Curragh September 14 (Good to Firm)**

1 **One Cool Cat** 9-0		M J Kinane
2 **Wathab** 9-0		D P McDonogh
3 **Pearl Of Love** 9-0		D Holland

4-6f, 20-1, 13-8. 1l, nk. 8 ran. 1m 23.1 (b5.89)
S Magnier (A P O'Brien, Ireland).

Another step up the ladder from One Cool Cat, who cemented his position at the head of the market for the 2,000 Guineas. The trademark acceleration was still in evidence and, with Pearl Of Love back in third, the form looks very strong.

64 **Irish Stallion Farms EBF Premier Nursery Handicap, (1m) Listowel September 15 (Good)**

1 **Faasel** 8-3		M C Hussey (3)
2 **Alexander Goldrun** 9-0		K J Manning
3 **Broomfield Lad** 7-13		W J Lee (7)

3-1, 7-2, 12-1. $\frac{1}{2}$l, 2l. 8 ran. 1m 42.0 (b4.26)
Hamdan Al Maktoum (K Prendergast, Ireland).

Faasel was up with the pace throughout and, having challenged on the inside, was never going to be reeled in, hard though Alexander Goldrun tried. The latter has gone up markedly in the weights.

65 **Christine Sadler Jewellery Harry Rosebery Stakes (Listed), (5f) Ayr September 18 (Good)**

1 **Boogie Street** 8-11		R Hughes
2 **Nights Cross** 8-11		A Culhane
3 **Moss Vale** 8-11		J Carroll

5-2j, 5-2j, 4-1. 1$\frac{1}{4}$l, 1l. 9 ran. 57.0 (b3.02)
Hippodrome Racing (R Hannon, Marlborough).

Boogie Street reversed Flying Childers form (61) with Nights Cross, although he may have been flattered by this outcome, as he ran down the favoured stands rail. Still, he pulled it out when required and won nicely at the line.

66 **Dubai Duty Free Mill Reef Stakes (Group 2), (6f8yds) Newbury September 19 (Good to Firm)**

1 **Byron** 8-12		J P Spencer
2 **Grand Reward** 8-12		M J Kinane
3 **Tahreeb** 8-12		Martin Dwyer

9-1, 4-9f, 16-1. $\frac{3}{4}$l, nk. 10 ran. 1m 12.7 (b4.34)
Sheikh Mohammed (D Loder, Newmarket).

Byron gained just reward after good efforts in the July Stakes (15) and the Gimcrack (37). Although the winning margin was narrow, Grand Reward never looked like catching him. The consistent **Holborn** was back in fourth.

67 **Sioexho Prestige Firth Of Clyde Stakes (Listed), (6f) Ayr September 20 (Good)**

1		**Ruby Rocket** 8-8
K Darley		
2 **Unshooda** 8-8		R Hills
3 **Tentative** 8-8		R Hughes

7-2, 7-4f, 14-1. 1$\frac{1}{4}$l, 1$\frac{1}{4}$l. 6 ran. 1m 11.8 (b2.15)
Thurloe Thoroughbreds IX (H Morrison, East Ilsley).

Ruby Rocket really stamped her authority on this race, never looking like getting beaten and confirming the recent improvement she has made. Unshooda would have been suited by further but wasn't disgraced, stepping up in trip.

68 **C L Weld Park Stakes (Group 3), (7f) Curragh September 21 (Good)**

1 **Venturi** 8-11		R Hughes
2 **Misty Heights** 8-11		P J Smullen
3 **Opera Comique** 8-11		J P Murtagh

10-1, 9-10f, 11-2. $\frac{3}{4}$l, $\frac{1}{2}$l. 10 ran. 1m 25.5 (b3.49)
Mrs Paul Shanahan (D Wachman, Ireland).

Misty Heights had Group 1 form, having finished fourth in the Moyglare Stud Stakes (48), but was well outpointed here. The winner was produced late and flew home.

69 **Watership Down Stud Sales Race, (6f110yds) Ascot September 26 (Good to Firm)**

1 **Nyramba** 9-1		L Dettori
2 **Dubaian Duel** 7-12		Martin Dwyer
3 **Valjarv** 8-8		I Mongan

4-1f, 9-2, 14-1. 1$\frac{1}{4}$l, 1l. 30 ran. 1m 22.8 (b4.86)
Salem Suhail (J Gosden, Manton).

Nyramba, drawn on the favoured side (30 of 30), only came off the fence to take the measure of Dubaian Duel in the final two furlongs. Conceding 17lb to the runner-up, this was no mean performance. It was her third win from her last four starts.

70 **Hackney Empire Royal Lodge Stakes (Group 2), (1m) Ascot September 27 (Good to Firm)**

1 **Snow Ridge** 8-11		Martin Dwyer
2 **Moscow Ballet** 8-11		M J Kinane
3 **Rule Of Law** 8-11		J P Spencer

15-8f, 11-2, 7-2. $\frac{3}{4}$l, shd. 10 ran. 1m 41.2 (b6.09)
Exors of the late Lord Weinstock (M Tregoning, Lambourn).

A remarkable show from Snow Ridge, who came from an unpromising position turning in to win going away. He was still very green, but on this evidence looks every inch a potential Classic winner. Moscow Ballet had no answers to the winner's surge, but held off Rule Of Law close home on only his second outing.

71 **Meon Valley Stud Fillies' Mile (Group 1), (1m) Ascot September 27 (Good to Firm)**

1 **Red Bloom** 8-10		K Fallon
2 **Sundrop** 8-10		L Dettori
3 **Punctilious** 8-10		P Robinson

3-1, 10-1, 13-8f. 1$\frac{1}{4}$l, shd. 7 ran. 1m 40.8 (b6.47)
Cheveley Park Stud (Sir M Stoute, Newmarket).

Red Bloom won this race in authoritative fashion and is the type of material from which Sir Michael Stoute can fashion a fine three-year-old. She pricked her ears close home, indicating that she found this all rather easy. Sundrop suffered a troubled passage but wouldn't have got to the winner.

72 **El Gran Senor Stakes (Listed), (7f) Cork September 27 (Firm)**
1   **Simple Exchange** 9-0
P J Smullen
2 **Cornwall** 9-0   C O'Donoghue
3 **Amalie Bay** 9-0   J A Heffernan
Evensf, 6-4, 6-1. 4¹/₂l, 1¹/₂l. 4 ran. 1m 24.1 (b6.22)
Moyglare Stud Farm (D Weld, Ireland).

Only four runners in this and a simple task for favourite Simple Exchange, who found this easier than when tackling One Cool Cat last time out *(63)*. He looks well suited by fast ground.

73 **Sky Bet Cheveley Park Stakes (Group 1 Fillies), (6f) Newmarket October 2 (Good to Firm)**
1 **Carry On Katie** 8-11   L Dettori
2 **Majestic Desert** 8-11   K Fallon
3 **Badminton** 8-11   D Holland
13-8f, 16-1, 12-1. shd, 1³/₄l. 10 ran. 1m 13.0 (b2.03)
Mohammed Rashid (J Noseda, Newmarket).

Temperament doubts surround Carry On Katie but there is no doubting her class, as she again led from pillar to post and just managed to repel the late charge of Majestic Desert. Stamina would be the big issue regarding a 1,000 Guineas challenge for the winner, judged on this showing. **Ruby Rocket** again ran well to be fourth, but **Nyramba** was disappointing, finishing plum last.

74 **Somerville Tattersall Stakes (Group 3), (7f) Newmarket October 2 (Good to Firm)**
1 **Milk It Mick** 8-9   Pat Eddery
2 **Bayeux** 8-9   L Dettori
3 **Bachelor Duke** 8-9   S Sanders
12-1, 9-4f, 25-1. nk, nk. 8 ran. 1m 24.9 (b6.31)
Paul J Dixon (J A Osborne, Upper Lambourn).

The seemingly-exposed Milk It Mick began his Indian summer with this stubborn defeat of Bayeaux and Bachelor Duke by two shortheads. It was his eleventh race of the season, but he still looked fantastic and deserved his success.

75 **Shadwell Stud Middle Park Stakes (Group 1), (6f) Newmarket October 3 (Good to Firm)**
1 **Three Valleys** 8-11   R Hughes
2 **Balmont** 8-11   Pat Eddery
3 **Holborn** 8-11   D Holland

2-1f, 8-1, 50-1. ³/₄l, ¹/₂l. 12 ran. 1m 10.7 (b4.38)
K Abdulla (R Charlton, Beckhampton).

A return to form from Three Valleys, who won well enough, without showing the brilliance of his Royal Ascot win *(5)*. He has since been disqualified, however, due to a banned substance being found in his sample, so Balmont claims a belated victory, with **Auditorium** third.

76 **Finnforest Oh So Sharp Stakes (Listed Fillies), (7f) Newmarket October 4 (Good to Firm)**
1 **Top Romance** 8-9   J P Spencer
2 **Spotlight** 8-9   Pat Eddery
3 **Kelucia** 8-9   R Ffrench
6-1, 3-1, 20-1. nk, 1l. 9 ran. 1m 24.2 (b6.99)
Mrs Denis Haynes (Sir M Stoute, Newmarket).

A good ride from Jamie Spencer, who dictated matters from the front and gradually increased the pace, leaving enough in reserve to hold off late finishers. **Unshooda**, sent off favourite, ran too freely to do herself justice.

77 **Redcar Two-Year-Old Trophy, (6f) Redcar October 4 (Good to Firm)**
1 **Peak To Creek** 9-0   S W Kelly
2 **Local Poet** 9-0   G Gibbons
3 **Imperial Echo** 8-3   P Fessey
13-2, 25-1, 100-1. hd, 3l. 23 ran. 1m 12.1 (b1.73)
C Fox & J Wright (J Noseda, Newmarket).

A long season didn't seem to bother Peak To Creek, who finished with a late rattle to get up in the closing stages. He is almost certainly suited by further, so this was a particularly smart effort, although the race in itself wasn't a great contest.

78 **Prix Marcel Boussac-Criterium des Pouliches (Group 1 Fillies), (1m) Longchamp October 5 (Soft)**
1 **Denebola** 8-11   C P Lemaire
2 **Green Noon** 8-11   Y Lerner
3 **Tulipe Royale** 8-11   S Pasquier
5-1, 6-1, 66-1. hd, 2l. 16 ran. 1m 40.9 (a5.90)
Fam Niarchos (P Bary, France).

A fine performance by Denebola, who relished this soft ground and who went through the pack like a hot knife through butter. The winning distance of a head doesn't reveal her superiority, and she could be as good for the stable as Six Perfections was in 2003. **Necklace**, sent off favourite could only manage tenth.

79 **Prix Jean-Luc Lagardere (Grand Criterium) (Group 1), (7f) Longchamp October 5 (Soft)**
1 **American Post** 9-0   R Hughes
2 **Charming Prince** 9-0   O Peslier
3 **Ximb** 9-0   I Mendizabal
4-1, 3-1, 11-4f. 4l, 2¹/₂l. 6 ran. 1m 24.5 (a5.50)

K Abdullah (C Head-Maarek, France)

An impressive performance from American Post, who (being a son of Bering), loved the soft ground. He quickened clear two out and quickly had the race won, with Richard Hughes able to ease down close home. It remained to be seen if he could reproduce this showing on a faster surface, but he would get his chance in the Racing Post Trophy (95).

80 **Danehill Dancer Tipperary Stakes (Listed), (5f) Tipperary October 5 (Good to Firm)**

1 Nights Cross 9-0	A Culhane
2 Blue Crush 8-11	W J Lee
3 Miss Serendipity 8-11	T P O'Shea

7-4f, 3-1, 6-1. 4¹/₄l, 1l. 10 ran. 56.8 (b2.82)
Ridgeway Downs Racing (M Channon, West Ilsley)

Nights Cross was running in his 15th race of the season here, but you wouldn't have thought it as he scampered clear. Blue Crush, chasing a hat-trick, had no answers in second.

81 **Tom McGee Autumn Stakes (Group 3), (1m) Ascot October 11 (Good to Firm)**

1	Fantastic View 9-0
P Dobbs	
2 Menokee 8-11	K Fallon
3 Temple Place 8-11	R Mullen

13-8f, 7-2, 8-1. 4l, 2¹/₄l. 5 ran. 1m 45.6 (b1.73)
Flying Tiger Partnership (W Haggas, Newmarket)

Fantastic View confirmed his improvement with an afternoon stroll. There was a slow early pace but, once Pat Dobbs sent his mount to the front, there was only ever going to be one result. Menokee kept on but looks nothing special.

82 **Willmott Dixon Cornwallis Stakes (Group 3), (5f) Ascot October 11 (Good to Firm)**

1 Majestic Missile 9-1	K Fallon
2 Nights Cross 8-12	T E Durcan
3 Fast Heart 8-12	E Ahern

11-4, 8-1, 66-1. 3¹/₄l, 1³/₄l. 11 ran. 1m 1.9 (b3.12)
Malih L Al Basti (R Hannon, Marlborough)

Having been well beaten in the 6f Gimcrack (37), Majestic Missile was returned to his best trip of 5f and won easily. He seems to be a specialist at the minimum trip. The remarkable Nights Cross was sent out again, just six days after winning a Listed race in Tipperary (80), and didn't disappoint.

83 **Irish Stallion Farms EBF Premier Nursery Handicap, (1m) Gowran Park October 11 (Good to Firm)**

1 Anchor 8-12	M J Kinane
2 Alexander Goldrun 9-4	K J Manning
3 Soul Legacy 7-13	M A Cleere (7)
4 German Malt 8-1	N G McCullagh

5-4f, 5-1, 25-1, 14-1. shd, 3l, 2l. 16 ran. 1m 34.2 (b7.19)

Michael Tabor (A P O'Brien, Ireland)

Alexander Goldrun looked to have this won, but Mick Kinane on Anchor never gave up and just got there. The winner needed every yard of this trip and will do better over further next season.

84 **Newton Fund Managers Rockingham Stakes (Listed), (6f3yds) York October 11 (Good to Firm)**

1 Peak To Creek 9-0	Pat Eddery
2 Mac Love 8-11	A Culhane
3 Blue Tomato 8-11	S Drowne

7-2, 16-1, 7-2. hd, 1¹/₄l. 8 ran. 1m 11.3 (b4.30)
C Fox & J Wright (J Noseda, Newmarket)

Peak To Creek showed that he was still improving, with his third consecutive win and his first in Listed company. He again came late with his usual flourish and it was just enough to get the better of Mac Love, who, like the winner, has also been having a busy time of it.

85 **Juddmonte Beresford Stakes (Group 2), (1m) Curragh October 12 (Good)**

1 Azamour 9-0	J P Murtagh
2 Relaxed Gesture 9-0	P J Smullen
3 Mustameet 9-0	D P McDonogh

6-4f, 11-2, 7-1. nk, 2l. 6 ran. 1m 42.0 (b2.55)
H H Aga Khan (J Oxx, Ireland)

This race was won by Alamshar the year before and John Oxx appeared to have unleashed another smart type in the unbeaten Azamour, who showed admirable resolution to hold off Relaxed Gesture. Unlike Alamshar, however, this winner looks as though trips short of middle distances will suit ideally.

86 **EBF Flame Of Tara Stakes (Listed fillies), (6f) Curragh October 12 (Good)**

1	Kanisfluh 8-11
W M Lordan	
2 Dangle 8-11	N G McCullagh
3 Summer Sunset 8-11	P J Smullen

16-1, 8-1, 5-1. shd, ¹/₂l. 13 ran. 1m 15.3 (b0.79)
Benedikt Fassbender (T Stack, Ireland)

A shock result and probably not a race to get carried away about. Kanisfluh finished last of ten on her latest start, but stuck on well in the final furlong to defeat Dangle, who looks sure to win races in future.

87 **£100,000 Tattersalls Autumn Auction Stakes, (6f) Newmarket October 16 (Good to Firm)**

1 Milly Waters 8-2	R Mullen
2 Ticker Tape 9-0	L Dettori
3 Magical Mimi 8-2	Lisa Jones

33-1, 7-2f, 10-1. 1¹/₂l, 1¹/₄l. 29 ran. 1m 14.4 (b0.70)
John E Oldknow (W Brisbourne, Baschurch)

Milly Waters, racing in the stands-side group, was held up in the early stages before hitting the front a furlong out and running on all the way to the line. Ticker Tape is consistent and again ran a good race, although a longer trip is probably needed nowadays.

88 Darley Dewhurst Stakes (Group 1), (7f) Newmarket October 18 (Good to Firm)

1 Milk It Mick 9-0	D Holland
2 Three Valleys 9-0	R Hughes
3 Haafhd 9-0	R Hills

33-1, 11-4f, 7-1. hd, 1¼l. 12 ran. 1m 25.2 (b5.99)
Paul J Dixon (J A Osborne, Upper Lambourn)

Three Valleys, trying 7f for the first time, looked sure to win approaching the final furlong but was outgunned by the late-developing Milk It Mick, who has conjured phenomenal improvement from somewhere. Neither particularly appeal as Classic winners, though Haafhd ran a good race in third and will be useful next term.

89 Owen Brown Rockfel Stakes (Group 2), (7f) Newmarket October 18 (Good to Firm)

1 Cairns 8-9	T E Durcan
2 Snow Goose 8-9	Pat Eddery
3 Kelucia 8-9	R Ffrench

12-1, 11-4f, 14-1. 1¼l, nk. 10 ran. 1m 25.9 (b5.33)
Sheikh Mohammed (M Channon, West Ilsley)

With **Bay Tree** and **Tarot Card** disappointing, this may not have taken much winning, although Cairns did it nicely, coming from last to first and going away. **Gracefully** ran slightly flat in fourth.

90 Derrinstown Stud EBF Birdcatcher Premier Nursery Handicap, (6f) Naas October 19 (Good to Firm)

1 Colossus 9-7	J A Heffernan
2 Sheltingham 8-3	N G McCullagh
3 Amourallis 7-12	R P Cleary (5)

9-4f, 9-2, 10-1. 2½l, ½l. 10 ran. 1m 9.5 (b3.17)
S Magnier (A P O'Brien, Ireland)

Colossus led from halfway and won as he was entitled to do, having run well in the Middle Park *(75)* last time out. He is clearly useful but probably not a star in the making. Amourallis was last early on and did well to finish as close as she did.

91 Tote Bookmakers Silver Tankard Stakes, (1m4yds) Pontefract October 20 (Good to Firm)

1 New Mexican 8-11	J P Spencer
2 Makfool 8-11	A Culhane
3 Carte Sauvage 8-11	K Dalgleish

2-1f, 16-1, 7-2. ½l, 1l. 10 ran. 1m 44.2 (b4.87)

J Musgrave (L Ramsden, Thirsk)

Having run in some useful races, New Mexican deserved this win, although he made harder work of it than at one stage looked likely. He edged right under pressure and didn't look overly enthusiastic when asked to close out his race.

92 Prix des Reservoirs (Group 3), (1m) Deauville October 21 (Good)

1 Via Milano 8-9	D Boeuf
2 Colony Band 8-9	O Peslier
3 Agata 8-9	C Soumillon

4.9-1, 3-1, 5-1. 2½l, shd. 8 ran. 1m 41.4 (a5.40)
A Capozzi (J Laurent-Joye Rossi, France)

Via Milano has a fine turn of foot, which she displayed here. Only sixth turning in, she squeezed through a narrow gap a furlong out and went on to score readily. She could add to her Group race tally next season.

93 Vodafone Horris Hill Stakes (Group 3), (7f) Newbury October 24 (Good to Firm)

1 Peak To Creek 8-9	Pat Eddery
2 Josephus 8-9	S Drowne
3 Millbag 8-9	T E Durcan

5-1, 12-1, 8-1. 3½l, 2l. 9 ran. 1m 26.7 (b4.20)
C Fox & J Wright (J Noseda, Newmarket)

A marvellous autumn for Peak To Creek was capped with a fine victory. Josephus looked the probable winner until Peak To Creek came late and swamped them all. He is clearly going the right way and looks one to follow next term, as does the lightly-raced runner-up.

94 Gerrardstown House Stud Silken Glider Stakes (Listed), (1m) Curragh October 25 (Soft)

1 Alexander Goldrun 8-11	K J Manning
2 Poetical 8-11	N G McCullagh
3 Treasure The Lady 8-11	F Berry

4-1, 9-1, 2-1f. ½l, 1½l. 12 ran. 1m 45.2 (a0.65)
N O'Callaghan (J Bolger, Ireland)

A gutsy success for Alexander Goldrun, who rarely seems to run a bad race. This was her third win from nine starts and she looks capable of adding to that tally in future, particularly if sent over further.

95 Racing Post Trophy (Group 1), (1m) Doncaster October 25 (Good to Firm)

1 American Post 9-0	C Soumillon
2 Fantastic View 9-0	P Dobbs
3 Magritte 9-0	J P Spencer

5-6f, 7-2, 11-4. 1¾l, 1½l. 4 ran. 1m 39.6 (b8.27)
K Abdulla (C Head-Maarek, France)

American Post proved that he could do it on fast ground with an easy success against a good yardstick in Fantastic View. At this stage, however, he looks more likely to make his mark in the top French events, where a more forgiving surface can normally be guaranteed. Magritte was well-beaten.

96 Constant Security Doncaster Stakes (Listed), (6f) Doncaster October 25 (Good to Firm)

1 Nero's Return 8-9	K Dalgleish
2 Mac Love 8-9	A Culhane
3 Moonlight Man 8-12	P Dobbs

5-1, 3-1f, 4-1. shd, 1¹/₂l. 8 ran. 1m 12.3 (b6.40)
Christine E Budden (M Johnston, Middleham)

Nero's Return won by 10l on his debut and followed up here in this much better race, battling back bravely having looked likely to taste defeat entering the final furlong. He could be anything in 2004, but is unlikely to be the best of Mark Johnston's formidable three-year-old gang.

97 Punter Southall Radley Stakes (Fillies Listed), (7f) Newbury October 25 (Good to Firm)

1 Secret Charm 8-8	M Hills
2 Hathrah 8-8	R Hills
3 Ticker Tape 8-8	Pat Eddery

2-1f, 5-2, 15-2. 1³/₄l, 1¹/₄l. 12 ran. 1m 28.7 (b2.20)
Maktoum Al Maktoum (B Hills, Lambourn)

Secret Charm had won a good Newmarket maiden last time out and stepped up to Listed class with an ease which marks her out as being useful at least. She ought to stay 1m2f next season and be able to hold her own in Group company. The consistent Ticker Tape came home with some prizemoney yet again.

98 Killavullan Stakes (Group 3), (7f) Leopardstown October 27 (Good)

1 Grey Swallow 9-0	P J Smullen
2 Newton 9-0	M Kinane
3 Takrice 8-11	D McDonogh

4-9f, 10-3, 4-1. 8l, 1l. 4 ran. 1m 26.7 (b6.22)
Rochelle Quinn (D Weld, Ireland)

A stunning performance from Grey Swallow on only his second start. Newton wouldn't be the best Aidan O'Brien has got, but even the master of Ballydoyle must have been impressed with the way Dermot Weld's Daylami colt cruised 8l clear. He will surely be a major player in the Guineas and Derby next term.

99 Zetland Stakes (Listed), (1m2f) Newmarket November 1 (Good to Soft)

1 Fun And Games 8-6	T E Durcan
2 Cohn Blue 8-11	K Fallon
3 Carte Sauvage 8-11	J Fanning

12-1, 3-1f, 9-2. 1¹/₂l, nk. 13 ran. 2m 6.2 (b5.53)
Sheikh Mohammed (M Channon, West Ilsley)

A race which doesn't normally produce any-

100

thing out of the ordinary and this renewal looks no exception. Fun And Games came through late to win going away and obviously stays well.

100 EBF Montrose Fillies' Stakes (Listed), (1m) Newmarket November 1 (Good to Soft)

1 Spotlight 8-8	Pat Eddery
2 St Francis Wood 8-9	L Dettori
3 Ouija Board 8-8	J P Spencer

7-2, 7-1, 11-4f. 4l, shd. 12 ran. 1m 38.6 (b5.33)
Hesmonds Stud (J Dunlop, Arundel)

Spotlight was allowed an easy lead and was able to pick up the pace throughout, resulting in quite a soft victory. St Francis Wood missed the kick but came through late to snatch second and should improve.

101 Criterium International, (1m) Saint-Cloud November 1 (Good)

1 Bago 9-0	T Gillet
2 Top Seed 9-0	A Culhane
3 Acropolis 9-0	M Kinane

2-5f, 35-1, 7.3-1. 6l, 4l. 7 ran. 1m 47.0 (a9.00)
Fam Niarchos (J Pease, France)

What Bago achieved here is difficult to measure – suffice to say that this well-bred colt looks the part and connections are making all the right noises about his ability.

102 Irish Stallion Farms EBF Premier Nursery Handicap, (7f) Leopardstown November 8 (Good)

1 Alexander Duchess 9-7	M J Kinane
2 Armanatta 8-5	D M Grant
3 Battle Games 8-12	F M Berry
4 Dancing Colors 9-5	F Tylicki (10)

9-2, 7-2f, 7-1, 14-1. shd, ³/₄l, 2l. 17 ran. 1m 28.5 (b4.42)
N O'Callaghan (J Burns, Ireland)

A narrow win for the topweight Alexander Duchess, who stayed on well after being strongly pressed in the final two furlongs. She could well be up to Listed class next season.

103 Eyrefield Stakes (Listed), (1m1f) Leopardstown November 8 (Good)

1 Mikado 9-0	M J Kinane
2 Tarakala 8-11	F M Berry
3 Liss Ard 9-0	D M Grant

4-5f, 7-2, 33-1. 1¹/₂l, 4l. 11 ran. Time not taken.
S Magnier (A P O'Brien, Ireland)

Mick Kinane didn't really need to exert himself here to any great degree as Mikado won comfortably. He looks as though staying will be his forte next season and he appeals for the St Leger, especially when you take his breeding into account – he's by Sadler's Wells out of a Shirley Heights mare.

Two-year-olds Index

All horses placed or commented on in our two-year-old review section, with race numbers

Outlook

Time Test *with Mark Nelson*

Feeling the need for speed

FOLLOWING the untimely loss of speed figure guru Ken Hussey last year, I was honoured to be called on to preserve the popular *Time Test* column in *Racing & Football Outlook*.

I've used Ken's methodology to produce speed figures during the autumn and winter for jump racing fans, but it is on the eve of the 2004 turf racing season where the action really begins.

Thoroughbreds trained to the minute, the potency of sprinters waiting to unfurl their power on the racetrack, plus the Classic aspirations of the juveniles – this is no place for the faint-hearted, just the fleet of foot. The dawn of a new Flat racing season turns a normal day into a special one and, armed with *Time Test* speed figures, we can reap the rewards.

Although many punters appear to have more of an affinity with the equine heroes of the National Hunt game, there seems to be a bit more precision to the action on the level. I'm quite certain it has everything to do with speed.

There's something not quite right about standing in a wet and muddy field, stopwatch poised whilst three-mile chasers, strung out across a whole county, walk towards the finish line.

That's not to say that speed figures over jumps aren't informative, far from it. It's just that strongly-run races in that sphere are thin on the ground.

Action on the Flat is a different matter entirely, a clock-watcher's paradise no less.

The majority of Flat races are run at a sound pace, producing speed figures which are far more reliable, and consequently profitable. Especially so the juvenile races, where the two-year-olds generally run flat out

DO YOU PREFER FINISHES LIKE THIS . . . the Stewards Cup takes just over a minute

. . . OR LIKE THIS? Red Marauder's National took over 11mins

> *"By far the strongest hint of an exceptional performer is when the speed figure exceeds those recorded by other, more proven performers, over course and distance on the same day"*

and to the best of their ability, time and time again.

It's enough to start polishing one's betting boots just thinking about it.

For those readers who have picked up this book for Classic clues and stable interviews and have no knowledge of speed figures, you may require some clarification as to the meaning and use of such numbers.

I wouldn't want you to thumb through to a different part of the book before I have the chance to explain that, for me, they are the most potent tool in our war against the men with big satchels.

Put simply, by looking at the winning time of each race and taking into account the going and weather on the day it was recorded, together with the distance the horse travelled, speed figures transform each performance into a number. This number will then reflect the ability of the horse in question.

In this way, you can compare performances of horses that have yet to meet and hopefully get an idea of who will run faster when they do.

By far the strongest hint of an exceptional performer is when the speed figure exceeds those recorded by other, more proven performers, over course and distance on the same day.

These instances may be few and far between, but when they arise the information is priceless.

One perfect example that provides a fond memory (for both me and my bank manager) was the performance of a three-year-old in a maiden at Folkestone a few years back.

Three races were run over 7f at the track on this particular day; two divisions of a three-year-old maiden and a classified stakes race for older horses.

The winner of the first division not only powered home in a time four seconds faster than the other three-year-old maiden, but also a second faster than the older horses had recorded earlier in the day.

The horse in question didn't even open as favourite on his next start and, although admittedly his price did tumble before the off, any serious clockwatcher would have waded in early.

The fact that the colt subsequently won and finished placed in five Group 1s, only once finishing out of the frame in his entire career, suggests that his second success was as near a certainty as you can get in this tricky game.

To think that this potential was apparent from the moment he first stepped onto a racecourse on a wet Tuesday in the spring of 1999, courtesy of timings on a trusty stopwatch! Oh, and the horse's name?

It was Kalanisi.

So, for those of you who only indulge with horses at the weekend, let this be a lesson. Days like that are a firm reminder that the weekend is always too far off.

Never overlook the current day, it is always too good to waste. Go and immerse yourself in speed figures, whether you calculate them for yourself or follow my column in the *Outlook*.

The top juveniles of 2003 with their *Time Test* ratings are shown on the opposite page. To keep up with developments throughout the season, either read my thoughts in the *Outlook* or subscribe to the Masterlist for a comprehensive list of speed figures which are updated each week.

Armed with such information and with betting boots on, we can give the old enemy hell. If the bookmakers have any sense, they may even stay at home this season.

Now, where's that polish gone?

Top Two-year-olds of 2003

	Horse	Speed rating	Distance in furlongs	Going	Track	Date achieved
1	**One Cool Cat** *(above)*	**66**	**6**	**G**	**Curragh**	**Aug 10**
2	Attraction	65	5	GF	Ascot	Jun 8
3	Three Valleys	64	6	GF	Ascot	Jun 17
4	Red Bloom	63	8	GF	Ascot	Sep 27
5	Old Deuteronomy	62	6	G	Curragh	Aug 10
6	Pearl Of Love	60	7	GF	Curragh	Aug 23
7	Balmont	59	6	GF	Newmarket	Oct 3
	Sundrop	59	8	GF	Ascot	Sep 27
	Haafhd	59	7	GF	Newbury	Aug 15
	Kinnaird	59	8	G	Doncaster	Sep 11
	Majestic Missile	59	5	G	Goodwood	Jul 31
	Necklace	59	7	GF	Curragh	Aug 31
	Snow Ridge	59	8	GF	Ascot	Sep 27
	Whipper	59	6	S	Deauville	Aug 31
15	Holborn	58	6	GF	Newmarket	Oct 3
	Lucky Story	58	7	GS	Goodwood	Jul 30
17	Byron	57	6	GF	Newbury	Sep 19
	Carrizo Creek	57	6	G	Goodwood	Jul 29
	Chester Le Street	57	7	GF	Newmarket	Jul 10
	Fokine	57	6	GF	York	Aug 20
	Kings Point	57	7	GF	Newmarket	Jul 10
	Milk It Mick	57	7	GF	Newmarket	Oct 18
	Orcadian	57	6	GF	Windsor	Jul 28
	Punctilious	57	8	GF	Ascot	Sep 27
	Rum Shot	57	6	GF	Windsor	Oct 6

Going key: VF = very firm, F = firm, GF = good to firm, G = good, GS = good to soft, S = soft

2004 Preview

Outlook

Ante-Post

by
Steffan Edwards

Finding those shorteners

I THINK we can count ourselves a touch unlucky not to have copped at least one result from last season's selections. After all, we got 33-1 about Lateen Sails for the 2,000 Guineas (he started at 9-2), we burgled some 25-1 about eventual 5-1 shot Intercontinental for the 1,000 Guineas, we had 16-1 Yesterday for the Oaks (she started 100-30 favourite) and finally we nabbed 33-1 Alamshar for the Derby, in which he lined up at 4-1.

Okay, Lateen Sails ran a shocker and Intercontinental didn't stay, but Yesterday would have won the Oaks with a clear run, and for once the best horse didn't win the Derby. Sometimes the punting gods just aren't with you.

Anyway, those of you shrewd enough to have layed off those bets on the exchanges prior to the races will have done alright, and here's hoping that the prices of the following selections collapse in similar fashion.

2,000 Guineas

In contrast to the fillies' version, the first colts' Classic has less of an open feel to it – the Irish pair at the head of the market look like they're a league above the British-trained entries.

Personally, I believe **One Cool Cat** should have been recognised as champion two-year-old last season, and his form entitles him to Guineas favouritism. Possessor of a fine turn of foot, he has the best form on offer, having won two Group 1s in Ireland, including the National Stakes (a significant pointer in recent years, with recent winners including Refuse To Bend, Hawk Wing and King Of Kings).

It's difficult to knock his chance, but the bookies now have him on their side and you'll struggle to beat 5-2.

Dermot Weld won the Guineas last year with Refuse To Bend and can repeat the trick with *GREY SWALLOW*.

A ten-length winner of a Galway maiden on his debut, he created quite an impression, prompting his normally reticent trainer to comment that "this is a racehorse, and he could be very special".

He then skipped a tilt at one of the autumn Group 1s in favour of a Group 3 at Leopardstown. Once again, he showed a rare ability to quicken and instantly put distance between himself and the opposition.

In beating **Newton**, whose form ties in with horses such as **Pearl Of Love** and **American Post**, by 8l, he stamped himself a class performer and, at a shade over twice the price of One Cool Cat, he represents decent value.

The plan is apparently to go the Refuse To Bend route, i.e. Leopardstown's Guineas Trial, then straight to Newmarket. If, as I expect, he wins on his reappearance, he could well be disputing favouritism on the big day.

Whatever you do, don't touch the 10-1 about American Post. His owner has Three Valleys for this race and the Racing Post Trophy winner is being aimed at the French Guineas.

The same goes for champion two-year-old **Bago**, whose trainer has intimated that the English Guineas is not really on the agenda, despite him having a precautionary entry in the race.

Although breeding suggests that **Three Valleys** could, in theory, get as far as 1m4f, his performances to date pose a big question mark regarding his chances of seeing out a mile. He has always been highly thought-of at home and works brilliantly by all accounts.

We punters got our first viewing of that ability when he ran out an impressive winner of the Coventry Stakes at Royal Ascot. His defeat in Ireland by One Cool Cat can be excused, as he returned with mucus in his lungs, but in winning the Middle Park (he was subsequently disqualified when testing positive for a banned substance), he appeared to put himself firmly back in the Guineas picture.

However, as a guide to the Guineas, the Middle Park has a poor recent record, with most of its winners turning out to be sprinters, and his performance when stepped up to 7f in the Dewhurst didn't convince me that he will get a mile this year.

I wouldn't have **Milk It Mick** on my mind for this. He'd looked an exposed sort prior to his shock win in the Dewhurst and his success suggests that the race was a far-from-vintage renewal. For that reason, I'm also happy to take on third-placed **Haafhd**, whose failure to handle the

Rowley Mile's undulations gives cause for concern, Guineas-wise.

In fact, it would be no surprise if Sir Michael Stoute's **Imperial Stride**, who could only finish sixth, were to reverse the form with those in front of him. Inexperience beat him in the Dewhurst, but he has plenty of scope for improvement and is sure to stay the trip.

Mark Johnston holds a strong hand on paper, with **Lucky Story**, Pearl Of Love and **Russian Valour**.

The last-named looks the weakest of the three, as he was forced to miss the second half of the season following a setback, and on breeding is a doubtful stayer.

Pearl Of Love enjoyed a successful season last year, winning a Listed race at Royal Ascot, a Group 2 in Ireland and a Group 1 in Italy.

However, he probably put up his best performance when third to One Cool Cat, an effort which suggests that a minor role is the best he can hope for at Newmarket.

Johnston's strongest claims come in the form of Lucky Story. A brother to St James's Palace Stakes winner Dr Fong, he impressed in winning the Vintage Stakes and Champagne Stakes despite running green, and the impression given was that he was winning with a little bit up his sleeve.

He'll get the mile alright and should be more the finished article this season, so 14-1 isn't a bad each-way price.

2,000 Guineas								
	Bet365	Chandler	Coral	Hills	Lads	PPower	SJames	Tote
One Cool Cat	**5-2**	2	9-4	7-4	9-4	2	**5-2**	2
Grey Swallow	5	5	**6**	11-2	**6**	5	11-2	5
American Post	8	**10**	-	8	-	**10**	**10**	8
Three Valleys	**10**	**10**	**10**	**10**	**10**	9	8	8
Lucky Story	**14**	12	10	8	12	12	12	**14**
Pearl Of Love	14	**16**	14	14	12	**16**	**16**	**16**
Milk It Mick	16	20	16	16	16	16	**25**	20
Snow Ridge	20	20	20	16	**25**	16	16	20
Diamond Green	14	-	16	**33**	-	16	-	25
Akimbo	25	25	25	25	25	**33**	20	**33**
Haafhd	25	**33**	25	25	25	25	20	25
Auditorium	25	**33**	25	**33**	25	20	25	25
Fantastic View	**33**	**33**	**33**	**33**	**33**	**33**	16	**33**
Peak To Creek	**33**	**33**	25	**33**	**33**	**33**	16	**33**
each-way 1/4 odds, 1-2-3								
Others on application, prices correct at time of going to press								

Newmarket, 1st May 2004

Most of the layers have John Oxx's **Azamour** priced up for the Derby, but not the Guineas. Frankly, I can't see him staying 1m4f and would far sooner back him for Newmarket.

Unbeaten in two starts as a two-year-old, he won the Group 2 Beresford Stakes on his last start, displaying admirable battling qualities to beat Relaxed Gesture, who Dermot Weld considered good enough to contest the Breeders' Cup Juvenile.

Azamour has the potential to develop into a serious contender if showing up well in the Guineas Trial at Leopardstown.

The Prix Morny hero **Whipper** has shown a distinct preference for a soft surface. He ran on well to finish fifth in the Middle Park on good to firm ground, but showed a rounded action that day and it's hard to believe he's going to get his ideal conditions.

Balmont is almost certainly going to be a sprinter this year, as is **Peak To Creek**, despite a win in the 7f Horris Hill Stakes, while **Snow Ridge** looks more of a Derby horse on breeding.

Fantastic View and **Auditorium** have some solid Group form to their names but look just short of the class required, while the Mill Reef form, represented by **Byron** and **Grand Reward**, doesn't look strong enough.

Akimbo's presence in the bookies' lists owes little to form and far more to rumoured ability on the gallops, as well as his high-profile connections.

One potential steamer, though, is the Andre Fabre-trained *DIAMOND GREEN*. Unbeaten in three starts in France, he won a Group 3 on his final start with plenty in hand, his rider spending most of the final furlong looking over his shoulder for non-existent dangers.

He bypassed a clash with American Post in the Grand Criterium due to the testing conditions, which suggests the probable better ground at Newmarket will suit this son of Green Desert. His trainer has already stated that he favours bringing the colt over for the 2,000 Guineas and, with big-name jockey Gary Stevens likely to be in the plate, there's plenty of scope for his current price to shorten before May 1.

1,000 Guineas

Every 1,000 Guineas winner over the last 22 years had Group form as a juvenile. Four races in particular stand out as throwing up Guineas winners year after year – Ascot's Fillies' Mile, Longchamp's Prix Marcel Boussac and Newmarket's Cheveley Park Stakes and Rockfel Stakes.

Sixteen of the last 22 Guineas winners had won and/or started favourite for one of these four races. Another three finished second in one of these key races.

Given the strength of this statistic, the chances are very strong that this year's 1,000 will be won by one of the following ten: **Red Bloom**, **Sundrop**, **Punctilious**, **Denebola**, **Green Noon**, **Necklace**, **Carry On Katie**, **Majestic Desert**, **Cairns** or **Snow Goose**.

It's a very manageable list and one that can be whittled down even further. First for the chop are the Cheveley Park pair.

Carry On Katie looks a sprinter. Her breeding gives some encouragement that she'll get a mile, but her free style of running totally undermines that hope. I'd rather have 12-1 for the July Cup than for the Guineas.

Majestic Desert was a cheap purchase and is unfashionably bred. While in theory she should improve for the step up to a mile at three, it's more than likely that we saw the best of her at two.

In Boussac winner Denebola we have the ideal Guineas candidate – on paper. By Storm Cat, out of the 1994 Guineas third Coup De Genie, she's bred to be a top-class miler and, so far, she's looked it.

After her running-on third in the Prix Morny over a trip too short, the step up to a mile for the Boussac was always going to suit. She travelled supremely well and cut through the field inside the final two furlongs, eventually scoring even more cosily than the short-neck winning distance implies.

Two things temper enthusiasm. First, she has never run on anything quicker than good to soft. The ground at Newmarket invariably rides good or faster during Guineas weekend, and her trainer's comment after the Boussac that he "knew she would love the soft going" is consequently worrying.

Second, and more importantly, Pascal

110

Bary has hinted that, following the Six Perfections debacle last season, he's more likely to play safe and keep Denebola at home for the French equivalent. If he has a change of heart, have a saver.

Boussac runner-up Green Noon is trained by Carlos Lerner, who's had just one runner in this country over the last six years, so the odds are that she, too, will be aimed at the French race.

Necklace was sent off favourite at Longchamp following her Moyglare Stud Stakes win, but ran disappointingly. On breeding, she strikes me as more of an Oaks filly than a Guineas contender.

The Rockfel looked a weak renewal last season. Cairns could do no more than run out a clear winner but it must be doubtful whether she wants a mile.

Snow Goose enjoyed a successful juvenile campaign but looks short of the class required to win a Classic in this country.

The one I like is the Fillies' Mile winner *RED BLOOM*. Her maiden win has been boosted by the success of the second and third in better grade, and her performance in winning at Ascot was superb – she bettered the new course record for juveniles set earlier in the day by Snow Ridge in the Royal Lodge Stakes.

A miler all over on breeding, one might expect her, as a daughter of Selkirk, to want some give in the ground, but all the evidence points the opposite way. She relishes a fast surface and that's a big plus.

It's difficult to see how Sundrop and Punctilious can reverse the form with Sir Michael Stoute's filly. Sundrop will be better suited by the demands of Epsom.

She may not fit the traditional profile for this, but I do like the look of **Badminton** (was Clive Brittain, now with Godolphin).

Beaten by Carry On Katie in both the Lowther and the Cheveley Park, she was nonetheless staying on well at the end of both those contests. In contrast to the winner, she's bred to appreciate a mile, but news of a minor injury in February tempers enthusiasm for her at this stage.

Attraction proved herself a classy filly during the first half of last season, running away with the Queen Mary and the Cherry Hinton in impressive style.

However, she wasn't seen after July due to a pedal-bone injury and, intriguingly, "changes to her knees". Whatever that means, it doesn't sound like a positive, and her breeding suggests that a mile will be too far for her this year.

Secret Charm has impressed in her two outings to date but her trainer Barry Hills, despite his high profile, has not enjoyed the success one would have expected in the Classics. He has just two successes in the first four Classics of the season to his name, and they were way back in the late 1970s.

Of the rest, **Much Faster** disappointed on fast ground in the Cheveley Park and is a doubtful stayer, while **Well Known** is an Oaks filly on breeding.

1,000 Guineas							Newmarket, 2nd May 2004
	Bet365	Chandler	Coral	Hills	Lads	PPower	SJames	Tote
Red Bloom	10	8	7	8	10	8	8	8
Denebola	10	10	8	10	8	8	10	10
Carry On Katie	10	10	9	10	12	10	9	10
Attraction	10	12	10	10	12	12	9	10
Cairns	16	16	10	14	16	14	16	12
Majestic Desert	20	20	20	16	20	16	20	20
Secret Charm	14	20	16	20	16	20	-	16
Green Noon	14	-	16	-	25	20	-	16
Necklace	25	25	25	20	25	25	20	25
Sundrop	25	25	20	20	25	20	20	25
Well Known	25	20	-	-	25	25	20	20
Badminton	25	25	20	20	25	20	20	33
Catstar	14	-	25	-	33	25	14	25
Phantom Wind	33	33	-	33	25	-	25	33

each-way 1/4 odds, 1-2-3
Others on application, prices correct at time of going to press

Oaks

Taking the best prices, there are three 20-1 co-favourites for the Oaks, and two of them (Secret Charm **and** Red Bloom) **are almost certain not to stay 1m4f. Neither is likely to want to go any farther than 1m2f at most, if breeding is anything to go by, and can be dismissed immediately.**

NECKLACE, on the other hand, has all the attributes one looks for in a possible Oaks filly. By Darshaan out of a half-sister to Opera House and Kayf Tara, she's bred to come into her own over middle distances, but is clearly not short on speed either, as her win in the Group 1 Moyglare Stud Stakes over 7f suggests.

A poor subsequent run in France, on ground (holding) which was meant to suit, was put down to her having not recovered from an aborted trip to Ascot the previous week. It sounded like a bit of a lame excuse but, whatever the reason, one can always forgive a horse one bad run.

We know she acts on good to firm ground, is a lock to get the trip and has top-class form, so she represents a solid bet at the current price.

Sundrop's breeding gives plenty of encouragement stamina-wise, while her experience of running at Lingfield on her debut will be a plus point when it comes to tackling Tattenham Corner.

Well Known will start the season a maiden, but ran with plenty of promise in a 7f conditions race on her debut. Being by Sadler's Wells out of a mare who won a Group race in France over 12 furlongs, she's sure to be in her element when stepped up in trip.

A number of fillies quoted by the bookmakers have plenty to prove on the book. For example, **Treasure The Lady** owes her place in the market to the fact that she's a half-sister to High Chaparral.

All Too Beautiful is a full-sister to Galileo and Black Sam Bellamy, while her stablemate **Because** is a full-sister to Quarter Moon, but neither has run a yard in public.

Spotlight's breeding suggests 1m2f might be her optimum trip this season, as does that of **Punctilious**.

Hathrah has plenty going for her in theory but, as I mentioned in the 1,000 Guineas preview, her trainer Barry Hills has a disappointing record in the Classics.

Kinnaird's breeding gives her every chance of staying 1m4f, but she almost certainly lacks the class required.

An interesting filly is Sir Michael Stoute's **Poise**. By Rainbow Quest out of a Sadler's Wells mare, her trainer thought enough of her to throw her in against two previous winners on her debut in a little 7f conditions event at Newbury.

She ended up sandwiched by the two

Oaks

Epsom, 4th June 2004

	Bet365	Betfred	Chandler	Hills	Lads	PPower	SJames	Tote
Necklace	**20**	16	16	16	12	16	16	**20**
Red Bloom	-	20	20		20	16	**20**	**20**
Secret Charm	14	16	20		-	20	**20**	20
Spotlight	**25**	20	-		-	-	**25**	
Sundrop	16	20	14	12	20	14	**28**	25
All Too Beautiful	25	**33**	**33**		20	25	25	**33**
Hathrah	**33**	**33**	**33**		**33**	25	**33**	**33**
Ithaca	**33**	**33**	**33**	33	**33**	-	**33**	25
Punctilious	**33**	**33**	25		25	25	25	25
Well Known	25	**33**	**33**		**33**	**33**	**33**	25
Poise	25	**40**	25	33	25	25	25	33
Treasure The Lady	25	**40**	**40**		**33**	-	**33**	33
Baraka	-	**40**	**40**		-	33	33	-
New Morning	-	**40**	**40**		**40**	-	**40**	40

each-way 1/4 odds, 1-2-3
Others on application, prices correct at time of going to press

form horses in second place and came out of the race with plenty of credit. A middle-distance filly in the making, she fits into the 'could be anything' category.

Top Romance may be flattered by her win in a slowly-run Oh So Sharp Stakes, as she got the run of the race in front, but she's bred to get middle distances, so could improve on the bare form.

She's a possible player.

Derby

Every year, a whole host of horses are quoted for the Derby who, on breeding, will never stay the trip.

Some people say you can win at Epsom with a ten-furlong horse, just as some stick to the old theory that a 2m4f type is what you want for the Grand National.

It's nonsense.

This year is no different, so to begin with I'm going to put a line through the following list of fancied entrants, many of whom one could argue will get 1m2f, but for whom 1m4f will surely prove too far.

They are: **One Cool Cat**, **Grey Swallow**, **Azamour**, **Akimbo**, **Lucky Story**, **Pearl Of Love**, **Duke Of Venice**, **Fantastic View**.

By contrast, **American Post** has an appealing middle-distance pedigree, and top-class two-year-old form to boot.

I have two worries, though. First, the reason he ran in the Racing Post Trophy at Doncaster was not because his French connections were committed to campaigning him here at three years, but rather so that Khalid Abdullah could secure the British owners' title.

Secondly, despite winning comfortably at Doncaster, the colt carried his head high and didn't seem to enjoy the fast ground.

Having seen that, how keen will Criquette Head-Maarek be to race him on the probable quick ground at Epsom in June? The chances are, it'll be the French Derby for him.

Although **Bago** is clearly an exciting prospect and should get 1m4f alright, the chances of him running in this country are also slim. His trainer has had just one runner in this country in the past five years and I suspect that this colt's June destination is Chantilly.

Following his win in the Royal Lodge Stakes, Marcus Tregoning described **Snow Ridge** as the best two-year-old he had trained.

He certainly impressed that day in coming from way off the pace to win cosily, but his performance when well fancied for the Dewhurst was disappointing, even allowing for the steady early pace.

His dam stayed 2m so there shouldn't be any stamina worries, and one can see quite clearly why Godolphin stepped in to purchase the colt at the end of the season.

	Bet365	Chandler	Coral	Hills	Lads	PPower	SJames	Tote
American Post	**10**	**10**	**10**	7	**10**	**10**	8	**10**
Yeats	10	10	10	8	10	**12**	8	10
Grey Swallow	**14**	12	12	12	**14**	12	11	12
One Cool Cat	**14**	-	-	-	-	-	12	12
Snow Ridge	10	14	14	8	**16**	10	14	12
Bago	14	14	**16**	-	12	14	**16**	12
Magritte	16	**20**	**20**	-	16	16	16	12
Wolfe Tone	20	**33**	25	-	25	**33**	**33**	-
Azamour	25	20	-	-	**33**	20	28	-
Apsis	25	**33**	**33**	-	20	-	-	-
Akimbo	25	33	33	-	33	33	**40**	25
Duke Of Venice	33	33	33	25	33	33	**40**	33
Antonius Pius	33	-	-	33	**40**	**40**	33	33
Mister Monet	40	**50**	-	-	-	33	-	-

Derby   Epsom, 5th June 2004

each-way 1/4 odds, 1-2-3
Others on application, prices correct at time of going to press

Imperial Stride ran well given his inexperience when sixth in the Dewhurst on his final start and, as a brother to High Pitched, he should get 1m4f this year. It's probable that he will be at his best when he can get his toe in, though, and that must be a worry with Epsom in mind.

As usual, Aidan O'Brien has a number of interesting entries. Chief among them is **YEATS**, who scooted home by 4l in a Curragh maiden on his only start to date.

O'Brien, who clearly holds him in high regard, has chosen what he calls the "Galileo route" for the colt, which means he will start off in the Ballysax Stakes and go on to the Derrinstown Derby Trial, before heading for Epsom.

He certainly has the pedigree for the job, being by Sadler's Wells out of a 1m6f winner, and looks a must for the shortlist.

Magritte is a brother to last year's Derby runner-up The Great Gatsby, who had looked more exposed than some of his stablemates at two but improved past them at three.

Whether Magritte can emulate his brother remains to be seen, but the evidence of his Racing Post run suggests he will be happiest with some ease in the ground.

The form of **Wolfe Tone**'s maiden win hasn't worked out at all well, but he's another who has the pedigree – he's bred along similar lines to Singspiel – to develop into a serious candidate.

Antonius Pius's dam won the Yorkshire Oaks but his sire rarely gets winners over middle distances.

Mikado, **Tycoon** and **Cobra** each have the pedigree for the job but will probably be playing in Ballydoyle's second XI this season. Ditto **Moscow Ballet**, who may spend a productive summer pot-hunting minor Classics on the continent.

Apsis is an interesting contender. An impressive winner of a French Group 3 on his final start, his pedigree gives plenty of hope that he will get 1m4f this term, for his dam was a Group 3 winner over the trip and his sire is by Sadler's Wells.

There are worse outsiders in the field than **Salford City**. A half-brother to Salford Express, who won the Dante in 1999, he created a big impression when running away with a Newbury maiden last backend, and success in one of the spring trials will soon

see his price collapse.

However, there's plenty of speed in his pedigree and I've a suspicion that 1m2f might be as far as he will want to go.

Let The Lion Roar, a half-brother to St Leger hero Millenary, showed enough last year to suggest he will be a force over middle distances at Group level this term, but whether he's Derby class must be pretty doubtful.

Both **Sussex** and **North Light** are by Danehill but are out of mares who stayed particularly well, so there's a fair chance they'll get the trip.

MISTER MONET catches the eye, as he showed plenty in two starts at two, despite being bred to appreciate middle distances.

Recommended Bets

2,000 Guineas

3pts Grey Swallow 6-1
(Betfred, Coral, Ladbrokes, Sean Graham)
1pt Diamond Green 33-1
(Hills)

1,000 Guineas

3pts Red Bloom 10-1
(Bet365, Betfred, Ladbrokes)

Oaks

2pts Necklace 20-1
(Bet365, Tote)

Derby

2pts Yeats 12-1
(Paddy Power)
1pt Mister Monet 50-1
(Chandlers)

All bets to win.
Prices correct at time of going to press.

A half-brother to Irish 1,000 Guineas winner Tarascon, he's by Peintre Celebre out of a mare who won over as far as 2m.

His trainer is planning to run him in a Guineas trial prior to the first Classic itself, and a decent effort in either or both of those races will see his odds tumble for the Derby. He's a speculative selection, but we're being offered a generous price.

Sponsored by Stan James

Dave Nevison
Read Dave's diary every week in the RFO

More racing is a lot less

AFTER a cracking 2003, *Outlook* readers may be surprised to hear that I have a white flag tucked in my inside pocket in case I have to wave it at some point during the summer.

My attitude to betting has always been that if I work hard enough, I will be able to keep on top of things and keep myself fully on top of the form book. Well, I have been waving the white flag frantically during the All-Weather season and I am fearing the worst for the turf.

It wasn't so long ago that I felt strong enough to cover Flat and jumps, but I decided three years ago that the jumping had to be ditched if my sanity and also my ability to turn a profit was to be preserved. I am now wondering whether I made the right decision or whether I should cut out the All-Weather, as there just seems to be about 100 per cent more, with the threat of tons more on the horizon.

The main problem with this ever-increasing amount of racing is that all the increase is in the lower levels. The amount of racing has gone up by perhaps 30 per cent but the amount of good racing has stayed the same.

We are getting overwhelmed by a tidal wave of flotsam and I guarantee that not many punters will survive it. The fact is, we are not meant to survive it.

The aim of more racing is not to provide exercise facilities for horses barely capable of putting one leg in front of the other, it is purely an attempt to siphon more money out of the punter.

The people who control the sport that we love obviously believe that the more times the wheel spins, the more profit the bookies and ultimately racing will make.

They have obviously looked at the success of virtual racing in forming this opinion and, I suppose, who can blame them?

Personally, I think this is a poor argument, certainly for anyone who genuinely cares about racing.

Lowering the overall quality of the game does not, in my view, generate increased enthusiasm for it. In fact, it will ultimately prove the reverse, with horseracing regarded as the domain of the chancer with the dog-end in his mouth.

Virtual racing caters for the idler who is wasting his day away in the betting shop of an afternoon. He is hardly the most discerning or, I would have thought, the most affluent customer.

I believe (and I hope I am right) that more money is actually bet on horseracing by people a few links higher up the food chain, who actually do some amount of work on

> *"It wasn't so long ago that I felt strong enough to cover Flat and jumps, but I decided three years ago that the jumping had to be ditched. I am now wondering whether I made the right decision"*

their selections and believe they have some sort of chance as a result. At the moment, these punters are being treated with contempt by the authorities.

Unless there is a change of attitude, I fear they may disappear eventually.

One thing is for certain, I will be concentrating my efforts on the top end of the range for this coming turf season.

I simply cannot wait for Doncaster to start the ball rolling and, from that moment on, you will be finding me on-course, at places where you would expect to find the BBC and Channel 4 cameras.

The horses that run at the Grade 1 tracks are the glamorous set and are unlikely to be dipping their toes in the murky waters of the Regional Racing tracks – this should enable me to concentrate on a smaller pool of decent, consistent horses.

Unless you have a supreme memory or a perverse appetite for watching endless dross, then I really would advise readers to do the same.

The fact that a rotten dish is served up to you does not mean you have to eat it!

If you can get your area of specialisation right, then I am absolutely sure that the chances of making a profit have never been any better.

We may well have lost a few of the internet bookmaking firms but the betting exchanges have grown phenomenally, despite the best efforts of the bookmakers to discredit them.

The High Street firms are being forced to compete to survive and the Tote has had to cut its margins to keep its market share as well.

All this adds up to the fact that things have never ever been better for the punter, who should find himself betting to minimal margins if he hits the right price.

There has been much talk about integrity in the last year and indeed it is a major concern for 2004.

I have raised my voice a couple of times during the last year about lack of action by the stewards on what I believe were pretty blatant cases of horses not doing as much as they could, and I think punters should be vigilant.

However, I am firmly of the belief that horseracing in this country is inherently straight and that claims of mass non-triers are wide of the mark.

It costs too much to stop a horse, for one thing, and too many people are involved in the process to make it worthwhile.

As ever, the majority of skulduggery goes on at the bottom of the market and, by staying at the top end, you will be largely protected.

Finally, my tips for the 2004 season.

Andrew Balding is expected to maintain his progress up the trainers' table. Like his father before him, he had a dream start to his career, with a Classic win in his first season under his own name.

Cynics would say that he has had a massive leg-up, and this is undeniably true, but he's not a one-hit wonder in my view and his placing of his horses shows a great depth of knowledge of the programme book. Balding is premier league stuff.

I am sure **Hughie Morrison** will continue his rise thorough the ranks and I would advise particular note of his horses when they are coming back from a lay-off. It seems the longer the lay-off, the better he gets them.

Lastly among the trainers I have great hopes for, **John Best** starts the year with some decent two-year-olds for once, instead of the bargain basement stuff he has been dealing with in the past.

Jockeys who will be coming though this winter include **Steve Donohoe**, who has shown himself to be strong and tactically very savvy for his age this All-Weather season.

Attached to David Evans' yard, he will be making an impact in the south this year.

In the north, **Mark Lawson** (who works for Mel Brittain) has had less opportunities so far but is certainly capable of making the most of any chances he gets.

The season really kicks off for me with the 2,000 Guineas, for which I am heavily involved in Mark Johnston's **Lucky Story** at big prices. I backed him after he showed tremendous battling qualities at Goodwood, despite being green.

He did much the same at Doncaster and, although his form may not amount to that of One Cool Cat or Grey Swallow, they will certainly know they have been in a race when they beat him.

With such a tough attitude, it is hard to believe we will lose money backing Lucky Story throughout 2004.

RACING & FOOTBALL
Outlook

Wherever you are, remember to call...

Call Dave Nevison every day and make your bookie pay

0906 911 0234
From Ireland:1570 924351
CALLS COST £1/MIN – RACEFORM – RG20 6NL

Luca back in the big time

ONE OF the things that made the 2003 Flat season so enjoyable was the way the main prizes were spread around.

Coolmore and Godolphin had moderate years by their own standards and, although Sir Michael Stoute was as big as ever, plenty of other trainers got their share of the limelight.

I've nothing against the two big battalions. Bar their policy of cherry-picking, Godolphin in particular have been good for racing.

Their horses are campaigned aggressively, every one is there to do its best, they're very open with the public (something you can't always say about Coolmore) and they have been largely responsible for older horses being kept in training.

Nonetheless, it can get a bit tiresome to see the same connections in the winner's enclosure after every big race.

Such is the power of these two mighty operations, with their huge breeding empires and their massive wealth which makes them so dominant at the sales, that last year's moderate season should probably be seen as a mere hiccup.

Their lack of success, though, in the big two-year-old races suggests 2004 may also be a difficult year for them.

So who are the men and horses to look out for?

Last year I put up Andrew Balding as a trainer to watch and Liam Keniry as a jockey.

Balding had a great season on both sides of the pond. Casual Look gave him his first Classic, while Phoenix Reach landed him a Canadian International at Woodbine.

Keniry's season, in contrast, was a bit of a disappointment and it could fairly be said that he marked time. I've no doubt he has the ability but he'll need better opportunities if he's going to break into the big time.

My two to watch this year are **Luca Cumani** (left) and **Eddie Ahern**. Cumani is hardly a new name (he's been near the top of the tree for 20 years) but, after a few quiet seasons, he showed how well he can do the job with his brilliant handling of Falbrav.

If last year's exploits don't attract the big owners back to his yard, nothing will.

Ahern impresses me more as a jockey every time I see him. He's as brave as anyone riding, more than happy to take the inside route if necessary, and is really strong in a finish.

Of all the young riders around, none appeal more as a future champion jockey.

Morning Mole's horses to follow

AKIMBO
3yo bay colt
Kingmambo – All At Sea (Riverman)
Henry Cecil

One of the saddest aspects of the past few seasons has been the rapid decline in fortunes of Henry Cecil.

Without doubt one of the greatest post-war trainers, personal problems and the loss of the Maktoum horses has seen his stock fall to an all-time low. He needs a star to take him back to the big time and, if he has one, it's surely Akimbo.

This beautifully-bred colt, by Kingmambo out of Oaks runner-up All At Sea, was the talk of the track when he appeared at Newbury last August. His homework had been top class by all accounts and a winning debut was fully expected.

Unfortunately, he threw away his chance in the preliminaries, being coltish in the paddock and green going to post.

In the race, he ran a cracker to finish a close second. With the experience behind him, he'll leave this form far behind.

A medium-sized, athletic horse, he wasn't seen out again due to a slight setback. I expect him to make up for lost time and will be disappointed if he doesn't make up into a Group horse.

A VERY GOOD YEAR
4yo bay colt
Indian Ridge – Ma N'Ieme Biche
(Key To The Kingdom)
Terry Mills

This big, good-looking colt could make up into a top sprint handicapper this season.

In two years' racing, he's only had eight starts and his career to date has been one of steady improvement. His first five runs were over 7f and, although he managed a maiden win at Salisbury, it soon became apparent that speed, not stamina, was his forte.

His performance when routing 16 rivals to take a Kempton handicap was most impressive and marked him down as a sprinter to watch. He would have followed up at Ascot but endured a terrible passage and went down by 2l.

Though expensive for his supporters

(Mole among them), that defeat won't have harmed his handicap mark and he'll start the new season well treated. He's a lightly-raced horse who should continue to improve for some time yet, so don't be surprised if a big handicap comes his way.

HILLS SPITFIRE
3yo bay or brown colt
Kahyasi – Questina (Rainbow Quest)
Peter Harris

I saw this youngster make his debut in a big field of maidens at Newmarket last autumn.

He took my eye in the paddock beforehand. He was a lengthy, well-made colt with plenty of scope but he looked much in need of the run.

Given his appearance, it was no surprise to see him freely available at 33-1 in the ring. He belied those odds, though, with a tremendous run.

After getting outpaced and running green, he flew up the hill to be a short-head second. He looked every inch a stayer there and confirmed that impression when stepped up to 1m2f and raised in class for the Listed Zetland Stakes.

Once again he looked green and once again he was outpaced but he really got going in the final furlong to finish a rapidly-closing fourth.

His breeding suggests that stamina was always going to be his strong suit – he'll want 1m4f or more this year.

Come the summer, races like the Ebor could be on the agenda.

IMPERIAL STRIDE
3yo bay colt
Indian Ridge – Place De L'Opera
(Sadler's Wells)
Sir Michael Stoute

Here is my idea of a lively outsider for the first colts' Classic.

This 375,000gns colt had three runs as a juvenile, winning his first two before finishing sixth in the Dewhurst. When taking his second start by 5l at Doncaster from White Hawk (a winner before and since), he impressed me more than any youngster I saw all year.

MUBTAKER'S BIG MOMENT: he chases home Dalakhani in last year's Arc de Triomphe

Due to a slight setback, he was off the track for three months after this win before reappearing in the Dewhurst. His slightly lacklustre effort that day is easily forgiven and I'm sure we'll see a much better animal this season.

The furthest he's run to date is 7f but his breeding (he's related to a couple of useful middle-distance performers) strongly suggests he'll be suited by further. Around 1m2f will be the order of the day come summer but Newmarket's stiff Rowley Mile in early May should be fine.

MUBTAKER
7yo chestnut horse
Silver Hawk – Gazayil (Irish River)
Marcus Tregoning

Tregoning has quickly established himself as a fine trainer and he's done especially well with older horses. He and Hamdan Al Maktoum, his principal owner, are prepared to give their charges all the time they need.

In my travels to the racecourses, I see so many horses that win or show promise on their debuts but then are swiftly raised in class and asked to do too much too soon. Within a short time, these animals are sweaty and edgy, often with headgear on, and never fulfil their initial promise – this is something Tregoning is rarely guilty of.

In my fantasies (the horseracing kind, not the more lurid type) I imagine winning the lottery and buying three expensive yearlings. I'd place them with Luca Cumani, Alec Stewart and Tregoning, safe in the knowledge that they'd be given every chance to reach their full potential.

Mubtaker has really benefited from this sort of approach. Very lightly-raced, he was better than ever as a six-year-old, winning three times and putting up his best ever performance when second on his final start in the Arc.

Only the top class Dalakhani denied him at Longchamp and who's to say that he won't go one better this season, as he appears to be still improving.

PHANTOM WIND
3yo bay filly
Storm Cat – Ryafan (Lear Fan)
John Gosden

This filly's two runs have been like chalk and cheese.

First time out at Nottingham, she was mulish beforehand and, despite starting a well-backed 100-30 second-favourite, she came stone-bonking last in an ordinary 15-runner maiden. She showed next to nothing that day but that didn't stop punters backing her down to favouritism a couple of weeks later in a better race at Newmarket.

This time her supporters were right, as, after travelling well throughout, she stormed 8l clear once given the office below the distance.

The merit of this performance was further enhanced by an excellent time and I've no doubt she's a Group horse in the making.

The Newmarket win was over 6f and she certainly isn't short of speed. Her breeding suggests she should stay further and, if she does, she could develop into a 1,000 Guineas contender.

Outlook's Horses to Follow

KEY

Name → **GENEROUS** 4 ch c ← age, colour & sex

Sire → **Caerleon – Doff The Derby (Master Derby)** ← Dam

123011/41118- Good, Good to Firm

Career form — Going preference (if any) — Dam's sire

AKIMBO 3 b c
Kingmambo – All At Sea (Riverman)
2-

Backed for the 2,000 Guineas before his debut at Newbury last August, he was sent off 8-11 in a field of 11 and made most of the running. Only inside the final furlong did Mukafeh get to him and Henry Cecils's colt went down by a head, the pair clear. Three of the next four went on to win maidens, so it was almost certainly a decent race. Akimbo is by the sire of Russian Rhythm, out of a mare who was second in the Oaks.

Henry Cecil, Newmarket

ALL TOO BEAUTIFUL 3 b f
Sadler's Wells – Urban Sea (Miswaki)
Unraced

This is probably the best-bred filly in training, being a full-sister to both Derby winner Galileo and Group 1 winner Black Sam Bellamy. Urban Sea, who won the Arc in 1993, also gave birth to Melikah and Urban Ocean, both of whom won good races. So it is almost inconceivable that All Too Beautiful, owned by Michael Tabor, isn't top drawer. She was entered in several Irish maidens last October but never ran. Word from across the sea is that she'll make up for her absence.

Aidan O'Brien, Ireland

ALMUTASADER 4 b c
Sadler's Wells – Dreamawhile (Known Fact)
047/1114- Good, Good to Firm

After three poor runs as a two-year-old, he began the season on a handy mark of 67 and exploited it to the full with a handicap hat-trick. The third of these wins came in a 1m6f event at Sandown, where he stayed on strongly. The assessor put him up 12lb and it was hardly surprising that next time he was anchored in Doncaster's Mallard Handicap. But, with only seven races under his belt, he has scope for improvement. He could be a contender for decent staying handicaps such as the Ebor.

John Dunlop, Arundel

BALTIC KING 4 b c
Danetime – Lindfield Belle (Fairy King)
4241/122043100- Good to Firm

Began last season by winning a 6f classified stakes at Leicester and went from strength to strength, although he only won one more race. That was a Class B handicap at Ascot over the minimum trip, when he beat Salviati by two and a half lengths. Other good runs included his second behind Deportivo in the 5f Balmoral Handicap at Royal Ascot and his third in Doncaster's Portland. Unlucky on three occasions, he is a Group-class sprinter waiting to happen. He hates any stickiness in the ground.

Hughie Morrison, East Ilsley

BAY TREE 3 b f
Daylami – My Branch (Distant Relative)
1100- Good to Firm

Looked promising after her first two starts, the second of which was the Sweet Solera Stakes at Newmarket over 7f, in which she put up a good time. She then had two months off before returning for the Prix Marcel Boussac over a mile at Longchamp. A poor run there was followed by an equally poor one in Newmarket's Rockfel Stakes 12 days later. Fillies are none too predictable and it may pay to forgive this one her disappointments and concentrate on her achievements. She's been switched to Loder from Barry Hills, a move which, at the least, is unlikely to result in deterioration.

David Loder, Newmarket

DALISAY 3 b f
Sadler's Wells – Dabiliya (Vayrann)
0-

The Beech House Stud Maiden Stakes, run at Newmarket's Cambridgeshire meeting, is invariably a source of future winners. Sir Michael Stoute uses it for his better two-year-olds and had three runners this time. Dalisay, who earned the comment "good sort" from Raceform for her paddock-looks, also caught the eye going to post. She wasn't nearly so impressive coming back, though, finishing 20th of 23. She is choicely-bred, being by the world's greatest sire and out of a mare who is closely-related to Darshaan. It will be a major surprise if she doesn't turn out half-decent in time.

Sir Michael Stoute, Newmarket

DENEBOLA 3 br f
Storm Cat – Coup de Genie (Mr Prospector)
4131-

Pascal Bary, who had such bad luck last season with Six Perfections, could be forgiven if he keeps this star in France this season. Should she run in the 1,000 Guineas, however, she would have a great chance, especially as the English fillies look below average. She showed her true self in the Prix Marcel Boussac at Longchamp, when she stepped up to a mile after three races over 6f or less. She quickened up nicely and, though only beating Green Noon by a 'short-neck', was always holding her off.

Pascal Bary, France

DOYEN 4 b c
Sadler's Wells – Moon Cactus (Kris)
5/11124-

With only six runs under his belt, the best has yet to be seen of Doyen, who finished off last season with a fourth in the Arc when with Andre Fabre. He's a tall, unfurnished sort and looks like a balloon that's only been three-quarters blown up – another year on his back and he could be the real deal. He was second to Dalakhani in an Arc trial and he didn't get the best of runs in the Arc itself. A superbly-bred colt out of a Lupe winner, he should stay at least 1m4f and act on a range of goings.

Saeed Bin Suroor, Newmarket

DUBAI SUCCESS 4 b c
Sadler's Wells – Crystal Spray (Beldale Flutter)
17513- Soft

In running a 4l third to Imperial Dancer in the St Simon Stakes at Newbury at the end of October, Dubai Success indicated his potential as a stayer. The race was run in a decent time and the second horse was the consistent High Accolade. Previously, Dubai Success had won the Listed Troy Stakes on good ground and been down the field in the Great Voltigeur and Gordon Stakes. Dubai Success has a pronounced knee action, so the more cut the better. The Yorkshire Cup is his early-season target.

Barry Hills, Lambourn

ELSHADI 3 b c
Cape Cross – Rispoto (Mtoto)
114- Good to Firm

Big and weak as a two-year-old, this one wanted every yard of a mile. His second victory came in the Haynes Hanson & Clark over that trip at Newbury, the race in which so many future stars have run. His stablemate Nayef made his debut in this and Elshadi could be just as talented – at no stage in last year's renewal did he look like being beaten. It was a different story at Ascot, however, because he was found out by the over-watered soft ground (it was officially good to firm). His pedigree is an interesting mixture of speed and stamina.

Marcus Tregoning, Lambourn

FAVOURABLE TERMS 4 b f
Selkirk – Fatefully (Private Account)
11215- Good, Good to Firm

In an effort to keep more fillies in training as four-year-olds, the BHB has raised the Falmouth Stakes to Group 1 status, a fact that won't have escaped the notice of Sir Michael Stoute, who may well aim Favourable Terms at this Newmarket race in July. Unraced at two, she won three of her five as a three-year-old, including the Group 2 Matron Stakes at Leopardstown over a mile. That race will also be Group 1 this year and is another obvious target. She's going to have to improve a little to be involved at the highest level but there are few better exponents of training older fillies than Stoute.

Sir Michael Stoute, Newmarket

HIGH ACCOLADE 4 b c
Mark Of Esteem – Generous Lady (Generous)
3183/111626212- Good to Firm

You should have a lot of fun following this fellow in 2004, especially as, if last season is anything to go by, he will be kept busy. It wasn't a vintage St Leger in which he came second to Brian Boru but he achieved Classic success of a sort when he won the 'Ascot Derby' (aka the King Edward VII Stakes) by a clear two lengths. His backers were unfortunate not to collect at the juicy price of 9-2 in the Gordon Stakes, when he was hampered in midfield and also received a crack over the nose. He could start off in the Hardwicke Stakes and take it from there.

Marcus Tregoning, Lambourn

MAJESTIC MISSILE 3 b c
Royal Applause – Tshusick (Dancing Brave)
211161- Good, Good to Firm

This colt will bid for top honours in the sprint division and there's every reason to think he could be successful, if his running in the Cornwallis Stakes at Ascot is to be believed. The hallmark of a top sprinter is to find a turn of foot entering the final furlong, and Majestic Missile did just that when beating Nights Cross by three and a half lengths over 5f. The only time he tried 6f, in the Gimcrack, he failed to see it out, although the margin was only two and a half lengths. He may get 6f as a three-year-old, which would widen his opportunities. One thing he must have, though, is a fast surface.

William Haggas, Newmarket

MILLENNIUM JUNIOR 2 ch c
Dubai Millennium – Zelanda (Night Shift)
Unraced

Sheikh Mohammed considers this colt one of the best from Dubai Millennium's first and only crop of foals – of which there were 56. The sire was a brilliant racehorse and the Sheikh was devastated when he died of grass sickness before his full potential as a stallion could be realised. Junior is a half-brother to Pearl Grey, the runner-up to Attraction in the Cherry Hinton. We can expect results from this one.

Saeed Bin Suroor, Newmarket

MR LAMBROS 3 ch c
Pivotal – Magical Veil (Majestic Light)
3-1

Made his debut in November on the All-Weather in a Lingfield conditions race, and refused to leave the stalls properly. He also ran green, so did well to come within two necks of Petardias Magic. Next time, in January, he did much better. Despite being slowly away again, he completely dominated an above-average 7f Lingfield maiden. Martin Dwyer hit the front after two furlongs and never looked back to win by 4l. When we spoke to the trainer over the winter, he was really looking forward to campaigning this colt. There's a mixture of speed and stamina in the pedigree.

Andrew Balding, Kingsclere

MUKAFEH 3 b c
Danzig – Bint Salsabil (Nashwan)
13-

This could be a Group contender over distances between 6f and a mile. He made his debut at Newbury, upsetting the highly-regarded Akimbo by a head, the pair well clear of the third. Three of the next four home won maidens soon afterwards. His subsequent Doncaster run was a tad disappointing but Mukafeh was always going to do better at three. John Dunlop knows his family well and trained both the dam and the grand-dam, Salsabil. Danzig is an outstanding sire of sprinters and milers and Mukafeh is a Group winner waiting to happen. Pencil him in for the Jersey Stakes.

John Dunlop, Arundel

NORTH LIGHT 3 b c
Danehill – Sought Out (Rainbow Quest)
21-

Here's a lightly-raced colt with potential, breeding and a great trainer. He made his debut in a 7f Sandown maiden, coming second to Post And Rail (see below), with the third horse 3l away. This was the race in which Rimrod beat Oasis Dream in 2002 and the field looked equally strong in 2003. The third, fourth, fifth, eighth and 12th were all next-time-out winners. North Light went on to take a Goodwood maiden at 1-5. He's out of the top-class French-trained stayer Sought Out and is a full-brother to Researched. He should make his mark in the best company.

Sir Michael Stoute, Newmarket

PERSIAN MAJESTY 4 b c
Grand Lodge – Spa (Sadler's Wells)
1/1-

Peter Harris has had nothing but trouble from this colt of the utmost potential. He went into last year's 'To Follow' list on the strength of a maiden victory at Newmarket's Cesarewitch meeting. A bruised foot kept him off the track until Royal Ascot, where he won the Listed Hampton Court Stakes over 1m2f. He should be rated much better than the neck margin by which he beat Foodbroker Founder, because he ran green and was looking about him. Another injury meant that he missed the rest of the campaign but he'll be back (fingers crossed) for a Group-race programme.

Peter Harris, Berkhamsted

PHANTOM WIND 3 b f
Storm Cat – Ryafan (Lear Fan)
01- Good to Firm

Plum last on her Nottingham debut in September, when she was extremely slowly away, she returned just over two weeks later to win a maiden at Newmarket by 8l. The runner-up franked the form by scoring next time. John Gosden trained her dam to win the Prix Marcel Boussac as a two-year-old, as well as the Falmouth and the Nassau Stakes at three. The evidence suggests Phantom Wind will be most effective at around a mile.

John Gosden, Manton

Sponsored by Stan James

PHOENIX REACH 4 b c
Alhaarth – Carroll's Canyon (Hatim)
2/1131-

The form of a Salisbury maiden in June 2002 has worked out well; first and second were Norse Dancer and Phoenix Reach. The former was third in the 2,000 Guineas, the latter won the Canadian International. The Salisbury race was Phoenix Reach's only outing at two. As a three-year-old, he also won a Newbury maiden and the Gordon Stakes at Goodwood, as well as being placed in the St Leger. He will contest Group 1 races over 1m4f and 1m2f, with the King George as the main objective. There's more to come.

Andrew Balding, Kingsclere

POST AND RAIL 3 b c
Silver Hawk – Past The Post (Danzig)
1-

This Derby entry's win was, on the face of it, nothing of note, just a Class D maiden at Sandown. Yet the second, third, fourth, fifth, eighth and 12th were all next-time-out winners. Furthermore, Rimrod had beaten Oasis Dream in the same contest the previous year. Post And Rail travelled strongly throughout on the soft ground and was only hand-ridden by Richard Hughes. He has plenty of scope and Silver Hawk's offspring tend to do better at three than as juveniles. He should win races at 1m2f and possibly even 1m4f.

Ed Dunlop, Newmarket

RAKTI 5 b h
Polish Precedent – Ragera (Rainbow Quest)
11/1111630/1212- Good to Firm

Rakti suffered a fetlock crack after his second to Nayef at Royal Ascot. On his comeback in October, he won the Champion Stakes and then came second to Falbrav in the Hong Kong Cup. Trained in Italy before joining Michael Jarvis at four, he offers the Newmarket elder statesman a serious chance of mopping up Group 1 events over 1m2f. Even though Rakti won the Derby Italiano in 2002, Jarvis may be more inclined to drop him back in trip rather than return to 1m4f. Rakti has a good turn of foot and goes on most grounds, though good to firm seems ideal.

Michael Jarvis, Newmarket

RUSSIAN VALOUR 3 b c
Fasliyev – Vert Val (Septieme Ciel)
31211-

Made a name for himself in the Norfolk Stakes by upsetting hot favourite Kheleyf, who was meant to be David Loder's best two-year-old. This one also attracted attention because of his exceptional size. Johnston reported that his racing weight was 560kg, making him the heaviest horse that the Middleham man has trained to win a race. Ascot was the last we saw of him but he is reported to have done well. He's entered in the 2,000 Guineas but sprinting could be his game. All his races have been over 5f.

Mark Johnston, Middleham

SAHOOL 3 b f
Unfuwain – Mathaayl (Shadeed)
01-

A big filly, she made an inauspicious debut in the New Ham Maiden Fillies Stakes at Glorious Goodwood, coming sixth to Ithaca. By November, she had started to fill that enormous frame and charged home the three-and-a-half-length winner of a Nottingham maiden on good to soft. The ground suited her much better than some of the 16 others but that's not to say she won't be just as effective on a faster surface. Expect her to make an impact at below top class over middle distances.

Marcus Tregoning, Lambourn

SALFORD CITY 3 b c
Desert Sun – Summer Fashion (Moorestyle)
1-

A Derby entry and a half-brother to Dante winner Salford Express, also trained by Elsworth, he has had one race. It was at Newbury in late October, a maiden over a mile, and Salford City fell out of the stalls. So to win the race by 7l was some feat, especially as the ground was good to firm and there were some nice sorts among the 16 others. A week later, the sixth-placed runner won at Lingfield. It's difficult to assess a horse on just one run, but he looks an exciting prospect.

David Elsworth, Whitsbury

SILK FAN 3 b f
Unfuwain – Alikhlas (Lahib)
2211- Good to Firm

At first sight, Silk Fan's claim to fame appears to be a second to 1,000 Guineas favourite Red Bloom in a Newmarket maiden. But her run next time at Salisbury was much more striking. It was only a Class D event but she won it with authority and there were 16 other nice sorts behind her. She made most of the running and stretched out to come home 2l clear. Similar tactics were employed next time at Newbury in a 7f conditions event, where they worked a treat. Races at a mile and further on quick ground will suit her. Note that Walter Swinburn is among the owners.

Peter Harris, Berkhamsted

SNOW RIDGE 3 b c
Indian Ridge – Snow Princess (Ela-Mana-Mou)
110- Good to Soft

Having won on his debut at Kempton, he went straight to Ascot's Royal Lodge Stakes. Still fifth at the furlong pole, Snow Ridge swept past his rivals and won going away. In the post-race interview Tregoning upped the ante: "He's the best two-year-old I have trained," he asserted. Snow Ridge was a big letdown in the Dewhurst, beaten 4l. He can act on fast ground but, like many Indian Ridges, he goes better with some cut. Brilliantly bred, he is now with Saeed Bin Suroor and should be on all shortlists for the 2,000 Guineas and the Derby. If it comes up soft in the former, we will be betting.

Saeed Bin Suroor, Newmarket

Sponsored by Stan James

UNSHAKABLE 5 b g
Eagle Eyed – Pepper And Salt (Double Schwartz)
52/11823/7628007- Good

Seven runs over either a mile or 7f brought no reward last season but there is surely a big pot waiting for this genuine sort. He ran a blinder in the Royal Hunt Cup, finishing about 6l behind Macadamia, and was only beaten in the last strides next time. Bob Jones had him gelded over the winter to calm him down. The trainer reports that Unshakable has lost a bit of weight but none of his wellbeing. The Lincoln is the early-season target (assuming he gets in) and 1m2f handicaps are also on the agenda.

Bob Jones, Newmarket

VAUGHAN 3 b c
Machiavellian – Labibeh (Lyphard)
01-

This one was beaten 15 lengths at Newbury on his debut but was a different proposition at Nottingham next time, when he beat Rarefied by 5l to land a mile maiden. The good to soft ground may have exaggerated his superiority but it was an impressive second run and he should act on faster ground if he takes after his sire. Described by Raceform's racereader as a "massive individual", he has only to put muscle onto his frame to make up into a formidable beast. He is entered in the Derby.

Amanda Perrett, Pulborough

YEATS 3 b c
Sadler's Wells – Lyndonville (Top Ville)
1-

Either we've been given it straight up or we've been put away big time. We're referring to the Galileo comparison espoused by Aidan O'Brien after Yeats's maiden win at The Curragh in September. "We'll go the Galileo route with him," said O'Brien, "taking in the Derrinstown Stud Derby Trial." O'Brien is not one to get excited – indeed, he is the epitome of cool – and he is not one to misjudge a horse. It's fair to assume that Yeats showed him just as much as Galileo and if Yeats doesn't live up to Galileo standard, then it will be because he hasn't trained on. He's our idea of the Derby winner.

Aidan O'Brien, Ireland

RFO's top 10 to follow

Baltic King	North Light
Doyen	Phoenix Reach
Dubai Success	Unshakable
Elshadi	Vaughan
Mr Lambros	Yeats

Berkshire by Downsman

ROGER CHARLTON must have felt supremely satisfied with the 2003 season when Patavellian **crossed the line ahead of a strong field in the Group 1 Prix de l'Abbaye at Longchamp's Arc meeting in early October.**

That victory not only highlighted yet another brilliant training performance from the Beckhampton team, but set the seal on his campaign, which almost mirrored the amazing summer we all experienced in Lambourn. There were many, many highs, and not too many lows.

But the storm clouds were already gathering when the turf season drew to a close in early November.

Three Valleys, the stable's best juvenile, and an impressive winner of the Group 1 Middle Park Stakes, had failed a drugs test. Faint traces of a cough cure were found in the sample taken after that Newmarket triumph and he had to be disqualified.

Naturally, the Beckhampton team were bitterly disappointed, especially as they had worked so hard to keep him healthy after a midseason virus proved difficult to shake off. But it has made them equally determined to put the record straight this year.

Whether or not Three Valleys gets to make his mark in the Guineas remains to be seen. Although he has not grown much, he has thickened up, so he should have trained on.

But will he stay?

Matters should become clearer when he tackles the Craven Stakes over the Rowley Mile in April. If he lasts home, he heads for the first Classic – if not, he will go sprinting.

Which brings us back neatly to the afore-mentioned Patavellian. Yes, his Manton neighbour Oasis Dream should be given the mantle of best sprinter, but you can take it from me there was no more popular speedster among the locals than 'The Pat'.

Apart from his somewhat unlucky defeat in the Wokingham, he landed three very shrewd gambles, at Windsor (what a good thing he was there), in the Bunbury Cup and, most significant of all, in the Stewards' Cup.

Connections were left wondering if he could graduate to the very highest level after that success. His victory in the Abbaye, after a troubled autumn preparation, gave them their answer.

He looks a leading contender for top sprint honours, but it should also be borne in mind that the Charlton camp have two more

A CLASS APART: Patavellian mocks the handicapper, winning the Stewards' Cup easily

> *"Gosden's fillies seem particularly promising and one of the most exciting is Phantom Wind, who ran no race at all on her debut but then hacked up on her only subsequent star"*

potential Group 1 stars in this category, **Deportivo** and **Avonbridge**.

To add to this heady mix of sprinting talent, Charlton has a large number of maidens with which to go to war.

Alderney Race is a must for any list. He has delighted connections with his progress and should soon be improving on his fourth in what looked a very good backend maiden at Newbury.

Song Of Vala was another to show potential at our home track and should pay his way at trips around a mile or 1m2f, and there will be some long faces if **Extra Cover** cannot hit the bookies for six.

Motorway, an unraced colt owned by Martin Myers, should give that great supporter of racing plenty to cheer, and those looking for a potentially nicely-handicapped three-year-old should ink in **Worcester Lodge**. He was disappointing last season, but has been gelded.

Kind, and the very well-bred **Well Known** already have some high-grade juvenile form behind them and should make their presence felt in the top fillies events.

Oasis Dream apart, *JOHN GOSDEN* did not have the greatest season by his own high standards. The juveniles seemed quite backward and really did not cut too much mustard at the highest level.

That is not to say that they will not make their mark this term, however.

The fillies seem particularly promising and one of the most exciting is **Phantom Wind**, who ran no race at all on her debut but then hacked up on her only subsequent start at Newmarket. She is exceptionally well bred and looks sure to train on.

Other fillies to look out for are **Dream Scene**, **Moonlight Tango** and **Proud Tradition**, whilst **Slavonic** and **Preview** should ensure the fairer sex do not have everything their own way.

MARCUS TREGONING's season followed a similar path to that of his Beckhampton counterpart in that an extremely successful

summer was followed by an end-of-term setback. Snow Ridge, impressive winner of the Group 2 Royal Lodge Stakes at Ascot and generally considered a live hope for the Guineas and the Derby, found his way into the ever-eager arms of Godolphin in a private deal.

The Kingwood team were convinced he was their best two-year-old last season, but he was not the only star talent on show and hopes are high that they have others capable of developing into Group performers.

Two very high up the list are the closely-related **Thaminah** and **Oriental Warrior**. Both are from the amazingly successful Height Of Fashion female line and are expected to uphold the family tradition begun by the likes of Unfuwain and Nashwan in the late 1980s and carried on to a very high standard by Nayef over the past three seasons.

Both of Thaminah's outings came at the backend. She had "certain future winner" written all over her when she made her debut at the Newmarket Cesarewitch meeting and duly delivered at Doncaster in the closing week of the season.

Although she stepped back from 7f to 6f to record that success, Tregoning is confident she will both get the mile and improve sufficiently, when the spring gallops begin, to earn a tilt at one of the Guineas trials.

Oriental Warrior showed his quality when he won over 6f on his debut effort at Newbury. He was always going to win, despite the trip being short of his best, and there was even more to like about the manner of his follow-up success at Ascot.

Described as a really tough sort by his trainer, he (like Thaminah) is expected to come to hand quite early and will have one of the 2,000 Guineas trials on his agenda.

Mustajed was the first of the classy Kingwood juveniles into play last season, but he was unable to fulfil his potential after his debut win at Newbury. He injured a hind pastern, but that is now fully recovered and he is back in full work.

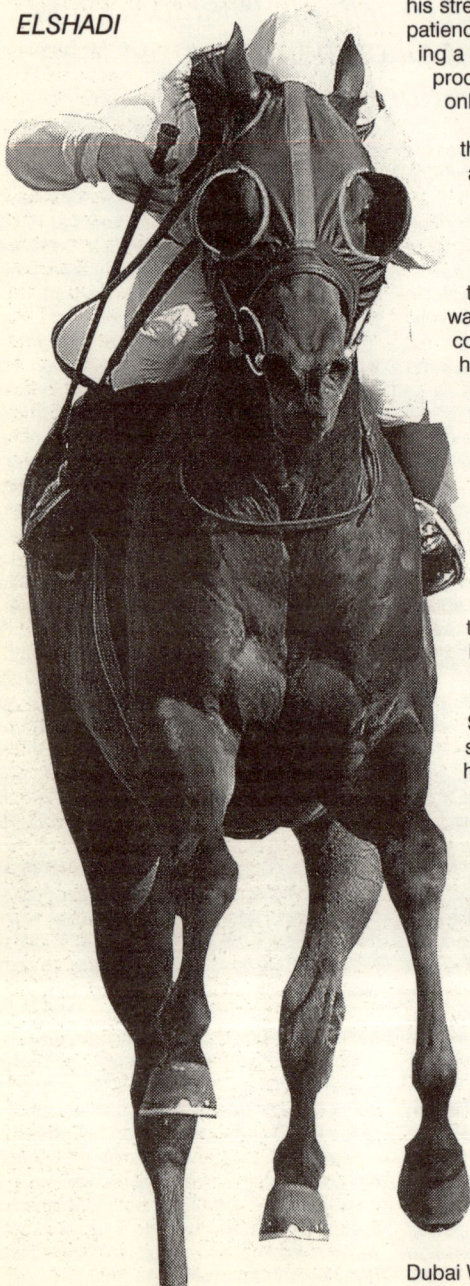

ELSHADI

Tregoning's determination over four seasons to give Nayef a full chance to grow into his strength highlighted the Cornishman's patience with his charges, and he is adopting a similar approach to **Manyana**, who produced an ultra-game effort to win his only race at Sandown in the summer.

He had his niggling problems after that win, so it was decided to put him away for the remainder of the campaign. He is back fit and firing now.

Elshadi won his first two last season before disappointing at Ascot and he will not be rushed into action this season. Although the ground was wrong for him at the Berkshire course, his trainer believes he outgrew his strength after an end-of-season "growth spurt". He should reappear in May.

So Will I is a slightly less exposed member of the line-up. He has been bought by Tregoning's boss Sheikh Hamdan after winning a maiden at Newbury on his second and final start of the campaign in October.

Tregoning really likes this colt and thinks he will stay sufficiently to run in a Guineas trial, despite having speed on both sides of his pedigree.

Two staying fillies to watch are **Sahool**, who impressed on her final start, and **Nuzooa**, who could well have the Cheshire Oaks on her agenda.

Once-raced **Meneef** and newcomer **Tettcott** are two maidens to note down.

Last, but no means least of the classy three-year-olds is **Tree Chopper**, a half-sister to **Mubtaker**, who, quite rightly, takes pride of place among the Kingwood older division this season.

What a grand horse Mubtaker is. As good at 1m2f as at 1m6f, his ultra-game run to finish second to Dalakhani in the Arc was one of the performances of the season.

Tregoning reasons with justification that Mubtaker will have a go at most of the top 1m4f races this season, but he will have a break after his intended first outing in the Sheema Classic at the Dubai World Cup meeting in March.

Sponsored by Stan James

Mubtaker spearheads a strong team of older horses. **High Accolade** developed into one of the very best middle-distance three-year-olds last season and will be looking to improve further this term. He will reappear in May and then go straight to Royal Ascot, where the Hardwicke will be his target.

The progressive **Alkaadhem**, a Godolphin throw-out, did really well for Tregoning in a light campaign last season and may give the Lincoln a try, whilst **Alrabab** will be attempting to consolidate her climb up the ladder in the second half of last term with more pattern victories. A big scopey mare, she should be up to the task.

BARRY HILLS is always the man to follow at the Doncaster Lincoln meeting and there is every chance **Pablo** will be back to try and follow up his 2003 success in the meeting's showpiece.

The Faringdon Place maestro is also very adept at getting his maidens ready to win at the three-day fixture, and three to watch (should they turn up) are **Flamboyant Lad** and **City Palace**, both of whom showed promise at the backend, and the unraced **News Sky**.

Also on the early beat are **Private Charter** (he may run in the Winter Derby on Lingfield's polytrack on March 20) and **Mutawassel**, who wants soft ground.

There is plenty of Classic potential in the yard this year.

The standout would have to be Radley Stakes winner **Secret Charm**, who could be very good. Other fillies for the short-list are **Tarot Card**, who is much stronger this year, and **Lucky Pipit**, who also showed promise in top company.

La Cucaracha, who looked a Queen Mary filly in the first half of last season until sustaining an injury, is healthy again, while very good things are expected of **Brindisi**.

Haafhd, a highly creditable third in the Dewhurst, is clearly top of the pile of the Hills three-year-old colts on racecourse form, and he is more than capable of making the improvement required to run a big race in the Guineas. It should be borne in mind that things were far from straightforward for him after his impressive Newbury win in August.

But there are much less exposed ones doing well enough to suggest they have plenty of class. One of their number is **Aqualung**.

Over The Rainbow will start off low, possibly in the north, but should do well over middle-distances and further, and another of the same ilk is **Coming Again**, a fair

SO CLASSY: High Accolade, jockey Martin Dwyer and trainer Marcus Tregoning at Ascot

second to So Will I at Newbury.

Oman Gulf, who beat a good field of maidens at Newmarket before giving his pelvis a nasty whack, is off the easy list and another out to make up for lost time.

MICK CHANNON surpassed Hills in both prizemoney and races won last season, to land the area's top trainer honours. He was beaten to the championship itself only by Sir Michael Stoute and Mark Johnston, a cracking performance from a trainer who so often loses his most talented three-year-olds to Godolphin.

Although Channon has plenty of ammunition in the Classic generation for the new campaign, pride of place must go to his remarkable stayer **Misternando**. The ultra-tough three-year-old had the handicapper reaching for the Anadin on a regular basis last season but, not content with winning nine handicaps, he compounded the assessor's problems by ending the campaign with a typically game success in a Listed event.

If he continues to progress, there is no telling how high up the ladder he can climb, but we get a note of warning from the trainer on expecting too much too soon. This is such a laid-back individual, he can take a race or two to get fit.

Channon's star juvenile last season had to be **Majestic Desert**, on the strength of her excellent second to Carry On Katie in the Cheveley Park Stakes. She was only just denied in that 6f dash and the improved performance suggests much better might await this season.

She's likely to go for a trial before a tilt at the Guineas.

The main strength among the West Ilsley three-year-old division lies with the fillies and there is quiet confidence concerning the prospects of **Catherine Howard**. She won her only race last term in style at Lingfield and, like Majestic Desert, has wintered very well.

San Lorenzo proved frustrating to train last season and did not manage to get onto the track, but she has ability in abundance and will make her mark if she can put the niggling problems behind her.

Mahmoom was touted as one of Channon's best colts very early on last season, but he also had to spend some time on the easy list. He enjoyed a backend campaign, however, and won two of his three starts.

Much better is to come, we are assured.

Seneschal beat the useful Bachelor Of Arts by an easy 6l on his second appearance at Windsor in April, but that was the last we saw of him. He is back in good nick now, however, and could be very good.

The same comment applies to **Gatwick**, who should not be long in losing his maiden tag.

BRIAN MEEHAN continues his climb up the prizemoney league. He won over £1 million in win and place money at home and abroad last term, and has more than 100 horses with which to do battle this term.

Meehan did particularly well with his forays to the United States and is keen to build on that success during the course of the new season.

But he will concentrate on the top prizes nearer to home with two of his star juveniles from last term, **Carrizo Creek** and **Cape Fear**. Both deserve to try their luck in the top races, but Cape Fear is likely to miss the Guineas and concentrate his attentions on Royal Ascot.

Although he finished only seventh in the Dewhurst, the ground was not right.

Among the list of Meehan maidens is **Gravardlax**, who was placed in good company on his only two outings last season, and **Pizazz**, who caught the eye on his only outing last season at Newbury.

Leitrim House, the winner of a Newmarket maiden on the first of two outings, should also pay his way, while a newcomer to bear in mind is **Instant Recall**.

Of the older contingent, **Chinkara** is a must for a mention. He developed into a smart handicapper before injury struck last season and, having recovered, he is expected to improve further.

The Newlands trainer is also delighted to have **Indian Country** in his care for the new season. This one was a very good sprinter for Jeremy Noseda two seasons ago.

RUSSIAN RHYTHM

Newmarket by Aborigine

SIR MICHAEL STOUTE is following the increasingly popular pattern of keeping a good filly in training as a four-year-old with his 1,000 Guineas winner Russian Rhythm **and she spearheads her trainer's bid to win a seventh trainer's championship.**

The daughter of Kingmambo was returned at a princely 12-1 for followers of Aborigine when lifting the Guineas, and followed up in both Royal Ascot's Coronation Stakes and the Nassau Stakes at Glorious Goodwood.

Cheveley Park Stud manager Chris Richardson told me: "Mr and Mrs Thompson decided to keep her in training as a four-year-old, as the Jockey Club's new races give older fillies more opportunities."

Like most of the Cheveley Park fillies, she had a winter break at their stud just outside town, but is now back at Freemason Lodge looking a picture. She will take all the beating in the top mile and 1m2f races.

While on the subject of the Stoute team, Classic prospects **Red Bloom** and **Auditorium** showed two-year-old promise and are going sweetly in their conditioning work just now.

LUCA CUMANI had a year to remember with Falbrav but at present there is no visible successor to the superstar, who is now at stud in Japan.

GLOBETROTTER: Rakti exercises on Sha Tin racecourse ahead of the Hong Kong Cup

That said, the highly professional Italian has a strong team and can be relied on to get the best out of the older trio **Ettrick Water**, **Kuster** and **King's County** in handicaps.

MICHAEL JARVIS brought **Rakti** back from injury to win the Champion Stakes and, though he was only second to the brilliant Falbrav when last seen in December's Hong Kong Cup, he was far from disgraced.

With Falbrav out of the way, Rakti will take all the beating in the top 1m2f Group 1 races, as he is the sort to improve with age.

Sadly for Jarvis, Godolphin have once again siphoned off his smart winning juveniles. This season, he will be without Cartography, Dunloskin, Sabbeeh, and Matloob.

DAVID LODER reversed his decision to quit the ranks of the trainers and is now safely ensconced in the historic Egerton House Stables near the July Course.

He has a team of 150 horses and the

Sheikh Mohammed-owned **Razkalla** is one of his best prospects. The six-year-old was working a treat on the All-Weather before competing in Dubai and will continue to pay his way both on the home and international front.

Two other Loder horses to note are the All-Weather winner **Dawn Piper** and **Shami**, who is expected to leave his 2003 form way behind. **Perfect Portrait** is also sure to pay his way.

It was great to see *CLIVE BRITTAIN* moving around the gallops with more fluency after his hip operation. Brittain has a way with older horses – remember Jupiter Island's Japan Cup triumph – and both **Warrsan** and **Santando** are likely to bring back prizes from around Britain and from foreign parts.

SAEED BIN SUROOR had a quiet time here, even though Godolphin's blue colours earned more foreign prizemoney than

Sponsored by Stan James

anyone else. The organisation bought a large number of promising two-year-olds from other yards and, though this policy has yet to yield the anticipated returns, surely **Sabbeeh**, **Matloob** and **Carry On Katie** are destined for rewarding campaigns.

JEREMY NOSEDA is Newmarket's brightest young trainer and, despite the death on the gallops of his potential 1,000 Guineas hope Park Affair, had a great year.

He also lost his unbeaten Cheveley Park Stakes winner Carry On Katie to Godolphin, but produced another potentially top-class filly in **St Francis Wood**.

She had been burning up the gallops before she made a belated debut at Newmarket. As she came into season just before that Listed race, she ran a blinder to be a nearest-finish second to the more experienced Spotlight.

She is a 1,000 Guineas challenger and good value at her current odds.

The Shalfleet trainer also has a smart team of three-year-old colts.

Balmont, his winner of the Gimcrack and (by default) the Middle Park, is entered in the 2,000 Guineas. There is no guarantee he will get a mile but, if he doesn't, there will be rich pickings on the sprinting front, judged on the speed I have seen him show here on the heath.

Peak To Creek is another smart three-year-

HARD TO CATCH: Balmont wins the Gimcrack – he was also awarded the Middle Park

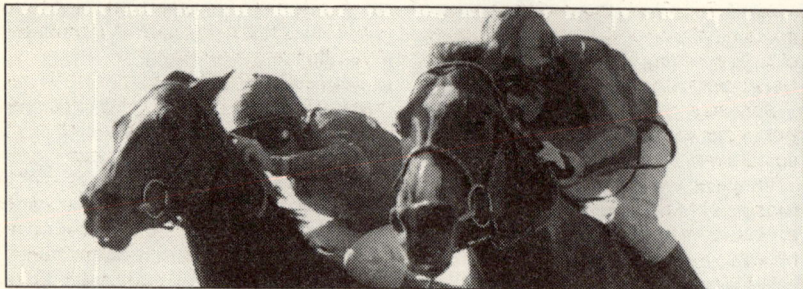

HARD-FOUGHT: Magistretti (right) edges out Dunhill Star for the Dante at York last May

old, who will ensure that Noseda continues to hit the headlines.

JAMES FANSHAWE had a quieter year but a lot of his horses were suffering from the equine flu.

This was the case with his 1,000 Guineas hope **Soviet Song**, who never fully lived up to her two-year-old promise. However, she has wintered a treat and the indications are that she will start making up for lost time around the mile mark.

High Reserve showed promise and, once she is stepped up in trip, can make her mark in decent company.

On the handicap front, Fanshawe should place **Heretic** and **Prins Willem** to advantage, with the latter being my idea of a serious Ebor contender.

NEVILLE CALLAGHAN's Dante Stakes hero **Magistretti** was arguably unlucky in the Derby and found only Falbrav too good for him in the York International.

He has done particularly well over the winter, as has the Solario Stakes winner **Barbajuan**, who is bordering on continental Classic class.

HENRY CECIL soldiers on without the material he used to be sent but, in **Akimbo** and **Ithaca**, his main supporter Khalid Abdullah has a couple of three-year-olds capable of making up into Classic performers.

Among the older horses, shock 50-1 York winner **Bagan** can again score in handicap company.

SIR MARK PRESCOTT always boasts one of the highest wins-to-runners percentages but reading his mind with his handicappers is no easy task!

Keep a weather watch on **Circassian**, **Habitual** and **Pedrillo**, as they will benefit

from being stepped up in trip after showing promise over shorter distances.

ED DUNLOP expects **Anani** to make his mark here after starting his season over in Dubai, while **Ouija Board** underlined her high potential with a staying-on third in a Newmarket Listed Race.

WILLIAM HAGGAS sends out a steady stream of winners and saddled **Chorist** to win three races, including the Group 3 Blandford Stakes at The Curragh.

Cheveley Park Stud keeps her in training and, on the three-year-old front, the speedy **Majestic Missile** will make his presence felt in top 5f events.

CHRIS WALL can make a bright start with his well-handicapped **Ace Of Hearts** being aimed at the Lincoln and **Fanny's Fancy** and **Cimyla** are two other members of the Induna Stables team worth bearing in mind.

JAMES TOLLER is highly capable and handled the Group 3 Pretty Polly Stakes winner Hanami skilfully last season.

His strapping Miswaki colt **Bachelor Duke** was fourth in the Dewhurst and it's not impossible that he could develop into a 2,000 Guineas dark horse.

Stable companions **Wyatt Earp** and **Flamjica** have also come through the winter a treat.

Hot off the Heath

Ace Of Hearts
Anduril
Anousa

Sponsored by Stan James

MARK TOMPKINS rounded the season off in a blaze of glory with his useful three-year-olds **Steenberg** and **Babodana** landing Listed races at Doncaster and Newmarket.

Both stay in training but remember that the former needs fast ground and the latter soft ground.

Tompkins will be hoping that his Oaks runner **Thingmebob** hits the winners' enclosure, as he trains the Bob Back filly for his wife, Angie!

HUGH COLLINGRIDGE's grey colt **Stormont** gave the respected older trainer a Group 2 triumph in the Goldene Peitsche at Baden Baden, and, along with **Hello It's Me**, can achieve more Pattern Race success.

PAUL D'ARCY landed a notable first Classic triumph with **Indian Haven** in last season's Irish 2,000 Guineas, though the rest of his year was a stop/start affair because of firm ground and various injuries.

Said Guineas winner now looks a million dollars and, along with **Forest Magic** (who was being readied for a tilt at the St Leger before injury struck), will pay his way.

JAMES EUSTACE has done readers of this annual many a good turn over the years and, as his horses usually start at decent odds, watch out for **Last Appointment**, **Orcadian** and **Anduril**.

PAUL HOWLING is set for one of his best seasons ever, as **Anousa** and **Nadir** did enough as two-year-olds to suggest they will pick up some top-class handicaps.

DECLAN DALY has made a bright start to his training career. Originally one of Sir Michael Stoute's head lads, he set up on his own after a short spell with Aidan O'Brien.

His list of owners makes for good reading and he is hoping that the exploits of **Hilltop Fantasy** and **Viola Da Braccio**, who made a highly promising debut when backward at Newmarket, will help him attract some more horses.

CONRAD ALLEN has had his fortunes resurrected by the advent of the Alan Brazil Racing Club and Geoff Huffer as assistant trainer. One of the yard's newest owners is the flamboyant Terry Ramsden.

If Ramsden's fluent All-Weather winner **Jake The Snake** wins an early-season conditions race on turf, he will take a tilt at the 2,000 Guineas, for which his punting owner has already backed him heavily!

Ireland
by Jerry M

While most of us were wrapped up in the jumps season and making ante-post bets for the Cheltenham Festival, *DERMOT WELD* was still able to focus on the big Flat handicaps of 2004.

During the winter, he secured **Akshar**, formerly based in Sir Michael Stoute's yard, for 170,000gns at Newmarket's Horses In Training Sale. "I'm open-minded about exactly where to go with him," the Curragh trainer advised at the time, "but I might look at a couple of decent handicaps."

Akshar won three races last season, and was placed in a Group 3 at York in September behind Naheef.

Perhaps his most impressive victory came at Goodwood last May, when beating Macadamia over a mile, but he supple-mented that with other wins at Epsom and York during the summer, as well as another placed effort behind In Times Eye in the Wolferton Handicap at Royal Ascot.

In fact, the only time he disappointed was on his last start in the Cambridgeshire, when he finished down the field despite being well fancied. He is sure to make his mark this coming season, and might well prove better than a handicapper in time.

The 2,000 Guineas at Newmarket has certainly been good to Irish raiders in recent years, with Rock Of Gibraltar and Refuse To Bend nailing the prize in the past two seasons, and it will be a surprise (nay, a disappointment) if we can't make it three in a row, for two reasons – **Grey Swallow** and **One Cool Cat**.

CLASSIC RIVALS: Grey Swallow is fancied for the Guineas but may prefer the Derby trip . . .

Grey Swallow, a son of Daylami in the hands of Weld, has only seen a racecourse twice in his life, but won both of his starts by an aggregate of 18l.

On his debut at Galway, he pulverised Rock Of Cashel by 10l and did the same by 8l to Newton on his final start in a Group 3 at Leopardstown, both wins coming over 7f.

The big question with this colt, however, is how far will he stay? After his Leopardstown win, Weld offered this opinion: "How far he will stay next year, I don't know. Daylami won at up to 1m4f, this horse relaxes and I would certainly see him getting 1m2f."

Grey Swallow has certainly not looked short of pace in his races thus far, so is a legitimate contender for 2,000 Guineas honours, but breeding suggests he should have little problem with 1m4f.

He's out of a mare by Derby winner The Minstrel, so maybe his best chance of Classic honours could come at Epsom, before taking in races such as the Eclipse and the Irish Champion later in the season.

On the other hand, One Cool Cat – by Storm Cat out of a Mr Prospector mare – probably wouldn't care to go further than a mile, and would probably be wholly effective at sprint distances.

He had quite a tough campaign as a two-year-old, winning four from five, with his last two victories coming in Group 1 events at the Curragh.

The first of those came in the Phoenix Stakes last August, where he made Three Valleys look very ordinary (although the latter was reportedly ill) and then on his last start he took in the National Stakes and beat Mark Johnston's Royal Ascot winner Pearl Of Love, amongst others, with ease.

A trademark of his seems to be the ability to make up a lot of ground in a short space of time, so he is very adaptable in a race, as his trainer *AIDAN O'BRIEN* himself

. . whereas One Cool Cat is full of pace and is unlikely to be asked to race beyond a mile

ONE FOR THE FUTURE: Celtic Cat (furthest left) is pipped by Rule Of Law (right) at York

eulogised: "I've never come across a horse with such a blast of speed as this fellow. Mick says he is dangerous."

Such comments provoke memories of King Of Kings – he took the 2,000 Guineas without a prep race, having won the National Stakes at two, and it wouldn't be hard to see One Cool Cat emulating him.

He has it all, and at this stage would be the selection over Grey Swallow if they both went for the Newmarket event. Don't be surprised if O'Brien changes tack through the season and has a crack at the July Cup with One Cool Cat.

The problem with O'Brien 's stable for the coming season is that he has such formidable strength in depth, it's hard to make accurate judgements on who might make it to the top of the tree and who will end up in the Sholokhov role as a near-permanent pacemaker.

One colt who probably hasn't invaded the public's consciousness as yet is **Celtic Cat** but he showed good form at two, is entered in the Derby and may yet emerge from the pack as a genuine Group-class animal.

He won on his debut at Cork last July over 5f, winning by 3l, and was subsequently thought good enough to take over to York's Ebor meeting for a crack at the Listed Acomb Stakes, which has been won by some useful types over the years.

He was outpaced for much of the journey, but two furlongs out the penny really started to drop and he flew at the death, only just failing by a neck behind Rule Of Law.

That was an excellent effort for one so inexperienced and earned him a crack at the Group 1 National Stakes on his third and final start, where he was obviously expected to play second fiddle to One Cool Cat. He went off at 12-1 on the day, so wasn't entirely unfancied and ran respectably in the hands of Seamus Heffernan to finish fifth behind his illustrious stablemate.

Being by Danehill, it's hard to predict his optimum trip, but the way he stayed on at York and the Derby entry suggest that middle-distances will see him at his best. O'Brien has already landed an Irish Derby with one of Danehill's progeny in Desert King, so it wouldn't surprise at all if Celtic Cat stayed well – perhaps even a St Leger trip?

MICHAEL GRASSICK is one of those trainers who don't often grab the headlines but know exactly how to handle a good horse when one comes through their hands – and he probably has one of the best maidens around in the filly **Poetical**.

She didn't start her career until September at the Curragh over 7f, where she ran a race full of promise to be second behind John Oxx's useful Treasure The Lady. On the strength of that, she was made favourite

142

for her next start at Navan in October, but narrowly failed to justify the odds, going under by half a length.

On her last start, she was upped to Listed class for a competitive race at the Curragh, where she again acquitted herself with distinction, running Jim Bolger's Alexander Goldrun to half a length.

Although, on the face of it, it was disappointing that she was unable to rid herself of her maiden tag, that does mean she retains it for the coming season and opportunities shouldn't be hard to find.

Her breeding suggests she will come into her own when sent over further, as she is by Croco Rouge (who was second in a French Derby) out of a Shadeed mare. She ought to be up to winning a Listed event and possibly more.

JOHN OXX showed again last season what a fine trainer he is with his handling of Alamshar. The Currabeg man has several good prospects for this season, best of whom may be the Aga Khan's **Azamour**.

This colt didn't see racecourse action last season until fairly late in the day, making his debut in September at the Curragh.

It was a winning debut, too. He was sent to the front three furlongs from home and responded well to win by two and a half lengths.

He then went for the Group 2 Beresford Stakes (a race that Oxx had won the previous season with Alamshar) and won that as well, showing immense determina-

AZAMOUR

tion to fend off Dermot Weld's Relaxed Gesture by a neck.

However, unlike Alamshar, who found his niche in middle-distance events, Oxx was keen to point out in the aftermath of the win that Azamour does have stamina limitations, so it may well be that a mile proves to be his best trip.

Having said that, the Aga Khan won a French Oaks a few seasons back with a Night Shift filly (Daryaba), so Azamour may yet be sent over further. Either way, he is an excellent prospect and Oxx is sure to find the right races to run him in.

EDWARD LYNAM's **Red Feather**, a Marju filly, should be able to make her mark this term also, having shown good form last season. She won a Limerick maiden last July by a staggering 10l, when the further she went the more she increased her advantage.

That performance meant a step up in grade, and she appeared next in a Group 3 at the Curragh, where she performed with merit to be third behind Necklace.

She was to lock horns again with Aidan O'Brien's filly on her next start in a Group 1 event at the Curragh and improved again, but not enough to turn the tables, going down by a length.

However she showed plenty of guts, throwing down a strong challenge and only giving best close home.

On her final start, she went over to Longchamp for a crack at the Prix Marcel Boussac. Here, she ran her only disappointing race of the campaign, finishing 12th of 16 behind Denebola.

That definitely wasn't her true form – the Curragh runs might have left their mark and it would be unwise to write her off on the strength of her Paris effort.

In any case, she wouldn't have to be up to that class in order to win plenty of races. She remains a bright middle-distance prospect for the season ahead.

Invincible Irish

Grey Swallow
One Cool Cat
Poetical

The North by Borderer

Borderer's annual look ahead to the new Flat season often starts with a close look at the all-conquering _MARK JOHNSTON_ stable and this year is no different.

The Scotsman continues his relentless pursuit of winners at all levels and he is sure to enjoy yet another great year.

His understanding of the racing calendar gives him a distinct advantage over his opponents and he was vociferous in attacking the introduction of 48-hour declarations last season. Johnston explained in detail how the new structure could severely interfere with a trainer's plans of capitalising on a horse's handicap mark.

Regardless of his pet hate, he goes into 2004 with a formidable team and his wife Deirdre issued the stable's wish list for the new campaign.

"It's a while since we won a Classic," she says, "but we've got a serious bunch of three-year-olds to realistically aim at the Guineas. We'll also aim at £2,000,000 in prizemoney again, and 100 winners."

She told Borderer about the stable's Classic hopefuls. "**Lucky Story** is very well and we gave him a long break after last season because he had a fairly long campaign. He had a very easy time before Christmas and we were walking and trotting him in January.

"We don't want to have him ready too soon because there is plenty of time before the 2,000 Guineas. He looks great and has wintered very well, so we're very pleased with him."

This imposing individual has an impressive stride. After winning minor events at Pontefract and Ayr, he went on to land the bubbly in Goodwood's Veuve Clicquot Vintage Stakes and Doncaster's Champagne Stakes, both Group 2s.

He still looked green in his races, yet this brother to Dr Fong will look more impressive this year, having grown into his huge frame. Deirdre told me: "He won the Champagne Stakes in real gritty fashion and

you would have to think he can only get better.

"He's fairly straightforward and is a lovely ride at home. We're just hoping for a good preparation, because his ability cannot be questioned."

Star filly **Attraction** was the subject of an injury scare towards the end of last season but this speedball is reportedly none the worse after her minor setback – she fractured a pedal bone.

Johnston said: "She looks absolutely incredible and is as strong as an ox. She looks like a colt and she's got such an enormous bottom.

"The fracture has healed very well and she was so fresh after four weeks of walking and trotting in the New Year that we had to give her a very slow canter before sending her off on the moor. She is magnificent."

Connections are hoping she stays the Guineas trip but they have an ideal second option of returning to the sprinting division if her limitations are exposed over a mile. She will go to Newmarket in May without a prep run and the rest of her campaign will be organised from there.

Deirdre also had encouraging words for **Pearl Of Love**:

"He was a very small individual last year and, although he has grown a bit, he is still not a big horse. However, he is like a tank and has lots of strength with a fantastic temperament.

"I get an awful lot of enjoyment riding him every day and he is the apple of my eye. You don't have to concentrate when riding him or Lucky Story because they do all the work for you and that can only benefit the jockeys who ride them in their races."

The Johnstons will again enjoy strong Arab patronage this season and there are several horses with top-class potential in the two-year-old division.

The pecking order will be more clearly defined after the first few weeks of the new campaign but, at the time of writing, Deirdre

144

is particularly keen on a filly called **Woodland Lodge**.

This daughter of Grand Lodge is worth looking out for. "She's a big, scopey filly and is a half-sister to Dramatic Quest, who we trained. We always thought that horse had a lot of ability but he struggled with his soundness.

"Woodland Lodge has a lot of size and strength, with a great attitude."

Of the older horses, **Bandari** hasn't been easy to predict. He didn't always take his races well and lacked the constitution to gain weight easily but connections have faith in his flying the flag for the more experienced brigade this term.

Systematic improved beyond recognition in 2002 and, although he wasn't as prolific at a higher level last term, Deirdre insists he has retained enough ability to win races over the coming months.

But the star in this department could be **Shanty Star**. This time last year connections were preparing him for a crack at the Derby, but they quickly learned that stamina was his forte.

Having been beaten when disappointing in the Lingfield Derby Trial, he won the Group 3 Queen's Vase at Royal Ascot on his next start. He hasn't been seen since, due to "niggling things", according to Mrs Johnston, who added: "We're hoping he is a Gold Cup horse this year."

Shanty Star is open to plenty of improvement and Borderer recommends that punters keep him in mind.

North of the border, *IAN SEMPLE* continues to win a high percentage of races with moderate animals, but has also proved he can do the job as well as any when given decent ammunition.

Last season was a very good one for the yard, considering the trainer lost stable star Kelburne, who was fatally injured on the gallops.

Chookie Heiton sustained an injury towards the backend and was seen only once after dead-heating at Doncaster in August but he will be back in action this term. Semple said: "He returned from Doncaster with a cut and was given 12 stitches, so you can forget his defeat at Newbury.

LUCKY STORY: has prospects of giving Mark Johnston a rare moment of Classic glory

> *"Templet was expected to be sold for a lot more than I paid for him. He looks like a real athlete with great balance. I'm hoping he turns out to be a bit better than handicapping class"*
>
> Ian Semple

"He always needs a run at the start of each season and, although I've got him more forward than he has been in previous years, he will do better on his second start when I send him to Newmarket's Craven meeting for the 6f Listed race.

"He needs to be held up for a late challenge, so the dip doesn't suit his style of running but he has finished second there on both starts."

Semple is a master of buying cast-offs from major stables and the success of recent seasons has resulted in an influx of new owners who have more money to spend. The Scotsman has bought a particularly interesting three-year-old maiden from the yard of his former governor, John Gosden.

The horse is called **Templet** and cost 45,000gns, which was reportedly his reserve price. Semple had his card marked before the sale and had been assured the purchase price would be beyond his limit.

He said: "This horse was expected to be sold for a lot more and he looks like a real athlete with great balance. I'm hoping he turns out to be a bit better than handicapping class.

"He finished fourth at Newbury a few days before the sale and Philip Robinson, who rode him, reckoned he was a 'proper' horse who shouldn't be sold.

"The plan is to win a poor maiden and get him handicapped before progressing. He's a big, strong horse with tons of ability and he'll handle most ground but I'd say his optimum trip is probably 1m2f."

Readers must write the name **Ridgeback** in their notebooks. Semple said: "He used to be trained by Barry Hills and went to the sales having not run since beating South Atlantic at Thirsk in May.

The runner-up put up an eye-catching performance that day and went on to land a valuable handicap at Newmarket in the summer.

Ridgeback's new handler told me: "He had a hairline fracture on the back of a knee but he has been cantering really well and I'm hoping to go to Doncaster for a 0-90 handicap over 6f in March.

"He gives me the impression he's a real tough, hard guy, who is going to win good handicaps. He is very sharp and excites me an awful lot.

"I'm hoping he turns into an Ayr Gold Cup horse, so he's one to stick with."

Silver Seeker is another inexpensive purchase from a high-profile yard. The master of Belstane Stables revealed: "I bought this fellow out of Godolphin for £6,000 – he was a giveaway.

The grey son of Seeking The Gold won his maiden at Newmarket two years ago but was really disappointing in the Group 3 Champagne Stakes at Goodwood on his next start.

He also failed to sparkle when beaten at Leicester in the spring of last year (his only subsequent start) but the combination of a hard training regime and an injury contributed to his low sales price.

Semple had him gelded and immediately adopted a different training strategy. He said: "He was used as a lead horse in the past but I've sweetened him up by dropping him in behind and letting him enjoy himself.

"If I can get his head right, there's no reason why this horse won't be winning because he was rated 96 last season."

He is lightly raced and will start in a Listed race over 6f at Doncaster. Although he was bought with the Lincoln in mind, his new owners are unsure whether he will stay 1m.

Semple added: "He'll definitely get 7f, so he could be suited by the Victoria Cup at Ascot in the spring, or the Bunbury Cup at Newmarket in the summer."

Appalachian Trail was bought out of John Gosden's yard for 18,000gns at Doncaster sales. He ran only twice last season, including when finishing fifth to Rule Of Law at York in July.

Semple said: "The ground was very fast that day and he might have hurt himself but he'll appreciate a bit of cut in the ground."

Connections resisted the temptation to have him gelded and, although he still has a bit of growing to do, he is thought capable of winning a maiden. The Scotsman trained Jordans Elect to finish second in the three-year-old maiden over a mile at Doncaster last year, and that is the initial target for Appalachian Trail.

There is another noteworthy recruit to this yard. "I bought a horse called **Vijay** in Ireland in the autumn and, though he is rated 60, he works on a par with 80-plus rated horses such as Maktavish and Viewforth, so I must have a bit to play with," says Semple.

Vijay disappointed on his first start for his new trainer when well beaten at Wolverhampton in November but there were excuses.

He explained: "I scoped him afterwards but he was filthy and suffering from anaemia.

"We've got him healthy and I just can't believe he won't win for me off his mark."

In the north-west, it is a travesty that *ERIC ALSTON* has only 20 horses for the new season. Despite this injustice, the likeable trainer is hoping **Piccled** can get back to the form that saw him progress through the handicap last term.

The Preston-based hander said: "He will bypass the sand this time but he is well handicapped on turf."

He had a long campaign, so connections purposely gave him a lengthy break and he will be much fresher when he returns. He is expected to be fit enough to win first time and will bid to win the handicap sprint at Doncaster in March for the second successive year.

Johnston's Diamond is a progressive type but disappointed on the All-Weather in January.

Alston said: "He had been off three months and was ring-rusty. Dean (McKeown) said he just didn't seem the same horse when he jumped out of the stalls.

"I thought he looked burly in the paddock, despite having done a lot of work with him at home, but you can forget that performance. He is on a good mark and 5f with

cut in the ground would be ideal – he is no good on fast ground."

Jadan is the horse to watch most closely from this yard. Alston insisted: "He must be followed!

"I always thought a lot of him as a two-year-old but we stepped him up to 7f and it didn't suit him.

"He didn't come off the bridle to win his maiden at Catterick and he could make up into a really smart sprinter this year. He stayed with me over the winter and has done really well.

"He could be my best horse this year and could win a decent prize."

Midnight Parkes didn't live up to expectations after joining Eric from Michael Jarvis in the summer. He said: "I don't know what went wrong with him but we ended up trying him over 7f. This horse needs 6f to show his best and he has a touch of quality – he must do well off his rating of 68.

"He never looked the finished product last year, but he does now and I'd be very disappointed if he didn't make up into a really good sprinter this year."

Alston paid more for **Allied Victory** than he has for any other horse throughout his long career. This one used to be trained by Jim Bolger but Eric gave 37,000gns for him.

He has yet to live up to his trainer's expectations and must build significantly upon a sole success in a modest race on the sand in January.

Alston tells me: "He looked weak last year but he has strengthened up a lot over the winter.

"If the handicapper gives him some respite, he will do well.

"He used to pull quite hard in his races but he is getting the hang of things, so I think he'll stay 1m4f, and I'm sure he'll recoup his purchase price because he's getting stronger by the day."

The West by Hastings

RICHARD HANNON managed yet another ton-up last term, churning out a typically impressive tally of 112 winners and netting £1.6million in win and place prizemoney in his 34th year as a trainer.

With the help of Richard Hannon Jnr (the trainer's son and assistant), the East Everleigh outfit has continued to be a major force on the Flat, particularly with its younger inmates.

Last year's juvenile crop proved no exception, with a plethora of talented individuals now expected to excel as three-year-olds this summer.

Top of the list has to be **Fantastic View**, who rates an exceptional each-way bet for the 2,000 Guineas at Newmarket on May 1.

Bought for just 35,000gns, the bargain buy quickly established himself as a class act. He fought well to beat subsequent winner Caracara in an Ascot maiden on his debut last July.

With some valuable experience to draw upon, he unleashed an electric turn of foot to leave Listed-class rivals in his wake in a mile contest at Goodwood in September. Even better was to come when pulling an easy 4l clear in a Group 3 contest on a return to Ascot later that month.

That exhilarating performance earned him the right to take on the best in Europe in the prestigious Racing Post Trophy at Doncaster. He once again excelled himself at Town Moor, finding only the impressive Grand Criterium scorer American Post too good.

That form is watertight and, given the wealth of experience accrued at two years, he'll know what is required of him at HQ this spring.

Another expected to bag some black-type in the months to come is **Vermilliann**, who found another gear for a shake of the reins when landing the odds in a Class C conditions race over 5f at Salisbury last spring.

She was next seen in the Group 3 Cornwallis Stakes at Ascot last autumn,

CLOSE TO THE BEST: Fantastic View (right) chases home American Post (left) at Donny

SUPER FAST: If Paradise is an impressive winner of Newbury's Super Sprint last summer

when the lack of a recent run took its toll on the youngster. Although not disgraced in sixth, it clearly wasn't her true running.

Expect significantly better from this Mujadil progeny in the months ahead.

Old Malt performed to a high level between July and October. Given his consistent profile, he rates a decent betting proposition for some of the big middle-distance handicaps this summer. The son of Ashkalani was impressive when opening the account at Brighton and responded gamely when joined for the lead during a gritty beating of stablemate Vienna's Boy in a 7f conditions race at Goodwood.

He ran too freely early on when upped to 1m114yds at Epsom when last seen, but that didn't stop him staying on resolutely into second with some highly-rated rivals behind.

Vienna's Boy managed two wins, three seconds and a third as a juvenile. It's a level of consistency that should stand him in good stead for his second term.

If Paradise led his rivals a merry dance when making virtually all to land a very valuable 22-strong sales race at Newbury last July.

He went on to chase home David Loder's subsequent Flying Childers winner Howick Falls in a Listed race at the York Ebor meeting.

As he's very closely related to Don Sebastian, who won over 1m1f as a three-year-old, we can expect even better from If Paradise when he faces a test of stamina.

Another consistent Hannon recruit to have enjoyed success as a juvenile is **Psychiatrist**. The chestnut gelding moves like a good sort and connections are confident he'll make up into a genuine Group performer this term.

He travelled and stayed well when putting daylight between himself and the also-rans on soft ground over a stiff mile at Sandown in August. He then upped his game to another plain when winning the race on the stands' side, only to be denied by Cape Fear on the far side, over an inadequate 6f in the competitive £200,000 St Leger Yearlings Stakes at Doncaster.

His breeding suggests 1m2f will be within range, leaving connections with plenty of options for the months ahead.

Sgt Pepper has been described as a "real galloper" and produced his best performance as a juvenile when allowed to bowl along from the front at Salisbury back in August.

The manner with which he dominated proceedings from the off in the Listed prize that day bodes well for the campaign ahead.

He wasn't quite ready for the stronger company faced in the Horris Hill and Criterium de Saint-Cloud last backend. After a winter's maturing and strengthening, expect a big prize to go his way at three.

Hannon described **Enford Princess** as "classy" after her cheeky debut win in a small Newmarket maiden last May. His high regard for the youngster was further validated by an equally comfortable success in a stronger conditions race at Windsor just a week later.

She didn't enjoy the best of runs when failing to live up to her status as market-leader in a Listed race on a return to Headquarters in June, and a run in a valuable sales race at the backend smacks of an afterthought. Granted an uninterrupted preparation, she can soon find her niche in Listed contests restricted to fillies and mares.

Of the lesser-known Hannon charges, watch out for **Bohola Flyer**, who could be the handicapper's bugbear this season. He lived up to his speedy pedigree when showing plenty of early dash before fading in stamina-stretching 7f contests on his first two starts, a maiden and a sales race.

More promise can be gleaned from his third and final start when just caught by the promising Miss Langkawi over 6f at Doncaster.

Of the older brigade, the one that stands out is **Nysaean**, who is held in the highest regard and will be a major force in all the top middle-distance championship events this summer. Described by Hannon Jnr as being the "real deal", the impeccably-bred entire has matured into a top-flight performer.

Despite having a light campaign last season, he still managed to make all for a couple of facile Group 3 wins in 1m2f events at The Curragh. He was far from disgraced in a long overdue return to action when finishing midfield at Longchamp in October.

Like a fine wine, he's matured well with age and even better things can be expected of him as a five-year-old, particularly with some juice in the ground.

Former useful juvenile **Tycoon Hall** wasn't right for much of his three-year-old campaign in 2003. The Lincoln entry possesses plenty of talent, is bred to improve with age and, given his lightly-raced profile, can step up to plunder a valuable purse for Hannon before long.

He wasn't given a hard time after his chance had gone when last seen at Goodwood and that kind of tender handling will have done his long-term prospects no harm.

MILTON BRADLEY, best known for the masterly placing of his handicappers, got a deserved shot at the big time when his ever-green speedball **The Tatling** emerged as a leading contender for the sprint crown.

This one was a model of consistency from the outset last term, kicking off with a second in a low-key conditions race in April and finishing with a gallant seventh in the fiercely competitive Group 1 Hong Kong Sprint at Sha Tin in November.

Highlights along the way included wins in a Listed contest at Sandown and the King George Stakes at Glorious Goodwood, plus a cracking second to Oasis Dream in the Nunthorpe at York and a fine third at 40-1 behind Patavellian in the Prix de l'Abbaye at Longchamp (when he was the reason for Bradley's first trip outside Britain in the trainer's 68 years).

To get involved and hold his form in so many high-profile speed tests shows what a tough nut The Tatling has become.

A smart handicapper confidently expected to pay his way for Bradley this summer is **Corridor Creeper**. The pacey seven-year-old chestnut likes to be up with the vanguard from the off in his races and did connections proud in cheekpieces last term.

He finished with a wet sail to plunder an Epsom sprint (off 85) last August. A subsequent half-length second to Halmahera in a fiercely competitive Portland Handicap at Doncaster further highlights his class and courage.

He will have been freshened up after a winter's rest and will come back raring to go for all of the top sprint handicaps on the racing calendar.

Devon-based *ROD MILLMAN* accrued a respectable tally of 19 winners last season, helping to amass total prizemoney in excess of £250,000. He's got some talented individuals housed at his Kentisbeare base and one

Sponsored by Stan James

MAN OF THE WORLD: Milton Bradley in Hong Kong to watch his top sprinter The Tatling

that should rank higher than most is **La Vie Est Belle**, sister to speed-merchant Maktavish.

She lived up to that breeding when a gallant third to Ticker Tape in a very competitive nursery over 7f at Doncaster last September. She's a proven fighter in a tight finish and can bag a big handicap.

Cop Hill Lad impressed pilot Kieren Fallon when outpacing his rivals in a Class C conditions race (second, third and fourth have won since) last May.

The classy chestnut proceeded to acquit himself with pride in stronger Group and sales races for the remainder of the season. Notable efforts included a second to If Paradise in a valuable sprint at Newbury, followed by a close fifth in the Richmond Stakes at Glorious Goodwood.

One from Millman's older brigade to watch out for is long-term Ebor hope **Sergeant Cecil**. He thrived during a consistent and successful campaign in staying handicaps.

He impressed when landing a couple of competitive events over a stiff 1m6f at Sandown

in the first half of last season. Despite steadily creeping up in the weights, he managed to maintain his form to finish a close second over an inadequate 1m4f at Ascot in August.

He reportedly lost his action when disappointing on his final start, a run that can be readily overlooked. He'll be freshened up by a winter break and can return, all guns blazing, in the months to come.

The rapidly-improving **Devon Flame** proved a flagbearer for *RON HODGES* last summer and confidence will be high for him to continue his upward progression as a five-year-old this term. A drop to 6f, once introduced into handicaps, proved the making of him, and he racked up a trio of convincing successes in the space of five weeks.

He was allowed the luxury of being eased down close to the line when scoring at Leicester last time we saw him. The lightly-raced gelding beat a competitive field of 13 rivals that day and it's worth noting that the third home won two of her next three, while the fourth also scored next time out.

The South
by Southerner

JOHN DUNLOP saddled 86 winners at a highly respectable 15 per cent strike-rate last year, and earned his patrons well over £1 million in prizemoney, but the master of Castle Stables still considered it a disappointing season.

Victories in Pattern races were far too few for Dunlop, whose laid-back exterior hides a fierce will to compete successfully at the highest level.

Perversely, the last campaign could not have started much better for Dunlop, as his first runner, **Dandoun**, swept home 4l clear of With Reason in the Listed Doncaster Mile on the opening day of the turf season.

The Halling entire was winning the race for the second year running and it would be no surprise to see him complete a hat-trick in the Town Moor event this term.

The current fashion of keeping good quality horses in training after their three-year-old careers is one of the most welcome recent trends in Flat rac-

JOHN DUNLOP

ing. A few years ago, Dunlop would have retained no more than half a dozen older horses – this year, he has 23 horses above the age of three still in training, headed by the St Leger hero of 2000, **Millenary**.

This son of Rainbow Quest won his second Princess Of Wales's Stakes at Newmarket in July and, on his final outing last term, he just lost out to the remarkable Persian Punch after an epic battle in 2m Group 3 Jockey Club Cup at HQ in October.

Almutasader and **Prince Tum Tum** are a couple of the more interesting members of Dunlop's senior squad.

The first-named won middle-distance handicaps at Leicester, Ripon and Sandown on his first three outings last year.

He was perhaps a shade disappointing on his final appearance when fourth to Shabernak in a valuable 1m6f132yds handicap at Doncaster in September, but at least that effort will have helped protect his Official Rating.

Almutasader is a big, rangy individual by Sadler's Wells, and will be stronger this year. He should be well worth following.

As should Prince Tum Tum, who looked all set for a profitable campaign in Group company last April after producing a smart turn of foot to land the Listed Easter Stakes over a mile at Kempton in April.

However, injury intervened and he did not appear again. Fully recovered now, the American-bred can make up for lost time in the months to come.

Dunlop has an exceptionally talented team of three-year-old fillies, headed by **Snow Goose**. A hat-trick scorer last term, the Polar Falcon filly signed off with a highly creditable second to Cairns in the 7f Group 2 Rockfel Stakes at Newmarket in October.

As she is from a family that improve with age, she should do even better this year.

There are also high hopes for the appealingly-bred **Ashwaaq**. A half-sister to the champion miler Bahri, she revealed bags of talent when staying on to be fourth in a

UNFINISHED BUSINESS I: Prince Tum Tum wins easily at Kempton, but has not run since

strongly-run 7f maiden at Newmarket last November on her debut.

Zaqrah is another well-related filly, who had just the one outing as a juvenile. The Silver Hawk offspring finished strongly, after encountering traffic problems, to be a close fourth to Josephus in a 7f maiden at Newmarket's July meeting.

The Rainbow Quest filly **Maid To Treasure**, who was runner-up to Si Si Amiga in a 7f juvenile maiden at Newmarket in November on her only visit to a racecourse last term, should not test Dunlop's placing skills too much.

Dunlop's three-year-old colts are headed by **Let The Lion Roar**. Having shown more as a juvenile than his half-brother Millenary, there are some ambitious plans for the Sadler's Wells colt this season.

He had no trouble landing a mile maiden at Newmarket on his debut in August before finding the concession of 5lb to Elshadi too much for him in the invariably informative Haynes, Hanson & Clark Stakes at Newbury over the same trip in September.

Let The Lion Roar will be given his chance in a Derby trial.

Mutahayya is another likely to start off in

"Having shown more as a juvenile than his half-brother Millenary, there are ambitious plans for Let The Lion Roar. He had no trouble landing a maiden and will get his chance in a Derby trial"

one of the Classic Trials. The Peintre Celebre colt was progressing well at the end of last term, winding up with a close second to subsequent Racing Post Trophy runner-up Fantastic View in a Listed race over a mile at Goodwood in September.

His breeding suggests he will really come into his own over 1m4f this year.

Thajja won a 7f maiden in good style at Newmarket last July on his sole start to date. As a son of King George VI & Queen Elizabeth Diamond Stakes winner Daylami, he should improve with age and experience.

The Danehill colt **Kodiac**, a half-brother to Group 1 winner Invincible Spirit (who was also by a Danzig stallion), had just the one outing last term and showed plenty of promise when an unlucky-in-running and strong-finishing third in a 6f maiden at Newmarket in July.

Jedburgh and **Iqte Saab** are two other three-year-old colts in Dunlop's care that should reward their followers this season.

The first-named went from strength to strength last year, signing off with a hat-trick of victories.

Iqte Saab created an excellent impression on his debut, quickening up after meeting trouble in running to land a 6f maiden at Salisbury in August.

The Bahri colt came up against the subsequent Royal Lodge Stakes winner Snow Ridge in a 7f conditions stakes at Kempton in September on his other outing as a juvenile.

Not surprisingly, he found trying to concede 4lb to Marcus Tregoning's Derby hope beyond him.

As ever, there are a host of blue-blooded youngsters at Castle Stables, including **Dancing In The Clouds**, a half-sister to Millenary.

AMANDA PERRETT has done very well to build the numbers back up to over 100 at Coombelands and she's in for a busy time in the months to come.

Taminoula is one of the best prospects in the yard. The Tagula filly ran away with a 7f Brighton maiden last August and supplemented that victory when getting up

JEDBURGH

UNFINISHED BUSINESS II: Persian Majesty (nearest) gets up at Ascot on his latest outing

close home to land a 7f nursery at Goodwood in October.

The speedy Machiavellian filly **Bread Of Heaven**, who won a 6f Redcar maiden in October on her final start last year, should pay her way this season.

Derby entry **Soulacroix** bolted home in a 1m2f maiden at Brighton at the end of last season. Whilst Epsom glory seems unlikely at this stage, the Kylian colt is expected to develop into a useful stayer.

The giant four-year-old **Westmoreland Road**, who disappointed when down the field in the St Leger on his final start last year, will be stronger this time and should have a profitable campaign.

PETER HARRIS has a powerful team for this year. The Berkhamsted trainer has particularly high hopes for **Persian Majesty**.

This Grand Lodge colt has only managed two appearances in his career so far but, as he won a mile maiden at Newmarket in 2002 as a juvenile and the 1m2f Listed Hampton Court Stakes at Royal Ascot last year, there is no doubt he has considerable talent.

Hills Spitfire will be suited by a thorough test of stamina and should more than pay his way this year.

The Kahyasi colt would have won at the first time of asking in another stride when beaten a short-head by **Lunar Exit** in a mile maiden at Newmarket last October.

He was again doing all his best work at the finish when fourth in the 1m2f Listed Zetland Stakes at Newmarket two weeks later.

The aforementioned Lunar Exit, who was just behind Hills Spitfire when fifth in the Zetland Stakes, is a very well-related grey gelding trained by *LADY HERRIES* at Angmering Park in West Sussex. He was only a shell of a horse last year and is another young stayer of abundant potential.

The Midlands
by John Bull

There are good racehorse trainers, excellent racehorse trainers . . . and then there is MARK BRISBOURNE.

Anyone who still had doubts as to the remarkable ability of our region's leading Flat trainer to get the best out of bargain basement buys should have been at Newmarket on October 16, when **Milly Waters**, bought as a yearling for just 800gns, landed the £100,000 Tattersalls Auction Stakes at odds of 33-1.

For those who said the result was a fluke, (believe it or not, there were such misguided souls), the daughter of Danzero repeated the performance a fortnight later in a Class D nursery at Newbury, a race in which our region chalked up a memorable one-two.

Milly Waters is only the latest in a long line of cheaply-bought horses that Brisbourne has trained to land lucrative prizes. Hannibal Lad, a John Gosden cast-off, won 11 times, including two valuable handicaps at Ascot and the Old Newton Cup at Haydock.

Last year was Brisbourne's best ever season (48 winners) and this time round the indefatigable master of Great Ness will be going all out to achieve the half-century.

When John Bull asked Brisbourne to single out two unexposed likely improvers, horses that RFO readers should be able to make good level-stakes profits from throughout the campaign, he put forward the names of **Roman Maze** and **Iftikhar**.

The former, a four-year-old Lycius gelding, finished an encouraging close-up fifth in a decent 7f Lingfield maiden on his first run for Brisbourne in October. He was stepped up to 1m1f110yds for his next outing at Wolverhampton in November, but didn't appear to stay before finishing lame. Returning to Dunstall Park, but this time dropped back to 7f, he ran out an easy winner of a maiden a fortnight later. His last run of the year, when he was slowly away and was short of room at the business end of affairs in a 7f classified stakes at Wolverhampton, is best forgotten.

Currently rated 68, Roman Maze is on a mark his astute trainer feels he can exploit, and the gelding has been working well on the grass gallops at home in preparation for his turf campaign.

"I really do think he's a very nice horse," Brisbourne told me. "He has enough pace for 7f and enough stamina for 1m. I'll be looking to pick up some decent handicaps over those distances.

"I think he'll want fairly fast ground."

Since being switched away from National Hunt Flat races, Iftikhar has only run in four maidens, finishing second twice (the first time going down by half a length at odds of 66-1 to a Newmarket-trained odds-on shot at Thirsk). He was last of four at Ripon when last seen in August.

But the bare form tells only half the story, as Brisbourne relates: "We tried him first in bumpers but he clearly wasn't getting home, and we discovered a wind problem,

MARK BRISBOURNE

and switched him to the Flat. He's 90 per cent okay now, and we've had him rescoped.

"I don't think we're ever going to get his wind 100 per cent right, but even so he's a horse of so much ability."

A current mark in the low 60s gives Brisbourne plenty of options and, with his wind problems hopefully a thing of the past, it would be no surprise to see the Storm Cat gelding chalk up a sequence of victories and climb up the ratings.

If the expected improvement does come, races such as the Gratwick Stakes at Goodwood in June or the Bonusprint Handicap at Ascot in July, which Brisbourne has targeted successfully in the past, could be possible midseason targets. Those are over 1m4f, but it would be no surprise to see Iftikhar makes his presence felt over further.

Regarding jockey bookings, Brisbourne will continue to use the services of George Baker, Keith Dalgleish, Richard Mullen, Shane Kelly and, when available, Kieren Fallon. But he will also be looking to give more opportunities to his promising young apprentice Ben Swarbrick.

"The boy is totally focused and dedicated" says Brisbourne. "He works like a demon. His 7lb claim is very useful, especially in tight handicaps, and the other advantage is that he knows the horses well."

As to last season's heroine, Brisbourne told me: "Milly Waters will run in small-field Listed Fillies Stakes races. You can't take away what she's already achieved, but this year things will be harder.

"The aim is to get some black type. Expect to see her out towards the end of April."

Although leading the way numerically, Brisbourne was not the only one of our region's trainers to get amongst the winners last year.

After a midseason lull, *JOHN SPEARING* finished 2003 strongly, and all those punters level-staking the yard throughout the season would have been rewarded with a healthy 29-points profit.

Star of the show was the evergreen **Thihn**, John Bull's favourite Flat handicapper, who notched up two wins in the last week of the season (having been tipped to do so by your correspondent in the pages of RFO).

He was returned at 12-1 when winning over 7f at Redcar and then, six days later, defied a 5lb penalty to land a competitive Newmarket handicap over a mile at 10-1. On the latter occasion he returned a time that was over a second faster than the preceding Listed Race over the same trip.

Thihn's first target of the new campaign will be the Lincoln on March 27. "Although he's done most of his winning in the autumn, this is more to do with the ground than any seasonal preferences," Spearing told me, "and if the ground does come up soft at

BRINGER OF FAT PROFITS: it's the mighty Thihn, scoring for the second time in a week

Doncaster he must go there with at least an each-way chance."

"He was fourth in the race on good to soft ground two years ago and fifth in the consolation race last year, and he'll be running off 90, the same mark as in 2002."

Unless we get a wet summer, we're unlikely to see Thihn to best effect until the back-end of the season but, when he does turn up in large-field HQ handicaps in the autumn, don't hesitate to wade in.

His record in such events bears repeating; in five runs, the worst he has finished is a 4l fifth in the 2001 Cambridgeshire. He has won once and been placed at double-figure odds on the other three occasions.

As to his younger horses, Spearing advises RFO readers to keep an eye on **Stokesies Wish**. This filly ran a total of 14 times last season and, although she only won once (in a maiden at Goodwood in October when given a peach of a ride by Lisa Jones), she was placed in five other races, each time at double-figure, each-way prices.

She went up 14lb for her Goodwood success to a mark of 63, but proved she could still get competitive off her new mark when running a close second at Brighton on her last run of the season.

With that all-important first win under her belt, Spearing predicts further improvement this year and, although she'll start off in 0-70s, she could be dangerous running off a low weight in 0-95s. She goes on all ground and is equally effective from 5f to 6f.

By his own standards, 2003 was a disappointing year for *BRYAN MCMAHON*, but there are solid grounds for believing that this season will be a better one for Britain's sixth-longest-serving trainer.

McMahon is renowned for his flying start to the Flat season and, when John Bull caught up with him in mid-January, he was already having his suit pressed and shoes polished for Town Moor.

The horse that McMahon is most excited about for the new campaign is **Local Poet**, who finished his two-year-old campaign in such promising fashion.

After a gentle introduction at Windsor in late July, the Robellino colt showed a big improvement on his second run, when giving an odds-on Newmarket raider a real run for his money in a maiden at Pontefract in August.

The potential highlighted by that performance was confirmed on his next outing, in the £150,000 Two-Year-Old Trophy at Redcar. Local Poet was backed in from 66-1 to 25-1 before the off, with owner John Fretwell standing to take £500,000 out of the ring.

Blazing a trail on the far side, Local Poet was still clear and looked set to land the gamble a furlong out, but was denied on the line by the late, late run of Peak To Creek. The pair had finished 4l clear of the third.

Peak to Creek went on to post successive wins in a Listed Race and the Group 3 Horris Hill at Newbury, and is now as low as 25-1 for the 2,000 Guineas. So to be beaten a head by such a horse, even in receipt of 6lb, was no mean achievement for McMahon's charge.

On his final run of the campaign, Local Poet was checked in running twice in the Listed Doncaster Stakes over 6f, yet still finished less than 4l back in fourth.

Winning his maiden should be a shoo-in, but the hope is that he can also go on to make his presence felt at a higher level. McMahon has no particular targets in mind, but reports that Local Poet has "wintered well" and will probably be out early on.

"I do believe he will improve and be capable of winning better races," he told me. We all know the pitfalls of interpreting end-of-season two-year-old form too literally, but Local Poet did post three good efforts last backend and McMahon certainly looks to have a horse to go to war with.

Regarding his more established campaigners, McMahon advises RFO readers to watch out for **El Coto**, particularly in the early weeks of the season. He's likely to start off in the Lincoln, where he'll carry 8st11lb, and it's worth bearing in mind that he won first time out at Doncaster last season and was only beaten a head into second at the same meeting the year before.

Midlands magic
Iftikhar
Local Poet
Roman Maze

Races and Racecourses

Fixtures

Key - **Flat**, ***Flat evening***, Jumps, *Jumps evening*

March

25	Thursday	**Doncaster,** Ludlow, Wincanton
26	Friday	**Doncaster, Lingfield,** Newbury
27	Saturday	Bangor, **Doncaster, Kempton,** Newbury, ***Wolverhampton***
28	Sunday	Kelso, Market Rasen
29	Monday	**Lingfield, Newcastle, Wolverhampton**
30	Tuesday	**Folkestone,** Sedgefield, **Southwell**
31	Wednesday	**Catterick, Lingfield, Nottingham**

April

1	Thursday	**Leicester,** Aintree, Taunton
2	Friday	**Lingfield,** Aintree, **Southwell**
3	Saturday	Hereford, **Lingfield,** Aintree, **Newcastle**
4	Sunday	Hexham, Lingfield, Wincanton
5	Monday	Kelso, **Southwell, Windsor**
6	Tuesday	Exeter, **Lingfield, Pontefract**
7	Wednesday	**Folkestone,** Fontwell, **Warwick**
8	Thursday	**Bath, Musselburgh,** Ludlow
10	Saturday	Carlisle, **Haydock, Kempton,** Newton Abbot
11	Sunday	**Musselburgh,** Plumpton, Towcester
12	Monday	Fakenham, Huntingdon, **Kempton,** Plumpton, **Redcar,** Sedgefield, **Warwick, Yarmouth**
13	Tuesday	Chepstow, Exeter, **Newmarket**
14	Wednesday	**Beverley,** Cheltenham, **Newmarket**
15	Thursday	Cheltenham, *Lingfield,* Newmarket, Ripon, *Southwell*
16	Friday	Ayr, **Newbury,** *Southwell,* *Taunton,* **Thirsk**
17	Saturday	Ayr, Bangor, **Newbury,** *Nottingham,* Thirsk, *Wolverhampton*
18	Sunday	Carlisle, Stratford, Wincanton
19	Monday	Hexham, **Lingfield, Pontefract,** *Windsor,* *Wolverhampton*
20	Tuesday	**Folkestone, Newcastle, Southwell**
21	Wednesday	**Catterick, Epsom,** *Lingfield,* Perth, *Worcester*
22	Thursday	**Beverley,** Fontwell, Perth, *Salisbury,* *Wolverhampton*
23	Friday	*Chepstow,* Perth, **Sandown,** *Warwick,* Wolverhampton
24	Saturday	*Haydock,* Leicester, Market Rasen, **Ripon, Sandown,** *Wolverhampton*
25	Sunday	**Brighton,** Ludlow, Wetherby
26	Monday	**Hamilton,** *Newcastle,* Towcester, *Windsor,* **Wolverhampton**
27	Tuesday	**Bath,** *Lingfield,* Newton Abbot, **Southwell**
28	Wednesday	**Ascot,** *Cheltenham,* Exeter, *Kelso,* **Pontefract**
29	Thursday	*Ayr,* Hereford, *Lingfield,* **Redcar, Southwell**
30	Friday	*Bangor,* **Musselburgh, Nottingham,** *Sedgefield,* Worcester

May

1	Saturday	**Haydock,** *Hexham,* **Newmarket,** *Southwell,* **Thirsk,** Uttoxeter
2	Sunday	**Hamilton, Newmarket, Salisbury**
3	Monday	**Doncaster,** Fontwell, **Kempton, Newcastle, Warwick**

4	Tuesday	**Bath, Brighton, Carlisle,** *Catterick,* *Exeter*
5	Wednesday	Chepstow, **Chester,** *Fakenham,* Kelso, ***Wolverhampton***
6	Thursday	**Chester, Folkestone,** *Ludlow,* **Southwell,** *Wetherby*
7	Friday	**Chester,** *Hamilton,* **Lingfield, Nottingham,** *Wincanton*
8	Saturday	**Beverley,** Hexham, **Lingfield,** *Thirsk,* **Warwick,** Worcester
9	Sunday	Market Rasen, Plumpton, Uttoxeter
10	Monday	**Kempton, Redcar,** *Towcester,* **Windsor, Wolverhampton**
11	Tuesday	Hereford, Huntingdon, *Newton Abbot,* **Wolverhampton,** York
12	Wednesday	**Brighton,** Exeter, **Newcastle,** *Perth,* **York**
13	Thursday	**Lingfield,** *Ludlow,* Perth, **Salisbury,** York
14	Friday	**Hamilton,** *Aintree,* **Newbury, Nottingham,** Yarmouth
15	Saturday	Bangor, **Newbury, Nottingham,** *Southwell,* **Thirsk,** *Uttoxeter*
16	Sunday	Fakenham, **Ripon,** Worcester
17	Monday	**Bath,** *Musselburgh,* Newton Abbot, *Windsor,* **Wolverhampton**
18	Tuesday	**Beverley, Goodwood,** *Leicester,* **Redcar,** *Towcester*
19	Wednesday	*Folkestone,* **Goodwood,** Kelso, *Sedgefield,* **Southwell**
20	Thursday	*Doncaster,* **Goodwood,** *Kelso,* **Newcastle,** Wetherby
21	Friday	**Ayr,** *Bath,* **Haydock, Newmarket,** *Stratford*
22	Saturday	**Ascot, Catterick, Haydock,** *Kempton,* **Newmarket,** *Stratford*
23	Sunday	**Brighton,** Hereford, Southwell
24	Monday	**Beverley, Carlisle, Leicester,** *Thirsk,* **Windsor**
25	Tuesday	*Bangor,* **Lingfield, Nottingham, Ripon,** *Sedgefield*
26	Wednesday	Cartmel, Fontwell, **Lingfield,** *Nottingham,* **Ripon**
27	Thursday	**Ayr, Bath,** *Huntingdon,* Newton Abbot, *Wetherby*
28	Friday	**Brighton, Catterick,** *Pontefract,* *Towcester,* **Wolverhampton**
29	Saturday	*Cartmel,* **Doncaster, Musselburgh,** Hexham, **Kempton,** *Lingfield*
30	Sunday	Fontwell, **Newmarket,** Uttoxeter
31	Monday	Cartmel, **Chepstow, Leicester, Redcar, Sandown**

June

1	Tuesday	*Hexham,* **Leicester, Redcar,** *Sandown*
2	Wednesday	*Beverley, Kempton,* Newcastle, Nottingham, Yarmouth
3	Thursday	**Chepstow, Hamilton, Haydock,** *Sandown,* *Uttoxeter*
4	Friday	**Catterick, Epsom,** *Goodwood,* **Haydock,** Wolverhampton
5	Saturday	**Doncaster, Epsom, Haydock,** *Newmarket,* *Perth,* Worcester
6	Sunday	**Brighton,** Perth, Stratford
7	Monday	**Folkestone,** Newton Abbot, *Pontefract,* **Windsor**
8	Tuesday	**Chester,** *Huntingdon,* **Redcar,** Salisbury
9	Wednesday	**Beverley,** *Hamilton,* Hereford, Market Rasen, **Newbury**
10	Thursday	*Brighton,* **Newbury, Southwell,** *Uttoxeter,* **Yarmouth**
11	Friday	*Chepstow, Goodwood,* **Sandown, Wolverhampton, York**
12	Saturday	**Bath,** Hexham, *Leicester, Lingfield,* **Sandown, York**
13	Sunday	**Doncaster, Salisbury,** Stratford
14	Monday	**Brighton, Carlisle,** *Warwick,* **Windsor**
15	Tuesday	**Ascot,** *Hereford, Newton Abbot,* **Thirsk**
16	Wednesday	**Ascot, Hamilton,** *Ripon,* **Southwell,** *Worcester*
17	Thursday	**Ascot,** *Ayr, Beverley,* **Ripon, Southwell**
18	Friday	**Ascot, Ayr,** *Goodwood, Newmarket,* **Redcar**
19	Saturday	**Ascot, Ayr,** *Lingfield,* **Newmarket, Redcar,** *Warwick*
20	Sunday	Hexham, **Pontefract, Warwick**
21	Monday	*Chepstow,* **Musselburgh, Nottingham,** *Windsor*
22	Tuesday	**Beverley, Brighton,** *Newbury, Newton Abbot*

23 Wednesday ....*Bath*, Carlisle, *Kempton*, Salisbury, Worcester
24 Thursday ....*Hamilton*, *Leicester*, Newcastle, Salisbury, Thirsk
25 Friday...Folkestone, *Newmarket*, Market Rasen,
....*Newcastle*, Wolverhampton
26 Saturday ....Chester, *Doncaster*, *Lingfield*, Newcastle,
....*Newmarket*, Windsor
27 Sunday ....Goodwood, Uttoxeter, **Windsor**
28 Monday ....*Musselburgh*, Pontefract, *Windsor*, Wolverhampton
29 Tuesday ....Brighton, Hamilton, Worcester
30 Wednesday...........................**Catterick**, *Kempton*, Lingfield, Perth, *Yarmouth*

July

1 Thursday ....*Epsom*, Haydock, *Newbury*, Perth, **Yarmouth**
2 Friday....................................*Beverley*, *Haydock*, Sandown, Southwell, **Warwick**
3 Saturday ......**Beverley**, *Carlisle*, **Haydock**, Leicester, *Nottingham*, **Sandown**
4 Sunday...Brighton, Market Rasen, **Redcar**
5 Monday...**Bath**, Musselburgh, *Ripon*, **Windsor**
6 Tuesday..............................Newmarket, Pontefract, *Uttoxeter*, **Wolverhampton**
7 Wednesday................**Catterick**, *Kempton*, Lingfield, Newmarket, *Worcester*
8 Thursday....................*Doncaster*, *Epsom*, Folkestone, Newmarket, **Warwick**
9 Friday...............................Ascot, *Chepstow*, *Chester*, Wolverhampton, **York**
10 Saturday...................**Ascot**, Chester, *Hamilton*, Nottingham, *Salisbury*, **York**
11 Sunday ....**Bath**, Haydock, Stratford
12 Monday..........................**Ayr**, Newton Abbot, *Windsor*, *Wolverhampton*
13 Tuesday..**Beverley**, Brighton
14 Wednesday ....**Catterick**, *Kempton*, Lingfield, Uttoxeter, *Worcester*
15 Thursday............................Cartmel, *Doncaster*, *Epsom*, Hamilton, Leicester
16 Friday ....**Carlisle**, *Hamilton*, Newbury, *Newmarket*, *Pontefract*, Southwell
17 Saturday....*Haydock*, *Lingfield*, Market Rasen, **Newbury**, **Newmarket**, Ripon
18 Sunday ....Newton Abbot, Stratford
19 Monday ....**Ayr**, *Beverley*, Brighton, *Windsor*
20 Tuesday ....**Ayr**, Uttoxeter
21 Wednesday ....**Catterick**, *Leicester*, Lingfield, *Sandown*, Worcester
22 Thursday ....**Bath**, *Doncaster*, *Folkestone*, Sandown, Yarmouth
23 Friday ....**Ascot**, *Chepstow*, *Newmarket*, Thirsk, Wolverhampton
24 Saturday...............**Ascot**, *Lingfield*, Newcastle, Nottingham, *Salisbury*, **York**
25 Sunday ....**Ascot**, Newmarket, Pontefract
26 Monday.................................Sedgefield, **Southwell**, *Windsor*, *Yarmouth*
27 Tuesday..**Beverley**, Goodwood
28 Wednesday ..**Musselburgh**, Goodwood, *Kempton*, *Leicester*, Newton Abbot
29 Thursday....................Carlisle, *Musselburgh*, *Epsom*, Goodwood, Stratford
30 Friday ....Bangor, **Goodwood**, *Newmarket*, *Nottingham*, Thirsk
31 Saturday....**Doncaster**, Goodwood, *Hamilton*, *Lingfield*, Newmarket, **Thirsk**

August

1 Sunday ....**Chester**, Market Rasen, **Newbury**
2 Monday..*Carlisle*, Newton Abbot, **Ripon**, *Windsor*
3 Tuesday ....**Brighton**, Catterick
4 Wednesday ....Brighton, *Kempton*, Newcastle, Pontefract, *Yarmouth*
5 Thursday....................*Brighton*, Chepstow, *Folkestone*, Haydock, Yarmouth
6 Friday ....*Haydock*, Lingfield, *Newmarket*, Sedgefield, Worcester
7 Saturday ....**Ascot**, *Ayr*, Haydock, *Lingfield*, Newmarket, **Redcar**

162   *Sponsored by Stan James*

8	Sunday	**Leicester, Redcar, Windsor**
9	Monday	Southwell, *Thirsk*, *Windsor*, **Wolverhampton**
10	Tuesday	**Bath,** Newton Abbot
11	Wednesday	**Beverley,** *Hamilton,* **Salisbury,** *Sandown,* **Yarmouth**
12	Thursday	**Beverley,** *Chepstow,* **Haydock, Salisbury, Sandown**
13	Friday	***Catterick,*** **Folkestone, Newbury, Newcastle,** *Newmarket*
14	Saturday	Bangor, *Market Rasen,* **Newbury, Newmarket, Ripon,** *Warwick*
15	Sunday	**Bath, Pontefract,** Stratford
16	Monday	**Brighton, Nottingham,** *Windsor,* *Yarmouth*
17	Tuesday	**Hamilton, York**
18	Wednesday	**Carlisle,** *Kempton,* *Nottingham,* Worcester, **York**
19	Thursday	*Chepstow,* **Chester,** Fontwell, **Wolverhampton, York**
20	Friday	**Ayr, Chester,** *Salisbury,* **Sandown,** *Wolverhampton*
21	Saturday	**Chester,** *Lingfield,* Market Rasen, *Newton Abbot,* **Ripon, Sandown**
22	Sunday	**Folkestone,** Newton Abbot, Southwell
23	Monday	**Hamilton, Leicester,** *Windsor,* **Wolverhampton**
24	Tuesday	**Brighton,** *Perth,* **Worcester, Yarmouth**
25	Wednesday	**Brighton, Catterick,** Perth
26	Thursday	Bangor, **Musselburgh, Lingfield**
27	Friday	***Bath,*** **Goodwood,** *Newcastle,* **Newmarket, Thirsk**
28	Saturday	**Beverley,** Cartmel, **Goodwood, Newmarket,** *Redcar,* *Windsor*
29	Sunday	**Beverley, Goodwood, Yarmouth**
30	Monday	Cartmel, **Chepstow, Epsom,** Huntingdon, **Newcastle, Ripon, Warwick**
31	Tuesday	**Ripon,** Sedgefield

September

1	Wednesday	**Lingfield,** Newton Abbot, **York**
2	Thursday	**Carlisle, Redcar, Salisbury**
3	Friday	**Chepstow, Haydock, Kempton**
4	Saturday	**Folkestone, Haydock, Kempton,** Stratford, **Thirsk,** *Wolverhampton*
5	Sunday	Fontwell, Worcester, **York**
6	Monday	**Bath, Newcastle, Warwick**
7	Tuesday	**Catterick, Leicester, Lingfield**
8	Wednesday	**Doncaster, Epsom,** Hereford
9	Thursday	**Chepstow, Doncaster, Epsom**
10	Friday	Bangor, **Doncaster, Sandown**
11	Saturday	**Carlisle, Chester, Doncaster, Musselburgh, Goodwood**
12	Sunday	**Goodwood,** Hexham, Stratford
13	Monday	**Bath, Musselburgh, Redcar**
14	Tuesday	**Salisbury, Thirsk, Yarmouth**
15	Wednesday	**Beverley, Sandown, Yarmouth**
16	Thursday	**Ayr, Pontefract, Yarmouth**
17	Friday	**Ayr, Newbury, Nottingham**
18	Saturday	**Ayr, Catterick, Lingfield, Newbury, Warwick,** *Wolverhampton*
19	Sunday	**Hamilton,** Plumpton, Uttoxeter
20	Monday	**Chepstow, Kempton, Leicester**
21	Tuesday	**Beverley,** Fontwell, **Newmarket**
22	Wednesday	**Goodwood,** Perth, Southwell
23	Thursday	**Brighton,** Perth, **Pontefract**
24	Friday	**Ascot, Haydock,** Worcester

25	Saturday	**Ascot, Haydock, Kempton**, Market Rasen, **Ripon**
26	Sunday	**Ascot, Musselburgh**, Huntingdon
27	Monday	**Bath, Hamilton, Windsor**
28	Tuesday	Exeter, **Nottingham**, Sedgefield
29	Wednesday	**Newcastle, Nottingham, Salisbury**
30	Thursday	**Goodwood**, Hereford, **Newmarket**

October

1	Friday	Hexham, **Lingfield, Newmarket**
2	Saturday	**Brighton**, Chepstow, **Epsom, Newmarket,**
		Redcar, *Wolverhampton*
3	Sunday	Kelso, Market Rasen, Uttoxeter
4	Monday	Plumpton, **Pontefract, Windsor**
5	Tuesday	**Catterick**, Huntingdon, Stratford
6	Wednesday	Exeter, **Lingfield**, Towcester
7	Thursday	Ludlow, **Southwell**, Wincanton
8	Friday	**Ascot**, Carlisle, **York**
9	Saturday	**Ascot**, Bangor, Hexham, **Warwick, York**
10	Sunday	**Bath, Goodwood, Newcastle**
11	Monday	**Ayr, Leicester, Windsor**
12	Tuesday	**Ayr**, Fontwell, **Leicester**
13	Wednesday	**Lingfield**, Uttoxeter, Wetherby
14	Thursday	**Newmarket**, Taunton, Worcester
15	Friday	**Brighton, Newmarket, Redcar**
16	Saturday	**Catterick**, Kelso, **Newmarket**, Stratford, **Yarmouth**
17	Sunday	**Musselburgh**, Hereford, Market Rasen
18	Monday	Plumpton, **Pontefract, Wolverhampton**
19	Tuesday	**Bath**, Exeter, **Southwell**
20	Wednesday	Chepstow, **Newcastle, Nottingham**
21	Thursday	**Brighton**, Haydock, Ludlow
22	Friday	**Doncaster**, Fakenham, **Newbury**
23	Saturday	Carlisle, **Doncaster**, Kempton, **Newbury, Wolverhampton**
24	Sunday	Aintree, Towcester, Wincanton
25	Monday	**Leicester, Lingfield, Wolverhampton**
26	Tuesday	**Catterick**, Cheltenham, **Nottingham**
27	Wednesday	Cheltenham, Sedgefield, **Yarmouth**
28	Thursday	**Lingfield**, Stratford, Taunton
29	Friday	**Newmarket**, Uttoxeter, Wetherby
30	Saturday	Ascot, **Ayr**, Chepstow, Kelso, **Newmarket,**
		Wetherby, *Wolverhampton*
31	Sunday	Carlisle, Huntingdon, **Lingfield**

November

1	Monday	Plumpton, **Redcar**, Warwick
2	Tuesday	**Catterick**, Exeter, Folkestone
3	Wednesday	**Musselburgh**, Kempton, Newton Abbot
4	Thursday	Haydock, **Nottingham**, Towcester
5	Friday	Fontwell, Hexham, **Yarmouth**
6	Saturday	Ayr, **Doncaster**, Sandown, Wincanton, *Wolverhampton*
7	Sunday	Ayr, Market Rasen, Southwell
8	Monday	Carlisle, **Southwell, Wolverhampton**
9	Tuesday	Huntingdon, Sedgefield, **Southwell**

164

10	Wednesday	Kelso, **Lingfield**, Newbury
11	Thursday	Lingfield, Ludlow, Taunton
12	Friday	Cheltenham, Newcastle, **Wolverhampton**
13	Saturday	Cheltenham, **Lingfield**, Uttoxeter, Wetherby, *Wolverhampton*
14	Sunday	Cheltenham, Fontwell, Haydock
15	Monday	Folkestone, Leicester, **Wolverhampton**
16	Tuesday	**Lingfield**, Newton Abbot, Towcester
17	Wednesday	Hexham, Kempton, **Southwell**
18	Thursday	Hereford, Market Rasen, Wincanton
19	Friday	Ascot, Exeter, **Wolverhampton**
20	Saturday	Ascot, Huntingdon, **Lingfield**, Aintree, *Wolverhampton*
21	Sunday	Fakenham, Aintree, Plumpton
22	Monday	**Lingfield**, Ludlow, **Southwell**
23	Tuesday	Sedgefield, **Southwell**, Warwick
24	Wednesday	Chepstow, Lingfield, Wetherby
25	Thursday	Carlisle, Taunton, Uttoxeter
26	Friday	Bangor, Musselburgh, **Wolverhampton**
27	Saturday	**Lingfield**, Newbury, Newcastle, Towcester, *Wolverhampton*
28	Sunday	Doncaster, Leicester, Newbury
29	Monday	Folkestone, Newcastle, **Wolverhampton**
30	Tuesday	Hereford, **Lingfield**, Newton Abbot

December

1	Wednesday	Catterick, Plumpton, **Southwell**
2	Thursday	Leicester, Market Rasen, Wincanton
3	Friday	Exeter, Sandown, **Wolverhampton**
4	Saturday	Chepstow, Haydock, **Lingfield**, Sandown, Wetherby, *Wolverhampton*
5	Sunday	Kelso, Warwick
6	Monday	Ayr, Newcastle, **Wolverhampton**
7	Tuesday	Fontwell, Sedgefield, **Southwell**
8	Wednesday	Leicester, **Lingfield**, Newbury
9	Thursday	Huntingdon, Ludlow, Taunton
10	Friday	Cheltenham, Doncaster, **Wolverhampton**
11	Saturday	Cheltenham, Doncaster, Lingfield, **Southwell**, *Wolverhampton*
12	Sunday	Musselburgh, **Southwell**
13	Monday	Plumpton, Towcester, **Wolverhampton**
14	Tuesday	Folkestone, **Southwell**, **Wolverhampton**
15	Wednesday	Bangor, Hexham, **Lingfield**
16	Thursday	Catterick, Exeter, **Southwell**
17	Friday	Ascot, Uttoxeter, **Wolverhampton**
18	Saturday	Ascot, Haydock, **Lingfield**, Newcastle, Warwick
20	Monday	Fakenham, **Lingfield**, **Wolverhampton**
21	Tuesday	Fontwell, **Lingfield**, **Southwell**
22	Wednesday	**Lingfield**, Ludlow, **Wolverhampton**
26	Sunday	Kempton, Market Rasen, Towcester, Uttoxeter, Wetherby, Wincanton
27	Monday	Ayr, Huntingdon, Kempton, Wetherby, **Wolverhampton**
28	Tuesday	Catterick, Chepstow, Leicester, **Southwell**
29	Wednesday	Musselburgh, **Lingfield**, Newbury
30	Thursday	Haydock, **Lingfield**, Taunton
31	Friday	Sedgefield, Warwick, **Wolverhampton**

Big-race Dates

March

27 Sat Doncaster ....Freephone Stanley Lincoln Handicap (1m)

April

13 Tue Newmarket......................................Shadwell Stud Nell Gwyn Stakes (7f)
14 Wed Newmarket...........................Weatherbys Earl Of Sefton Stakes (1m1f)
       Newmarket......................Victor Chandler European Free Handicap (7f)
15 Thu Newmarket.......................Macau Jockey Club Craven Stakes (1m)
17 Sat Newbury ....Dubai Irish Village John Porter Stakes (1m4f)
       Newbury ....Lane's End Greenham Stakes (7f)
       Newbury ....Dubai Duty Free Fred Darling Stakes (7f)
23 Fri Sandown ....Sandown Park Classic Trial (1m2f)
24 Sat Sandown ....attheraces Mile (1m)
       Sandown ....attheraces.co.uk Gordon Richards Stakes (1m2f)
28 Wed Ascot.......................................Bovis Homes Sagaro Stakes (2m)
       Ascot...Sony Victoria Cup (7f)

May

1 Sat Newmarket ....Jockey Club Stakes (1m4f)
      Newmarket ....2,000 Guineas Stakes (1m)
      Newmarket................................Victor Chandler Palace House Stakes (5f)
2 Sun Newmarket ....1,000 Guineas Stakes (1m)
      Newmarket...........................R L Davison Pretty Polly Stakes (1m2f)
5 Wed Chester.....................Victor Chandler Chester Vase (1m4f66yds)
6 Thu Chester ....Tote Chester Cup (2m2f117yds)
      Chester ....UPM-Kyemmene Cheshire Oaks (1m3f79yds)
7 Fri Chester ....betfair.com Ormonde Stakes (1m5f89yds)
      Chester ....Philip Leverhulme Dee Stakes (1m2f75yds)
8 Sat Lingfield ....atttheraces Derby Trial Stakes (1m3f106yds)
      Lingfield ....attheraces Racing Oaks Trial Stakes (1m3f106yds)
11 Tue York..Tattersalls Musidora Stakes (1m2f)
      York..Duke Of York Stakes (6f)
12 Wed York...Tote Dante Stakes (1m2f)
13 Thu York...Yorkshire Cup (1m5f194yds)
14 Fri Newbury.........................Swettenham Stud Fillies' Trial Stakes (1m2f)
15 Sat Newbury ....Juddmonte Lockinge Stakes (1m)
      Newbury ....Aston Park Stakes (1m5f61yds)
18 Tue Goodwood ....Letheby & Christopher Predominate Stakes (1m2f)
19 Wed Goodwood ....Victor Chandler Lupe Stakes (1m2f)
22 Sat Haydock ....Tote Credit Club Silver Bowl (1m)
      Haydock Dunwoody Sports Marketing Sandy Lane Rated Handicap (6f)
31 Mon Sandown ....Bonusprint Henry II Stakes (2m)
      Redcar.....................Freephone Stanley Zetland Gold Cup Stakes (1m2f)
      Sandown ....Tripleprint Temple Stakes (5f)

June

1 Tue Sandown....................................Brigadier Gerard Stakes (1m2f)
4 Fri Epsom ....Vodafone Oaks (1m4f10yds)

Sponsored by Stan James

4	Fri	Epsom	Vodafone Coronation Cup (1m4f10yds)
5	Sat	Epsom	Vodafone Derby (1m4f10yds)
		Epsom	Vodafone Diomed Stakes (1m114yds)
		Haydock	betfair.com John Of Gaunt Stakes (7f30yds)
10	Thu	Newbury	Ballymacoll Stud Stakes (1m2f)
12	Sat	York	William Hill Trophy (6f)
15	Tue	Royal Ascot	St James's Palace Stakes (1m)
		Royal Ascot	Queen Anne Stakes (1m)
		Royal Ascot	Coventry Stakes (6f)
16	Wed	Royal Ascot	Prince Of Wales's Stakes (1m2f)
		Royal Ascot	Royal Hunt Cup (1m)
		Royal Ascot	Jersey Stakes (7f)
		Royal Ascot	Chesham Stakes (6f)
		Royal Ascot	Queen Mary Stakes (5f)
17	Thu	Royal Ascot	Gold Cup (2m4f)
		Royal Ascot	Ribblesdale Stakes (1m4f)
		Royal Ascot	Norfolk Stakes (5f)
18	Fri	Royal Ascot	Coronation Stakes (1m)
		Royal Ascot	King Edward VII Stakes (1m4f)
		Royal Ascot	Queen's Vase (2m45yds)
19	Sat	Royal Ascot	Hardwicke Stakes (1m4f)
		Royal Ascot	Golden Jubilee Stakes (6f)
26	Sat	Newcastle	Foster's Lager Northumberland Plate (2m19yds)
		Newmarket	Criterion Stakes (7f)
		Newmarket	Ladbrokes Fred Archer Stakes (1m4f)

July

3	Sat	Haydock	Lancashire Oaks Stakes (1m4f)
		Haydock	Old Newton Cup (1m4f)
		Sandown	Coral Eurobet Eclipse Stakes (1m2f)
6	Tue	Newmarket	Princess of Wales's Stakes (1m4f)
		Newmarket	Cherry Hinton Stakes (6f)
7	Wed	Newmarket	Falmouth Stakes (1m)
		Newmarket	TNT July Stakes (6f)
8	Thu	Newmarket	Darley July Cup (6f)
		Newmarket	Ladbrokes Bunbury Cup (7f)
10	Sat	York	John Smith's Cup (1m2f85yds)
		York	Webster's Silver Cup Rated Handicap (1m5f194yds)
16	Fri	Newbury	Shadwell Stud Rose Bowl Stakes (6f)
17	Sat	Newbury	Weatherbys Super Sprint (5f34yds)
19	Mon	Ayr	Daily Record Scottish Derby (1m2f)
24	Sat	Ascot	King George VI and Queen Elizabeth Diamond Stakes (1m4f)
		Ascot	Princess Margaret Stakes (6f)
27	Tue	Glorious Goodwood	Peugot Gordon Stakes (1m2f)
28	Wed	Glorious Goodwood	Sussex Stakes (1m)
		Glorious Goodwood	Tote Gold Trophy (1m4f)
		Glorious Goodwood	Veuve Cliquot Vintage Stakes (7f)
29	Thu	Glorious Goodwood	William Hill Mile (1m)
		Glorious Goodwood	Betfair Molecomb Stakes (5f)
		Glorious Goodwood	Lady O Goodwood Cup (2m)
30	Fri	Glorious Goodwood	Oak Tree Stakes (6f)

30	Fri	Glorious Goodwood ....Glorious Rated Handicap (1m4f)
31	Sat	Glorious Goodwood...................................Vodafone Stewards' Cup (6f)
		Glorious Goodwood ....Vodafone Nassau Stakes (1m2f)

August

7	Sat	Newmarket ....Sweet Solera Stakes (7f)
		Haydock ....Petros Rose Of Lancaster Stakes (1m2f120yds)
13	Fri	Newbury.................Newbury Racecourse Washington Singer Stakes (7f)
14	Sat	Newbury ....Stan James St Hugh's Stakes (5f)
		Newbury ....Stan James Hungerford Stakes (7f64yds)
		Newbury ....Stan James Geoffrey Freer Stakes (1m5f61yds)
		Ripon...................................William Hill Great St Wilfrid Handicap (6f)
17	Tue	York...............................Juddmonte International Stakes (1m2f85yds)
		York..Great Voltigeur Stakes (1m4f)
		York...............................Weatherbys Insurance Lonsdale Stakes (2m)
18	Wed	York...Aston Upthorpe Yorkshire Oaks (1m4f)
		York...............................Scottish Equitable Gimcrack Stakes (6f)
		York..Tote Ebor Stakes (1m6f)
19	Thu	York...Peugot Lowther Stakes (6f)
		York...............................Victor Chandler Nunthorpe Stakes (5f)
		York..EBF Galtres Stakes (1m4f)
21	Sat	Sandown...Iveco Daily Solario Stakes (7f)
28	Sat	Goodwood...Celebration Mile (1m)
		Goodwood ....San Migel March Stakes (1m6f)
29	Sun	Goodwood...........................Touchdown in Malaysia Prestige Stakes (7f)
30	Mon	Ripon.................betfair.com Ripon Champion Two Years Old Trophy (6f)

September

4	Sat	Kempton ....Sirenia Stakes (6f)
		Kempton ....Milcars September Stakes (1m3f)
8	Wed	Doncaster ....Park Hill Stakes (1m6f132yds)
		Doncaster ....£200,000 St Leger Yearling Stakes (6f)
		Doncaster...............................Tote Trifecta Portland Handicap (1m)
9	Thu	Doncaster ....Scarbrough Stakes (5f)
		Doncaster ....GNER Park Stakes (1m)
		Doncaster...GNER Doncaster Cup (2m2f)
		Doncaster..May Hill Stakes (1m)
10	Fri	Doncaster...Champagne Stakes (7f)
		Doncaster...............................DBS St Leger Yearling Stakes (1m6f132yds)
11	Sat	Doncaster ....Polypipe Flying Childers Stakes (5f)
		Doncaster...St Leger Stakes (1m6f)
12	Sun	Goodwood ....Select Stakes (1m2f)
17	Fri	Newbury ....Dubai Duty Free Cup (7f)
		Newbury ....Dubai Duty Free Mill Reef Stakes (6f)
18	Sat	Newbury ....Dubai International Airport World Trophy (5f34yds)
		Newbury ....Dubai Duty Free Arc Trial (1m3f5yds)
		Ayr ....Tote Ayr Gold Cup (6f)
		Ayr...Doonside Cup (1m2f192yds)
25	Sat	Ascot...Queen Elizabeth II Stakes (1m)
		Ascot...............................Meon Valley Stud Fillies' Mile (1m)
		Ascot ....Hackney Empire Royal Lodge Stakes (1m4f)
		Ascot...Diadem Stakes (6f)

26 Sun Ascot..........................Young Vic Theatre Cumberland Lodge Stakes (1m)
         Ascot ....Mail On Sunday Mile Final (1m)
30 Thu Goodwood ....Charlton Hunt Supreme Stakes (7f)
         Newmarket ....Cheveley Park Stakes (6f)

October

 1 Fri   Newmarket....................................Shadwell Stud Middle Park Stakes (6f)
 2 Sat   Newmarket ....Tote Cambridgeshire Handicap (1m1f)
         Newmarket..................................Peugot Sun Chariot Stakes (1m2f)
         Redcar...Betabet Two-Year-Old Trophy (7f)
 9 Sat   Ascot ....Princess Royal Willmott Dixon Stakes (1m4f)
         Ascot...Willmott Dixon Cornwallis Stakes (5f)
15 Fri   Newmarket ....£100,000 Tatersalls Autumn Auction Stakes (1m)
16 Sat   Newmarket ....Emirates Airline Champion Stakes (1m2f)
         Newmarket...Tote Cesarewitch (2m2f)
         Newmarket..................................Victor Chandler Challenge Stakes (1m)
         Newmarket...Darley Dewhurst Stakes (6f)
         Newmarket...Owen Brown Rockfel Stakes (7f)
         Newmarket...Jockey Club Cup (2m)
22 Fri   Doncaster ....Vodafone Horris Hill Stakes (7f)
23 Sat   Doncaster...Racing Post Trophy (1m)
         Newbury...St Simon Stakes (1m4f)

November

 6 Sat   Doncaster ....Tote Scoop6 November Handicap (1m4f)

Ireland

May	22 Sat	Curragh ....Entenmann's Irish 2,000 Guineas (1m)
	23 Sun	Curragh ....Entenmann's Irish 1,000 Guineas (1m)
June	27 Sun	Curragh ....Budweiser Irish Derby (1m4f)
July	18 Sun	Curragh ....Darley Irish Oaks (1m4f)
August	15 Sun	Curragh ...Waterford Wedgewood Phoenix Park Stakes (6f)
September	5 Sun	Curragh ....Moyglare Stud Stakes (7f)
		Curragh...Flying Five Stakes (5f)
	11 Sat	Leopardstown ....Irish Champion Stakes (1m2f)
	18 Sat	Curragh...Irish St Leger (1m6f)
	19 Sun	Curragh...National Stakes (7f)

Overseas

March	27 Sat	Nad Al Sheba, UAE ....Dubai World Cup (1m2f)
May	1 Sat	Churchill Downs, USA ....Kentucky Derby (1m2f)
	15 Sat	Pimlico, USA ....Preakness Stakes (1m1f110yds)
	16 Sun	Longchamp, France ....Poule d'Essai des Poulains (1m)
		Longchamp, France........Poule d'Essai des Pouliches (1m)
June	5 Sat	Belmont Park, USA...........................Belmont Stakes (1m4f)
	6 Sun	Chantilly, France.......................Prix du Jockey Club (1m4f)
	13 Sun	Chantilly, France ....Prix de Diane Hermes (1m2f110yds)
October	3 Sun	Longchamp, France ....Prix de l'Arc de Triomphe (1m4f)
	30 Sat	Lone Star Park, USA........................Breeders Cup meeting
November	2 Tue	Flemington, Australia...........................Melbourne Cup (2m)
	28 Sun	Fuchu, Japan ....Japan Cup (1m4f)

Outlook

Group One Records

Year	Winner	Age (if appropriate)	Trainer	Jockey	SP	draw/ran

2,000 Guineas (1m) Newmarket

Year	Winner	Trainer	Jockey	SP	draw/ran
1994	**Mister Baileys**	M Johnston	J Weaver	16-1	21/23
1995	**Pennekamp**	A Fabre	T Jarnet	9-2	11/11
1996	**Mark Of Esteem**	S bin Suroor	L Dettori	8-1	2/13
1997	**Entrepreneur**	Sir M Stoute	M Kinane	11-2	4/16
1998	**King Of Kings**	A O'Brien	M Kinane	7-2	17/18
1999*	**Island Sands**	S bin Suroor	L Dettori	10-1	3/16

(*run on July course)

Year	Winner	Trainer	Jockey	SP	draw/ran
2000	**King's Best**	Sir M Stoute	K Fallon	13-2	12/27
2001	**Golan**	Sir M Stoute	K Fallon	11-1	19/18
2002	**Rock Of Gibraltar**	A O'Brien	J Murtagh	9-1	22/22
2003	**Refuse To Bend**	D Weld	P Smullen	9-2	18/20

THE FIRST colts' Classic was first run in 1809 and is usually held on the first Saturday in May. It's often a specialist miler's race. As with the 1,000 Guineas, you don't get many winners who haven't earned themselves a high place in the International Classifications, although Island Sands bucked that trend. King Of Kings was rated 111 and was already a Group 1 winner at two, as was Rock Of Gibraltar, who had won the Dewhurst, which has proved the best of the two-year-old trials. The race currently known as the Racing Post Trophy has produced only one winner, High Top. Newmarket's Craven Stakes has proved a far better guide than Newbury's Greenham in recent years. It appears that horses having their seasonal debut in the race are not disadvantaged, with Rock Of Gibraltar, Golan, King Of Kings, Entrepreneur, Mark Of Esteem and Mister Baileys all making their seasonal reappearances when triumphing here. There was evidence of a pronounced draw bias favouring high numbers in the 2002 renewal – to combat this, the 2003 race was run over a much narrower strip of ground, producing no clear bias.

1,000 Guineas (1m) Newmarket

Year	Winner	Trainer	Jockey	SP	draw/ran
1994	**Las Meninas**	T Stack	J Reid	12-1	1/15
1995	**Harayir**	W Hern	R Hills	5-1	2/14
1996	**Bosra Sham**	H Cecil	Pat Eddery	10-11f	11/13
1997	**Sleepytime**	H Cecil	K Fallon	5-1	3/15
1998	**Cape Verdi**	S bin Suroor	L Dettori	10-3	7/16
1999*	**Wince**	H Cecil	K Fallon	4-1	19/22

(*run on July course)

Year	Winner	Trainer	Jockey	SP	draw/ran
2000	**Lahan**	J Gosden	R Hills	14-1	10/18
2001	**Ameerat**	M Jarvis	P Robinson	11-1	10/18

| 2002 | **Kazzia** | S bin Suroor | L Dettori | 9-2 | 12/17 |
| 2003 | **Russian Rhythm** | Sir M Stoute | K Fallon | 12-1 | 2/19 |

FIRST RUN in 1814, since 1995 the first fillies' Classic has been run on a Sunday. A high place in the International Classifications has been critical – very few winners register less than 112. Ameerat (106) and Cape Verdi (109) count against this theory but the latter was campaigned at distances short of her best at two, which may explain the extent of her apparent improvement. The Marcel Boussac and the Cheveley Park are the races to study from the previous year. Two key trials are Newbury's Fred Darling and Newmarket's Nell Gwyn, but don't necessarily be put off by horses beaten in those. Cape Verdi was an unusual winner at the time, not having had a prep-run, but the last three winners have all been making their seasonal reappearances.

Lockinge (1m) Newbury

1994	**Emperor Jones**	4	J Gosden	L Dettori	11-2	9/11
1995	**Soviet Line**	5	Sir M Stoute	W Swinburn	2-1f	4/5
1996	**Soviet Line**	6	Sir M Stoute	T Quinn	13-2	1/7
1997	**First Island**	5	G Wragg	M Hills	11-4	1/10
1998	**Cape Cross**	4	S bin Suroor	D O'Donohoe	20-1	8/10
1999	**Fly To The Stars**	5	S bin Suroor	W Supple	9-1	6/6
2000	**Aljabr**	4	S bin Suroor	L Dettori	8-13f	1/7
2001	**Medicean**	4	Sir M Stoute	K Fallon	3-1	5/7
2002	**Keltos**	4	C Laffon-Parias	O Peslier	9-1	7/10
2003	**Hawk Wing**	4	A O'Brien	M Kinane	2-1f	4/6

Formerly Group 2, Group 1 from 1995.

OFTEN QUITE weak for a Group 1 (something which was conveniently forgotten amid all the hype after Hawk Wing won the latest renewal), the Lockinge was a Godolphin benefit in the late 1990s. It's worth noting, however, that both Cape Cross and Fly To The Stars were perceived to be their second-strings, with their Intikhab getting turned over at 4-7 in the 1999 race. Godolphin's Noverre was also beaten at odds-on behind Keltos. Four-year-olds seem to have the call over their older rivals. This race is often run on ground with plenty of give, and can therefore provide a rare chance at this level for horses who like to get their toe in.

Coronation Cup (1m4f) Epsom

1994	**Apple Tree**	5	A Fabre	T Jarnet	12-1	10/11
1995	**Sunshack**	4	A Fabre	Pat Eddery	10-1	2/7
1996	**Swain**	4	A Fabre	L Dettori	11-10f	2/4
1997	**Singspiel**	5	Sir M Stoute	L Dettori	5-4f	3/5
1998	**Silver Patriarch**	4	J Dunlop	Pat Eddery	7-2	2/7
1999	**Daylami**	5	S bin Suroor	L Dettori	9-2	3/7
2000	**Daliapour**	4	Sir M Stoute	K Fallon	11-8f	2/4
2001	**Mutafaweq**	5	S bin Suroor	L Dettori	11-2	1/6
2002	**Boreal**	4	P Schiergen	K Fallon	4-1	3/6
2003	**Warrsan**	5	C Brittain	P Robinson	9-2	4/9

IT'S HARD to escape the conclusion that this race is suffering a fall from grace, with the quality of winner dropping markedly, even within the last ten years. Almost always featuring a small field, the combination of a false pace and the tricky course have produced some funny results, perhaps none more so than Silver Patriarch beating Swain. In general, the call has got to be to oppose the market-leader.

The Oaks (1m4f) Epsom

1994	Balanchine	H Ibrahim	L Dettori	6-1	9/10
1995	Moonshell	S bin Suroor	L Dettori	3-1	9/10
1996	Lady Carla	H Cecil	Pat Eddery	100-30	9/11
1997	Reams Of Verse	H Cecil	K Fallon	5-6f	6/12
1998	Shahtoush	A O'Brien	M Kinane	12-1	5/8
1999	Ramruma	H Cecil	K Fallon	3-1	5/10
2000	Love Divine	H Cecil	T Quinn	9-4f	3/16
2001	Imagine	A O'Brien	M Kinane	3-1f	10/14
2002	Kazzia	S bin Suroor	L Dettori	100-30f	13/14
2003	Casual Look	A Balding	Martin Dwyer	10-1	7/15

FIRST RUN in 1779, the Oaks is one year older then the Derby. Breeding is just as important as in the Derby, particularly since so few three-year-old fillies stay so far at this time of the year. The 1,000 Guineas has provided the best guide, followed by the Musidora at York. In 1998, Shahtoush kept up the good record of 1,000 Guineas runners – she had finished second in the first fillies' Classic, while Kazzia provided a further boost by winning both. Casual Look was sixth in the Guineas on her only previous outing that season. Ramruma won the Lingfield Oaks Trial, while Imagine was the first filly to do the Irish Guineas/Oaks double since 1966.

The Derby (1m4f) Epsom

1994	Erhaab	J Dunlop	W Carson	7-2f	15/25
1995	Lammtarra	S bin Suroor	W Swinburn	14-1	7/15
1996	Shaamit	W Haggas	M Hills	12-1	9/20
1997	Benny The Dip	J Gosden	W Ryan	11-1	8/13
1998	High-Rise	L Cumani	O Peslier	20-1	14/15
1999	Oath	H Cecil	K Fallon	13-2	1/16
2000	Sinndar	J Oxx	J Murtagh	7-1	15/15
2001	Galileo	A O'Brien	M Kinane	11-4j	10/12
2002	High Chaparral	A O'Brien	J Murtagh	7-2	9/12
2003	Kris Kin	Sir M Stoute	K Fallon	6-1	4/20

MANY HIGH-CLASS colts are beaten here due to lack of stamina. It's important to have a top-class sire (Sadler's Wells took an age to get a Derby winner but has now produced two of the last three winners, as well as last year's runner-up), plus a staying pedigree on the dam's side. Since the golden years of Nijinsky and Mill Reef (1970 and 1971) only one horse, Nashwan, has won both the 2,000 Guineas and Derby, although Dancing Brave was unlucky at Epsom having landed the Newmarket race. Key races include York's Dante Stakes and the Lingfield Derby Trial, High-Rise winning the latter. In three of the last four years, Leopardstown's Derby Trial has been the key pointer. Oath warmed up by winning a Listed race at Chester, while Kris Kin's final prep was in a Group 3 race at the same track. Generally this is a race for fancied runners in the first four in the betting – 20-1 winner High-Rise was the biggest priced winner for 25 years. Having said that, outright favourites don't have a strong record, with 4-6 Entrepreneur among the beaten jollies. Kris Kin was the subject of a huge gamble on the morning of the race.

Queen Anne Stakes (1m) Royal Ascot

1994	Barathea	4	L Cumani	M Kinane	3-1	1/10
1995	Nicolotte	4	G Wragg	M Hills	16-1	2/7
1996	Charnwood Forest	4	S bin Suroor	M Kinane	10-11	6/9

1997	**Allied Forces**	4	S bin Suroor	L Dettori	10-1	11/11
1998	**Intikhab**	4	S bin Suroor	L Dettori	9-4	6/9
1999	**Cape Cross**	5	S bin Suroor	G Stevens	7-1	2/8
2000	**Kalanisi**	4	Sir M Stoute	K Fallon	11-2	11/11
2001	**Medicean**	4	Sir M Stoute	K Fallon	11-2	8/10
2002	**No Excuse Needed**	4	Sir M Stoute	J Murtagh	13-2	11/12
2003	**Dubai Destination**	4	S bin Suroor	L Dettori	9-2	10/10

Formerly Group 3. Group 2 from 1985, Group 1 from 2003.

THE FIRST race of the Royal Ascot meeting, usually run at a furious pace. Four-year-olds who were once considered Classic contenders fit the bill and the age group has taken ten of the last 11 runnings. Three-year-olds have a dreadful record and few of them attempt the race these days – only one in the last five years. Godolphin won the race four times in a row before Kalanisi's success in 2000 and they again hit the target in 2003; Sir Michael Stoute won all three renewals in the intervening years. The Lockinge Stakes (Newbury, May, a Group 1 for the first time in 1996) is a key race; Medicean won both races, while No Excuse Needed ran a feeble race behind Keltos in the Lockinge before landing this. Dubai Destination was given a low-key warm-up at Nottingham last year, when Lockinge winner Hawk Wing let down the record of the Newbury race by beating only three home.

Prince Of Wales's Stakes (1m2f) Royal Ascot

1994	**Muhtarram**	5	J Gosden	W Carson	6-4f	8/11
1995	**Muhtarram**	6	J Gosden	W Carson	5-1	5/6
1996	**First Island**	4	G Wragg	M Hills	9-1	3/12
1997	**Bosra Sham**	4	H Cecil	K Fallon	4-11f	1/6
1998	**Faithful Son**	4	S bin Suroor	J Reid	11-2	7/8
1999	**Lear Spear**	4	D Elsworth	M Kinane	20-1	5/8
2000	**Dubai Millennium**	4	S bin Suroor	J Bailey	5-4	7/6
2001	**Fantastic Light**	5	S bin Suroor	L Dettori	100-30	8/9
2002	**Grandera**	4	S bin Suroor	L Dettori	4-1	3/12
2003	**Nayef**	5	M Tregoning	R Hills	5-1	6/10

FIRST RUN in 1968 and now one of the races of the week. Four-year-olds have mostly proved successful in recent years. Three-year-olds have won only twice since the inception of the race, while three horses have doubled up – Muhtarram, Mtoto and Connaught. For the above reason, a key race is the previous year's running, a fact underlined by Nayef, who'd been fourth in 2002. The Brigadier Gerard Stakes, won by Bosra Sham, the Gordon Richards Stakes and the Tattersalls Gold Cup (won by Fantastic Light in 2001) are other key pointers. Grandera came into the race from a spring international campaign taking in Dubai, Hong Kong and Singapore, while Nayef's only prep-run was also in Dubai.

St James's Palace Stakes (1m) Royal Ascot

1994	**Grand Lodge**	W Jarvis	M Kinane	6-1	3/9
1995	**Bahri**	J Dunlop	W Carson	11-4f	7/9
1996	**Bijou d'Inde**	M Johnston	J Weaver	9-1	7/9
1997	**Starborough**	D Loder	L Dettori	11-2	5/8
1998	**Dr Fong**	H Cecil	K Fallon	4-1	4/8
1999	**Sendawar**	A de Royer-Dupre	G Mosse	2-1f	11/11
2000	**Giant's Causeway**	A O'Brien	M Kinane	7-2f	3/11
2001	**Black Minnaloushe**	A O'Brien	J Murtagh	8-1	1/11
2002	**Rock Of Gibraltar**	A O'Brien	M Kinane	4-5f	4/9
2003	**Zafeen**	M Channon	D Holland	8-1	5/11

FIRST RUN in 1925, this is restricted to three-year-olds. Winners and also-rans from the Irish, French and English Guineas often line up for this valuable prize. The last four winners all ran in the Irish Guineas, Black Minnaloushe and Rock Of Gibraltar having won on the Curragh, while Giant's Causeway had been second and Zafeen a dismal fourteenth. Six of the last eight winners had made the frame in the English version. Less exposed types such as Persian Heights and Shavian can make a breakthrough. Derby runners have a mixed record; Marju was second in the Derby and won, but Rodrigo De Triano flopped in both races.

Coronation Stakes (1m) Royal Ascot

1994	**Kissing Cousin**	H Cecil	M Kinane	13-2	2/10
1995	**Ridgewood Pearl**	J Oxx	J Murtagh	9-2	8/10
1996	**Shake The Yoke**	E Lellouche	O Peslier	Evensf	4/7
1997	**Rebecca Sharp**	G Wragg	M Hills	25-1	3/6
1998	**Exclusive**	Sir M Stoute	W Swinburn	5-1	10/9
1999	**Balisada**	G Wragg	M Roberts	16-1	8/9
2000	**Crimplene**	C Brittain	P Robinson	4-1j	6/9
2001	**Banks Hill**	A Fabre	O Peslier	4-1j	4/13
2002	**Sophisticat**	A O'Brien	M Kinane	11-2	3/11
2003	**Russian Rhythm**	Sir M Stoute	K Fallon	4-7f	11/9

A CHAMPIONSHIP race for three-year-old fillies, first run in 1870. Winners and runners from all the Guineas races fare well (Exclusive was third in English version, while the 2002 running was a triumph for the form of the French Guineas), but Irish 1,000 Guineas winners have the best record through Ridgewood Pearl, Kooyonga and Crimplene. English 1,000 Guinness winners have been worth opposing – failures include Harayir, Las Meninas, Shadayid and Sleepytime. Russian Rhythm was the first Newmarket winner to take this since 1979.

Golden Jubilee Stakes (6f) Royal Ascot

1994	**Owington**	3	G Wragg	M Hills	4-1f	2/17
1995	**So Factual**	5	S bin Suroor	L Dettori	9-2	9/11
1996	**Atraf**	3	D Morley	W Carson	12-1	2/17
1997	**Royal Applause**	4	B Hills	M Hills	11-2f	16/23
1998	**Tomba**	4	B Meehan	M Tebbutt	4-1	13/12
1999	**Bold Edge**	4	R Hannon	D O'Neill	16-1	16/19
2000	**Superior Premium**	6	R Fahey	J Murtagh	20-1	17/16
2001	**Harmonic Way**	6	R Charlton	S Drowne	10-1	1/21
2002	**Malhub**	4	J Gosden	K Darley	16-1	12/12
2003	**Choisir**	4	P Perry	J Murtagh	13-2	20/17

AKA 'The Cork And Orrery'. Formerly Group 3. Group 2 from 1999, Group 1 from 2002.
ALWAYS A fiercely competitive race and one that has thrown up more than its share of shocks in recent seasons. Four-year-olds have won most often, but then they usually make up most of the field. By contrast, three-year-olds haven't won since 1996 but one or two often run well at big prices, notably Baron's Pit (third at 50-1 last year), Indian Country (fourth at the same price the year before) and Freud (third at 25-1 in 2001).

Gold Cup (2m4f) Royal Ascot

1994	**Arcadian Heights**	6	G Wragg	M Hills	20-1	5/9
1995	**Double Trigger**	4	M Johnston	J Weaver	9-4	6/7
1996	**Classic Cliche**	4	S bin Suroor	M Kinane	3-1	7/7
1997	**Celeric**	5	D Morley	Pat Eddery	11-2	2/13

1998	**Kayf Tara**	4	S bin Suroor	L Dettori	11-1	17/16
1999	**Enzeli**	4	J Oxx	J Murtagh	20-1	16/17
2000	**Kayf Tara**	6	S bin Suroor	M Kinane	11-8f	6/11
2001	**Royal Rebel**	5	M Johnston	J Murtagh	8-1	10/12
2002	**Royal Rebel**	6	M Johnston	J Murtagh	16-1	8/15
2003	**Mr Dinos**	4	P Cole	K Fallon	3-1	6/12

THE ONLY British Group 1 race run over 2m4f. Many winners, including most recently Royal Rebel, have followed up from the year before, probably because winners have to possess a blend of speed and stamina that is very rare in modern racing stock. Apart from the winner of the previous year's heat, the key races are the St Leger and Sandown's Henry II Stakes. Mr Dinos had been fifth in the Leger and warmed up for this by landing the Sandown race.

Eclipse (1m2f) Sandown

1994	**Ezzoud**	5	Sir M Stoute	W Swinburn	5-1	6/8
1995	**Halling**	4	S bin Suroor	W Swinburn	7-1	3/8
1996	**Halling**	5	S bin Suroor	J Reid	100-30	1/7
1997	**Pilsudski**	5	Sir M Stoute	M Kinane	11-2	1/5
1998	**Daylami**	4	S bin Suroor	L Dettori	6-4f	5/7
1999	**Compton Admiral**	3	G Butler	D Holland	20-1	7/8
2000	**Giant's Causeway**	3	A O'Brien	G Duffield	8-1	4/8
2001	**Medicean**	4	Sir M Stoute	K Fallon	7-2	7/8
2002	**Hawk Wing**	3	A O'Brien	M Kinane	8-15f	6/5
2003	**Falbrav**	5	L Cumani	D Holland	8-1	14/15

CHANGES IN the weight-for-age scale meant that, from 1990 onwards, three-year-olds became 2lb worse off with their elders, but that didn't stop Environment Friend, Compton Admiral, Giant's Causeway or Hawk Wing (though the latter won a very weak renewal). Derby winners and fillies have a poor record. Pebbles, in the mid-Eighties, was the first filly to succeed since the nineteenth century. Proven Group 1 form is a major asset. Daylami and Falbrav, both beaten in the Prince of Wales's Stakes, kept up the good record of runners from that race and Royal Ascot form in general is a key to this race; Giant's Causeway won the St James's Palace and Medicean won the Queen Anne.

July Cup (6f) Newmarket

1994	**Owington**	3	G Wragg	Paul Eddery	3-1	1/9
1995	**Lake Coniston**	4	G Lewis	Pat Eddery	13-8f	9/9
1996	**Anabaa**	4	C Head	F Head	11-4	2/10
1997	**Compton Place**	3	J Toller	S Sanders	50-1	1/9
1998	**Elnadim**	4	J Dunlop	R Hills	3-1f	18/17
1999	**Stravinsky**	3	A O'Brien	M Kinane	8-1	6/17
2000	**Agnes World**	5	H Mori	Y Take	4-1f	6/10
2001	**Mozart**	3	A O'Brien	M Kinane	4-1f	19/18
2002	**Continent**	5	D Nicholls	D Holland	12-1	2/14
2003	**Oasis Dream**	3	J Gosden	R Hughes	9-2	11/16

THE BLUE RIBAND event of Newmarket's July meeting, it was first staged in 1876. Horses dropping down in distance succeeded in 1987, 1988, 1999 and 2001. Mozart had won the 7f Jersey Stakes and finished second in the Irish Guineas. However, in the main over the last 10 years it is specialist sprinters who have been doing well in this race. The Cork and Orrery (Royal Ascot, June), the King's Stand (also Royal Ascot), the Duke of York (York, May), the 2,000 Guineas (Newmarket, May) and the 1,000 Guineas (also Newmarket, May) give the most helpful clues.

King George VI and Queen Elizabeth Diamond Stakes (1m4f) Ascot

1994	King's Theatre	3	H Cecil	M Kinane	12-1	7/12
1995	Lammtarra	3	S bin Suroor	L Dettori	9-4f	3/7
1996	Pentire	4	G Wragg	M Hills	100-30	7/8
1997	Swain	5	S bin Suroor	J Reid	16-1	5/8
1998	Swain	6	S bin Suroor	L Dettori	11-2	5/8
1999	Daylami	5	S bin Suroor	L Dettori	3-1	8/8
2000	Montjeu	4	J Hammond	M Kinane	1-3f	5/7
2001	Galileo	3	A O'Brien	M Kinane	1-2f	7/12
2002	Golan	4	Sir M Stoute	K Fallon	11-2	8/9
2003	Alamshar	3	J Oxx	J Murtagh	13-2	5/12

ALTHOUGH IT has less prestige than the Arc, the King George is always won by a top-class horse. It was first run in 1951. Lammtarra and Galileo came into this race as Derby winners, while King's Theatre had been second at Epsom and Alamshar third. Although a top-class older horse, trained by an established handler, best fits the bill, (1999, 2000, 2002), a seriously good three-year-old is almost given a head-start by the weight-for-age scale – but note that no three-year-old has won this in the last decade without having made the frame in the Derby. The Eclipse is also a big influence, while, for the older horses, the Coronation Cup is a good pointer. Golan was the first horse ever to win this on his seasonal debut, though few serious contenders will have attempted such a feat.

Sussex Stakes (1m) Goodwood

1994	Distant View	3	H Cecil	Pat Eddery	4-1	9/9
1995	Sayyedati	5	C Brittain	B Doyle	11-2	4/6
1996	First Island	4	G Wragg	M Hills	5-1	9/10
1997	Ali-Royal	4	H Cecil	K Fallon	13-2	3/9
1998	Among Men	4	Sir M Stoute	M Kinane	4-1	10/10
1999	Aljabr	3	S Bin Suroor	L Dettori	11-10f	6/8
2000	Giant's Causeway	3	A O'Brien	M Kinane	3-1j	6/10
2001	Noverre	3	S Bin Suroor	L Dettori	9-2	11/10
2002	Rock Of Gibraltar	3	A O'Brien	M Kinane	8-13f	3/5
2003	Reel Buddy	5	R Hannon	Pat Eddery	20-1	7/9

THIS GENERALLY features a glamorous three-year-old, who is sent off a well-backed favourite. As well as winners Rock Of Gibraltar, Aljabr and Giant's Causeway, losing jollies Trade Fair, Lend A Hand, Starborough, Bahri and Mister Baileys would fall into this category. This race is dominated by the big-league yards and big-name jockeys.

Nassau Stakes (1m1f192yds) Goodwood

1994	Hawajiss	3	Sir M Stoute	W Swinburn	4-1j	4/9
1995	Caramba	3	R Hannon	M Roberts	5-2f	3/6
1996	Last Second	3	Sir M Prescott	G Duffield	7-4f	1/8
1997	Ryafan	3	J Gosden	M Hills	9-4f	5/7
1998	Alborada	3	Sir M Prescott	G Duffield	4-1	5/9
1999	Zahrat Dubai	3	S bin Suroor	G Stevens	5-1	3/8
2000	Crimplene	3	C Brittain	P Robinson	7-4f	3/7
2001	Lailani	3	E Dunlop	L Dettori	5-4f	5/7
2002	Islington	3	Sir M Stoute	K Fallon	100-30	6/10
2003	Russian Rhythm	3	Sir M Stoute	K Fallon	4-5f	7/8

AN AMAZINGLY good race for favourites, pointing up a real lack of strength in depth among fillies at this distance and at this level. The only losing jolly of the last four years has been Quarter Moon, who had become a very unreliable sort by the time of this race and was fairly beaten by a subsequent Breeders' Cup winner. Russian Rhythm was the first Guineas winner to add this for many a year. Three-year-olds have dominated to the exclusion of their elders.

Juddmonte International Stakes (1m2f85yds) York

1994	Ezzoud	5	Sir M Stoute	W Swinburn	4-1	4/8
1995	Halling	4	S bin Suroor	W Swinburn	9-4f	2/6
1996	Halling	5	S bin Suroor	L Dettori	6-4f	1/6
1997	Singspiel	5	Sir M Stoute	L Dettori	4-1	2/4
1998	One So Wonderful	4	L Cumani	Pat Eddery	6-1	5/8
1999	Royal Anthem	4	H Cecil	G Stevens	3-1f	9/12
2000	Giant's Causeway	3	A O'Brien	M Kinane	10-11f	5/6
2001	Sakhee	4	S bin Suroor	L Dettori	7-4f	5/8
2002	Nayef	4	M Tregoning	R Hills	6-4f	5/7
2003	Falbrav	5	L Cumani	D Holland	5-2	2/8

FAMOUS FOR its many upsets since its first running in 1972 when Roberto beat Grundy. Bosra Sham in 1997 was one of many hot favourites to be beaten in this race. That said, favourites won four on the reel before Kalaman proved a big let-down in the latest renewal. Older horses, especially lightly-raced ones, have mostly kept on top of the three-year-olds, though Giant's Causeway bucked the trend in 2000. Note the previous year's running and the Eclipse.

Yorkshire Oaks (1m3f195yds) York

1994	Only Royale	5	L Cumani	L Dettori	15-2	5/7
1995	Pure Grain	3	Sir M Stoute	J Reid	11-10f	2/8
1996	Key Change	3	J Oxx	J Murtagh	7-1	1/9
1997	My Emma	4	R Guest	D Holland	7-1	7/8
1998	Catchascatchcan	3	H Cecil	K Fallon	2-1f	7/6
1999	Ramruma	3	H Cecil	Pat Eddery	5-6f	9/11
2000	Petrushka	3	Sir M Stoute	J Murtagh	5-4f	1/6
2001	Super Tassa	5	V Valiani	K Darley	25-1	7/9
2002	Islington	3	Sir M Stoute	K Fallon	2-1	9/11
2003	Islington	4	Sir M Stoute	K Fallon	8-11f	5/8

SIR MICHAEL STOUTE has a good grip on what it takes to land this, with four victories from the last ten, albeit all at short odds. Super Tassa, the only non-Stoute-trained winner of the last four years, was also remarkable for being the first Italian-trained winner in Britain for 41 years. The Classic generation have the edge, with six wins in the last decade, though only one of them was returned at bigger than 2-1, whereas only one of the older winners was shorter than 7s.

Nunthorpe Stakes (5f) York

1994	Piccolo	3	M Channon	J Reid	14-1	4/10
1995	So Factual	5	S bin Suroor	L Dettori	9-2	5/8
1996	Pivotal	3	Sir M Prescott	G Duffield	100-30	5/8
1997 {	Coastal Bluff	5	T D Barron	K Darley	6-1	6/15
	Ya Malak	6	D Nicholls	A Greaves	11-1	4/15
1998	Lochangel	4	I Balding	L Dettori	6-1	2/17
1999	Stravinsky	3	A O'Brien	M Kinane	Evensf	13/16
2000	Nuclear Debate	5	J Hammond	G Mosse	5-2f	1/13
2001	Mozart	3	A O'Brien	M Kinane	4-9f	4/10
2002	Kyllachy	4	H Candy	J Spencer	3-1f	15/17
2003	Oasis Dream	3	J Gosden	R Hughes	4-9f	2/8

A RUN of five consecutive winning favourites (including two at the very skimpy price of 4-9) suggests that the sprinting division is not so competitive as it has been, despite the healthy field-sizes. Three-year-olds have punched above their weight, with half of the last ten winners. Recent results hint at a draw bias towards low numbers – Kyllachy was switched around the entire field and finished up the far rail, where you'd expect the low-drawn runners to be.

Stanley Leisure Sprint Cup (6f) Haydock

1994	Lavinia Fontana	5	J Dunlop	J Weaver	11-2	8/8
1995	Cherokee Rose	4	J Hammond	C Asmussen	5-1	4/6
1996	Iktamal	4	E Dunlop	W Ryan	10-1	9/11
1997	Royal Applause	4	B Hills	M Hills	15-8f	9/9
1998	Tamarisk	3	R Charlton	T Sprake	13-2	5/13
1999	Diktat	4	S bin Suroor	L Dettori	13-8f	16/16
2000	Pipalong	4	T Easterby	K Darley	3-1	7/13
2001	Nuclear Debate	6	J Hammond	G Mosse	11-2	9/12
2002	Invincible Spirit	5	J Dunlop	J Carroll	25-1	10/14
2003	Somnus	3	T Easterby	T Durcan	12-1	7/10

CAN OFTEN be run on ground with plenty of give, including two stagings on heavy going in the last four years – plus last year's renewal, which appeared to feature significantly deeper ground than the official good to soft. Older horses appear to have the call over the Classic generation, though the only three three-year-olds in the latest renewal finished 1-2-3. High numbers have the edge.

St. Leger (1m6f127yds) Doncaster

1994	Moonax		B Hills	Pat Eddery	40-1	3/8
1995	Classic Cliche		S bin Suroor	L Dettori	100-30	7/10
1996	Shantou		J Gosden	L Dettori	8-1	10/11
1997	Silver Patriarch		J Dunlop	Pat Eddery	5-4f	9/10
1998	Nedawi		S bin Suroor	J Reid	5-2	1/9
1999	Mutafaweq		S bin Suroor	R Hills	11-2	6/9
2000	Millenary		J Dunlop	T Quinn	11-4	5/11
2001	Milan		A O'Brien	M Kinane	13-8f	7/10
2002	Bollin Eric		T Easterby	K Darley	7-1	3/8
2003	Brian Boru		A O'Brien	J Spencer	5-4f	9/12

THE OLDEST of the five Classics, first run in 1776, and the last to be staged each year. You don't have to have a Classic profile to win and you don't necessarily have to be a stayer. Horses such as Bob's Return, Commanche Run, Silver Patriarch and Millenary returned to shorter distances after winning this, while others such as Le Moss went on to be Cup horses. Two of the last eight winners were placed in the Epsom Derby and Mutafaweq was fifth in the Irish version. The key race, aside from the Epsom Classics, has been the Great Voltigeur at York in August (won by Milan in 2001, when the first three went on to finish 1-2-3 in the Leger in 2002; Brian Boru was second in the Voltigeur).

Queen Elizabeth II Stakes (1m) Ascot

1994	Maroof	4	R Armstrong	R Hills	66-1	3/9
1995	Bahri	3	J Dunlop	W Carson	5-2	1/6
1996	Mark Of Esteem	3	S bin Suroor	L Dettori	100-30	5/7
1997	Air Express	3	C Brittain	O Peslier	9-1	7/9
1998	Desert Prince	3	D Loder	O Peslier	100-30f	1/7
1999	Dubai Millennium	3	S bin Suroor	L Dettori	4-9f	3/4
2000	Observatory	3	J Gosden	K Darley	14-1	6/12

2001	Summoner	4	S bin Suroor	R Hills	33-1	7/8
2002	Where Or When	3	T Mills	K Darley	7-1	3/5
2003	Falbrav	5	L Cumani	D Holland	6-4f	4/8

THE TWO stunning results, Maroof and Summoner, were both the result of Richard Hills stealing the race on a supposed pacemaker. Those renewals apart, three-year-olds have been firmly in command, with only the exceptional Falbrav interrupting their hegemony. That doesn't mean that the winners are necessarily short odds, with Observatory turning over 11-10 hotpot Giant's Causeway and Where Or When embarrassing the 1-2 shot Hawk Wing.

Prix De l'Arc De Triomphe (1m4f) Longchamp

1994	Carnegie	3	A Fabre	T Jarnet	3-1c	2/20
1995	Lammtarra	3	S bin Suroor	L Dettori	21-10f	7/16
1996	Helissio	3	E Lellouche	O Peslier	18-10f	5/16
1997	Peintre Celebre	3	A Fabre	O Peslier	22-10f	2/18
1998	Sagamix	3	A Fabre	O Peslier	5-2j	7/14
1999	Montjeu	3	J Hammond	M Kinane	6-4c	4/14
2000	Sinndar	3	J Oxx	J Murtagh	6-4	7/10
2001	Sakhee	4	S bin Suroor	L Dettori	22-10f	15/17
2002	Marienbard	5	S bin Suroor	L Dettori	158-10	3/16
2003	Dalakhani	3	A de Royer-Dupre	C Soumillon	9-4	14/13

RESULTS HAVE usually been more reliable over the last decade or so, perhaps a reflection of the fact that winners have been trained specifically for the race from the summer. Three-year-olds have dominated recently and, though four-year-old Sakhee succeeded in 2001, he was still lightly-raced. Note that Godolphin have trained both of the only two older winners. Andre Fabre has trained four of the last 12 winners. There are three key trials for the Arc at Longchamp, three weeks prior to the race; the Prix Vermeille, for three-year-old fillies, the Prix Niel, for three-year-old colts – won by Montjeu, Sinndar and Dalakhani – and the Prix Foy. The Derbys all have a major bearing. Marienbard was something of an aberration, being prepared with two races in Germany.

Dubai Champion Stakes (1m2f) Newmarket

1994	Dernier Empereur	4	A Fabre	S Guillot	8-1	2/8
1995	Spectrum	3	P Chapple-Hyam	J Reid	5-1	1/8
1996	Bosra Sham	3	H Cecil	Pat Eddery	9-4	4/6
1997	Pilsudski	5	Sir M Stoute	M Kinane	Evensf	1/7
1998	Alborada	3	Sir M Prescott	G Duffield	6-1	5/10
1999*	Alborada	4	Sir M Prescott	G Duffield	5-1	10/13
					*(*run on July course)*	
2000	Kalanisi	4	Sir M Stoute	J Murtagh	5-1	3/15
2001	Nayef	3	M Tregoning	R Hills	3-1	1/12
2002	Storming Home	4	B Hills	M Hills	8-1	4/11
2003	Rakti	4	M Jarvis	P Robinson	11-1	3/12

FRENCH CONTENDERS and fillies have an excellent record in the last 10 years and more. Guineas winners of the same year or the year before have a good record. The overseas races with influence are the Irish Champion Stakes, the Arc de Triomphe and the Coupe de Maisons-Laffitte, which was won by Hatoof and Dernier Empereur. Rakti had only had one run outside Italy before landing this, when runner-up to Nayef in the Prince Of Wales's Stakes.

Outlook

Big Handicap Records

Lincoln Handicap (1m) Doncaster

Year	Winner		Trainer	Jockey	SP		Draw/ran
1994	**Our Rita**	5	8st5lb	Dr J Scargill	D Holland	16-1	6/24
1995	**Roving Minstrel**	4	8st3lb	B McMahon	K Darley	33-1	11/23
1996	**Stone Ridge**	4	8st7lb	R Hannon	D O'Neill	33-1	6/24
1997	**Kuala Lipis**	4	8st6lb	P Cole	T Quinn	11-1	21/24
1998	**Hunters Of Brora**	8	9st	J Bethell	J Weaver	16-1	23/23
1999	**Right Wing**	5	9st5lb	J Dunlop	T Quinn	9-2f	8/24
2000	**John Ferneley**	5	8st10lb	P Cole	J Fortune	7-1j	1/24
2001	**Nimello**	5	8st9lb	P Cole	J Fortune	9-2f	1/23
2002	**Zucchero**	6	8st13lb	D Arbuthnot	S Whitworth	33-1	7/23
2003	**Pablo**	4	8st11lb	B Hills	M Hills	5-1	6/24

BET ANTE-POST or, better still, take a morning price but, whatever you do, don't bet at SP. The perennial question is what effect the draw will have, though recent years appear strongly to indicate that low numbers are favoured. The best thing is to watch the Spring Mile, run a day earlier. The 1998 winner, Hunters Of Brora, was the exception; she was the oldest winner since 1963, the first to carry 9st or more to victory since 1985 and was winning for the first time in three years. Form on a straight course over a stiff 1m or further is ideal, as is experience of the hurly burly of a big race – both applied to the 1999 winner, Right Wing, hence his 9-2 starting price. The vast majority of both winners and runners were having their first outings of the season. Northern-based trainers no longer seem to dominate and Paul Cole has done particularly well in recent years. Both his last two winners had won a 1m Class B handicap run at Wolverhampton on the All-Weather a fortnight earlier. See also *By The Numbers*, pages 186-7.

Royal Hunt Cup Handicap (1m) Royal Ascot

Year	Winner		Trainer	Jockey	SP		Draw/ran
1994	**Face North**	6	8st3lb	R Akehurst	A Munro	25-1	30/32
1995	**Realities**	5	9st	G Harwood	M Kinane	11-1	30/32
1996	**Yeast**	4	8st6lb	W Haggas	K Fallon	8-1f	3/31
1997	**Red Robbo**	4	8st6lb	R Akehurst	O Peslier	16-1	17/32
1998	**Refuse To Lose**	4	7st11lb	J Eustace	J Tate	20-1	6/32
1999	**Showboat**	5	8st6lb	B Hills	N Pollard	14-1	30/32
2000	**Caribbean Monarch**	5	8st10lb	Sir M Stoute	K Fallon	11-2	28/32
2001	**Surprise Encounter**	5	8st9lb	E Dunlop	L Dettori	8-1	29/30
2002	**Norton**	5	8st9lb	T Mills	J Fortune	25-1	10/30
2003	**Macadamia**	4	8st13lb	J Fanshawe	D O'Neill	8-1	6/32

A GREAT betting race in which the draw can play a crucial part, especially if the ground is soft – no less than five of the last ten winners have run from stall 28 or higher. There are few pointers and plots are thick on the ground, so most winners are a working man's price. Watch the Victoria Cup at Ascot in May. See also *By The Numbers*, pages 188-9.

Sponsored by Stan James

Wokingham Handicap (6f) Royal Ascot

1994	Venture Capitalist	5	8st12lb	R Hannon	J Reid	20-1	30/30
1995	Astrac	4	8st7lb	R Akehurst	S Sanders	14-1	16/30
1996	Emerging Market	4	8st13lb	J Dunlop	K Darley	33-1	7/29
1997	Selhurstpark Flyer	6	8st9lb	J Berry	P Roberts	25-1	5/30
1998	Selhurstpark Flyer	7	9st7lb	J Berry	C Lowther	16-1	20/29
1999	Deep Space	4	8st7lb	E Dunlop	G Carter	14-1	3/30
2000	Harmonic Way	5	9st6lb	R Charlton	R Hughes	12-1	28/29
2001	Nice One Clare	5	9st3lb	J Payne	J Murtagh	7-1f	4/30
2002	Capricho	5	8st11lb	J Akehurst	T Quinn	20-1	21/28
2003{	Fayr Jag	4	9st6lb	T Easterby	W Supple	10-1	13/29
	Ratio	5	9st3lb	J Hammond	L Dettori	14-1	22/29

WAS FIRST run in 1896 and is a tough race in which to find a winner, though the *Outlook* tipped Nice One Clare on the front page ahead of the 2001 race. Winners are often long-priced and low-weighted. A key race is the Victoria Cup (Ascot, May). Winners tend to be aged four to six, with only two winners having been older. Favourites have a dismal record. See also *By The Numbers*, pages 190-1.

Northumberland Plate (2m) Newcastle

1994	Quick Ransom	6	8st8lb	M Johnston	J Weaver	25-1	4/20
1995	Bold Gait	4	9st10lb	J Fanshawe	D Harrison	12-1	5/17
1996	Celeric	4	9st4lb	D Morley	W Carson	2-1f	7/13
1997	Windsor Castle	3	8st10lb	P Cole	T Quinn	10-1	20/18
1998	Cyrian	4	7st13lb	P Cole	T Sprake	12-1	2/20
1999	Far Cry	4	8st10lb	M Pipe	K Darley	9-2j	6/20
2000	Bay Of Islands	8	8st4lb	D Morris	K Darley	7-1	4/18
2001	Archduke Ferdinand	3	8st4lb	P Cole	F Norton	12-1	17/18
2002	Bangalore	6	9st5lb	A Perrett	S Sanders	8-1	9/16
2003	Unleash	4	8st11lb	P Hobbs	J Spencer	10-1	1/20

HAS IN the past been known as a good race for older, experienced stayers but recent winners show a trend towards younger, less exposed types. Paul Cole does well with his three-year-old runners here but other trainers seem happy to stick with older runners. The first bend comes shortly after the start, so those drawn high can be disadvantaged, creating a significant bias towards low numbers that is probably not yet factored into the market. See also *By The Numbers*, pages 192-3.

Bunbury Cup (7f) Newmarket

1994	En Attendant	6	9st12lb	B Hanbury	L Piggott	14-1	7/20
1995	Cadeaux Tryst	3	9st1lb	E Dunlop	W Swinburn	20-1	17/19
1996	Crumpton Hill	4	8st12lb	N Graham	M Roberts	7-1	3/16
1997	Tumbleweed Ridge	4	9st6lb	B Meehan	M Tebbutt	20-1	19/20
1998	Ho Leng	3	9st7lb	L Perratt	M Kinane	14-1	20/20
1999	Grangeville	4	9st3lb	I Balding	K Fallon	13-2j	20/19
2000	Tayseer	6	9st9lb	D Nicholls	G Mosse	9-1	8/19
2001	Atavus	4	8st10lb	G Margarson	J Mackay (3)	10-1	14/19
2002	Mine	4	8st12lb	J D Bethell	K Fallon	5-1f	3/17
2003	Patavellian	5	9st1lb	R Charlton	S Drowne	4-1f	2/20

A PERSISTANT feature of this race used to be the draw bias towards high numbers, but the current course management appear to have successfully brought an end to that and only one of the last four winners has come from a double-figure draw. With six of the last ten winners carrying 9st or more, weight is clearly no barrier to success, while the bigger yards have failed to make their mark in recent renewals – this is a big race in which the smaller stables can put themselves on the map. Four of the last five winners have been returned at single-figure SPs. See also *By The Numbers*, pages 194-5.

John Smith's Cup (1m2f85yds) York

1994	Cezanne	5	9st12lb	H Ibrahim	G Hind	9-2	3/16
1995	Naked Welcome	3	8st4lb	M F'-Godley	D Holland	6-1	9/16
1996	Wilcuma	5	9st2lb	P Makin	Pat Eddery	10-1	2/17
1997	Pasternak	4	8st3lb	Sir M Prescott	G Duffield	13-2	1/21
1998	Porto Foricos	3	8st3lb	H Cecil	J Quinn	6-1	7/20
1999	Achilles	4	8st11lb	K Burke	J Weaver	25-1	6/15
2000	Sobriety	3	8st8lb	R F J'-Houghton	J Reid	20-1	8/22
2001	Foreign Affairs	3	8st6lb	Sir M Prescott	G Duffield	5-2f	8/19
2002	Vintage Premium	5	9st9lb	R Fahey	P Hanagan	20-1	9/20
2003	Far Lane	4	9st4lb	B Hills	M Hills	7-1	4/20

EVEN THOSE of you who are allergic to draw analysis must take care when playing in this race, which features a notorious bias towards low numbers – for almost the first half of the race, the field are turning left and those on the outside can struggle to get into the contest. Sir Mark Prescott has proved his liking for the race, and the fact that he won one of the most competitive handicaps twice in five years is testament to his skill in this type of race. Runners older than four increasingly struggle. It's almost always worth looking past the market-leader. See also *By The Numbers*, pages 196-7.

Stewards' Cup Handicap (6f) Goodwood

1994	For The Present	4	8st3lb	T Barron	J Fortune	16-1	16/26
1995	Shikari's Son	8	8st13lb	J White	R Hughes	40-1	30/27
1996	Coastal Bluff	4	8st5lb	T Barron	J Fortune	10-1j	29/30
1997	Danetime	3	8st10lb	N Callaghan	Pat Eddery	5-1	5/30
1998	Superior Premium	4	8st12lb	R Fahey	R Winston	14-1	28/29
1999	Harmonic Way	4	8st6lb	R Charlton	R Hughes	12-1	8/30
2000	Tayseer	6	8st11lb	D Nicholls	R Hughes	13-2	28/30
2001	Guinea Hunter	5	9st	T Easterby	J Spencer	33-1	19/30
2002	Bond Boy	5	8st2lb	B Smart	C Catlin	14-1	29/28
2003	Patavellian	5	8st11lb	R Charlton	S Drowne	4-1	27/29

INAUGURATED IN 1840, this is a major betting heat with a strong ante-post market. However, the race has been altered in recent seasons by the opening up of a fresh strip of ground on the far rail which has given high numbers a huge advantage, to the detriment of the ante-post market. A high draw is now thought essential and even a casual glance at the results above will tell you why. In 1998, winner Superior Premium was drawn 28 of 29, the second 25 and the third 29 and, though it was more even in 1999, in 2000 Tayseer (28) won from Bon Ami (24). Bond Boy (29) won from horses drawn 9, 22, 16, 7, 25, 30 and 28 in 2002, while Patavellian led home a 1-2-3 for three of the widest four stalls in the latest renewal. Do not bet ante-post in this race. The Wokingham Handicap has the most bearing; Knight Of Mercy pulled off the double, Danetime was an unlucky second in the Ascot race. See also *By The Numbers*, pages 198-9.

Ebor Handicap (1m6f) York

1994	Hasten To Add	4	9st3lb	Sir M Prescott	G Duffield	13-2	9/21
1995	Sanmartino	3	7st11lb	B Hills	W Carson	8-1	21/21
1996	Clerkenwell	3	7st11lb	Sir M Stoute	F Lynch	17-2	2/21
1997	Far Ahead	5	8st	J Eyre	T Williams	33-1	10/21
1998	Tuning	3	8st7lb	H Cecil	K Fallon	9-2	1/21
1999	Vicious Circle	5	8st4lb	L Cumani	K Darley	11-1	7/21

DRIVING FINISH: Saint Alebe (far left) comes late to take the Ebor from Sun Bird (centre)

2000	Give The Slip	3	8st8lb	Mrs A Perrett	Pat Eddery	8-1	16/22
2001	Mediterranean	3	8st4lb	A O'Brien	M Kinane	16-1	20/22
2002	Hugs Dancer	5	8st5lb	J Given	D McKeown	25-1	20/22
2003	Saint Alebe	4	8st8lb	D Elsworth	T Quinn	20-1	17/22

ONE OF the oldest and most famous handicaps, first run in 1847, with a strong ante-post market. Sea Pigeon brought the house down when lumping top-weight home in 1979. Stamina is a premium (as Sea Pigeon showed) and many Ebor winners, such as Further Flight, go on to be top stayers. Unexposed three-year-olds have come to the fore in recent years. Watch the Northumberland Plate (Newcastle, June) and the Duke Of Edinburgh Handicap (Royal Ascot, June).

Ayr Gold Cup Handicap (6f) Ayr

1994	Daring Destiny	3	8st	K Burke	J Tate	18-1	29/29
1995	Royale Figurine	4	8st9lb	M F'-Godley	D Holland	8-1	27/29
1996	Coastal Bluff	4	9st10lb	T Barron	J Fortune	3-1f	28/28
1997	Wildwood Flower	4	9st3lb	R Hannon	D O'Neill	14-1	24/29
1998	Always Alight	4	8st7lb	K Burke	J Egan	16-1	8/29
1999	Grangeville	4	9st	I Balding	K Fallon	11-1	17/28
2000	Bahamian Pirate	5	8st	D Nicholls	A Nicholls	33-1	7/28
2001	Continent	4	8st10lb	D Nicholls	D Holland	10-1	22/28
2002	Funfair Wane	3	9st3lb	D Nicholls	A Nicholls	16-1	16/28
2003	Quito	6	8st6lb	D Chapman	A Culhane	20-1	10/26

A HISTORIC race first run in 1804, for which there is a lively ante-post book. The effect of the draw can be gleaned from the Ayr Silver Cup, run the day before. A horse with good recent form who can settle in large fields and who can come from off the pace is required. Key races are; the Wokingham Handicap (Royal Ascot, June), the Tote Portland Handicap (Doncaster, September) and the Stewards' Cup (Goodwood, August). See also *By The Numbers*, pages 200-1.

Cambridgeshire Handicap (1m1f) Newmarket

| 1994 | Halling | 3 | 8st8lb | J Gosden | L Dettori | 8-1c | 24/30 |

1995	**Cap Juluca**	3	9st10lb	R Charlton	R Hughes	11-1	26/39
1996	**Clifton Fox**	4	8st2lb	J Glover	N Day	14-1	17/38
1997	**Pasternak**	4	9st1lb	Sir M Prescott	G Duffield	4-1f	17/36
1998	**Lear Spear**	3	7st13lb	D Elsworth	N Pollard	20-1	33/35
1999*	**She's Our Mare**	6	7st12lb	A Martin	F Norton	11-1	14/33

*(*run on July course)*

2000	**Katy Nowaitee**	4	8st8lb	P Harris	J Reid	6-1	34/35
2001	**I Cried For You**	6	8st6lb	J Given	M Fenton	33-1	11/35
2002	**Beauchamp Pilot**	4	9st5lb	G Butler	E Ahern	9-1	26/30
2003	**Chivalry**	4	8st1lb	Sir M Prescott	G Duffield	14-1	17/34

THE FIRST leg of the Autumn Double, dating back to 1839. Because of its unusual distance and its straight course, the Cambridgeshire has thrown up a number of specialists. Apart from perennials, look for a late-maturing three-year-old bred to find improvement over longer trips which are not attempted until after the weights are set. Two races at Doncaster on St Leger day, a 0-105 handicap over the straight mile and a 0-95 over an extended 1m2f should provide clues. Longer-priced horses often do well. See also *By The Numbers*, pages 202-3.

Cesarewitch Handicap (2m2f) Newmarket

1994	**Captain's Guest**	4	9st9lb	G Harwood	A Clark	25-1	28/32
1995	**Old Red**	5	7st11lb	Mrs M Reveley	L Charnock	11-1	18/21
1996	**Inchcailloch**	7	7st3lb	J King	R Ffrench	20-1	15/26
1997	**Turnpole**	6	7st10lb	Mrs M Reveley	L Charnock	16-1	6/30
1998	**Spirit Of Love**	3	8st8lb	M Johnston	O Peslier	11-1	19/29
1999*	**Top Cees**	9	8st10lb	I Balding	K Fallon	7-1	17/32

*(*run on July course)*

2000	**Heros Fatal**	6	8st1lb	M Pipe	G Carter	11-1	18/33
2001	**Distant Prospect**	4	8st8lb	I Balding	M Dwyer	14-1	32/31
2002	**Miss Fara**	7	8st	M Pipe	R Moore	12-1	36/36
2003	**Landing Light**	8	9st4lb	N Henderson	Pat Eddery	12-1	36/36

THE SECOND leg of the Autumn Double. Normally a race won by five-year-olds and above, Spirit Of Love being a rare three-year-old winner. Fresh horses at the lower end of the weights have a good record. The Tote Ebor and previous runnings of this race itself have the most influence. Go for horses who have shown good autumn form in the past. See also *By The Numbers*, pages 204-5.

November Handicap (1m4f) Doncaster

1994	**Saxon Maid**	3	8st9lb	L Cumani	J Weaver	16-1	20/24
1995	**Snow Princess**	3	8st2lb	Lord Huntingdon	R Hills	5-1	10/18
1996	**Clifton Fox**	4	8st10lb	J Glover	N Day	9-1	14/22
1997	**Sabadilla**	3	7st8lb	J Gosden	R Ffrench	10-1	22/24
1998	**Yavana's Pace**	6	9st10lb	M Johnston	D Holland	8-1	12/23
1999	**Flossy**	3	7st7lb	C Thornton	A Beech	5-1	10/16
2000	**Batswing**	5	8st8lb	B Ellison	R Winston	14-1	14/20
2001	**Royal Cavalier**	4	7st10lb	R Hollinshead	P Quinn	50-1	5/14
2002	**Red Wine**	3	8st1lb	J Osborne	M Dwyer	16-1	20/23
2003	**Turbo**	4	9st2lb	G Balding	A Clark	25-1	14/24

THE LAST big ante-post race of the season traces back to 1876. Three-year-olds, lightly raced, progressive and with stout pedigrees, are most likely to succeed. The 1m4f Ladbroke Handicap run over course and distance at the previous meeting is worth studying.

For this year's big-race dates, see page 166

Outlook

By The Numbers
by **Chris Cook**

In profit after a year!

BY THE NUMBERS recently celebrated the first anniversary of its appearance in RFO. And what better way to sum up the feature's first 12 months than by expressing it numerically – so that's six winners from 31 tips (a strike-rate of 19 percent), producing a £20 profit to £1 level stakes, a 65 per cent profit on turnover.

But the tips that go alongside our stats boxes are very much an individual interpretation of what the stats mean and how they are best applied. Having pored over the same stats boxes, it's perfectly possible that you may come to a different, more successful conclusion.

For every big handicap that comes along, there will be dozens of different tipsters rushing into print with their conflicting theories about how the race will pan out. The aim of this feature is to give you some hard data to get your teeth into, so you can test how well-founded some of these theories are.

Once you've formed an idea about the kind of horse likely to be suited by a particular race's conditions, it's easy to check your conclusions against this year's entrants – the *Racing Post* and its associated website (*racingpost.co.uk*) carry all the information you need to work out where each runner fits in each of the *By The Numbers* categories.

Over the next 20 pages, we've got all the stats you need to analyse ten of the biggest betting races of the coming Flat season. For the first time in an RFO annual, we've found space to include ten-year figures in each of the categories that normally appear in the feature.

Each race is spread across two pages. On the left page are stats showing how many of the last ten winners have come from each band of runners within each category, together with full details of those winners.

On the right page, our stats relate to how many placed horses have come from each band, plus there's a commentary offering some insight into the bare numbers.

Let's take the Lincoln as an example.

In our 'Win stats' on the left page, the first box shows that 95 runners in the last ten years have been four-year-olds. Four of them have won, at a strike-rate of four per cent. By betting £1 on all of those four-year-olds, you'd have made a net loss of £9, alternatively expressed as a loss of 9 per cent of total stakes.

Over on the right page, our 'Place stats' show that, of those 95 four-year-olds, 17 made the frame, a place-rate of 18 per cent.

In the 'Win stats', all bands that have returned a level-stakes profit over the last ten years are shaded. So, for the Lincoln, the stats for horses aged eight or over are shaded, because they returned a £13 profit to £1 stakes.

In the 'Place stats', bands of runners are shaded if their place-rate is above average. So, for the Lincoln, there is shading over the bands for four-year-olds, for seven-year-olds and for runners aged eight or over; all three of these bands have achieved place rates above the average of 17 per cent.

Here's hoping our numbers lead you to profitable conclusions.

Win stats

Age

Age	Wins/runs	%	£+-	% of stakes
4	4/95	4	-£9.00	-9
5	4/74	5	-£38.00	-51
6	1/48	2	-£14.00	-29
7	0/15	0	-£15.00	-100
8+	1/4	25	+£13.00	+325

Weight

Weight	Wins/runs	%	£+-	% of stakes
Under 8st	0/8	0	-£8.00	-100
8st-8st6lb	3/77	4	-£14.00	-18
8st7lb-8st13lb	5/92	5	-£4.50	-5
9st-9st5lb	2/32	6	-£9.50	-30
9st6lb-9st10lb	0/27	0	-£27.00	-100

Official Ratings

OR	Wins/runs	%	£+-	% of stakes
Under 80	1/12	8	+£5.00	+42
80-84	1/46	2	-£12.00	-26
85-89	3/80	4	-£28.50	-36
90-94	3/49	6	+£10.00	+20
95-99	1/30	3	-£24.00	-80
100+	1/19	5	-£13.50	-71

Wins

Wins	Wins/runs	%	£+-	% of stakes
0	No runners			
1	1/36	3	-£24.00	-67
2	3/58	5	+£15.50	+27
3	2/56	4	-£44.50	-79
4+	4/86	5	-£10.00	-12

Starting Prices

SP	Wins/runs	%	£+-	% of stakes
Under 5-1	2/4	50	+£7.00	+175
5-1 to 7-1	2/11	18	+£3.00	+27
15-2 to 9-1	0/11	0	-£11.00	-100
10-1 to 12-1	1/31	3	-£19.00	-61
14-1 to 18-1	2/45	4	-£11.00	-24
20-1 to 25-1	0/55	0	-£55.00	-100
28-1 to 33-1	3/33	9	+£69.00	+209
40-1to 66-1	0/43	0	-£43.00	-100
80-1+	0/3	0	-£3.00	-100

Draw

Draw	Wins/runs	%	£+-	% of stakes
1-8	7/79	9	+£31.00	+39
9-16	1/79	1	-£45.00	-57
17-24	2/78	3	-£49.00	-63

Sex

Sex	Wins/runs	%	£+-	% of stakes
Entires	4/58	7	-£0.50	-1
Females	2/22	9	+£12.00	+55
Geldings	4/156	3	-£74.50	-48

Handicap wins

Wins	Wins/runs	%	£+-	% of stakes
0	2/76	3	-£30.00	-39
1	3/61	5	-£16.00	-26
2	2/46	4	-£32.00	-70
3	2/28	7	+£6.00	+21
4+	1/25	4	+£9.00	+36

	Winner	Age	Weight	OR	SP	Wins	H'caps	Sex	Draw
2003	Pablo	4	8st11lb	97	5-1	3	2	entire	6/24
2002	Zucchero	6	8st13lb	91	33-1	5	5	gelding	7/23
2001	Nimello	5	8st9lb	89	9-2f	2	1	gelding	1/23
2000	John Ferneley	5	8st10lb	90	7-1j	4	2	gelding	1/24
1999	Right Wing	5	9st5lb	100	9-2f	3	1	entire	8/24
1998	Hunters Of Brora	8	9st	90	16-1	4	3	female	23/23
1997	Kuala Lipis	4	8st6lb	86	11-1	1	0	entire	21/24
1996	Stone Ridge	4	8st7lb	87	33-1	2	1	gelding	6/24
1995	Roving Minstrel	4	8st3lb	82	33-1	2	0	entire	11/23
1994	Our Rita	5	8st5lb	76	16-1	6	3	female	6/24

Place stats

I FIRMLY believe that the numbers in this feature are particularly useful in analysing draw biases.

This runs counter to the views of my respected colleague Graham Wheldon, who remains clear of the field in draw analysis. He feels that his specialist subject is so much of an art that crude stats can only rarely (and then by chance) capture the true nature of a bias.

Well, I accept that stats should be tested before being trusted and they may well require a deal of interpretation but, for me, as long as a sample is large enough, then the bare stats are your best possible starting point in finding where a bias lies.

Our draw numbers on the Lincoln are as clear as can be - the bottom eight stalls dominate.

You could have made a very healthy profit backing them blindly, collecting in seven of the last ten years. Last year, Paddy Power went odds-against that the winner

	Age	Wins/runs	%
Age	4	17/95	18
	5	11/74	15
	6	8/48	17
	7	3/15	20
	8+	1/4	25

	Weight	Wins/runs	%
Weight	Under 8st	0/8	0
	8st-8st6lb	10/77	13
	8st7lb-8st13lb	19/92	17
	9st-9st5lb	8/32	25
	9st6lb-9st10lb	3/27	11

	OR	Wins/runs	%
Official Ratings	Under 80	1/12	8
	80-84	7/46	15
	85-89	15/80	19
	90-94	9/49	18
	95-99	4/30	13
	100+	4/19	21

	Wins	Wins/runs	%
Wins	0	No runners	
	1	5/36	14
	2	10/58	17
	3	13/56	23
	4+	12/86	14

	SP	Wins/runs	%
Starting Prices	Under 5-1	3/4	75
	5-1 to 7-1	6/11	55
	15-2 to 9-1	4/11	36
	10-1 to 12-1	5/31	16
	14-1 to 18-1	11/45	24
	20-1 to 25-1	5/55	9
	28-1 to 33-1	5/33	15
	40-1to 66-1	1/43	2
	80-1+	0/3	0

	Draw	Wins/runs	%
Draw	1-8	25/79	32
	9-16	10/79	13
	17-24	5/78	6

	Sex	Wins/runs	%
Sex	Entires	16/58	28
	Females	2/22	9
	Geldings	22/156	14

	Wins	Wins/runs	%
Handicap wins	0	12/76	16
	1	11/61	18
	2	8/46	17
	3	3/28	11
	4+	6/25	24

would come from these stalls – if they do that again, pile in!

Uniquely among the ten races in this section, you could have made a level-stakes profit by following all runners who'd won three or more handicaps. In theory, such horses should be exposed and an unlikely source of value, but for some reason that doesn't apply here.

Though only three such runners have won, they've all been 16-1 or higher and our place stats confirm that those with plenty of prior handicap success fare better than the rest.

Those at the head of the market have almost invariably run as their SP suggested they would. In the last decade, Adiemus (7-2f in the latest renewal) has been the only starter at 5s or less to have missed the places.

Win stats

	Age	Wins/runs	%	£+-	% of stakes
Age	3	0/4	0	-£4.00	-100
	4	4/167	2	-£111.00	-66
	5	5/77	7	-£8.50	-11
	6	1/40	3	-£14.00	-35
	7	0/18	0	-£18.00	-100
	8+	0/9	0	-£9.00	-100

	OR	Wins/runs	%	£+-	% of stakes
Official Ratings	Under 80	0/3	0	-£3.00	-100
	80-84	2/46	3	+£1.00	+2
	85-89	2/79	3	-£53.00	-67
	90-94	3/80	4	-£30.00	-38
	95-99	3/44	7	-£16.50	-38
	100+	0/63	0	-£63.00	-100

	Draw	Wins/runs	%	£+-	% of stakes
Draw	1-8	3/79	4	-£40.00	-51
	9-16	1/78	1	-£52.00	-67
	17-24	1/78	1	-£61.00	-78
	25-32	5/80	6	-£11.50	-14

	Wins	Wins/runs	%	£+-	% of stakes
Wins	0	0/7	0	-£7.00	-100
	1	2/49	4	-£11.00	-22
	2	2/86	2	-£70.50	-82
	3	4/80	5	-£21.00	-26
	4+	2/93	2	-£55.00	-59

	SP	Wins/runs	%	£+-	% of stakes
Starting Prices	Under 5-1	0/2	0	-£2.00	-100
	5-1 to 7-1	1/6	17	+£0.50	+8
	15-2 to 9-1	3/10	30	+£17.00	+170
	10-1 to 12-1	1/26	4	-£14.00	-54
	14-1 to 18-1	2/41	5	-£9.00	-22
	20-1 to 25-1	3/91	3	-£18.00	-20
	28-1 to 33-1	0/64	0	-£64.00	-100
	40-1 to 66-1	0/71	0	-£71.00	-100
	80-1+	0/4	0	-£4.00	-100

	Weight	Wins/runs	%	£+-	% of stakes
Weight	Under 8st	1/34	3	-£13.00	-38
	8st-8st6lb	4/103	4	-£36.00	-35
	8st7lb-8st13lb	4/97	4	-£46.50	-48
	9st-9st5lb	1/46	2	-£34.00	-74
	9st6lb-9st10lb	0/35	0	-£35.00	-100

	Sex	Wins/runs	%	£+-	% of stakes
Sex	Entires	4/99	4	-£34.00	-34
	Females	1/19	5	-£10.00	-53
	Geldings	5/197	3	-£120.50	-61

	Wins	Wins/runs	%	£+-	% of stakes
Handicap wins	0	4/85	5	-£31.50	-37
	1	3/91	3	-£41.00	-45
	2	2/62	3	-£41.00	-66
	3	1/44	2	-£18.00	-41
	4+	0/33	0	-£33.00	-100

	Winner	Age	Weight	OR	SP	Wins	H'caps	Sex	Draw
2003	Macadamia	4	8st13lb	93	8-1	3	0	female	6/32
2002	Norton	5	8st9lb	91	25-1	3	1	gelding	10/30
2001	Surprise Encounter	5	8st9lb	95	8-1	3	2	gelding	29/30
2000	Caribbean Monarch	5	8st10lb	96	11-2	2	0	gelding	28/32
1999	Showboat	5	8st6lb	92	14-1	3	1	entire	30/32
1998	Refuse To Lose	4	7st11lb	83	20-1	1	0	entire	6/32
1997	Red Robbo	4	8st6lb	88	16-1	1	0	entire	17/32
1996	Yeast	4	8st6lb	87	8-1f	2	1	gelding	3/31
1995	Realities	5	9st	99	11-1	4	2	entire	30/32
1994	Face North	6	8st3lb	83	25-1	6	3	gelding	30/32

Place stats

THE numbers for the Hunt Cup are more in line with what I expected when we started collecting 'previous win' statistics.

My elementary theory was that the best handicaps would typically be won by horses who were very unexposed.

The more often a horse runs in handicaps, the easier it becomes for the official assessor to measure his ability.

Winners of handicaps quickly have their burdens escalated and even those on the upgrade are usually brought back to the level of the herd in short order. It takes clever campaigning for a horse to run up a sequence in handicaps.

This is pretty straightforward stuff and it's not sophisticated enough to apply generally to all horse handicaps, but it works for this one.

Four of the last ten winners had never won such a race before. Almost a quarter of all starters had previously won three or more handicaps – just one of those managed to add this prize and that was ten years ago now.

Age	Wins/runs	%
3	0/4	0
4	25/167	15
5	10/77	13
6	4/40	10
7	1/18	6
8+	0/9	0

OR	Wins/runs	%
Under 80	0/3	0
80-84	4/46	9
85-89	11/79	14
90-94	11/80	14
95-99	9/44	20
100+	5/63	8

Draw	Wins/runs	%
1-8	17/79	22
9-16	7/78	9
17-24	6/78	8
25-32	10/80	13

Wins	Wins/runs	%
0	0/7	0
1	7/49	14
2	13/86	15
3	12/80	15
4+	8/93	9

SP	Wins/runs	%
Under 5-1	0/2	0
5-1 to 7-1	3/6	50
15-2 to 9-1	4/10	40
10-1 to 12-1	6/26	23
14-1 to 18-1	10/41	24
20-1 to 25-1	9/91	10
28-1 to 33-1	4/64	6
40-1 to 66-1	4/71	6
80-1+	0/4	0

Weight	Wins/runs	%
Under 8st	3/34	9
8st-8st6lb	13/103	13
8st7lb-8st13lb	16/97	16
9st-9st5lb	5/46	11
9st6lb-9st10lb	3/35	9

Sex	Wins/runs	%
Entires	23/99	23
Females	2/19	11
Geldings	15/197	8

Wins	Wins/runs	%
0	8/85	9
1	17/91	19
2	10/62	16
3	3/44	7
4+	2/33	6

Runners aged four and five have dominated, with 90 per cent of the winners and 88 per cent of those in the frame. Still, they've made up most of the field.

The draw matters, though not in such an obvious way as for the Lincoln. Our place stats show that, although those drawn low have the edge, it's much better to be drawn near a rail than in the middle.

Five of the last ten winners were drawn within three places of a rail. It may be hard to say which rail will be favoured but some of the results have shown extreme biases - the first four were drawn 3,2,1 and 4 in 1996, while the first three in 1999 came from stalls 30, 31 and 29.

Win stats

Age	Wins/runs	%	£+-	% of stakes
3	0/14	0	-£14.00	-100
4	4/106	4	-£31.00	-29
5	5/76	7	+£2.00	+3
6	1/52	2	-£26.00	-50
7	1/26	4	-£9.00	-35
8+	0/20	0	-£20.00	-100

OR	Wins/runs	%	£+-	% of stakes
Under 80	No runners			
80-84	0/19	0	-£19.00	-100
85-89	3/77	4	-£26.00	-34
90-94	2/78	3	-£31.00	-40
95-99	3/63	5	-£6.00	-10
100+	3/57	5	-£16.00	-28

Draw	Wins/runs	%	£+-	% of stakes
1-8	4/79	5	+£4.00	+5
9-16	2/77	3	-£51.00	-66
17-24	3/78	4	-£25.00	-32
25-32	2/60	3	-£26.00	-43

Wins	Wins/runs	%	£+-	% of stakes
0	0/3	0	-£3.00	-100
1	0/17	0	-£17.00	-100
2	3/63	5	-£1.00	-2
3	5/59	8	+£21.00	+36
4+	3/152	2	-£98.00	-64

SP	Wins/runs	%	£+-	% of stakes
Under 5-1	0/2	0	-£2.00	-100
5-1 to 7-1	1/5	20	+£3.00	+60
15-2 to 9-1	0/12	0	-£12.00	-100
10-1 to 12-1	2/30	7	-£6.00	-20
14-1 to 18-1	4/44	9	+£18.00	+41
20-1 to 25-1	3/68	4	Level	Level
28-1 to 33-1	1/65	2	-£31.00	-48
40-1 to 66-1	0/66	0	-£66.00	-100
80-1+	0/2	0	-£2.00	-100

Weight	Wins/runs	%	£+-	% of stakes
Under 8st	0/6	0	-£6.00	-100
8st-8st6lb	0/53	0	-£53.00	-100
8st7lb-8st13lb	6/117	5	+£15.00	+13
9st-9st5lb	2/72	3	-£49.00	-68
9st6lb+	3/46	7	-£5.00	-11

Sex	Wins/runs	%	£+-	% of stakes
Entires	1/35	3	-£22.00	-63
Females	1/43	2	-£35.00	-81
Geldings	9/216	4	-£41.00	-19

Handicap wins	Wins/runs	%	£+-	% of stakes
0	2/66	3	-£17.00	-26
1	2/53	4	-£19.00	-36
2	4/56	7	+£14.00	+25
3	1/32	3	-£17.00	-53
4+	2/87	2	-£59.00	-68

	Winner	Age	Weight	OR	SP	Wins	H'caps	Sex	Draw
2003{	*Fayr Jag*	4	9st6lb	102	10-1	5	4	gelding	13/29
	Ratio	5	9st3lb	99	14-1	3	0	gelding	22/29
2002	*Capricho*	5	8st11lb	87	20-1	3	2	gelding	21/28
2001	*Nice One Clare*	5	9st3lb	98	7-1f	3	2	female	4/30
2000	*Harmonic Way*	5	9st6lb	102	12-1	2	1	entire	28/29
1999	*Deep Space*	4	8st7lb	88	14-1	3	3	gelding	3/30
1998	*Selhurstpark Flyer*	7	9st7lb	100	16-1	9	4	gelding	20/29
1997	*Selhurstpark Flyer*	6	8st9lb	94	25-1	7	2	gelding	5/30
1996	*Emerging Market*	4	8st13lb	95	33-1	2	0	gelding	7/29
1995	*Astrac*	4	8st7lb	89	14-1	2	2	gelding	16/30
1994	*Venture Capitalist*	5	8st12lb	91	20-1	3	1	gelding	30/30

Place stats

AS we'll see with the Stewards' Cup, it can really help when interpreting these statistics to identify which winners don't fit the general trend.

For the Wokingham, that would definitely be Selhurstpark Flyer. Jack Berry's popular sprinter has been the only dual winner of this race in the last 70 years.

More immediately, he's been the only winner aged over five in the last ten years. A total of 96 other runners aged six or over have tried their luck here since 1994, but he's been the only one to beat the youngsters - and he did it twice!

On the question of exposure, only he and Fayr Jag have managed to take this after having won as many as four previous handicaps. Fayr Jag, of course, only managed a share of first place last year.

This hasn't been much of a race for market-leaders. Nice One Clare, the only filly or mare to triumph in the last decade,

Age	Wins/runs	%
3	3/14	21
4	18/106	17
5	9/76	12
6	8/52	15
7	2/26	8
8+	0/20	0

OR	Wins/runs	%
Under 80	No runners	
80-84	2/19	11
85-89	9/77	12
90-94	9/78	12
95-99	9/63	14
100+	11/57	19

Draw	Wins/runs	%
1-8	19/79	24
9-16	8/77	10
17-24	7/78	9
25-32	6/60	10

Wins	Wins/runs	%
0	0/3	0
1	6/17	35
2	7/63	11
3	10/59	17
4+	17/152	11

SP	Wins/runs	%
Under 5-1	0/2	0
5-1 to 7-1	4/5	80
15-2 to 9-1	3/12	25
10-1 to 12-1	10/30	33
14-1 to 18-1	10/44	23
20-1 to 25-1	6/68	9
28-1 to 33-1	5/65	8
40-1 to 66-1	2/66	3
80-1+	0/2	0

Weight	Wins/runs	%
Under 8st	1/6	17
8st-8st6lb	5/53	9
8st7lb-8st13lb	16/117	14
9st-9st5lb	8/72	11
9st6lb+	10/46	22

Sex	Wins/runs	%
Entires	6/35	17
Females	4/43	9
Geldings	30/216	14

Wins	Wins/runs	%
0	14/66	21
1	4/53	8
2	10/56	18
3	6/32	19
4+	6/87	7

has also been the only winner to be returned at a single-figure SP, from 19 who have tried.

That said, 45 per cent of all starters have been sent off at 28-1 or bigger, yielding just one winner, a cripplingly low strike-rate.

This race is run over the last three-quarters of the Royal Hunt Cup, so one might expect the draw bias to be similar, but in fact the bias towards the stands' side is much more pronounced.

The bottom eight stalls have filled almost half the places, and are more than twice as likely to make the frame as runners from other draws. You could have made a fractional level-stakes profit by backing them blindly, though many winners have come from other parts of the course.

Win stats

Age	Wins/runs	%	£+-	% of stakes
3	2/7	29	+£17.00	+243
4	5/87	6	-£41.50	-48
5	0/33	0	-£33.00	-100
6	2/27	7	+£8.00	+30
7	0/11	0	-£11.00	-100
8+	1/15	7	-£7.00	-47

OR	Wins/runs	%	£+-	% of stakes
Under 80	0/32	0	-£32.00	-100
80-84	0/38	0	-£38.00	-100
85-89	2/33	6	-£14.50	-44
90-94	2/29	7	-£10.00	-34
95-99	3/18	17	+£20.00	+111
100+	3/30	10	+£7.00	+23

Draw	Wins/runs	%	£+-	% of stakes
1-5	5/49	10	+£22.00	+45
6-10	3/47	6	-£29.50	-63
11-15	0/47	0	-£47.00	-100
16+	2/37	5	-£13.00	-35

Wins	Wins/runs	%	£+-	% of stakes
0	0/8	0	-£8.00	-100
1	3/30	10	+£1.50	+5
2	1/42	2	-£31.00	-74
3	1/40	3	-£29.00	-73
4+	5/60	8	-£1.00	-2

SP	Wins/runs	%	£+-	% of stakes
Under 5-1	2/11	18	-£2.50	-23
5-1 to 7-1	1/18	6	-£10.00	-56
15-2 to 9-1	1/12	8	-£3.00	-25
10-1 to 12-1	5/31	16	+£30.00	+97
14-1 to 18-1	0/26	0	-£26.00	-100
20-1 to 25-1	1/47	2	-£21.00	-45
28-1 to 33-1	0/16	0	-£16.00	-100
40-1 to 66-1	0/15	0	-£15.00	-100
80-1+	0/4	0	-£4.00	-100

Weight	Wins/runs	%	£+-	% of stakes
Under 8st	1/58	2	-£45.00	-78
8st-8st6lb	2/34	6	-£13.00	-38
8st7lb-8st13lb	4/40	10	+£13.50	+34
9st-9st5lb	2/26	8	-£14.00	-54
9st6lb+	1/22	5	-£9.00	-41

Sex	Wins/runs	%	£+-	% of stakes
Entires	1/28	4	-£17.00	-61
Females	0/13	0	-£13.00	-100
Geldings	9/139	7	-£37.50	-27

Handicap wins	Wins/runs	%	£+-	% of stakes
0	2/39	5	-£15.00	-38
1	3/48	6	-£18.50	-39
2	0/29	0	-£29.00	-100
3	2/26	8	-£9.00	-35
4+	3/38	8	+£4.00	+11

	Winner	Age	Weight	OR	SP	Wins	H'caps	Sex	Draw
2003	*Unleash*	4	8st11lb	91	10-1	2	1	gelding	1/20
2002	*Bangalore*	6	9st5lb	99	8-1	4	3	gelding	9/16
2001	*Archduke Ferdinand*	3	8st4lb	100	12-1	1	0	gelding	17/18
2000	*Bay Of Islands*	8	8st4lb	90	7-1	4	3	gelding	4/18
1999	*Far Cry*	4	8st10lb	89	9-2j	1	1	gelding	6/20
1998	*Cyrian*	4	7st13lb	85	12-1	1	1	gelding	2/20
1997	*Windsor Castle*	3	8st10lb	104	10-1	3	0	entire	20/18
1996	*Celeric*	4	9st4lb	96	2-1f	5	5	gelding	7/13
1995	*Bold Gait*	4	9st10lb	105	12-1	4	4	gelding	5/17
1994	*Quick Ransom*	6	8st8lb	95	25-1	7	7	gelding	4/20

Place stats

THIS is the first of three midsummer handicaps, covered in this feature last season, in which we found that three-year-olds were an excellent source of value, albeit from low samples; the other two, also featured here, were the John Smith's Cup and the Bunbury Cup.

The reason we should be cautious in applying this stat to the Northumberland Plate is that both winning three-year-olds of the last decade have come from the same stable, that of Paul Cole. He must be conscious of an affinity with the race, having also saddled the three-year-old Mr Dinos to be a short-head runner-up in 2002.

Mr Dinos was sent off the 3-1 favourite, as opposed to the 10-1 and 12-1 of Cole's winners, so it seems clear that punters have latched onto what's happening.

Regardless of age, lack of exposure is also important – five of the last seven winners had won no more

Age	Wins/runs	%
3	3/7	43
4	23/87	26
5	5/33	15
6	4/27	15
7	2/11	18
8+	3/15	20

OR	Wins/runs	%
Under 80	6/32	19
80-84	5/38	13
85-89	7/33	21
90-94	7/29	24
95-99	8/18	44
100+	7/30	23

Draw	Wins/runs	%
1-5	18/49	37
6-10	11/47	23
11-15	9/47	19
16+	2/37	5

Wins	Wins/runs	%
0	1/8	13
1	6/30	20
2	9/42	21
3	10/40	25
4+	14/60	23

SP	Wins/runs	%
Under 5-1	8/11	73
5-1 to 7-1	2/18	11
15-2 to 9-1	3/12	25
10-1 to 12-1	12/31	39
14-1 to 18-1	6/26	23
20-1 to 25-1	7/47	15
28-1 to 33-1	1/16	6
40-1 to 66-1	1/15	7
80-1+	0/4	0

Weight	Wins/runs	%
Under 8st	9/58	16
8st-8st6lb	7/34	21
8st7lb-8st13lb	10/40	25
9st-9st5lb	10/26	38
9st6lb+	4/22	18

Sex	Wins/runs	%
Entires	7/28	25
Mares	2/13	15
Geldings	31/139	22

Handicap wins	Wins/runs	%
0	6/39	15
1	9/48	19
2	8/29	28
3	9/26	35
4+	8/38	21

than one previous handicap. This used to be a good race for those with four or more handicap wins but recent renewals seem to show that such horses now struggle.

Sixty per cent of all starters have gone off at SPs of 14-1 or higher, but only one such has actually won. A huge 73 per cent of all starters at less than 5-1 have made the frame, a figure bettered only by the Stewards Cup and the Lincoln among the races in this feature – and both of those are based on much smaller samples.

Topweights haven't necessarily done well but you could have made an excellent profit (over 50 per cent on turnover) by backing all those rated 95 or over on Official Ratings.

Win stats

	Age	Wins/runs	%	£+-	% of stakes
Age	3	2/22	9	+£14.00	+64
	4	5/83	6	-£29.50	-36
	5	1/40	2.5	-£35.00	-88
	6	2/24	8	+£1.00	+4
	7	0/13	0	-£13.00	-100
	8+	0/7	0	-£7.00	-100

	OR	Wins/runs	%	£+-	% of stakes
Official Ratings	Under 80	0/20	0	-£20.00	-100
	80-84	0/19	0	-£19.00	-100
	85-89	4/46	9	-£11.00	-24
	90-94	3/41	7	-£7.50	-18
	95-99	1/40	3	-£19.00	-48
	100+	2/23	9	+£7.00	+30

	Draw	Wins/runs	%	£+-	% of stakes
Draw	1-5	3/49	6	-£30.00	-61
	6-10	2/49	4	-£24.00	-49
	11-15	1/47	2	-£36.00	-77
	16+	4/44	9	+£20.50	+47

	Wins	Wins/runs	%	£+-	% of stakes
Wins	0	0/1	0	-£1.00	-100
	1	2/34	6	-£5.50	-16
	2	3/41	7	+£3.00	+7
	3	2/48	4	-£31.00	-65
	4+	3/65	5	-£35.00	-54

	SP	Wins/runs	%	£+-	% of stakes
Starting Prices	Under 5-1	1/6	17	-£1.00	-17
	5-1 to 7-1	3/15	20	+£6.50	+43
	15-2 to 9-1	1/16	6	-£6.00	-38
	10-1 to 12-1	1/32	3	-£21.00	-66
	14-1 to 18-1	2/39	5	-£9.00	-23
	20-1 to 25-1	2/52	4	-£10.00	-19
	28-1 to 33-1	0/18	0	-£18.00	-100
	40-1 to 66-1	0/11	0	-£11.00	-100
	80-1+	No runners			

	Weight	Wins/runs	%	£+-	% of stakes
Weight	Under 8st	0/8	0	-£8.00	-100
	8st-8st6lb	0/25	0	-£25.00	-100
	8st7lb-8st13lb	4/54	7	-£19.00	-35
	9st-9st5lb	3/54	6	-£20.50	-38
	9st6lb+	3/48	6	+£3.00	+6

	Sex	Wins/runs	%	£+-	% of stakes
Sex	Entires	4/40	10	+£19.00	+48
	Females	0/17	0	-£17.00	-100
	Geldings	6/132	5	-£71.50	-54

	Wins	Wins/runs	%	£+-	% of stakes
Handicap wins	0	2/45	4	-£3.00	-7
	1	3/48	6	-£17.50	-36
	2	2/35	6	-£19.00	-54
	3	2/32	6	-£16.00	-50
	4+	1/29	3	-£14.00	-48

	Winner	Age	Weight	OR	SP	Wins	H'caps	Sex	Draw
2003	Patavellian	5	9st1lb	90	4-1f	4	2	gelding	2/20
2002	Mine	4	8st12lb	87	5-1f	3	3	entire	3/17
2001	Atavus	4	8st9lb	86	10-1	3	2	entire	14/19
2000	Tayseer	6	8st9lb	86	9-1	5	3	gelding	8/19
1999	Grangeville	4	9st3lb	92	13-2j	1	1	gelding	20/19
1998	Ho Leng	3	9st7lb	102	14-1	2	1	gelding	20/20
1997	Tumbleweed Ridge	4	9st6lb	94	20-1	2	0	entire	19/20
1996	Crumpton Hill	4	8st12lb	86	7-1	2	1	gelding	3/16
1995	Cadeaux Tryst	3	9st1lb	97	20-1	1	0	entire	17/19
1994	En Attendant	6	9st12lb	102	14-1	7	5	gelding	7/20

Sponsored by Stan James

Place stats

AS with the Northumberland Plate and the John Smith's Cup, three-year-olds have turned a level-stakes profit.

Again, as with the Plate, this system relies on only two winners out of the last ten. While you can't knock a profit, it requires a special kind of patience to wait five years for a winner that may not come.

As with all systems that appear to offer a reliable return, it would be a help to know why this should work, so that we could have some kind of reassurance that it will keep on working. The best I can offer in this regard is that the Classic generation are improving quickly at this time of year and can take advantage of the fact that the assessor has not been able to get a bead on their ability – punters, of course, would also be taken by surprise by such rapid improvement, so such horses would often start at bigger prices than they should.

In any case, our

Age	Wins/runs	%
3	9/22	41
4	17/83	20
5	9/40	23
6	4/24	17
7	1/13	8
8+	0/7	0

OR	Wins/runs	%
Under 80	3/20	15
80-84	2/19	11
85-89	14/46	30
90-94	9/41	22
95-99	6/40	15
100+	6/23	26

Draw	Wins/runs	%
1-5	10/49	20
6-10	11/49	22
11-15	6/47	13
16+	13/44	30

Wins	Wins/runs	%
0	1/1	100
1	7/34	21
2	10/41	24
3	9/48	19
4+	13/65	20

SP	Wins/runs	%
Under 5-1	2/6	33
5-1 to 7-1	8/15	53
15-2 to 9-1	3/16	19
10-1 to 12-1	7/32	19
14-1 to 18-1	9/39	23
20-1 to 25-1	8/52	15
28-1 to 33-1	1/18	6
40-1 to 66-1	2/11	18
80-1+	No runners	

Weight	Wins/runs	%
Under 8st	3/8	38
8st-8st6lb	3/25	12
8st7lb-8st13lb	16/54	30
9st-9st5lb	12/54	22
9st6lb+	6/48	13

Sex	Wins/runs	%
Entires	12/40	30
Females	2/17	12
Geldings	26/132	20

Wins	Wins/runs	%
0	11/45	24
1	7/48	15
2	11/35	31
3	6/32	19
4+	5/29	17

place statistics (drawn from a much larger sample than our win stats) back up the simple fact that three-year-olds punch well above their weight in these three races; their place-rate is over 40 per cent in each case.

Placed three-year-olds in this race recently have included Needwood Blade (fourth at 16-1 in 2001), Grizedale (beaten a head at 20-1 in 2002) and Commission (fourth at 14-1 last year).

The stats show that high draws have done well in the past but recent results have gone against that trend, which may now be a thing of the past. It seems that Newmarket's new management team have intervened to minimise the bias.

For more on this subject, I refer you to the specialist knowledge of Graham Wheldon (page 245).

Win stats

Age	Wins/runs	%	£+-	% of stakes
3	4/36	11	+£2.50	+7
4	3/62	5	-£20.50	-33
5	3/49	6	-£11.50	-23
6	0/19	0	-£19.00	-100
7	0/12	0	-£12.00	-100
8+	0/8	0	-£8.00	-100

OR	Wins/runs	%	£+-	% of stakes
Under 80	0/25	0	-£25.00	-100
80-84	0/29	0	-£29.00	-100
85-89	2/39	5	-£20.50	-53
90-94	3/33	9	+£7.00	+21
95-99	2/37	5	-£25.50	-69
100+	3/23	13	+£24.50	+107

Draw	Wins/runs	%	£+-	% of stakes
1-6	5/56	9	+£2.00	+4
7-12	5/59	9	+£0.50	+1
13-18	0/53	0	-£53.00	-100
19+	0/18	0	-£18.00	-100

Wins	Wins/runs	%	£+-	% of stakes
0	0/3	0	-£3.00	-100
1	2/44	5	-£29.00	-66
2	6/49	12	+£21.50	+44
3	0/37	0	-£37.00	-100
4+	2/53	4	-£21.00	-40

SP	Wins/runs	%	£+-	% of stakes
Under 5-1	2/11	18	-£2.00	-18
5-1 to 7-1	4/16	25	+£13.50	+84
15-2 to 9-1	0/19	0	-£19.00	-100
10-1 to 12-1	1/20	5	-£9.00	-45
14-1 to 18-1	0/25	0	-£25.00	-100
20-1 to 25-1	3/52	6	+£16.00	+31
28-1 to 33-1	0/16	0	-£16.00	-100
40-1 to 66-1	0/27	0	-£27.00	-100
80-1+	No runners			

Weight	Wins/runs	%	£+-	% of stakes
Under 8st	0/33	0	-£33.00	-100
8st-8st6lb	4/57	7	-£32.00	-56
8st7lb-8st13lb	2/43	5	+£4.00	+9
9st-9st5lb	2/29	7	-£10.00	-34
9st6lb+	2/24	8	+£2.50	+10

Sex	Wins/runs	%	£+-	% of stakes
Entires	4/46	9	-£20.00	-43
Females	0/13	0	-£13.00	-100
Geldings	6/127	5	-£35.50	-28

Handicap wins	Wins/runs	%	£+-	% of stakes
0	5/58	9	+£11.00	+19
1	3/45	7	-£28.50	-63
2	0/34	0	-£34.00	-100
3	1/21	5	Level	Level
4+	1/28	4	-£17.00	-61

	Winner	Age	Weight	OR	SP	Wins	H'caps	Sex	Draw
2003	Far Lane	4	9st4lb	99	7-1	1	0	entire	4/20
2002	Vintage Premium	5	9st9lb	101	20-1	5	3	gelding	9/20
2001	Foreign Affairs	3	8st6lb	97	5-2f	2	1	entire	8/19
2000	Sobriety	3	8st8lb	100	20-1	2	0	gelding	8/22
1999	Achilles	4	8st11lb	90	25-1	2	0	gelding	6/15
1998	Porto Foricos	3	8st3lb	90	6-1	1	0	entire	7/20
1997	Pasternak	4	8st3lb	85	13-2	2	1	entire	1/21
1996	Wilcuma	5	9st2lb	89	10-1	4	4	gelding	2/17
1995	Naked Welcome	3	8st4lb	90	6-1	2	0	gelding	9/16
1994	Cezanne	5	9st12lb	105	9-2	2	1	gelding	3/16

Place stats

THIS race features what has become probably the most famous draw bias in the racing year.

Shortly after the 1m2f start at York, the track starts turning left and continues to do so for the next half-mile.

In a race with guaranteed pace, like this one, it's extremely difficult to get across to the rail from an outside (high) draw - but if you don't get across, you'll be running a lot further than everything on your inside.

The net result is that nothing has won this from a wider draw than stall nine in the last ten years. You could have made a tiny profit by backing all those drawn in the bottom 12.

Stalls one to six have made up only 30 per cent of the runners in the last ten years, but they've nabbed 56 per cent of the places.

Kirovski and Man O'Mystery have gone close from outside draws but even their stout efforts couldn't quite overcome the bias. Most famously, Medicean, who won two Group 1s and two Group 2s in subsequent outings, could finish only 14th from stall 21 of 22 in the 2000 renewal.

This race seems to attract fancied runners from big-name stables, and the trend is for them to be overbet. Medicean has been one of three losing favourites for Sir Michael Stoute over the last four years, while Henry Cecil's Killer Instinct was well beaten from a good draw at 7-4 in 1999.

As with the two previous races in this feature, three-year-olds have hit good strike-rates and returned a profit, though a slim one in this case.

Half of the last ten winners had not previously won a handicap, returning a level-stakes profit.

Age	Wins/runs	%
3	15/36	42
4	14/62	23
5	8/49	16
6	1/19	5
7	1/12	8
8+	0/8	0

OR	Wins/runs	%
Under 80	2/25	8
80-84	4/29	14
85-89	7/39	18
90-94	12/33	36
95-99	9/37	24
100+	5/23	22

Draw	Wins/runs	%
1-6	22/56	39
7-12	10/59	17
13-18	5/53	9
19+	2/18	11

Wins	Wins/runs	%
0	0/3	0
1	9/44	20
2	12/49	24
3	7/37	19
4+	11/53	21

SP	Wins/runs	%
Under 5-1	6/11	55
5-1 to 7-1	8/16	50
15-2 to 9-1	7/19	37
10-1 to 12-1	8/20	40
14-1 to 18-1	3/25	12
20-1 to 25-1	6/52	12
28-1 to 33-1	1/16	6
40-1 to 66-1	0/27	0
80-1+	No runners	

Weight	Wins/runs	%
Under 8st	5/33	15
8st-8st6lb	15/57	26
8st7lb-8st13lb	8/43	19
9st-9st5lb	7/29	24
9st6lb+	4/24	17

Sex	Wins/runs	%
Entires	14/46	30
Mares	3/13	23
Geldings	22/127	17

Wins	Wins/runs	%
0	13/58	22
1	7/45	16
2	9/34	26
3	6/21	29
4+	4/28	14

Handicap wins

Win stats

Age	Wins/runs	%	£+-	% of stakes
3	1/45	2	-£39.00	-87
4	4/95	4	-£39.00	-41
5	3/66	5	-£12.00	-18
6	1/41	2	-£33.50	-82
7	0/24	0	-£24.00	-100
8+	1/18	6	+£23.00	+128

OR	Wins/runs	%	£+-	% of stakes
Under 80	0/20	0	-£20.00	-100
80-84	2/46	4	-£14.00	-30
85-89	0/64	0	-£64.00	-100
90-94	4/59	7	+£13.50	+23
95-99	3/47	6	+£7.00	+15
100+	1/53	2	-£47.00	-89

Draw	Wins/runs	%	£+-	% of stakes
1-8	2/79	3	-£60.00	-76
9-16	1/75	1	-£58.00	-77
17-24	1/78	1	-£44.00	-56
25+	6/57	11	+£37.50	+66

Wins	Wins/runs	%	£+-	% of stakes
0	0/2	0	-£2.00	-100
1	1/24	4	-£11.00	-46
2	1/52	2	-£46.00	-88
3	2/54	4	-£26.00	-48
4+	6/157	4	-£39.50	-25

SP	Wins/runs	%	£+-	% of stakes
Under 5-1	1/4	25	+£1.00	+25
5-1 to 7-1	2/12	17	+£1.50	+13
15-2 to 9-1	0/9	0	-£9.00	-100
10-1 to 12-1	2/26	8	-£2.00	-8
14-1 to 18-1	3/41	7	+£6.00	+15
20-1 to 25-1	0/64	0	-£64.00	-100
28-1 to 33-1	1/48	2	-£14.00	-29
40-1 to 66-1	1/80	1	-£39.00	-49
80-1+	0/5	0	-£5.00	-100

Weight	Wins/runs	%	£+-	% of stakes
Under 8st	0/66	0	-£66.00	-100
8st-8st6lb	4/92	4	-£36.00	-39
8st7lb-8st13lb	5/64	8	+£10.50	+16
9st-9st5lb	1/41	2	-£7.00	-17
9st6lb+	0/26	0	-£26.00	-100

Sex	Wins/runs	%	£+-	% of stakes
Entires	3/39	8	-£5.00	-13
Females	0/33	0	-£33.00	-100
Geldings	7/217	3	-£86.50	-40

Handicap wins	Wins/runs	%	£+-	% of stakes
0	1/54	2	-£41.00	-76
1	3/68	4	-£13.00	-19
2	2/51	4	-£23.00	-45
3	2/34	6	-£14.00	-41
4+	2/82	2	-£33.50	-41

	Winner	Age	Weight	OR	SP	Wins	H'caps	Sex	Draw
2003	*Patavellian*	5	8st11lb	95	4-1	5	3	gelding	27/29
2002	*Bond Boy*	5	8st2lb	83	14-1	5	3	gelding	29/28
2001	*Guinea Hunter*	5	9st	98	33-1	4	1	gelding	19/30
2000	*Tayseer*	6	8st11lb	93	13-2	6	4	gelding	28/30
1999	*Harmonic Way*	4	8st6lb	92	12-1	1	0	entire	8/30
1998	*Superior Premium*	4	8st12lb	99	14-1	5	1	entire	28/29
1997	*Danetime*	3	8st10lb	100	5-1f	2	1	entire	5/30
1996	*Coastal Bluff*	4	8st5lb	91	10-1j	3	2	gelding	29/30
1995	*Shikari's Son*	8	8st13lb	92	40-1	11	9	gelding	30/27
1994	*For The Present*	4	8st3lb	81	16-1	3	2	gelding	16/26

Place stats

IT'S hard to get away from the fact that, among our ten recent winners here, we have a couple of cuckoos.

Danetime stands out from the others for several reasons. The only successful three-year-old, he has also been the only outright favourite to score. No other winner has come into the race on such a high mark; no other winner has managed to overcome such a low draw.

The other weird winner is Shikari's Son, a Brighton specialist who was helped to his shock success by a very high draw. He was two years older than any other winner during the period and the only one to overcome having previously won more than four handicaps.

By setting this pair to one side, we get a much clearer idea of what we're looking for. The ideal composite candidate will be four or five years old, rated in the 90s and carrying somewhere between 8st2lb and 9st.

Age	Wins/runs	%
3	4/45	9
4	19/95	20
5	4/66	6
6	6/41	15
7	5/24	21
8+	2/18	11

OR	Wins/runs	%
Under 80	2/20	10
80-84	6/46	13
85-89	8/64	13
90-94	10/59	17
95-99	7/47	15
100+	7/53	13

Draw	Wins/runs	%
1-8	8/79	10
9-16	6/75	8
17-24	10/78	13
25+	16/57	28

Wins	Wins/runs	%
0	0/2	0
1	2/24	8
2	5/52	10
3	8/54	15
4+	25/157	16

SP	Wins/runs	%
Under 5-1	3/4	75
5-1 to 7-1	6/12	50
15-2 to 9-1	2/9	22
10-1 to 12-1	6/26	23
14-1 to 18-1	8/41	20
20-1 to 25-1	6/64	9
28-1 to 33-1	6/48	13
40-1 to 66-1	3/80	4
80-1+	0/5	0

Weight	Wins/runs	%
Under 8st	5/66	8
8st-8st6lb	18/92	20
8st7lb-8st13lb	6/64	9
9st-9st5lb	8/41	20
9st6lb+	3/26	12

Sex	Wins/runs	%
Entires	11/39	28
Females	4/33	12
Geldings	25/217	12

Wins	Wins/runs	%
0	7/54	13
1	11/68	16
2	9/51	18
3	4/34	12
4+	9/82	11

Our place stats throw up something interesting regarding previous wins. It seems that, the more races a horse has won before showing up here, the more likely he is to make the frame. Or at least, that's true so long as his prior successes doesn't include too many handicaps. If he's won more than two of those, his chances of going close fall off quite steeply.

Back to that draw bias, which gives a major edge to high numbers. The only two to overcome low draws in the last decade have been Danetime (subsequently placed at Group 1 level) and Harmonic Way (who went on to win a Group 2). Six of the last ten winners have come from one of the top three stalls (10 per cent of total fields) and the first three home in the latest renewal were drawn 27,29,28.

Sponsored by Stan James

Win stats

	Age	Wins/runs	%	£+-	% of stakes
	3	2/67	3	-£31.00	-46
	4	6/84	7	-£16.00	-19
Age	5	1/51	2	-£17.00	-33
	6	1/47	2	-£26.00	-55
	7	0/17	0	-£17.00	-100
	8+	0/16	0	-£16.00	-100

	OR	Wins/runs	%	£+-	% of stakes
	Under 80	No runners			
	80-84	0/15	0	-£15.00	-100
Official Ratings	85-89	3/65	5	+£5.00	+8
	90-94	2/81	3	-£49.00	-60
	95-99	3/49	6	-£13.00	-27
	100-104	2/45	4	-£24.00	-53
	105+	0/27	0	-£27.00	-100

	Draw	Wins/runs	%	£+-	% of stakes
	1-8	2/80	3	-£29.00	-36
Draw	9-16	2/80	3	-£42.00	-53
	17-24	3/76	4	-£38.00	-50
	25+	3/46	7	-£14.00	-30

	Wins	Wins/runs	%	£+-	% of stakes
	0	0/1	0	-£1.00	-100
	1	1/13	8	-£2.00	-15
Wins	2	3/50	6	-£2.00	-4
	3	1/56	2	-£22.00	-39
	4+	5/162	3	-£96.00	-59

	SP	Wins/runs	%	£+-	% of stakes
	Under 5-1	1/4	25	Level	Level
	5-1 to 7-1	0/7	0	-£7.00	-100
	15-2 to 9-1	1/9	11	Level	Level
Starting Prices	10-1 to 12-1	2/29	7	-£6.00	-21
	14-1 to 18-1	4/41	10	+£27.00	+66
	20-1 to 25-1	1/70	1	-£49.00	-70
	28-1 to 33-1	1/48	2	-£14.00	-29
	40-1 to 66-1	0/69	0	-£69.00	-100
	80-1+	0/5	0	-£5.00	-100

	Weight	Wins/runs	%	£+-	% of stakes
	Under 8st	0/17	0	-£17.00	-100
	8st-8st6lb	3/83	4	-£9.00	-11
Weight	8st7lb-8st13lb	3/94	3	-£57.00	-61
	9st-9st5lb	3/54	6	-£10.00	-19
	9st6lb+	1/34	3	-£30.00	-88

	Sex	Wins/runs	%	£+-	% of stakes
	Entires	2/38	5	+£4.00	+11
Sex	Females	3/49	6	-£6.00	-12
	Geldings	5/195	3	-£121.00	-62

	Wins	Wins/runs	%	£+-	% of stakes
	0	2/54	4	-£26.00	-48
	1	1/57	2	-£38.00	-67
Handicap wins	2	4/53	8	+£23.00	+43
	3	1/34	3	-£30.00	-88
	4+	2/84	2	-£52.00	-62

	Winner	Age	Weight	OR	SP	Wins	H'caps	Sex	Draw
2003	Quito	6	8st6lb	92	20-1	4	2	entire	10/26
2002	Funfair Wane	3	9st3lb	100	16-1	2	0	gelding	16/28
2001	Continent	4	8st10lb	92	10-1	1	0	entire	22/28
2000	Bahamian Pirate	5	8st	86	33-1	3	2	gelding	7/28
1999	Grangeville	4	9st	98	11-1	2	2	gelding	17/28
1998	Always Alight	4	8st7lb	89	16-1	5	4	gelding	8/29
1997	Wildwood Flower	4	9st3lb	97	14-1	5	4	female	24/29
1996	Coastal Bluff	4	9st10lb	104	3-1f	4	3	gelding	28/28
1995	Royale Figurine	4	8st9lb	95	8-1	5	2	female	27/29
1994	Daring Destiny	3	8st	89	18-1	2	1	female	29/29

Place stats

TRAINER stats are not something this feature gets wound up about but it's necessary to concede the hold Dandy Nicholls has over this race.

Generally speaking, trainer trends will only guide you to big-name trainers who almost invariably have fancied runners - the sort of horse, in fact, that you'd have been considering anyway. It's hard to see the percentage in making much of them.

Mr Nicholls, however, appears to be fixated with this race, which he won three times in a row from 2000 to 2002. He's doing it his own way, though – two of his winners have been the only ones to take this without having previously won a handicap.

Knowing this helps us to distinguish between the general trend and a variation peculiar to a particular trainer (like Paul Cole winning the Northumberland Plate with three-year-olds). But it's hard to know what else to do with

Age	Wins/runs	%
3	7/67	10
4	13/84	15
5	9/51	18
6	8/47	17
7	1/17	6
8+	2/16	13

OR	Wins/runs	%
Under 80	No runners	
80-84	2/15	13
85-89	9/65	14
90-94	7/81	9
95-99	14/49	29
100-104	6/45	13
105+	2/27	7

Draw	Wins/runs	%
1-8	11/80	14
9-16	11/80	14
17-24	9/76	12
25+	9/46	20

Wins	Wins/runs	%
0	0/1	0
1	2/13	15
2	7/50	14
3	5/56	9
4+	26/162	16

SP	Wins/runs	%
Under 5-1	1/4	25
5-1 to 7-1	2/7	29
15-2 to 9-1	3/9	33
10-1 to 12-1	7/29	24
14-1 to 18-1	8/41	20
20-1 to 25-1	10/70	14
28-1 to 33-1	7/48	15
40-1 to 66-1	2/69	3
80-1+	0/5	0

Weight	Wins/runs	%
Under 8st	0/17	0
8st-8st6lb	15/83	18
8st7lb-8st13lb	11/94	12
9st-9st5lb	10/54	19
9st6lb+	4/34	12

Sex	Wins/runs	%
Entires	4/38	11
Females	6/49	12
Geldings	30/195	15

Wins	Wins/runs	%
0	8/54	15
1	5/57	9
2	9/53	17
3	6/34	18
4+	12/84	14

the knowledge of Nicholls' ability here – he always makes a block entry and only one of his three winners was clearly his most fancied runner.

This race used to feature a very strong bias in favour of high numbers, and at least one bookies' representative was still talking it up as if that bias persisted ahead of last year's renewal. Yet the truth is that only one winner since 1997 has been drawn higher than 17 – the first four home in 2003 came from 10, 14, 6 and 1.

Younger horses have had the call. Those aged three and four have made up 54 per cent of the runners and 80 per cent of the winners.

The market's been a good guide. Backing everything at 18-1 or shorter (averaging nine bets a year) would have turned you a profit.

Win stats

	Age	Wins/runs	%	£+-	% of stakes
Age	3	3/97	3	-£55.00	-57
	4	5/122	4	-£70.00	-57
	5	0/60	0	-£60.00	-100
	6	2/39	5	+£7.00	+18
	7	0/16	0	-£16.00	-100
	8+	0/11	0	-£11.00	-100

	OR	Wins/runs	%	£+-	% of stakes
Official Ratings	Under 80	1/40	3	-£28.00	-70
	80-84	0/57	0	-£57.00	-100
	85-89	3/83	4	-£19.00	-23
	90-94	4/65	6	-£23.00	-35
	95-99	1/54	2	-£44.00	-81
	100+	1/46	2	-£34.00	-74

	Draw	Wins/runs	%	£+-	% of stakes
Draw	1-10	0/95	0	-£95.00	-100
	11-20	5/97	5	-£16.00	-16
	21-30	3/97	3	-£66.00	-68
	31+	2/56	4	-£28.00	-50

	Wins	Wins/runs	%	£+-	% of stakes
Wins	0	0/7	0	-£7.00	-100
	1	1/46	2	-£25.00	-54
	2	1/90	1	-£81.00	-90
	3	3/82	4	-£58.00	-71
	4+	5/120	4	-£34.00	-28

	SP	Wins/runs	%	£+-	% of stakes
Starting Prices	Under 5-1	1/2	50	+£3.00	+150
	5-1 to 7-1	1/13	8	-£6.00	-46
	15-2 to 9-1	2/10	20	+£9.00	+90
	10-1 to 12-1	2/23	9	+£1.00	+4
	14-1 to 18-1	2/39	5	-£9.00	-23
	20-1 to 25-1	1/63	2	-£42.00	-67
	28-1 to 33-1	1/66	2	-£32.00	-48
	40-1 to 66-1	0/117	0	-£117.00	-100
	80-1+	0/12	0	-£12.00	-100

	Weight	Wins/runs	%	£+-	% of stakes
Weight	Under 8st	2/75	3	-£42.00	-56
	8st-8st6lb	3/102	3	-£38.00	-37
	8st7lb-8st13lb	2/105	2	-£89.00	-85
	9st-9st5lb	2/34	6	-£19.00	-56
	9st6lb+	1/29	3	-£17.00	-59

	Sex	Wins/runs	%	£+-	% of stakes
Sex	Entires	3/77	4	-£42.00	-55
	Females	2/49	4	-£30.00	-61
	Geldings	5/219	2	-£133.00	-61

	Wins	Wins/runs	%	£+-	% of stakes
Handicap wins	0	1/69	1	-£48.00	-70
	1	0/93	0	-£93.00	-100
	2	5/69	7	-£21.00	-30
	3	1/55	2	-£43.00	-78
	4+	3/59	5	Level	Level

	Winner	Age	Weight	OR	SP	Wins	H'caps	Sex	Draw
2003	*Chivalry*	4	8st1lb	87	14-1	4	2	gelding	17/34
2002	*Beauchamp Pilot*	4	9st5lb	99	9-1	5	4	gelding	26/30
2001	*I Cried For You*	6	8st6lb	88	33-1	6	4	gelding	11/35
2000	*Katy Nowaitee*	4	8st8lb	92	6-1	3	2	female	34/35
1999	*She's Our Mare*	6	7st12lb	78	11-1	3	3	female	14/33
1998	*Lear Spear*	3	7st13lb	90	20-1	1	0	entire	33/35
1997	*Pasternak*	4	9st1lb	91	4-1f	3	2	entire	17/36
1996	*Clifton Fox*	4	8st2lb	85	14-1	6	4	gelding	17/38
1995	*Cap Juluca*	3	9st10lb	107	11-1	4	2	gelding	26/39
1994	*Halling*	3	8st8lb	93	8-1c	2	2	entire	24/30

Place stats

VALUE-SEEKING is often confused with backing outsiders, when in fact it consists of looking for horses whose odds are bigger than they should be – such horses could be 66-1 or 4-7.

The expectation may be that value is more likely to be found among the long-shots but the stats on this race are conclusive proof that this is not necessarily the case. If you'd backed every runner that was sent off at 12-1 or less over the last ten years, you'd have made a profit of 15 per cent on turnover.

As it happens, this is also true of two other races covered in this section, viz the Royal Hunt Cup and the Northumberland Plate.

I must admit to being surprised by such clear evidence that the market-leaders in some of the biggest betting races of the year are generally being underbet. You'd have thought their prospects had been so thoroughly exposed by off-time that all hope of value would be long gone.

Contrast this with the 258 runners (75 per cent of all fields) who started at 20-1 or over, producing a dismal two winners for a net loss of almost 80 per cent of your investment.

Previous experience seems to count for a lot - Halling and Lear Spear have been the only winners of the last ten years with less than three previous wins, while Lear Spear has been the only one without at least two handicap wins. Both were subsequently multiple Group winners, so their sheer ability may arguably have helped them overcome a lack of prior success.

Over a quarter of runners have started from the bottom ten stalls but not one of them has won and their place-rate is half the average.

Age	Wins/runs	%
3	15/97	15
4	10/122	8
5	9/60	15
6	5/39	13
7	1/16	6
8+	0/11	0

OR	Wins/runs	%
Under 80	5/40	13
80-84	5/57	9
85-89	9/83	11
90-94	10/65	15
95-99	6/54	11
100+	5/46	11

Draw	Wins/runs	%
1-10	6/95	6
11-20	13/97	13
21-30	15/97	15
31+	6/56	11

Wins	Wins/runs	%
0	0/7	0
1	6/46	13
2	10/90	11
3	6/82	7
4+	18/120	15

SP	Wins/runs	%
Under 5-1	1/2	50
5-1 to 7-1	4/13	31
15-2 to 9-1	4/10	40
10-1 to 12-1	5/23	22
14-1 to 18-1	7/39	18
20-1 to 25-1	7/63	11
28-1 to 33-1	6/66	9
40-1 to 66-1	6/117	5
80-1+	0/12	0

Weight	Wins/runs	%
Under 8st	6/75	8
8st-8st6lb	12/102	12
8st7lb-8st13lb	16/105	15
9st-9st5lb	4/34	12
9st6lb+	2/29	7

Sex	Wins/runs	%
Entires	9/77	12
Females	7/49	14
Geldings	24/219	11

Handicap wins	Wins/runs	%
0	7/69	10
1	7/93	8
2	11/69	16
3	7/55	13
4+	8/59	14

Win stats

Age	Wins/runs	%	£+-	% of stakes
3	1/32	3	-£20.00	-63
4	2/105	2	-£64.00	-61
5	1/71	1	-£59.00	-83
6	2/45	4	-£16.00	-36
7	2/30	7	+£4.00	+13
8+	2/24	8	-£3.00	-13

OR	Wins/runs	%	£+-	% of stakes
Under 70	1/22	5	-£10.00	-45
70-74	2/31	7	+£7.00	+23
75-79	0/59	0	-£59.00	-100
80-84	1/68	2	-£56.00	-82
85-89	2/49	4	-£21.00	-43
90-94	1/35	3	-£9.00	-26
95-99	3/23	13	+£10.00	+43
100+	0/20	0	-£20.00	-100

Draw	Wins/runs	%	£+-	% of stakes
1-10	1/98	1	-£81.00	-83
11-20	5/99	5	-£34.00	-34
21-30	1/86	1	-£60.00	-70
31+	3/24	13	+£17.00	+71

Wins	Wins/runs	%	£+-	% of stakes
0	0/18	0	-£18.00	-100
1	1/36	3	-£24.00	-67
2	3/76	4	-£38.00	-50
3	4/49	8	+£21.00	+43
4+	2/128	2	-£99.00	-77

SP	Wins/runs	%	£+-	% of stakes
Under 5-1	0/6	0	-£6.00	-100
5-1 to 7-1	1/17	6	-£9.00	-53
15-2 to 9-1	0/10	0	-£10.00	-100
10-1 to 12-1	5/29	17	+£33.00	+114
14-1 to 18-1	2/27	7	+£5.00	+19
20-1 to 25-1	2/53	4	-£6.00	-11
28-1 to 33-1	0/28	0	-£28.00	-100
40-1 to 66-1	0/95	0	-£95.00	-100
80-1+	0/42	0	-£42.00	-100

Weight	Wins/runs	%	£+-	% of stakes
Under 8st	3/138	2	-£88.00	-64
8st-8st6lb	2/64	3	-£39.00	-61
8st7lb-8st13lb	3/52	6	-£17.00	-33
9st-9st5lb	1/36	3	-£23.00	-64
9st6lb+	1/17	6	+£9.00	+53

Sex	Wins/runs	%	£+-	% of stakes
Entires	0/27	0	-£27.00	-100
Females	1/45	2	-£32.00	-71
Geldings	9/235	4	-£99.00	-42

Wins	Wins/runs	%	£+-	% of stakes
0	0/53	0	-£53.00	-100
1	4/67	6	-£4.00	-6
2	2/58	3	-£28.00	-48
3	2/42	5	-£15.00	-36
4+	2/87	2	-£58.00	-67

	Winner	Age	Weight	OR	SP	Wins	H'caps	Sex	Draw
2003	*Landing Light*	8	9st4lb	98	12-1	2	1	gelding	36/36
2002	*Miss Fara*	7	8st	85	12-1	2	2	female	36/36
2001	*Distant Prospect*	4	8st8lb	88	14-1	3	3	gelding	32/31
2000	*Heros Fatal*	6	8st1lb	84	11-1	2	1	gelding	18/33
1999	*Top Cees*	9	8st10lb	95	7-1	8	7	gelding	17/32
1998	*Spirit Of Love*	3	8st8lb	95	11-1	3	3	gelding	19/29
1997	*Turnpole*	6	7st10lb	74	16-1	3	2	gelding	6/31
1996	*Inchcailloch*	7	7st3lb	70	20-1	5	4	gelding	15/26
1995	*Old Red*	5	7st11lb	66	11-1	1	1	gelding	18/21
1994	*Captain's Guest*	4	9st9lb	92	25-1	3	1	gelding	28/32

Place stats

AS DIFFERENT from the Cambridgeshire as you'd expect, considering one is twice as far as the other.

In particular, the stats on market-leaders are in direct contrast to those for the earlier race. Of the 33 starters returned at single-figure SPs, only Top Cees (the horse of many headlines) actually managed to get past the post first.

Having said that, runners who fell into the 28-1 or higher bracket didn't manage to win even once, despite making up over half of all starters.

In between these extremes, 90 per cent of winners since 1994 have been priced from 11-1 to 25-1. This section included over a third of all runners but the payouts have been so healthy that the net profit is just shy of 30 per cent on turnover.

Remarkably for a competitive handicap, six of the last eight winners have been six or older.

Weight takes more of a toll over longer distances, so it's no surprise that only two winners have managed to defy burdens of over 9st. However, the figures for percentage loss on turnover suggest that the topweights have been closer to being value than those below them in the handicap.

Runners rated in the 90s have won four times, producing a tiny profit.

Those with no previous handicap wins have struggled.

Oddly, for a race over 2m2f, there's a serious draw bias, in favour of high numbers. Indeed, the last two winners have been drawn right next to the rail, while only one runner was drawn wider than Distant Prospect. Graham Wheldon's explanation for this is that horses have to settle early on in order to see out marathon trips to best effect. Only those drawn well can do this – the rest have to be asked for an effort right from the start, to get a good position.

Age	Wins/runs	%
3	4/32	13
4	13/105	12
5	12/71	17
6	5/45	11
7	3/30	10
8+	3/24	13

OR	Wins/runs	%
Under 70	3/22	14
70-74	3/31	10
75-79	9/59	15
80-84	9/68	13
85-89	5/49	10
90-94	6/35	17
95-99	4/23	17
100+	1/20	5

Draw	Wins/runs	%
1-10	6/98	6
11-20	19/99	19
21-30	10/86	12
31+	5/24	21

Wins	Wins/runs	%
0	2/18	11
1	3/36	8
2	7/76	9
3	12/49	24
4+	16/128	13

SP	Wins/runs	%
Under 5-1	3/6	50
5-1 to 7-1	3/17	18
15-2 to 9-1	2/10	20
10-1 to 12-1	10/29	34
14-1 to 18-1	4/27	15
20-1 to 25-1	6/53	11
28-1 to 33-1	2/28	7
40-1 to 66-1	9/95	9
80-1+	1/42	2

Weight	Wins/runs	%
Under 8st	17/138	12
8st-8st6lb	7/64	11
8st7lb-8st13lb	11/52	21
9st-9st5lb	3/36	8
9st6lb+	2/17	12

Sex	Wins/runs	%
Entires	3/27	11
Females	6/45	13
Geldings	31/235	13

Handicap wins	Wins/runs	%
0	5/53	9
1	10/67	15
2	5/58	9
3	9/42	21
4+	11/87	13

Track Facts

WANT TO size up the layout and undulations of the course where your fancy's about to line up? Over the next 30-odd pages, we bring you three-dimensional maps of all Britain's Flat tracks, allowing you to see at a glance task facing your selection. The maps come to you courtesy of the *Racing Post*'s website (www.racingpost.co.uk).

We've listed the top dozen trainers and jockeys at each course, ranked by strike-rate, with a breakdown of their relevant statistics over the last three years. The record of favourites is here as well – Folkestone (36.8%) has seen the best strike-rate for jollies, while Ascot (23.2%) has produced the worst. Note that market leaders generated a profit (to level stakes of £1) at only four of the 35 tracks, underlining a basic fact of racing; as a general rule, favourites offer little in the way of value.

We've included addresses, phone numbers, directions and fixture lists for each track, together with Time Test's standard times for all you clock-watchers.

And Graham Wheldon, whose *Sprintline* column is a popular feature of RFO, has chipped in with his views on the draw at every course – see page 245. As his analysis has repeatedly shown, most tracks feature a bias of some kind, so check whether the beast on your betting slip is running on the right side before you hand it over.

ASCOT

Royal Enclosure, Ascot, Berks,
SL5 7JN. Tel 01344 622 211

How to get there – Road: M4 Jct 6, M3 Jct 6, M25 Jct 13. Rail: Ascot from London Waterloo
Features: Stiff, galloping RH 1m6f circuit
2004 Flat fixtures: Apr 28, May 22, June 15-19, July 9-10, 23-25, Aug 7, Sep 24-26, Oct 8-9
Pointers: A solid performance from Marcus Tregoning, who can be backed blind. Aidan O'Brien should be avoided - Hawk Wing's flop in the Queen Anne last year being a case in point. Johnny Murtagh has good figures. He was leading jockey at the Royal meeting two years ago and rode Choisir to win twice, at 25-1 and 13-2, last year. Frankie Dettori may have ridden seven through the card here but he strikes at under 10 per cent.

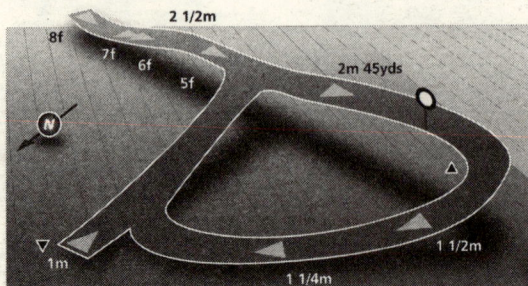

Time Test standard times

5f	59.4	1m2f	2min3.4
6f	1min13	1m4f	2min27.3
6f110yds	1min19.5	2m45yds	3min25.3
7f	1min26	2m4f	4min18
1m (str)	1min38.7	2m6f34yds	4min48
1m (rnd)	1min39.4		

Favourites

2-y-o	31.3%	-£9.35
3-y-o+	20.7%	-£85.22
Overall	23.2%	-£94.57

Trainers

Trainers	Wins-Runs	%	2yo	3yo+	£1 level stks
J.E.Hammond	3-10	30.0	0-0	3-10	+24.00
M.Tregoning	14-48	29.2	3-10	11-38	+25.03
M.Johnston	32-137	23.4	9-29	23-108	+105.22
Sir M.Stoute	19-114	16.7	2-17	17-97	-22.56
J.Eustace	3-19	15.8	2-3	1-16	+12.00
H.Morrison	4-28	14.3	0-1	4-27	+4.00
M.Pipe	4-28	14.3	0-0	4-28	+15.00
J.Fanshawe	6-43	14.0	1-2	5-41	-10.40
T.Mills	9-65	13.8	2-5	7-60	+47.00
J.Jenkins	3-22	13.6	0-1	3-21	+14.00
G.Wragg	3-22	13.6	0-0	3-22	-3.62
J.Gosden	12-96	12.5	2-17	10-79	+14.88

Jockeys

Jockeys	Wins-Rides	%	£1 level stks	Best Trainer	W-R
J.Murtagh	18-69	26.1	+105.75	Sir M.Stoute	4-13
P.Fitzsimons	4-17	23.5	+28.00	J.M.Bradley	2-11
K.Dalgleish	7-35	20.0	+39.50	M.Johnston	5-27
P.Dobbs	3-16	18.8	+6.63	R.Hannon	3-12
J.Tate	3-19	15.8	+12.00	J.Eustace	3-13
K.Darley	22-142	15.5	+19.61	M.Johnston	12-35
R.Hughes	20-134	14.9	+23.38	R.Hannon	5-34
K.Fallon	27-187	14.4	-26.93	Sir M.Stoute	12-66
O.Urbina	3-21	14.3	-8.90	J.Fanshawe	3-17
R.Hills	14-103	13.6	+12.27	M.Tregoning	3-16
W.Supple	6-50	12.0	-22.39	M.Tregoning	4-11
M.Dwyer	13-122	10.7	+6.50	M.Tregoning	6-17

Sponsored by Stan James

Whitletts Road Ayr KA8 0JE.
Tel 01292 264 179

AYR

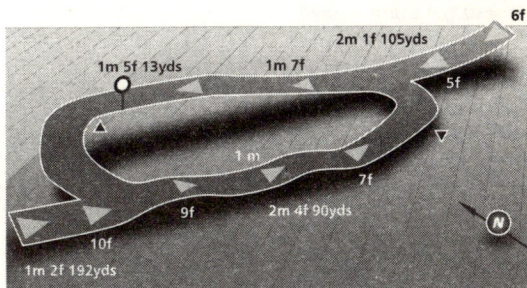

How to get there – Road: south from Glasgow on A77 or A75, A70, A76. Rail: Ayr, bus service from station on big race days

Features: LH 1m4f oval, easy turns, generally flat, suits galloping types

2004 Flat fixtures: Apr 29, May 21, 27, June 17-19, Jul 12, 19-20, Aug 7, 20, Sep 16-18, Oct 11-12, 30

Pointers: Southern trainers dominate the top half of the list but their runners are few and far between and there's no obvious betting strategy. Mark Johnston is the man to base a system around, because he has a meaningful amount of runners and a strike-rate close to 25 per cent, the benchmark percentage figure.

Time Test standard times

5f	57.7	1m2f	2min4.4
6f	1min9.7	1m2f192yds	2min14.3
7f	1min25	1m5f13yds	2min45.4
7f50yds	1min28	1m7f	3min13.2
1m	1min37.7	2m1f105yds	3min46
1m1f20yds	1min50	2m4f90yds	4min25

Favourites

2-y-o	41.2%	+£2.30
3-y-o+	29.0%	-£34.03
Overall	32.5%	-£31.73

Trainers	Wins-Runs	%	2yo	3yo+	£1 level stks
L.Cumani	5-9	55.6	0-0	5-9	+9.60
M.Tregoning	3-8	37.5	2-5	1-3	-1.87
M.Bell	5-16	31.3	3-6	2-10	+10.50
M.Brittain	3-10	30.0	1-1	2-9	+22.00
J.Noseda	3-11	27.3	1-2	2-9	-4.69
Sir.M.Stoute	4-16	25.0	0-3	4-13	+0.37
B.Hills	11-45	24.4	4-20	7-25	-3.87
M.Johnston	26-108	24.1	18-57	8-51	+38.12
W.Haggas	4-17	23.5	0-4	4-13	+3.50
Mrs.M.Reveley	6-28	21.4	0-1	6-27	+9.50
Mrs.L.Stubbs	3-15	20.0	2-7	1-8	+10.50
E.Dunlop	7-37	18.9	4-19	3-18	+7.82

Jockeys	Wins-Rides	%	£1 level stks	Best Trainer	W-R
L.Dettori	6-14	42.9	+4.62	J.Gosden	2-5
R.Hughes	4-12	33.3	+7.25	R.Hannon	2-2
S.Sanders	9-27	33.3	+62.50	B.McMahon	1-1
K.Fallon	12-42	28.6	+16.80	Sir.M.Stoute	3-4
M.Hills	3-13	23.1	-5.86	B.Hills	3-11
L.Keniry	3-14	21.4	+15.00	J.Goldie	1-1
D.Holland	8-40	20.0	+14.70	Mrs.L.Stubbs	1-1
W.Supple	9-45	20.0	+33.45	E.Dunlop	4-7
N.Mackay	7-38	18.4	+68.63	L.Cumani	2-4
K.Darley	21-120	17.5	+0.82	M.Johnston	7-23
T.E.Durcan	11-68	16.2	-15.09	M.Tompkins	6-31
M.Fenton	7-49	14.3	+20.50	M.Bell	4-10

BATH

How to get there – Road: M4, Jctn 18, then A46 south.

Rail: Bath Spa, special bus service to course on race-days

Features: LH oval, uphill straight of 4f.

2004 Flat fixtures: Apr 8, 27, May 4, 17, 21, 27, June 12, 23, July 5, 11, 22, Aug 10, 15, 27, Sep 6, 13, 27, Oct 10, 19

Pointers: Sir Michael Stoute and Roger Charlton are strike-rate trainers per se and it's no surprise that their percentages are good. The former has further to travel, so won't be time-wasting. Keep an eye on Darryll Holland and Manton-based Jimmy Fortune.

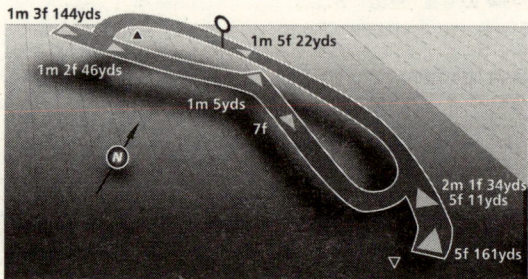

1m 3f 144yds
1m 5f 22yds
1m 2f 46yds
1m 5yds
7f
2m 1f 34yds
5f 11yds
5f 161yds

Time Test standard times

5f11yds	1min0.5	1m3f144yds	2min26
5f161yds	1min9	1m5f22yds	2min47.3
1m5yds	1min38	2m1f34yds	3min44
1m2f46yds	2min6.2		

Favourites

2-y-o	43.9%	-£2.84
3-y-o+	32.4%	+£14.64
Overall	35.2%	+£11.80

Trainers

Trainers	Wins-Runs	%	2yo	3yo+	£1 level stks
N.Callaghan	3-6	50.0	2-3	1-3	+5.75
R.Cowell	4-9	44.4	0-0	4-9	+27.50
M.Tregoning	6-16	37.5	1-4	5-12	+5.65
J.Akehurst	6-18	33.3	0-4	6-14	+31.00
R.Charlton	9-29	31.0	3-9	6-20	+8.85
Sir.M.Stoute	7-24	29.2	0-0	7-24	+8.42
J.Cullinan	3-11	27.3	0-0	3-11	+7.83
G.Bravery	3-11	27.3	2-4	1-7	+23.50
Mrs.A.L.King	3-12	25.0	0-0	3-12	+27.50
L.Cumani	4-16	25.0	0-3	4-13	+4.50
A.Balding	5-21	23.8	4-6	1-15	+9.63
Sir.M.Prescott	3-15	20.0	2-11	1-4	-4.22

Jockeys

Jockeys	Wins-Rides	%	£1 level stks	Best Trainer	W-R
L.Dettori	5-9	55.6	+7.51	J.Boyle	1-1
D.Holland	6-16	37.5	+8.82	S.Keightley	1-1
A.Quinn	3-9	33.3	+7.50	R.Cowell	2-3
J.Fanning	3-10	30.0	+12.25	M.Johnston	2-4
D.McGaffin	3-10	30.0	+17.50	B.Palling	2-8
R.Hills	3-12	25.0	-1.52	B.Hills	1-1
K.Fallon	10-42	23.8	-13.68	G.A.Butler	3-5
G.Duffield	3-13	23.1	-2.84	Sir.M.Prescott	2-5
R.Hughes	17-91	18.7	-9.30	R.Charlton	5-10
M.Hills	8-43	18.6	-2.10	B.Hills	7-26
J.Fortune	11-63	17.5	-14.35	B.Meehan	2-3
B.Doyle	5-29	17.2	-0.67	B.Meehan	3-8

York Road, Beverley, E Yorkshire,
HU17 8QZ. Tel 01482 867 488

BEVERLEY

How to get there – Road:
Course is signposted from
the M62.
Rail: Beverley, bus service
to course on race-days
Features: RH, uphill finish
2004 Flat fixtures: Apr 14,
22, May 8, 18, 24, June 2,
9, 17, 22, July 2-3, 13, 19,
27, Aug 11-12, 28-29,
Sep 15, 21

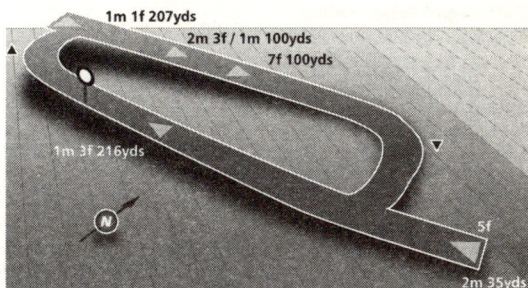

Pointers: The top 13 trainers, percentage-wise, are
southern-based and only
send a handful of horses
each year to the Yorkshire
track. Mick Channon
sends the most, with an
average of close to seven
runners per season, so consider a system involving his
two-year-olds. Watch Kevin Darley's mounts.

Time Test standard times

5f	1min0.5	1m3f216yds	2min30.6
7f100yds	1min29.5	1m4f16yds	2min32
1m100yds	1min42.4	2m35yds	3min29.5
1m1f207yds	2min0	2m3f100yds	4min16.7

Favourites

2-y-o	45.3%	+£0.93
3-y-o+	30.5%	-£29.73
Overall	34.1%	-£28.79

Trainers	Wins-Runs	%	2yo	3yo+	£1 level stks
A.Balding	3-7	42.9	1-2	2-5	+2.62
D.Loder	3-7	42.9	2-5	1-2	+0.60
M.Tregoning	6-15	40.0	1-3	5-12	+17.75
L.Cumani	5-13	38.5	0-1	5-12	+14.00
W.Jarvis	3-8	37.5	0-0	3-8	+26.08
M.Jarvis	7-19	36.8	3-4	4-15	+5.64
Sir.M.Prescott	6-19	31.6	3-11	3-8	+3.07
M.Bell	5-17	29.4	2-4	3-13	+19.62
Mrs.A.Perrett	4-14	28.6	1-5	3-9	-2.88
M.Channon	10-36	27.8	6-17	4-19	-1.01
H.Cecil	3-11	27.3	2-3	1-8	-5.05
H Candy	3-13	23.1	1-3	2-10	+5.25

Jockeys	Wins-Rides	%	£1 level stks	Best Trainer	W-R
K.Fallon	12-39	30.8	+1.99	I.Balding	2-4
T.Quinn	4-15	26.7	+15.25	H.Cecil	2-4
K.Darley	27-114	23.7	+5.70	T.Easterby	5-23
R.Hills	3-13	23.1	+13.86	M.Tregoning	2-4
N.Mackay	3-14	21.4	+4.50	L.Cumani	2-2
J.P.Spencer	7-36	19.4	-6.31	L.Cumani	2-5
D.Holland	6-32	18.8	-5.35	D.Loder	1-1
R.Ffrench	9-50	18.0	-2.92	M.Johnston	4-12
J.Mackay	3-17	17.6	+6.88	G.M.Moore	2-2
T.E.Durcan	9-53	17.0	+30.95	M.Tompkins	3-21
A.Nicholls	9-55	16.4	+1.35	D.Nicholls	6-30
M.Tebbutt	4-27	14.8	-12.96	M.Jarvis	2-4

BRIGHTON

Freshfield Road, Brighton,
E Sussex BN2 2XZ.
Tel 01273 603 580

How to get there – Road: Signposted from A23 London Road and A27. Rail: Brighton, bus to course on race-days

Features: LH, sharp and undulating, mainly down-hill for last 7f, suitable for handy, speedy types

2004 Flat fixtures: Apr 25, May 4, 12, 23, 28, June 6, 10, 14, 22, 29, July 4, 13, 19, Aug 3-5, 16, 24-25, Sep 23, Oct 2, 15, 21

Pointers: There's always an edge supporting Sir Mark Prescott's runners and he has maintained a high strike-rate here for far longer than the five-year period in question. Seb Sanders is far and away the winningmost jockey. Prescott is partly responsible but it is the lightweight's partnership with Andrew Reid that catches the eye.

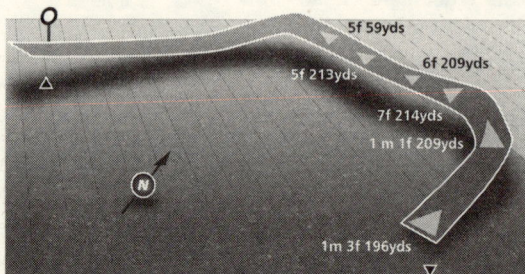

Time Test standard times

5f59yds	59.5	7f214yds	1min32
5f213yds	1min7.5	1m1f209yds	1min57.5
6f209yds	1min19.6	1m3f196yds	2min26

Favourites

2-y-o	42.9%	-£4.21
3-y-o+	28.8%	-£36.84
Overall	31.7%	-£41.04

Trainers

	Wins-Runs	%	2yo	3yo+	£1 level stks
R.Charlton	6-11	54.5	2-3	4-8	+22.37
L.Montague Hall	4-8	50.0	0-0	4-8	+26.75
H.Cecil	4-9	44.4	1-1	3-8	+8.87
Sir.M.Stoute	5-13	38.5	2-3	3-10	+0.03
Sir.M.Prescott	12-32	37.5	4-15	8-17	+2.69
P.Blockley	6-19	31.6	1-7	5-12	+46.50
C.Wall	6-19	31.6	1-1	5-18	+2.63
G.A.Butler	9-30	30.0	1-6	8-24	+21.42
A.Stewart	5-18	27.8	1-5	4-13	+5.43
D.Nicholls	7-26	26.9	0-0	7-26	+13.50
J.Noseda	4-15	26.7	1-2	3-13	-7.95
M.Jarvis	3-12	25.0	1-3	2-9	-2.25

Jockeys

	Wins-Rides	%	£1 level stks	Best Trainer	W-R
R.FitzPatrick	5-10	50.0	+11.08	R.Wilman	4-4
M.Hills	7-15	46.7	+10.25	B.Hills	4-8
R.Hills	6-15	40.0	+1.05	A.Stewart	2-2
D.Nolan	4-12	33.3	+39.25	P.Blockley	4-8
W.Ryan	6-23	26.1	-1.80	H.Cecil	2-2
Claire Stretton	3-12	25.0	+31.00	R.Spicer	2-2
S.Sanders	38-161	23.6	+79.73	A.Reid	5-13
K.Fallon	4-18	22.2	-10.66	M.Wallace	1-1
A.Nicholls	3-14	21.4	+11.50	D.Nicholls	2-7
J.P.Spencer	11-52	21.2	+23.28	L.Cumani	3-14
E.Ahern	13-67	19.4	+62.17	G.A.Butler	7-17
R.Hughes	15-80	18.8	+9.20	R.Hannon	7-26

Sponsored by Stan James

Durdar Road, Carlisle, Cumbria,
CA2 4TS. Tel 01228 554 700

CARLISLE

How to get there – Road: M6 Jctn 42, follow signs on Dalston Road.
Rail: Carlisle, 66 bus to course on race-days
Features: RH, undulating, uphill finish
2004 Flat fixtures: May 4, 24, June 14, 23, July 3, 16, 29, Aug 2, 18, Sep 2, 11

Pointers: Not a track for systems. Mark Johnston's three-year-olds are worth a second look and Alan Berry's two-year-olds are best avoided. Kevin Darley is his usual excellent self.

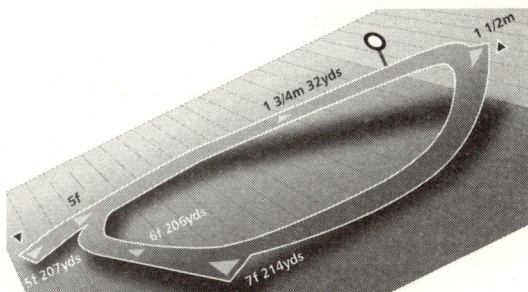

Time Test standard times

5f	59.6	1m1f61yds	1min55
5f193yds	1min11.8	1m3f206yds	2min28.7
6f192yds	1min24.7	1m6f32yds	2min59.2
7f200yds	1min37.6	2m1f52yds	3min42

Favourites

2-y-o	52.4%	+£1.17
3-y-o+	30.6%	-£14.35
Overall	34.1%	-£13.18

Trainers	Wins-Runs	%	2yo	3yo+	£1 level stks
R.Wilman	3-4	75.0	0-0	3-4	+42.00
Sir.M.Prescott	3-8	37.5	0-2	3-6	-1.79
Mrs.L.Stubbs	3-10	30.0	0-2	3-8	+6.63
Mrs.J.Ramsden	3-13	23.1	2-4	1-9	-4.19
M.Channon	3-14	21.4	2-4	1-10	+7.11
M.Johnston	5-28	17.9	0-6	5-22	-11.25
J.J.Quinn	3-17	17.6	1-1	2-16	+8.00
I.Semple	3-17	17.6	0-1	3-16	-1.33
D.Nicholls	5-34	14.7	1-1	4-33	-6.13
R.Fahey	5-37	13.5	1-8	4-29	-10.33
M.Dods	4-31	12.9	0-3	4-28	+8.00
T.D.Barron	3-24	12.5	2-6	1-18	-9.13

Jockeys	Wins-Rides	%	£1 level stks	Best Trainer	W-R
E.Ahern	3-8	37.5	+18.45	N.Bycroft	1-1
Alex Greaves	4-16	25.0	+9.00	D.Nicholls	4-16
K.Darley	7-38	18.4	-22.42	L.Cumani	2-2
K.Dalgleish	3-23	13.0	-8.75	M.Johnston	2-11
D.Allan	4-31	12.9	+5.75	J.O'Reilly	3-3
G.Duffield	6-48	12.5	-5.60	Sir.M.Prescott	2-7
P.Hanagan	8-67	11.9	-11.83	R.Fahey	5-25
F.Lynch	6-58	10.3	-32.26	Sir.M.Stoute	2-3
F.Norton	4-40	10.0	-1.00	A.Berry	4-29
R.Winston	6-62	9.7	-22.88	Mrs.L.Stubbs	2-2
D.McKeown	3-36	8.3	-12.00	Miss.I.Craig	1-1
J.Fanning	3-38	7.9	-12.50	I.A.Wood	1-1

CATTERICK

Catterick Bridge, Richmond,
N Yorkshire, DL10 7PE.
Tel 01748 811 478

How to get there – Road: A1, exit 5m south of Scotch Corner.
Rail: Darlington or Northallerton and bus.
Features: LH, undulating, tight turns, lends itself to course specialists
2004 Flat fixtures: Mar 31, Apr 21, May 4, 22, 28, June 4, 30, July 7, 14, 21, Aug 3, 13, 25, Sep 7, 18, Oct 5, 16, 26, Nov 2
Pointers: A couple of jockey/trainer combinations catch the eye, Alex Greaves for husband David Nicholls and Tony Culhane for Mary Reveley. Mick Channon fires a lot of short-priced blanks.

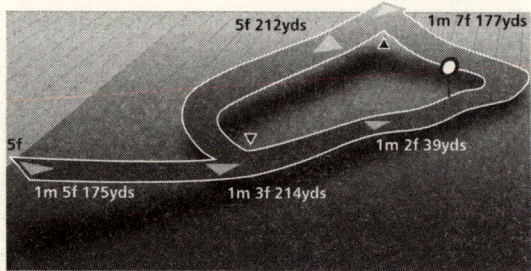

Time Test standard times

5f	57.5	1m3f214yds	2min31
5f212yds	1min10.5	1m5f175yds	2min55.3
7f	1min23.2	1m7f177yds	3min21.2

Favourites

2-y-o	39.1%	-£5.48
3-y-o+	29.9%	-£38.10
Overall	32.2%	-£43.59

Trainers

Trainers	Wins-Runs	%	2yo	3yo+	£1 level stks
E. Dunlop	6-13	46.2	3-5	3-8	+1.92
P. Cole	9-23	39.1	6-16	3-7	+8.64
Sir M. Stoute	5-14	35.7	2-4	3-10	+2.39
W. Haggas	4-16	25.0	2-6	2-10	-1.52
A. Turnell	4-17	23.5	0-3	4-14	+5.25
M. Bell	5-22	22.7	2-6	3-16	+6.88
Sir M. Prescott	8-37	21.6	3-19	5-18	-7.63
W. Muir	4-20	20.0	2-6	2-14	-5.68
M. Johnston	22-112	19.6	7-43	15-69	-32.71
B. Hills	7-39	17.9	2-10	5-29	-0.38
J. Glover	8-45	17.8	1-13	7-32	-2.38
B. Smart	6-35	17.1	2-14	4-21	+44.05

Jockeys

Jockeys	Wins-Rides	%	£1 level stks	Best Trainer	W-R
J. Fortune	6-15	40.0	+29.25	P. Cole	3-5
Paul Scallan	6-20	30.0	+70.44	B. Smart	3-11
G. Carter	5-19	26.3	+9.00	A. Berry	2-7
K. Fallon	11-43	25.6	+9.62	D. Nicholls	2-5
I. Mongan	3-12	25.0	-1.00	M. Jarvis	1-1
D. Holland	11-46	23.9	-17.08	M. Johnston	5-9
J.F. McDonald	3-14	21.4	+7.75	I.A. Wood	2-5
Alex Greaves	10-48	20.8	+12.58	D. Nicholls	10-47
J. Egan	3-16	18.8	+4.50	P.D. Evans	3-6
L. Fletcher	6-35	17.1	+38.00	Mrs. L. Stubbs	1-1
E. Ahern	3-18	16.7	-2.67	E. Alston	2-4
K. Darley	23-141	16.3	-32.20	M. Johnston	5-18

CHEPSTOW

How to get there – Road: M4 Jct 22 on west side of Severn Bridge, A48 north, then A446 Monmouth Rd. Rail: Chepstow, bus to course on race-days

Features: LH, undulating

2004 Flat fixtures: Apr 23, May 31, June 3, 11, 21, July 9, 23, Aug 5, 12, 19, 30, Sep 3, 9, 20

Pointers: The Welsh track has its fans among the training fraternity, not least the Dunlops John and Ed. They are the only two handlers striking at over 30 per cent. If we had to pick a system, though, it would be to back all of Martin Pipe's horses. Famous as champion jumps trainer, his Flat-race figures have stood up to scrutiny for more than the last five years here.

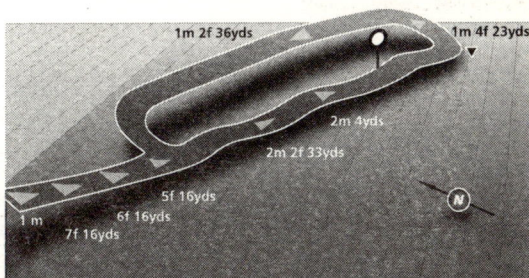

Time Test standard times

5f16yds	57	1m4f23yds	2min31.3
6f16yds	1min8.8	2m49yds	3min28
7f16yds	1min20.5	2m1f40yds	3min41
1m14yds	1min32.6	2m2f	3min52
1m2f36yds	2min4.2		

Favourites

2-y-o	36.7%	-£4.37
3-y-o+	19.0%	-£72.22
Overall	23.8%	-£76.59

Trainers

Trainers	Wins-Runs	%	2yo	3yo+	£1 level stks
J.Dunlop	8-25	32.0	3-10	5-15	+7.95
E.Dunlop	9-29	31.0	2-7	7-22	+17.30
H.Candy	6-21	28.6	1-5	5-16	+9.57
H.Howe	3-11	27.3	0-2	3-9	+30.00
M.Pipe	3-11	27.3	0-4	3-7	+20.00
B.Meehan	10-37	27.0	5-20	5-17	+43.88
Sir.M.Prescott	4-15	26.7	0-7	4-8	-0.74
P.Hiatt	3-12	25.0	0-1	3-11	+27.50
R.Johnson Houghton	3-12	25.0	2-5	1-7	+14.50
Sir.M.Stoute	3-14	21.4	1-2	2-12	-3.73
R.Charlton	4-19	21.1	0-5	4-14	+9.40
B Palling	10-53	18.9	3-19	7-34	+45.91

Jockeys

Jockeys	Wins-Rides	%	£1 level stks	Best Trainer	W-R
K.Fallon	7-20	35.0	+5.88	Sir.M.Stoute	2-4
R.Ffrench	3-10	30.0	+7.75	A Stewart	2-3
R.Hughes	5-17	29.4	+2.58	R Hannon	2-5
G.Duffield	3-12	25.0	+2.01	Sir.M.Prescott	2-5
F.Norton	8-32	25.0	+16.05	D.Haydn Jones	2-3
T.Quinn	6-27	22.2	-3.46	H.Cecil	2-4
G.Gibbons	5-23	21.7	+51.00	P.D.Evans	3-5
A.McCarthy	3-15	20.0	+36.63	P.L.Clinton	1-1
D.O'Neill	14-71	19.7	+32.08	R.Charlton	3-3
T.McLaughlin	3-18	16.7	0.00	M.Saunders	2-5
J.Egan	4-25	16.0	-6.59	J.Dunlop	2-4
N.Callan	3-20	15.0	-1.75	D.Cantillon	1-1

CHESTER

Steam Mill Street,
Chester, CH1 2LY.
Tel 01244 304 600

How to get there – Road: Join Inner Ring Road and A458 Queensferry Road. Rail: Chester General, bus to city centre

Features: LH, flat, almost circular

2004 Flat fixtures: May 5-7, June 8, 26, July 9-10, Aug 1, 19-21, Sep 11

Pointers: Two trainers to follow are Gerard Butler and Geoff Wragg. A great deal of fuss is made of Barry Hills' liking for the place but level-stakes support for him would have put you in the red. Sir Michael Stoute owes his position in the black to Kris Kin's 20-1 shock. Alan Bailey lands the occasional handicap coup, while Eric Alston snaps up more than his share for a small yard.

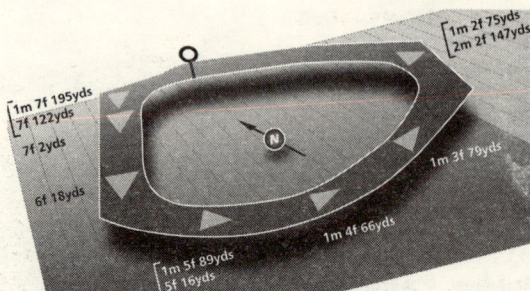

1m 2f 75yds
2m 2f 147yds
1m 7f 195yds
7f 122yds
7f 2yds
6f 18yds
1m 3f 79yds
1m 4f 66yds
1m 5f 89yds
5f 16yds

Time Test standard times

5f16yds	59.8	1m3f79yds	2min22.7
6f18yds	1min13	1m4f66yds	2min35
7f2yds	1min24.7	1m5f89yds	2min48.6
7f122yds	1min31.2	1m7f195yds	3min22
1m1f70yds	1min55	2m2f147yds	4min1
1m2f75yds	2min8		

Favourites

2-y-o	55.6%	+£25.28
3-y-o+	27.4%	-£35.65
Overall	35.1%	-£10.38

Trainers	Wins-Runs	%	2yo	3yo+	£1 level stks
M.Tregoning	3-4	75.0	0-0	3-4	+11.63
J.Noseda	4-6	66.7	2-4	2-2	+9.63
J.Gosden	5-13	38.5	0-1	5-12	+19.38
G.A.Butler	8-25	32.0	1-3	7-22	+19.63
G.Wragg	5-16	31.3	0-0	5-16	-2.87
W.G.M.Turner	3-12	25.0	3-7	0-5	+4.63
B.Hills	20-81	24.7	10-21	10-60	-5.09
Sir.M.Stoute	8-34	23.5	1-6	7-28	+9.15
J.M.Bradley	3-13	23.1	0-0	3-13	-1.25
M.W.Easterby	5-22	22.7	0-1	5-21	+14.00
M.Tompkins	4-18	22.2	2-5	2-13	-5.50
J.Dunlop	4-19	21.1	3-4	1-15	-4.75

Jockeys	Wins-Rides	%	£1 level stks	Best Trainer	W-R
R.Hills	7-16	43.8	+8.58	B.Hills	4-6
P.Dobbs	4-14	28.6	+5.00	R.Hannon	3-8
K.Fallon	22-84	26.2	+12.54	Sir.M.Stoute	6-23
E.Ahern	7-28	25.0	+12.62	G.A.Butler	4-9
D.Holland	17-72	23.6	-3.77	G.Wragg	5-13
A.Culhane	3-17	17.6	+8.33	S.Woods	1-1
R.Mullen	3-17	17.6	+20.50	P.D.Evans	2-9
P.Robinson	4-23	17.4	+19.50	C.Brittain	2-10
J.Fortune	3-18	16.7	+6.50	J.Gosden	1-1
K.Darley	12-76	15.8	-19.60	P.Cole	3-4
P.Hanagan	5-32	15.6	+5.50	R.Fahey	2-12
M.Hills	7-48	14.6	-16.46	B.Hills	6-41

Leger Way, Doncaster,
DN2 6BB. Tel: 01302 304 200

DONCASTER

How to get there – Road:
M18, Jncts 3 or 4
Rail: Doncaster, bus to
course
Features: LH, flat, easy
turns, suits galloping type
2004 Flat fixtures:
Mar 25-27, May 3, 20, 29,
June 5, 13, 26, July 8, 15,
22, 31, Sep 8-11, Oct 22-
23, Nov 6
Pointers: The first three
trainers in our list have
healthy strike-rates but
their horses don't start at
working men's prices.
John Gosden's two-year-
olds are worth a look.
Henry Cecil, who once
reigned supreme, is
notable by his absence.
The jockey/trainer combo is Joe Fanning for Mark
Johnston.

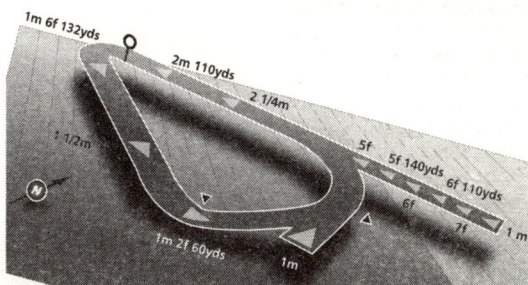

Time Test standard times

5f	58.7	1m(round)	1min37.2
5f140yds	1min7.4	1m2f60yds	2min6
6f	1min11.5	1m4f	2min30
6f110yds	1min18	1m6f132yds	3min3
7f	1min24.3	2m110yds	3min32
1m(str)	1min36.8	2m2f	3min53

Favourites

2-y-o	35.2%	-£7.23
3-y-o+	24.3%	-£72.26
Overall	27.5%	-£79.49

Trainers	Wins-Runs	%	2yo	3yo+	£1 level stks
A.P.O'Brien	5-18	27.8	3-11	2-7	+0.25
D.Loder	8-30	26.7	7-22	1-8	-12.60
S.Bin Suroor	6-23	26.1	0-3	6-20	-5.13
W.G.M.Turner	3-13	23.1	2-10	1-3	+8.00
J.Fanshawe	7-33	21.2	0-5	7-28	-10.28
J.Gosden	9-45	20.0	7-21	2-24	+25.27
J.A.Osborne	5-26	19.2	3-17	2-9	+25.50
G.Wragg	5-26	19.2	3-4	2-22	-5.50
Sir.M.Stoute	11-58	19.0	4-23	7-35	-11.60
M.Johnston	26-140	18.6	9-48	17-92	+23.85
Mrs.M.Reveley	4-23	17.4	1-1	3-22	+13.00
R.Beckett	5-30	16.7	3-12	2-18	-6.63

Jockeys	Wins-Rides	%	£1 level stks	Best Trainer	W-R
M.Henry	3-13	23.1	+25.00	J.Cullinan	1-1
F.P.Ferris	3-14	21.4	+42.00	P.D.Evans	2-6
L.Dettori	18-89	20.2	+7.39	D.Loder	6-14
J.Murtagh	4-21	19.0	-2.75	J.W.Payne	1-1
D.Holland	22-116	19.0	+3.20	B.Hills	4-12
K.Fallon	18-98	18.4	-16.26	Sir.M.Stoute	3-16
G.Carter	5-28	17.9	+15.37	P.S.McEntee	1-1
R.Hills	8-49	16.3	+12.96	M.Tregoning	2-8
M.Hills	14-86	16.3	+13.38	B.Hills	14-68
J.Fanning	12-78	15.4	+1.44	M.Johnston	9-33
S.Sanders	6-42	14.3	+25.62	B.McMahon	2-12
J.P.Spencer	13-91	14.3	-7.50	L.Cumani	4-15

Sponsored by Stan James

EPSOM

Epsom Downs,
Surrey, KT18 5LQ.
Tel 01372 726 311

How to get there – Road: M25 Jctn 8 (A217) or 9 (A24) 2m south of Epsom on B290

Rail: Epsom & raceday bus, Epsom Downs or Tattenham Corner

Features: LH, undulating, downhill 5f is fastest in the world

2004 Flat fixtures: Apr 21, June 4-5, July 1, 8, 15, 29, Aug 30, Sep 8-9, Oct 2

Pointers: Not a track with strong trends, so John Dunlop's eight winners from 30 runners is commendable, even if it didn't produce a profit. Andrew Balding, who supplied the Oaks winner Casual Look in his first season, should be a future force - four of his five scores were ridden by Martin Dwyer. The gradients take some navigating and it's no surprise to see two champion jockeys, Kieren Fallon and Frankie Dettori, heading the numbers.

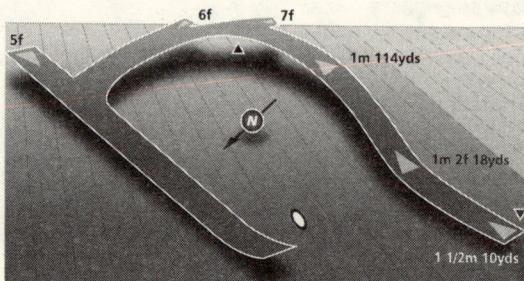

Time Test standard times

5f	53.8	1m114yds	1min41.6
6f	1min8	1m2f18yds	2min3.5
7f	1min20.2	1m4f10yds	2min33.6

Favourites

2-y-o	43.6%	-£5.86
3-y-o+	28.3%	+£10.78
Overall	30.8%	+£4.92

Trainers

Trainers	Wins-Runs	%	2yo	3yo+	£1 level stks
H. Morrison	5-11	45.5	0-1	5-10	+17.10
J. Fanshawe	3-8	37.5	0-1	3-7	+18.00
Mrs J. Ramsden	3-8	37.5	0-0	3-8	+5.00
S.C. Williams	6-18	33.3	0-1	6-17	+19.62
J. Dunlop	8-30	26.7	2-5	6-25	-4.66
G.A. Butler	5-21	23.8	0-1	5-20	+31.80
S. Bin Suroor	4-18	22.2	0-0	4-18	-2.28
Sir M. Stoute	5-23	21.7	0-1	5-22	-1.00
N. Callaghan	5-23	21.7	2-6	3-17	+0.75
A. Balding	5-24	20.8	1-4	4-20	+12.10
M. Jarvis	4-21	19.0	0-2	4-19	-2.97
A.P. O'Brien	3-16	18.8	0-0	3-16	-3.75

Jockeys

Jockeys	Wins-Rides	%	£1 level stks	Best Trainer	W-R
L. Dettori	14-55	25.5	-2.00	S. Bin Suroor	4-15
O. Urbina	3-12	25.0	+10.75	J. Fanshawe	2-3
K. Dalgleish	4-18	22.2	+4.00	M. Johnston	4-9
K. Fallon	14-66	21.2	-6.92	N. Callaghan	2-2
R. Miles	4-19	21.1	+15.50	T. Mills	2-6
T. Quinn	9-47	19.1	+17.93	J. Dunlop	2-2
E. Ahern	6-33	18.2	+0.55	G.A. Butler	3-11
M. Dwyer	11-62	17.7	+26.35	A. Balding	4-12
J. Egan	4-23	17.4	+1.75	J. Dunlop	2-4
R. Hills	4-23	17.4	-3.77	A. Stewart	1-2
D. Holland	9-55	16.4	-7.28	D. Nicholls	2-3
R. Mullen	4-25	16.0	-6.28	C. Wall	2-6

FOLKESTONE

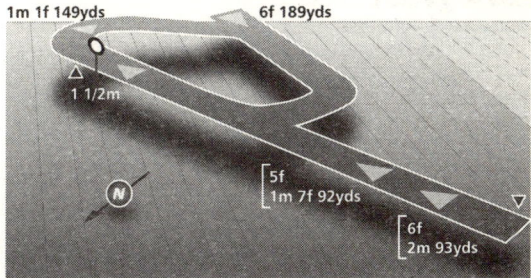

How to get there – Road: M20 Jctn 11, A20 south. Rail: Westenhanger from Charing Cross or Victoria
Features: RH, sharp turns
2004 Flat fixtures: Mar 30, Apr 7, 20, May 6, June 7, 25, July 8, 22, Aug 5, 13, 22, Sep 4
Pointers: You won't catch Sir Mark Prescott's horses napping at the Kent venue; they'll always give you a run. Amanda Perrett's father, Guy Harwood, had likeable percentages and his daughter follows in his path. Steve Drowne has the hang of the place and teams up successfully with Mick Channon.

Time Test standard times

5f	58.6	1m1f149yds	2min0.2
6f	1min11	1m4f	2min33.6
6f189yds (Rnd)	1min21.8	1m7f92yds	3min19.4
7f(str)	1min24	2m93yds	3min32.7

Favourites

2-y-o	39.2%	-£2.43
3-y-o+	36.0%	+£4.05
Overall	36.8%	+£1.62

Trainers	Wins-Runs	%	2yo	3yo+	£1 level stks
A.Berry	3-5	60.0	0-0	3-5	+15.50
H.Candy	3-6	50.0	1-2	2-4	+5.23
M.G.Quinlan	3-6	50.0	3-4	0-2	+47.00
Sir.M.Prescott	7-16	43.8	3-6	4-10	+25.07
R.Charlton	4-11	36.4	3-5	1-6	+0.54
J.W.Payne	5-14	35.7	0-2	5-12	+16.96
N.Callaghan	3-9	33.3	1-3	2-6	+7.50
D.Nicholls	3-9	33.3	0-1	3-8	+21.00
Mrs.A.Perrett	10-30	33.3	2-12	8-18	+6.18
A.Stewart	3-10	30.0	0-2	3-8	+13.60
B.Meehan	5-17	29.4	3-7	2-10	+3.73
J.Spearing	4-15	26.7	0-0	4-15	+2.58

Jockeys	Wins-Rides	%	£1 level stks	Best Trainer	W-R
J.Fortune	4-8	50.0	+11.88	P.Cole	2-2
R.Hughes	6-23	26.1	-5.38	Mrs A.Perrett	2-4
K.Fallon	5-20	25.0	-3.07	Lady Herries	1-1
S.Drowne	12-52	23.1	+5.68	M.Channon	5-14
J.P.Spencer	4-19	21.1	-1.65	S.Gollings	1-1
T.Quinn	9-43	20.9	-8.75	Mrs A.Perrett	3-4
S.Sanders	12-59	20.3	-2.68	Sir.M.Prescott	4-8
A.Mackay	3-15	20.0	-3.00	N.Littmoden	2-5
G.Carter	5-25	20.0	+12.51	S.C.Williams	2-3
P.Robinson	5-26	19.2	+8.50	G.Margarson	2-7
P.Dobbs	6-33	18.2	-9.40	S.Kirk	2-11
R.L.Moore	5-28	17.9	-1.50	I.A.Wood	2-2

GOODWOOD

Chichester, W Sussex,
PO18 0PS. Tel 01243 755 022

How to get there – Road: signposted from A27 south and A285 north
Rail: Chichester, bus to course on race-days
Features: RH, undulating
2004 Flat fixtures:
May 18-20, June 4, 11, 18, 27, July 27-31, Aug 27-29, Sep 11-12, 22, 30, Oct 10
Pointers: Marcus Tregoning is unreservedly nominated as a trainer to follow blindly on the picturesque Sussex downs. He's just below the 25 per cent benchmark but racing is so competitive here, he will hit the target with decently-priced animals. His followers had a big payday when Morahib and High Accolade both won at 8-1 on May 20 last year. At the Glorious meeting, add Mark Johnston's horses to the mix.

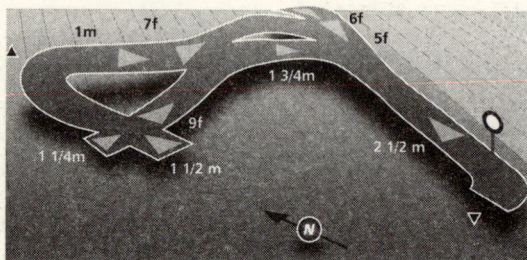

Time Test standard times

5f	56.4	1m3f	2min20
6f	1min10	1m4f	2min32.7
7f	1min24.4	1m6f	2min59
1m	1min36.8	2m	3min22
1m1f	1min52	2m4f	4min13
1m1f192yds	2min2.2	2m5f	4min27.3

Favourites

2-y-o	38.3%	+£5.06
3-y-o+	29.2%	-£8.15
Overall	31.4%	-£3.09

Trainers

Trainers	Wins-Runs	%	2yo	3yo+	£1 level stks
S.Bin Suroor	8-25	32.0	0-0	8-25	+3.43
D.Loder	5-17	29.4	3-9	2-8	+12.41
M.Ryan	3-11	27.3	0-1	3-10	+10.50
J.Given	5-19	26.3	1-3	4-16	+38.50
M.Tregoning	14-59	23.7	2-19	12-40	+33.17
J.Spearing	3-13	23.1	1-3	2-10	+11.50
B.Hanbury	4-18	22.2	1-3	3-15	+29.50
J.Fanshawe	6-28	21.4	0-1	6-27	-0.35
W.Jarvis	3-15	20.0	0-3	3-12	-0.25
Sir.M.Stoute	12-60	20.0	1-5	11-55	-11.52
J.Gosden	18-96	18.8	4-30	14-66	+12.01
L.Cumani	3-17	17.6	1-2	2-15	-4.00

Jockeys

Jockeys	Wins-Rides	%	£1 level stks	Best Trainer	W-R
S.Hitchcott	5-15	33.3	+22.38	M.Channon	5-11
L.Dettori	19-95	20.0	-4.08	S.Bin Suroor	6-19
M.Kinane	7-38	18.4	-4.94	A.P.O'Brien	2-10
J.P.Spencer	17-96	17.7	+50.17	L.Cumani	3-12
A.Daly	3-18	16.7	+16.00	J.Spearing	1-1
O.Urbina	3-18	16.7	-10.10	J.Fanshawe	2-13
D.Holland	21-132	15.9	+37.88	G.Wragg	4-26
S.Sanders	13-83	15.7	+33.51	E.Dunlop	2-5
K.Fallon	25-163	15.3	-54.32	Sir.M.Stoute	10-40
R.Hills	14-97	14.4	-29.48	M.Tregoning	5-22
J.Fanning	3-21	14.3	+0.50	M.Johnston	2-13
D.Corby	5-35	14.3	+8.50	M.Channon	4-20

HAMILTON

How to get there – Road: M74 Jctn 5, off the A74 Rail: Hamilton West

Features: RH, undulating, dip can become testing in wet weather

2004 Flat fixtures: Apr 26, May 2, 7, 14, June 3, 9, 16, 24, 29, July 10, 15-16, 31, Aug 11, 17, 23, Sep 19, 27

Pointers: The horses of George Moore and James Given must be on the shortlist at the Lanarkshire gaff. With 12 winners from 61 runners, David Barron is someone to keep the right side of, too. Chris Catlin and Ian Mongan are jockeys to note.

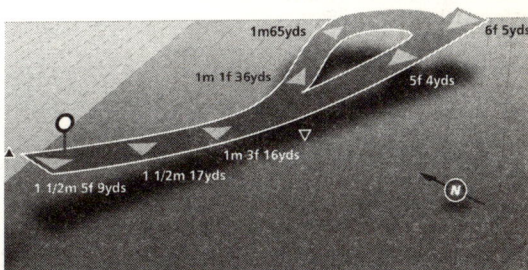

Time Test standard times

5f4yds	58.2	1m1f36yds	1min54.3
5f200yds	1min9.2	1m3f16yds	2min19.2
6f5yds	1min10	1m4f17yds	2min32.2
1m65yds	1min43.5	1m5f9yds	2min45.4

Favourites

2-y-o	38.9%	+£2.39
3-y-o+	30.7%	-£10.49
Overall	32.4%	-£8.10

Trainers	Wins-Runs	%	2yo	3yo+	£1 level stks
Sir M Stoute	4-8	50.0	0-1	4-7	+3.25
P Cole	5-13	38.5	2-3	3-10	+0.16
Sir M Prescott	6-17	35.3	1-4	5-13	-3.42
D Eddy	3-12	25.0	0-0	3-12	+61.00
G M Moore	5-21	23.8	0-5	5-16	+18.98
J Given	4-18	22.2	0-5	4-13	+22.41
G A Butler	4-18	22.2	1-3	3-15	+3.25
T Etherington	3-14	21.4	0-0	3-14	+23.50
M Channon	9-42	21.4	4-16	5-26	-2.71
M Bell	4-20	20.0	2-6	2-14	-2.15
K Ryan	7-35	20.0	3-9	4-26	+7.39
T D Barron	12-61	19.7	4-14	8-47	+15.00

Jockeys	Wins-Rides	%	£1 level stks	Best Trainer	W-R
C Catlin	5-12	41.7	+20.69	M Channon	3-5
K Fallon	5-12	41.7	+7.25	R Guest	1-1
T E Durcan	12-50	24.0	+31.50	M Tompkins	6-25
Darren Williams	11-49	22.4	+0.66	K R Burke	5-24
S Sanders	3-14	21.4	-8.63	P Makin	2-2
R Ffrench	7-33	21.2	+45.01	J Noseda	2-3
F P Ferris	4-22	18.2	+27.80	P D Evans	2-12
I Mongan	4-22	18.2	+2.50	N Littmoden	2-10
G Duffield	11-65	16.9	-13.68	Sir M Prescott	5-13
C Lowther	3-18	16.7	+20.50	Miss A Stokell	1-1
K Dalgleish	19-115	16.5	-9.56	M Johnston	8-32
K Darley	18-115	15.7	-39.50	G A Butler	3-3

HAYDOCK

Newton-Le-Willows, Merseyside, WA12 0HQ. Tel 01942 725 963

How to get there – Road: M6 Jctn 23, A49 to Wigan Rail: Wigan & 320 bus or Newton-le-Willows

Features: LH flat track, easy turns, suits the galloping type

2004 Flat fixtures: Apr 10, 24, May 1 (Mixed), 21-22, June 3-5, July 1-3, 11, 17, Aug 5-7, 12, Sep 3-4, 24-25

Pointers: The Newmarket big boys do well here, as does William Haggas, one of HQ's smaller trainers. Manton maestro John Gosden banged in 25-1 Place Rouge to win the Lancashire Oaks. Henry Cecil's star is firmly in decline.

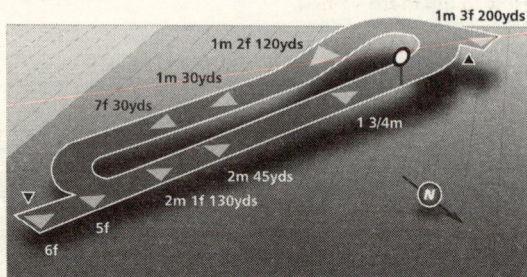

Time Test standard times

5f	59	1m3f200yds	2min28
6f	1min11.3	1m6f	2min54
7f30yds	1min27.4	2m45yds	3min28
1m30yds	1min40.2	2m1f130yds	3min47
1m2f120yds	2min10	2m3f	4min7

Favourites

2-y-o	31.0%	-£22.40
3-y-o+	31.3%	-£23.29
Overall	31.2%	-£45.69

Trainers

Trainers	Wins-Runs	%	2yo	3yo+	£1 level stks
D.Loder	3-5	60.0	0-1	3-4	+6.69
Miss J.A.Camacho	3-8	37.5	1-1	2-7	+25.00
H.Cecil	9-24	37.5	0-1	9-23	+2.07
Sir.M.Stoute	12-36	33.3	2-5	10-31	+10.56
M.Tompkins	5-16	31.3	2-4	3-12	+23.50
J.A.Osborne	5-16	31.3	4-11	1-5	+22.75
B.Hanbury	4-14	28.6	1-3	3-11	+5.55
W.Haggas	8-28	28.6	2-4	6-24	+23.77
L.Cumani	8-29	27.6	0-5	8-24	+13.78
Sir.M.Prescott	6-22	27.3	1-9	5-13	-1.50
M.Jarvis	11-46	23.9	2-7	9-39	+1.07
M.Johnston	21-98	21.4	2-25	19-73	+8.74

Jockeys

Jockeys	Wins-Rides	%	£1 level stks	Best Trainer	W-R
L.Dettori	4-9	44.4	+1.30	S.Bin Suroor	1-1.
K.Fallon	15-60	25.0	-4.28	Sir.M.Stoute	6-10.
D.Holland	9-38	23.7	-9.02	R.Charlton	2-2.
B.Doyle	4-17	23.5	+1.12	H.Morrison	1-1.
M.Henry	3-13	23.1	+8.75	J.Unett	2-2.
J.P.Spencer	11-48	22.9	+11.93	L.Cumani	3-10.
N.Mackay	4-18	22.2	+13.00	L.Cumani	2-6.
Darren Williams	6-31	19.4	+23.00	K.R.Burke	3-12.
R.Havlin	3-16	18.8	+29.63	J.Gosden	2-8.
R.Hills	6-32	18.8	-1.17	Sir.M.Stoute	2-2.
A.Culhane	14-81	17.3	+40.00	M.Channon	5-11.
D.McGaffin	3-18	16.7	+10.50	I.Semple	2-6.

Sponsored by Stan James

Staines Rd East, Sunbury-On-Thames,
Middlesex, TW16 5AQ. Tel 01932 782 292

KEMPTON

How to get there – Road:
M3 Jctn 1, A308 towards
Kingston-on-Thames
Rail: Kempton Park from
Waterloo
Features: RH, flat, sharp
turn into straight
2004 Flat fixtures:
Mar 27, Apr 10, 12, May 3,
10, 22, 29, June 2, 23, 30,
July 7, 14, 28, Aug 4, 18,
Sep 3-4, 20, 25
Pointers: When Martin
Pipe gets stuck into some
Flat action, it's time to be
involved. His Fortune
Island won the Queen's
Prize last year. Bank
Holiday Monday was
brilliant for David Elsworth
fans. They were on Bi
Polar at 12-1 and Foodbroker Fancy at 16s. Richard Hills
for Marcus Tregoning is a standout arrangement.

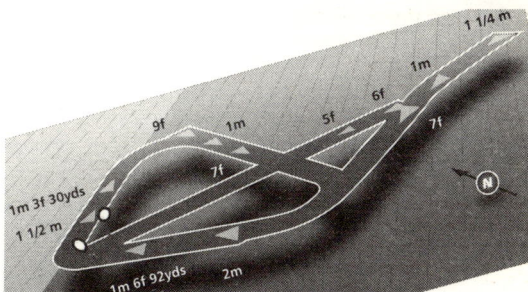

Time Test standard times

5f	58.2	1m1f	1min50
6f	1min10.3	1m2f	2min2
7f(round)	1min24.6	1m3f30yds	2min17.4
7f(Jubilee)	1min24	1m4f	2min30.3
1m(round)	1min37.4	1m6f92yds	3min2
1m(Jubilee)	1min36.6	2m	3min25.5

Favourites

2-y-o	35.6%	-£7.20
3-y-o+	30.2%	-£12.08
Overall	31.4%	-£19.27

Trainers	Wins-Runs	%	2yo	3yo+	£1 level stks
M.Pipe	4-12	33.3	0-0	4-12	+8.50
M.Tregoning	10-31	32.3	3-11	7-20	+5.76
A.Stewart	7-23	30.4	0-4	7-19	+15.17
H.Collingridge	5-17	29.4	0-1	5-16	+37.25
J.Fanshawe	11-43	25.6	2-5	9-38	+11.54
M.Jarvis	9-39	23.1	1-7	8-32	+18.36
Sir.M.Stoute	10-48	20.8	4-18	6-30	-9.52
T.Mills	10-49	20.4	1-5	9-44	+73.60
W.Haggas	3-17	17.6	2-3	1-14	-9.25
P.Makin	3-18	16.7	1-1	2-17	+29.00
D.Elsworth	11-66	16.7	0-4	11-62	+28.50
Miss.B.Sanders	3-19	15.8	0-1	3-18	+11.00

Jockeys	Wins-Rides	%	£1 level stks	Best Trainer	W-R
R.Hills	23-83	27.7	+41.00	M.Tregoning	8-12
R.Miles	6-24	25.0	+54.10	T.Mills	5-15
K.Fallon	28-150	18.7	-23.54	Sir.M.Stoute	5-24
P.Robinson	13-72	18.1	+30.03	M.Jarvis	8-31
D.Kinsella	8-46	17.4	+30.00	J.W.Payne	1-1
R.Hughes	18-109	16.5	-5.47	Mrs.A.Perrett	3-5
L.Dettori	6-40	15.0	-25.97	D.Loder	2-3
O.Urbina	5-35	14.3	-2.25	J.Fanshawe	4-17
R.L.Moore	8-57	14.0	+10.50	R.Hannon	3-17
J.Egan	4-31	12.9	+5.25	M.Dods	1-1
P.Dobbs	5-39	12.8	+3.30	R.Hannon	3-19
T.Quinn	13-109	11.9	-34.35	T.Mills	2-6

LEICESTER

London Road, Oadby, Leicester, LE2 4QH. Tel 0116 271 6515

How to get there – Road: M1 Jctn 21, A6, 2m south of city
Rail: Leicester, bus
Features: RH, straight mile is downhill for first 4f, then uphill to finish
2004 Flat fixtures: Apr 1, 24, May 18, 24, 31-June 1, 12, 24, July 3, 15, 21, 28, Aug 8, 23, Sep 7, 20, Oct 11-12, 25
Pointers: Mark Johnston has the most impressive statistics, closely followed by Sir Michael Stoute on the same amount of winners, but with a lesser strike-rate. Ryan Moore and Lisa Jones are two newish riders to keep an eye on. The former's partnership with Richard Hannon bears fruit.

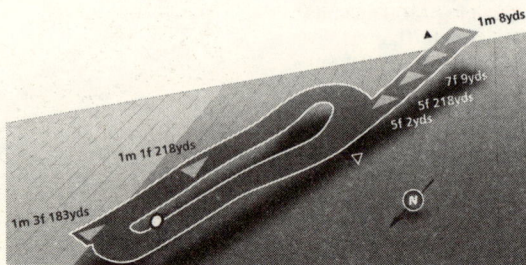

Time Test standard times

5f2yds	58.3	1m (rnd)	1min39.7
5f218yds	1min10.2	1m1f218yds	2min2.7
7f9yds	1min22.3	1m3f183yds	2min28.6
1m8yds	1min38.7		

Favourites

2-y-o	41.2%	+£2.63
3-y-o+	27.4%	-£36.59
Overall	31.0%	-£33.96

Trainers

Trainers	Wins-Runs	%	2yo	3yo+	£1 level stks
D.Loder	6-11	54.5	4-8	2-3	+1.06
M.Tregoning	5-10	50.0	3-3	2-7	+33.91
J.Eustace	4-10	40.0	0-3	4-7	+40.00
M.Johnston	13-47	27.7	4-15	9-32	+16.56
J.Fanshawe	10-39	25.6	1-9	9-30	+27.18
Sir.M.Stoute	13-54	24.1	8-36	5-18	+12.75
H.Cecil	5-21	23.8	1-5	4-16	-0.39
P.D'Arcy	4-17	23.5	0-1	4-16	+11.00
N.Tinkler	3-15	20.0	1-5	2-10	+48.25
N.Callaghan	4-20	20.0	2-10	2-10	-3.87
H.Candy	4-20	20.0	1-4	3-16	+10.40
J.Gosden	6-30	20.0	3-18	3-12	-15.76

Jockeys

Jockeys	Wins-Rides	%	£1 level stks	Best Trainer	W-R
L.Dettori	8-28	28.6	+3.22	D.Loder	3-5
K.Fallon	20-76	26.3	+26.69	Sir.M.Stoute	6-23
R.Hughes	10-47	21.3	+14.16	Mrs.A.Perrett	2-3
R.Hills	10-48	20.8	+3.14	J.Dunlop	3-16
J.P.Spencer	14-78	17.9	+4.43	D.Loder	3-4
R.L.Moore	4-23	17.4	-4.68	R.Hannon	3-4
T.Quinn	12-69	17.4	+13.11	H.Cecil	5-15
C.Rutter	5-29	17.2	-2.22	H.Candy	3-5
R.Smith	3-18	16.7	+1.13	R.Hannon	3-13
Lisa Jones	4-24	16.7	+10.00	T.Powell	1-1
O.Urbina	8-48	16.7	-3.83	J.Fanshawe	8-24
J.Fanning	5-32	15.6	-12.67	M.Johnston	5-12

Racecourse Road, Lingfield,
Surrey, RH7 6PQ.
Tel 01342 834 800

LINGFIELD turf

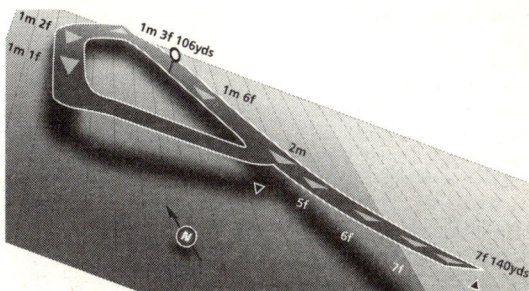

How to get there – Road:
M25 Jctn 6, south on A22,
then B2029.
Rail: Lingfield from London Bridge or Victoria

Features: LH, undulating,
straight runs downhill

2004 Flat fixtures:
Mar 29, May 7-8, 25-26,
29, June 12, 19, 26, 30,
July 7, 14, 17, 21, 24, 31,
Aug 6-7, 21, 26, Sep 1, 7,
18, Oct 1

Pointers: Roger
Charlton's seven from 23
steals the show and has
produced a decent profit.
It's not the most exciting
of systems, though, with
around four to five qualifiers per year. Avoid Barry Hills' three-year-olds and
upwards; one from 19 is disappointing from such a
big-name trainer. Richard Hughes and Richard Quinn
can exploit John Dunlop's ammunition now that Pat
Eddery has retired.

Time Test standard times

5f	56.3	1m2f	2min5.4
6f	1min9	1m3f106yds	2min24.4
7f	1min20.7	1m6f	2min58.6
7f140yds	1min28.2	2m	3min24.6
1m1f	1min52.5		

Favourites

2-y-o	33.3%	-£15.95
3-y-o+	28.4%	-£15.34
Overall	30.0%	-£31.29

Trainers	Wins-Runs	%	2yo	3yo+	£1 level stks
S.Bin Suroor	3-7	42.9	0-0	3-7	+2.40
Sheena West	4-10	40.0	0-0	4-10	+57.50
H.Collingridge	3-9	33.3	1-2	2-7	+10.80
M.Tregoning	4-12	33.3	2-3	2-9	+4.88
R.Charlton	7-23	30.4	2-9	5-14	+43.88
C.Wall	4-14	28.6	0-2	4-12	+25.00
B.Hanbury	3-12	25.0	0-2	3-10	+15.00
R.Guest	6-24	25.0	0-3	6-21	+6.00
Sir.M.Stoute	4-17	23.5	1-4	3-13	-7.33
N.Callaghan	3-14	21.4	1-10	2-4	+1.25
T.Mills	3-14	21.4	0-3	3-11	+9.25
J.Dunlop	10-49	20.4	2-21	8-28	-7.26

Jockeys	Wins-Rides	%	£1 level stks	Best Trainer	W-R
T.Quinn	9-39	23.1	+24.50	J.Given	1-1
R.Hughes	10-49	20.4	+6.68	J.Dunlop	2-3
P.Fitzsimons	3-17	17.6	+3.00	J.M.Bradley	3-9
K.Fallon	7-44	15.9	-21.11	Sir.M.Stoute	2-9
W.Supple	4-27	14.8	-10.50	I.A.Wood	1-1
W.Ryan	4-29	13.8	-2.12	Mrs A.Perrett	2-5
D.Holland	9-67	13.4	-26.14	T.Mills	2-2
O.Urbina	4-31	12.9	-8.50	J.Fanshawe	3-10
M.Hills	3-24	12.5	+12.63	R.Charlton	1-1
J.P.Spencer	4-32	12.5	-15.99	S.Bin Suroor	2-4
R.Mullen	5-41	12.2	-17.75	W.Muir	3-17
J.Mackay	4-34	11.8	-15.87	M.Bell	4-7

LINGFIELD sand

Features: LH, polytrack, tight

2004 Flat fixtures:
Mar 26, 31, Apr 2-3, 6, 15, 19, 21, 27, 29, May 13, Oct 6, 13, 25, 28, 31, Nov 10, 13, 16, 20, 22, 27, 30, Dec 4, 8, 15, 18, 20-22, 29-30

Pointers: With 243 runners, Gerard Butler is by far the biggest patron of the track, yet still achieved a strike-rate of 23.5 per cent. Keep him on the right side. Jeremy Noseda must also enter calculations, especially with Darryll Holland in the plate.

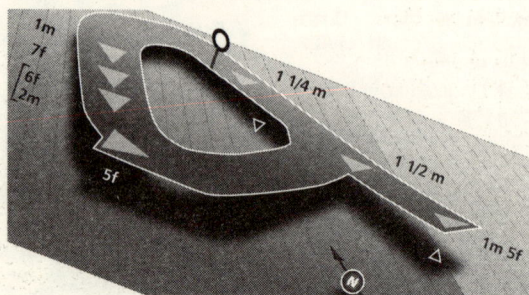

Time Test standard times

5f	58	1m2f	2min3
6f	1min11	1m4f	2min29.6
7f	1min23.2	1m5f	2min43
1m	1min36.6	2m	3min21.5

Favourites

2-y-o	37.0%	-£11.00
3-y-o+	28.9%	-£90.83
Overall	30.0%	-£101.83

Trainers

Trainers	Wins-Runs	%	2yo	3yo+	£1 level stks
D.Loder	7-21	33.3	2-5	5-16	+11.06
M.Wallace	4-14	28.6	1-7	3-7	+0.83
J.Noseda	24-91	26.4	4-19	20-72	-5.56
A.Turnell	4-17	23.5	0-2	4-15	+19.00
G.A.Butler	57-243	23.5	13-59	44-184	+44.68
M.Jarvis	12-54	22.2	5-18	7-36	+32.66
P.Haslam	7-33	21.2	2-4	5-29	+20.00
G.Enright	5-24	20.8	0-1	5-23	+14.25
C.Wall	15-72	20.8	1-8	14-64	+0.15
Miss E.Lavelle	3-15	20.0	1-3	2-12	+17.00
D.Cantillon	4-20	20.0	0-0	4-20	-5.62
B.Hanbury	5-25	20.0	0-1	5-24	+28.50

Jockeys

Jockeys	Wins-Rides	%	£1 level stks	Best Trainer	W-R
L.Dettori	13-39	33.3	+13.60	D.Loder	4-7
E.Dehdashti	3-10	30.0	+26.20	G.L.Moore	3-9
T.Best	3-10	30.0	+3.25	S.Dow	1-1
J.E.Moore	3-13	23.1	+14.50	G.L.Moore	3-9
J.P.Spencer	27-118	22.9	+20.32	G.A.Butler	9-20
D.Holland	31-144	21.5	+16.85	J.Noseda	6-14
M.Worrell	6-30	20.0	+4.00	Sir.M.Prescott	3-9
F.Lynch	8-41	19.5	+8.13	K.R.Burke	4-12
G.Duffield	7-36	19.4	-10.99	Sir.M.Prescott	3-8
J-P.Guillambert	20-109	18.3	+1.66	N.Littmoden	6-38
E.Ahern	48-270	17.8	+40.33	G.A.Butler	31-117
P.Robinson	8-47	17.0	+6.07	M.Jarvis	6-23

Linkfield Road,
Musselburgh,
E Lothian EH21 7RG.
Tel 0131 665 2859

MUSSELBURGH

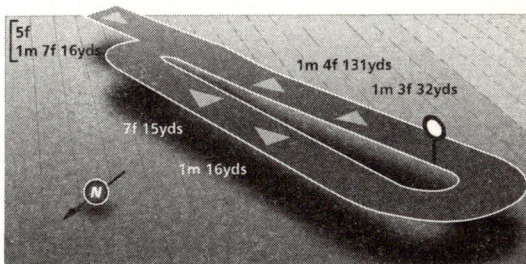

How to get there – Road:
M8 Jctn 2, A8 east, follow
Ring Road, A1 east.
Rail: Musselburgh from
Edinburgh Waverley
Features: RH, flat, tight
2004 Flat fixtures: Apr 8,
11, 30, May 17, 29,
June 21, 28, July 5, 28-29,
Aug 26, Sep 11, 13, 26,
Oct 17, Nov 3
Pointers: Not a track to
operate trainer systems.
Mick Channon's figures
are respectable and he
has eked out a small
profit. He's the biggest
source of winners for
Steve Drowne, Tony
Culhane and Chris Catlin.

Time Test standard times

5f	57.6	1m4f	2min32.4
7f15yds	1min26.3	1m5f	2min45.3
1m	1min38.3	1m6f	2min58.4
1m1f	1min50.7	1m7f16yds	3min11.3
1m3f32yds	2min20	2m	3min25

Favourites

2-y-o	32.6%	-£16.38
3-y-o+	32.3%	+£4.61
Overall	32.4%	-£11.78

Trainers	Wins-Runs	%	2yo	3yo+	£1 level stks
M.Bell	5-12	41.7	1-2	4-10	+18.25
Sir.M.Prescott	3-8	37.5	0-1	3-7	+15.50
M.Jarvis	3-8	37.5	1-3	2-5	-0.47
G.A.Butler	9-25	36.0	4-9	5-16	+9.50
W.Haggas	6-17	35.3	2-10	4-7	-1.06
M.Tompkins	4-14	28.6	1-2	3-12	+33.00
J.Balding	3-11	27.3	1-2	2-9	+9.50
L.Cumani	3-11	27.3	1-3	2-8	-1.50
R.Bastiman	3-11	27.3	0-1	3-10	+5.50
J.J.Quinn	3-11	27.3	1-3	2-8	+7.00
J.R.Best	4-15	26.7	0-7	4-8	-2.25
I.A.Wood	3-12	25.0	2-3	1-9	-2.52

Jockeys	Wins-Rides	%	£1 level stks	Best Trainer	W-R
E.Ahern	6-14	42.9	+10.63	G.A.Butler	6-8
S.Drowne	5-12	41.7	+23.10	M.Channon	3-5
D.Holland	6-28	21.4	-3.71	W.Haggas	2-4
P.Robinson	3-15	20.0	-8.73	M.Jarvis	2-5
J.P.Spencer	6-30	20.0	+2.25	J.J.Quinn	2-2
R.FitzPatrick	5-28	17.9	+1.75	J.Goldie	3-12
N.Mackay	4-23	17.4	+6.75	J.Goldie	2-8
G.Duffield	12-74	16.2	+0.46	I.A.Wood	3-5
J.Mackay	4-25	16.0	-6.25	B.Meehan	1-1
F.Norton	10-65	15.4	+3.05	A.Berry	9-37
A.Culhane	11-76	14.5	-22.45	M.Channon	3-10
K.Darley	16-110	14.5	-55.83	M.Johnston	7-23

NEWBURY

Newbury, Berkshire, RG14 7NZ.
Tel: 01635 400 15 or 01635 550 354

How to get there – Road: M4 Jctn 13 and A34 south
Rail: Newbury racecourse
Features: LH, wide, flat
2004 Flat fixtures: Apr 16-17, May 14-15, June 9-10, 22, July 1, 16-17, Aug 1, 13-14, Sep 17-18, Oct 22-23

Pointers: John Gosden has the most winners but you'd have made a thumping loss following them all. Better returns may be had by concentrating on the times he puts up Jimmy Fortune. Mark Johnston's horses have done well on their forays south, especially with Kevin Darley on board, as have those of Tim Easterby .

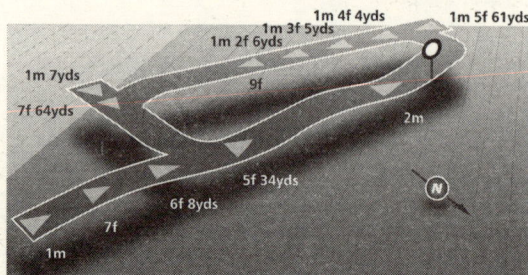

Time Test standard times

5f34yds	1min0	1m1f	1min49.7
6f8yds	1min11.2	1m2f6yds	2min2
7f	1min23	1m3f5yds	2min15.8
7f64yds(round)	1min26.4	1m4f4yds	2min29.3
1m(str)	1min36	1m5f61yds	2min45.8
1m7yds(round)	1min35.3	2m	3min23

Favourites

2-y-o	38.5%	-£2.82
3-y-o+	25.4%	-£50.09
Overall	28.8%	-£52.91

Trainers

Trainers	Wins-Runs	%	2yo	3yo+	£1 level stks
D.Loder	5-17	29.4	4-12	1-5	+9.94
S.Bin Suroor	3-12	25.0	0-1	3-11	-2.77
T.Easterby	3-13	23.1	1-7	2-6	+7.00
M.Tregoning	14-61	23.0	7-25	7-36	+1.25
M.Johnston	11-53	20.8	1-10	10-43	+8.44
N.Callaghan	3-15	20.0	0-1	3-14	+1.50
J.Fanshawe	5-25	20.0	0-2	5-23	-3.84
H.Cecil	8-42	19.0	1-3	7-39	+1.00
M.Jarvis	6-36	16.7	2-10	4-26	+10.13
Sir.M.Stoute	10-60	16.7	1-12	9-48	-3.25
B.Hanbury	4-25	16.0	1-2	3-23	+1.50
R.Charlton	12-75	16.0	5-24	7-51	-10.00

Jockeys

Jockeys	Wins-Rides	%	£1 level stks	Best Trainer	W-R
M.Kinane	4-14	28.6	-1.25	A.P.O'Brien	2-7
L.Dettori	16-78	20.5	-4.67	S.Bin Suroor	3-8
K.Dalgleish	5-26	19.2	-0.25	M.Johnston	3-16
R.Hills	21-120	17.5	-16.89	M.Tregoning	6-21
R.Hughes	24-155	15.5	-22.52	R.Hannon	7-48
J.P.Spencer	8-52	15.4	+7.58	M.Mullineaux	1-1
T.Quinn	17-118	14.4	-1.26	H.Cecil	7-35
J.Murtagh	4-29	13.8	+0.67	Sir.M.Stoute	3-9
D.Holland	13-94	13.8	+0.12	G.Wragg	4-22
M.Hills	15-114	13.2	-2.17	B.Hills	11-69
P.Robinson	8-64	12.5	-6.38	M.Jarvis	6-31
K.Darley	11-89	12.4	-26.89	M.Johnston	6-22

High Gosforth Park,
Newcastle-Upon-Tyne NE3 5HP.
Tel: 0191 236 2020 or 236 5508

How to get there – Road:
Signposted from A1
Rail: Newcastle Central,
metro to Regent Centre or
Four Lane End & bus

Features: LH, 1m6f round,
galloping, half-mile
straight is all uphill

2004 Flat fixtures:
Mar 29, Apr 3, 20, 26,
May 3, 12, 20, June 2, 24-
26, July 24, Aug 4, 13, 27,
30, Sep 6, 29, Oct 10, 20

Pointers: There are some
terrific strike-rates in the
trainers' table but they
must be treated with
caution, given how small
the data pool is. The
glaring exception is Mick
Channon, who sends an average of ten per year. The
booking of Darryll Holland is a big plus.

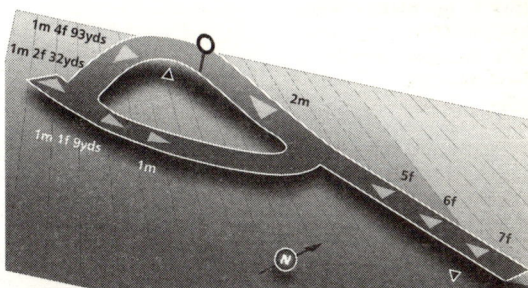

Time Test standard times

5f	59	1m1f9yds	1min52.5
6f	1min11.8	1m2f32yds	2min6.7
7f	1min24.2	1m4f93yds	2min37
1m(round)	1min39.7	1m6f97yds	3min2
1m3yds(str)	1min37.2	2m19yds	3min23.7

Favourites

2-y-o	37.6%	-£9.98
3-y-o+	26.6%	-£64.40
Overall	29.2%	-£74.38

Trainers

Trainers	Wins-Runs	%	2yo	3yo+	£1 level stks
H.Cecil	4-6	66.7	0-0	4-6	+2.25
R.Charlton	4-9	44.4	3-4	1-5	-0.99
W.Haggas	10-26	38.5	3-7	7-19	+13.48
M.Jarvis	3-8	37.5	0-1	3-7	+0.44
J.Dunlop	8-23	34.8	1-2	7-21	-7.48
M.Channon	16-49	32.7	5-16	11-33	+14.42
Sir M.Prescott	7-23	30.4	2-8	5-15	-7.45
P.Cole	4-14	28.6	1-3	3-11	+9.16
J.Noseda	3-12	25.0	0-3	3-9	-7.73
B.Hills	6-25	24.0	1-5	5-20	+2.91
Sir.M.Stoute	4-20	20.0	1-3	3-17	-5.14
M.Bell	5-25	20.0	2-10	3-15	+10.15

Jockeys

Jockeys	Wins-Rides	%	£1 level stks	Best Trainer	W-R
L.Dettori	3-6	50.0	+7.20	J.Noseda	1-1
W.Ryan	4-9	44.4	+5.42	H.Cecil	3-3
J.Mongan	3-8	37.5	+32.80	N.Littmoden	3-4
A.Beech	3-9	33.3	+40.00	D.Eddy	1-1
S.Drowne	8-27	29.6	-7.03	M.Channon	7-12
M.Hills	3-11	27.3	+8.08	B.Hills	3-7
S.Sanders	6-24	25.0	-2.57	R.Charlton	2-2
D.Holland	12-50	24.0	+23.91	Mrs.M.Reveley	2-2
P.Robinson	3-14	21.4	-5.56	M.Jarvis	3-4
S.W.Kelly	5-24	20.8	-4.14	M.Bell	1-1
T.Quinn	4-20	20.0	+11.27	P.Harris	2-6
K.Fallon	13-65	20.0	-22.89	T.Easterby	2-2

NEWMARKET

How to get there – Road: from south M11 Jctn 9, then A11, from east or west A45, from north A1 or A45

Rail: Newmarket

Features: RH, wide, galloping, uphill finish

2004 Flat fixtures: Apr 13-15, May 1-2, 21-22, 30, June 5, Sep 21, 30, Oct 1-2, 14-16, 29-30

Pointers: Racing is so competitive at HQ that no one trainer or rider can make the track his own. Sir Mark Prescott loves to line them up for the Cambridgeshire and the Cesarewitch, and landed the former with Chivalry last year. The French have been highly successful and, although neither Criquette Head-Maarek nor Olivier Peslier feature, they must be respected.

Rowley Mile Course

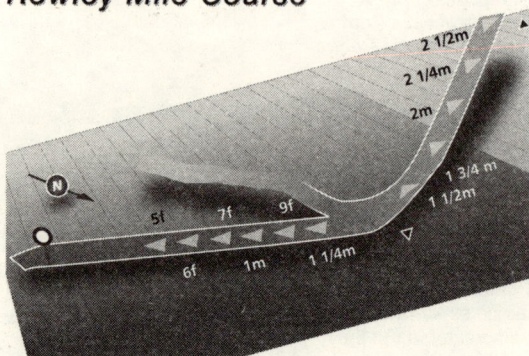

Time Test standard times

5f	57.5	1m2f	2min1.4
6f	1min10.5	1m4f	2min27.7
7f	1min22.7	1m6f	2min54.4
1m	1min35.7	2m	3min20.3
1m1f	1min48.6	2m2f	3min48

Trainer stats below apply for both Newmarket courses.

Trainers	Wins-Runs	%	2yo	3yo+	£1 level stks
Sir M Prescott	7-24	29.2	1-5	6-19	+15.58
D Loder	21-84	25.0	15-68	6-16	-37.81
J J Quinn	3-14	21.4	0-1	3-13	+6.25
J Gosden	32-151	21.2	13-66	19-85	+22.72
J Akehurst	5-24	20.8	0-1	5-23	+29.00
J Glover	3-15	20.0	0-1	3-14	+20.50
R Charlton	17-91	18.7	6-32	11-59	-0.72
Mrs A Perrett	20-120	16.7	5-38	15-82	+11.90
M Tregoning	13-80	16.3	1-21	12-59	-32.86
J A Osborne	5-33	15.2	3-14	2-19	+46.25
J Fanshawe	24-160	15.0	3-21	21-139	-35.96
M Johnston	21-141	14.9	4-34	17-107	+15.44
P Cole	15-109	13.8	6-30	9-79	+10.00
J Noseda	14-102	13.7	3-38	11-64	+24.17
J Dunlop	42-316	13.3	15-126	27-190	-54.09
S Bin Suroor	7-53	13.2	0-1	7-52	-10.33
J Jenkins	5-39	12.8	0-9	5-30	-1.00
P Harris	12-94	12.8	2-10	10-84	+10.91
N Callaghan	22-173	12.7	10-77	12-96	-2.65
C G Cox	3-24	12.5	1-6	2-18	+16.50

Westfield House, The Links,
Newmarket, Suffolk, CB8 0TG.
Tel 01638 663 482 or 01638 662 762

How to get there: see
facing page
Features: RH, wide,
galloping, uphill finish
2004 Flat fixtures:
June 18-19, 25-26, July
6-8, 16-17, 23, 25, 30-31,
Aug 6-7, 13-14, 27-28
Pointers: See facing
page.

July Course

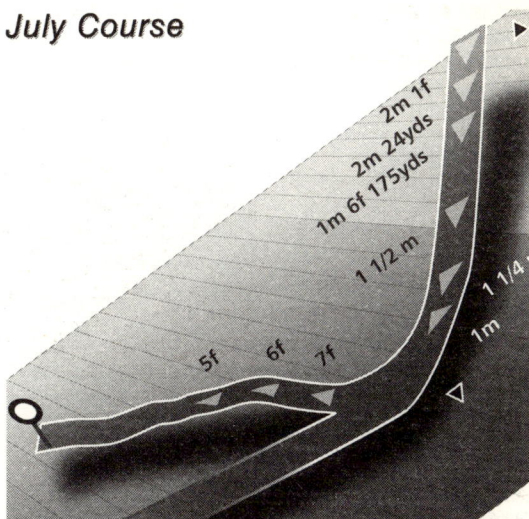

Time Test standard times

5f	57.7	1m2f	2min1
6f	1min10	1m4f	2min26.7
7f	1min22.8	1m6f175yds	3min3
1m	1min35.7	2m24yds	3min21.2
1m110yds	1min42	2m1f65yds	3min36

Favourites
(apply for both Newm't courses)

2-y-o	35.9%	-£17.31
3-y-o+	27.1%	-£71.64
Overall	29.7%	-£88.95

Jockey stats apply for both Newmarket courses.

Jockeys	Wins-Rides	%	£1 level stks	Best Trainer	W-R
L.Dettori	58-306	19.0	-78.06	D.Loder	18-56
R.Hills	45-250	18.0	-25.84	M.Tregoning	11-41
R.Hughes	49-288	17.0	+2.94	R.Hannon	17-82
K.Fallon	51-360	14.2	-81.47	Sir M.Stoute	15-115
D.McKeown	3-22	13.6	-3.50	T.D.Barron	1-1
T.Quinn	37-293	12.6	-4.35	H.Cecil	13-93
M.Kinane	11-89	12.4	+0.92	A.P.O'Brien	5-38
C.Rutter	3-25	12.0	-3.50	D.Haydn Jones	1-1
J.Fortune	21-192	10.9	-24.49	J.Gosden	8-44
J.Egan	8-75	10.7	-6.50	P.D'Arcy	3-18
M.Hills	27-253	10.7	-17.31	B.Hills	20-154
O.Urbina	12-114	10.5	-57.13	J.Fanshawe	12-61
K.Darley	23-225	10.2	-22.70	M.Johnston	10-58
J.P.Spencer	29-284	10.2	-73.99	J.Fanshawe	7-27
S.Hitchcott	3-30	10.0	+9.00	M.Channon	3-18
L.Keniry	3-30	10.0	+3.00	P.Felgate	1-1
S.Sanders	19-192	9.9	-39.67	Sir M.Prescott	4-13
S.W.Kelly	6-62	9.7	+9.00	J.Noseda	2-8

NOTTINGHAM

Colwick Park, Colwick Road, Nottingham, NG2 4BE.
Tel 0115 958 0620

How to get there – Road: M1 Jctn 25, A52 east to B686, signs for Trent Bridge, then Colwick Park
Rail: Nottingham

Features: LH, flat, easy turns

2004 Flat fixtures: Mar 31, Apr 17, 30, May 7, 14-15, 25-26, June 2, 21, July 3, 10, 24, 30, Aug 16, 18, Sep 17, 28-29, Oct 20, 26, Nov 4

Pointers: Two Godolphin trainers top the charts and David Loder, who has now broken formal links with the UAE syndicate, could be worth following. Expect him to have many more runners here than in the past. Darryll Holland is the winningmost rider by some lengths. His partnership with Geoff Wragg pays dividends.

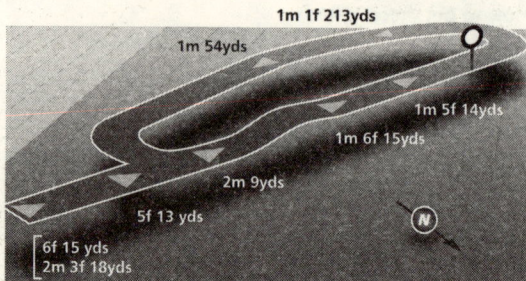

Racecourse map with distances: 1m 1f 213yds, 1m 54yds, 1m 5f 14yds, 1m 6f 15yds, 2m 9yds, 5f 13 yds, 6f 15 yds, 2m 3f 18yds

Time Test standard times

5f13yds	58.7	1m6f15yds	2min58.5
6f15yds	1min11.3	2m9yds	3min24.3
1m54yds	1min40.3	2m2f18yds	3min52.3
1m1f213yds	2min2.4		

Favourites

2-y-o	44.6%	+£1.56
3-y-o+	25.7%	-£70.78
Overall	30.5%	-£69.22

Trainers

Trainers	Wins-Runs	%	2yo	3yo+	£1 level stks
S. Bin Suroor	3-4	75.0	0-1	3-3	+1.22
D. Loder	4-9	44.4	4-8	0-1	+12.09
E.J.O'Neill	3-9	33.3	2-3	1-6	+5.25
M. Tregoning	4-12	33.3	1-3	3-9	+29.50
H. Candy	7-22	31.8	3-4	4-18	+29.98
J. Gosden	12-38	31.6	5-15	7-23	+0.86
R. Charlton	9-32	28.1	4-17	5-15	+11.53
Sir M. Prescott	8-31	25.8	1-11	7-20	-1.67
Mrs L. Stubbs	3-12	25.0	2-4	1-8	+14.00
J. Fanshawe	6-24	25.0	0-6	6-18	-0.22
Mrs A. Perrett	4-18	22.2	1-4	3-14	+10.61
G. Wragg	6-27	22.2	1-4	5-23	+2.88

Jockeys

Jockeys	Wins-Rides	%	£1 level stks	Best Trainer	W-R
B. Marcus	3-10	30.0	+6.00	B. Millman	3-6
L. Dettori	6-20	30.0	-9.52	J. Gosden	2-2
K. Darley	10-44	22.7	+41.89	J.M. Bradley	2-2
J.P. Spencer	13-60	21.7	+41.62	D. Loder	2-2
D. Holland	21-98	21.4	+26.36	G. Wragg	5-19
R. Hills	8-40	20.0	-12.11	D. Loder	1-1
M. Hills	6-31	19.4	+37.62	J. Hills	3-7
R. Hughes	12-62	19.4	-6.25	R. Charlton	4-7
J. Fortune	12-67	17.9	-31.34	J. Gosden	8-17
Stephanie Hollinshea	3-18	16.7	+34.50	R. Hollinshead	2-13
S. Sanders	15-97	15.5	-15.92	Sir M. Prescott	3-8
F. Lynch	4-27	14.8	+20.62	G.A. Swinbank	1-1

33 Ropergate, Pontefract,
WF8 1LE. Tel 01977 703 224

PONTEFRACT

How to get there – Road: M62 Jctn 32, then A539 Rail: Pontefract Monkhill or Pontefract Baghill from Leeds

Features: LH, undulating, sharp home turn, last half-mile is all uphill

2004 Flat fixtures: Apr 6, 19, 28, May 28, June 7, 20, 28, July 6, 16, 25, Aug 4, 15, Sep 16, 23, Oct 4, 18

Pointers: It's quite a surprise to see Sir Michael Stoute sending so many runners here (at least six a year) and his strike-rate and profit margin make for good reading. Kieren Fallon's strength saw many of them home up the Ponty hill. Mark Johnston saddles plenty of horses for small returns but he did have a treble last year in April, at 4-6, 14-1 and 100-30.

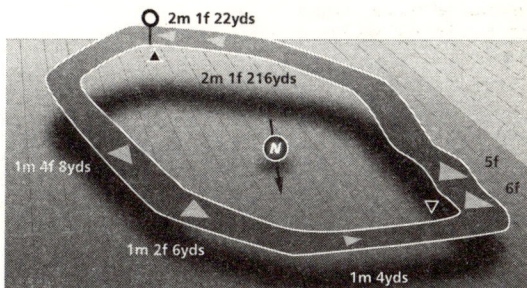

Time Test standard times

5f	1min1.3	1m4f8yds	2min34.5
6f	1min14.2	2m1f22yds	3min42.2
1m4yds	1min41.8	2m1f216yds	3min52
1m2f6yds	2min7.2	2m5f122yds	4min48

Favourites

2-y-o	44.9%	+£3.60
3-y-o+	27.5%	-£15.16
Overall	31.2%	-£11.56

Trainers	Wins-Runs	%	2yo	3yo+	£1 level stks
Sir M.Stoute	13-32	40.6	3-6	10-26	+23.92
Mrs A.Perrett	3-9	33.3	0-1	3-8	-1.00
L.Cumani	5-15	33.3	0-2	5-13	+11.04
M.Jarvis	7-22	31.8	1-4	6-18	+16.63
H.Cecil	5-16	31.3	0-1	5-15	-0.14
P.Cole	5-16	31.3	3-4	2-12	-2.98
W.Musson	4-14	28.6	0-2	4-12	+22.50
A.Stewart	9-32	28.1	2-5	7-27	+6.20
W.Haggas	7-25	28.0	4-12	3-13	+13.20
J.Dunlop	9-34	26.5	4-5	5-29	-1.94
Sir M.Prescott	5-20	25.0	2-9	3-11	-2.74
E.Dunlop	8-32	25.0	1-8	7-24	-7.51

Jockeys	Wins-Rides	%	£1 level stks	Best Trainer	W-R
L.Dettori	6-10	60.0	+8.74	D.Loder	2-3
K.Fallon	27-78	34.6	+28.14	Sir M.Stoute	6-11
T.Quinn	9-35	25.7	+30.42	H.Cecil	2-6
R.Hughes	3-13	23.1	-4.17	B.Hills	2-6
J.Fortune	5-23	21.7	+7.21	Sir M.Stoute	1-1
R.Hills	5-23	21.7	-8.68	Sir M.Stoute	2-3
D.O'Neill	3-15	20.0	+2.00	R.Hannon	2-5
J.P.Spencer	9-45	20.0	-1.64	Mrs J.Ramsden	3-4
M.Hills	4-22	18.2	-12.73	B.Hills	4-17
P.Robinson	7-39	17.9	+2.63	M.Jarvis	6-13
W.Ryan	3-18	16.7	-7.75	H.Cecil	3-9
Alex Greaves	4-24	16.7	+31.50	D.Nicholls	4-24

REDCAR

Redcar, Teesside,
TS10 2BY. Tel 01642 484 068

How to get there – Road:
A1, A168, A19, then A174
Rail: Redcar Central from
Darlington
Features: LH, flat, galloping
2004 Flat fixtures: Apr 12,
29, May 10, 18, 31-June 1,
8, 18-19, July 4, Aug 7-8,
28, Sep 2, 13, Oct 2, 15,
Nov 1

Pointers: Plenty of
impressive trainer
percentages, many of
them meaningless. It's a
favourite hunting ground
for Peter Harris, who
shouldn't be underestimated. Neil Callan knows his
way round and Ian
Mongan is learning fast.

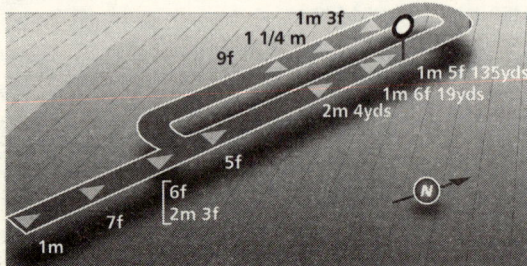

Time Test standard times

5f	56.7	1m3f	2min17
6f	1min9.4	1m4f	2min30
7f	1min22	1m5f135yds	2min54.7
1m	1min34.7	1m6f19yds	3min0
1m1f	1min49.3	2m4yds	3min25
1m2f	2min2.6	2m3f	4min5.3

Favourites

2-y-o	39.8%	-£17.35
3-y-o+	24.2%	-£55.11
Overall	28.1%	-£72.46

Trainers

Trainers	Wins-Runs	%	2yo	3yo+	£1 level stks
D.Loder	4-7	57.1	3-6	1-1	-1.39
M.Ryan	3-6	50.0	1-1	2-5	+8.07
J.Noseda	7-18	38.9	3-6	4-12	+15.53
N.Callaghan	3-8	37.5	1-4	2-4	+7.25
S.Gollings	3-8	37.5	0-0	3-8	+36.00
L.Cumani	5-14	35.7	1-3	4-11	+17.88
Sir M.Stoute	5-15	33.3	2-5	3-10	+18.23
R.Charlton	3-10	30.0	1-5	2-5	-0.49
J.Gosden	5-19	26.3	2-8	3-11	-4.50
B.Hills	4-20	20.0	1-8	3-12	-8.01
P.Harris	8-40	20.0	0-5	8-35	+30.17
M.Bell	3-16	18.8	2-6	1-10	-6.55

Jockeys

Jockeys	Wins-Rides	%	£1 level stks	Best Trainer	W-R
G.Faulkner	4-13	30.8	+30.00	T.D.Barron	4-8
D.Corby	3-10	30.0	+10.25	M.Channon	2-2
M.Henry	3-12	25.0	-0.05	M.Jarvis	2-2
N.Mackay	4-16	25.0	+6.75	L.Cumani	2-3
N.Callan	8-32	25.0	+15.51	K.Ryan	2-5
K.Darley	16-75	21.3	+0.55	G.A.Butler	2-4
S.Drowne	4-19	21.1	+7.12	R.Charlton	2-6
J.P.Spencer	6-29	20.7	+2.28	D.Loder	2-2
G.Bardwell	3-15	20.0	+57.00	M.Wigham	2-2
I.Mongan	5-25	20.0	+60.50	N.Littmoden	3-10
J.Egan	4-22	18.2	-3.13	P.L.Gilligan	1-1
T.E.Durcan	9-64	14.1	+10.62	Mrs M.Reveley	2-2

Sponsored by Stan James

How to get there – Road:
A1, then B6265
Rail: Harrogate, bus to
Ripon centre, 1m walk
Features: RH, sharp
2004 Flat fixtures: Apr 15,
24, May 16, 25-26,
June 16-17, July 5, 17,
Aug 2, 14, 21, 30, 31,
Sep 25

Pointers: Little fish are
sweet for Barry Hills.
John Dunlop also finds the
pickings to his taste. Willie
Supple is the top jock,
even if his strike-rate
isn't as good as Philip
Robinson's. The latter
enjoys the useful patron-
age of Michael Jarvis.

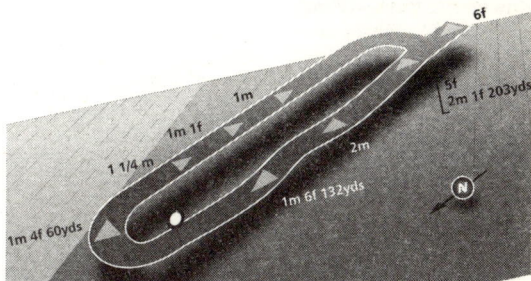

Time Test standard times

5f	57.8	1m2f	2min3.3
6f	1min10.6	1m4f60yds	2min34
1m	1min37.8	2m	3min27
1m1f	1min50.8	2m1f203yds	3min52

Favourites

2-y-o	40.9%	-£1.25
3-y-o+	33.6%	+£2.41
Overall	35.3%	+£1.17

Trainers	Wins-Runs	%	2yo	3yo+	£1 level stks
Sir M.Prescott	3-6	50.0	2-3	1-3	+5.25
H.Cecil	6-13	46.2	0-0	6-13	+4.42
M.Tregoning	5-14	35.7	1-2	4-12	+4.76
A.Stewart	3-9	33.3	0-0	3-9	+5.00
B.Hills	13-43	30.2	3-6	10-37	+11.34
J.Gosden	6-20	30.0	0-2	6-18	-0.06
P.Cole	5-17	29.4	0-2	5-15	+15.81
M.Jarvis	3-11	27.3	1-1	2-10	-4.45
P.Harris	4-16	25.0	1-4	3-12	+8.50
J.Dunlop	10-40	25.0	1-3	9-37	-9.19
Sir M.Stoute	6-25	24.0	1-1	5-24	-10.95
D.Eddy	3-14	21.4	0-1	3-13	+11.50

Jockeys	Wins-Rides	%	£1 level stks	Best Trainer	W-R
P.Robinson	6-16	37.5	+17.59	M.Jarvis	2-7
R.Hills	4-13	30.8	-2.80	J.Dunlop	2-5
T.Quinn	4-13	30.8	-1.08	H.Cecil	3-5
W.Ryan	4-14	28.6	+5.50	H.Cecil	3-6
R.Havlin	3-14	21.4	+0.94	J.Gosden	2-8
J.Fortune	4-19	21.1	-1.71	J.Gosden	3-5
J.P.Spencer	7-36	19.4	-14.38	L.Cumani	2-4
S.Sanders	5-26	19.2	-1.58	J.Fanshawe	2-2
D.Holland	6-32	18.8	-3.19	S.Gollings	1-1
W.Supple	14-75	18.7	-19.12	T.Easterby	4-23
Alex.Greaves	4-24	16.7	+0.50	D.Nicholls	4-23
T.Hamilton	3-21	14.3	+10.00	J.G.FitzGerald	1-1

SALISBURY

Netherhampton, Salisbury, Wilts, SP2 8PN. Tel 01722 326 461

How to get there – Road: 2m west of Salisbury on A3094
Rail: Salisbury, bus
Features: RH, uphill finish
2004 Flat fixtures: Apr 22, May 2, 13, June 8, 13, 23-24, July 10, 24, Aug 11-12, 20, Sep 2, 14, 29
Pointers: Richard Hannon is top of the numbers game but blanket support would have been loss-making in the extreme. Backing all of Roger Charlton's horses (bar his two-year-olds) has been profitable. For a fast-rising jockey, look no further than Paul Fitzsimons.

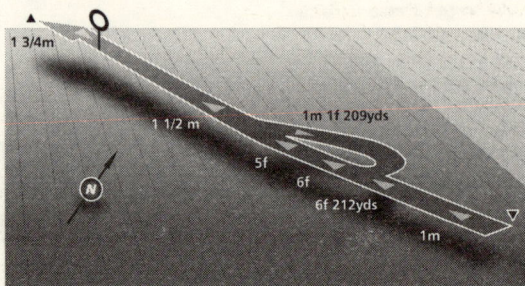

Time Test standard times

5f	59.6	1m1f209yds	2min5
6f	1min12	1m4f	2min32
6f212yds	1min25.2	1m6f15yds	2min58.3
1m	1min39.2		

Favourites

2-y-o	36.0%	-£2.36
3-y-o+	27.5%	-£41.93
Overall	29.9%	-£44.29

Trainers	Wins-Runs	%	2yo	3yo+	£1 level stks
W.Haggas	5-9	55.6	2-2	3-7	+20.88
P.L.Gilligan	3-7	42.9	0-0	3-7	+29.50
G.Wragg	5-12	41.7	0-1	5-11	+11.00
J.Gosden	19-60	31.7	9-26	10-34	+21.14
J.Fanshawe	4-15	26.7	1-3	3-12	+3.50
P.D.Evans	3-16	18.8	0-2	3-14	+21.50
R.Charlton	10-56	17.9	1-13	9-43	-1.77
M.Tregoning	6-34	17.6	1-12	5-22	-10.97
M.Bell	3-18	16.7	0-2	3-16	+7.00
H.Candy	5-34	14.7	1-8	4-26	+7.87
R.Hannon	34-236	14.4	16-103	18-133	-54.13
H.Howe	3-21	14.3	0-8	3-13	+17.33

Jockeys	Wins-Rides	%	£1 level stks	Best Trainer	W-R
L.Dettori	8-25	32.0	-3.58	J.Gosden	3-6
R.Hills	9-41	22.0	+3.78	M.Tregoning	4-11
K.Fallon	13-64	20.3	+3.74	Sir.M.Stoute	3-12
R.Hughes	24-121	19.8	+4.77	R.Hannon	9-31
M.Hills	7-42	16.7	-3.68	B.Hills	5-25
P.Fitzsimons	6-37	16.2	+8.00	J.M.Bradley	4-17
D.Holland	7-45	15.6	-5.50	G.Wragg	4-5
J.Fortune	14-91	15.4	-7.30	J.Gosden	9-20
J.Reid	3-20	15.0	-6.75	T.Mills	1-1
D.O'Neill	19-136	14.0	-5.34	R.Hannon	9-55
B.Doyle	5-36	13.9	+18.25	B.Meehan	2-10
J.P.Spencer	4-29	13.8	-1.50	P.Hobbs	1-1

SANDOWN

How to get there – Road: M25 Jctn 10 then A3
Rail: Esher from Waterloo
Features: RH, last 7f uphill
2004 Flat fixtures: Apr 23-24 (24 mixed), May 31-June 1, 3, 11-12, July 2-3, 21-22, Aug 11-12, 20-21, Sep 10, 15

Pointers: A real man's track, where you need a horse trained to the minute. Who better than Sir Michael Stoute, who leads the trainers by numbers? Alec Stewart is good for a handicap touch, while Geoff Wragg's older horses come here in tip-top shape. Kieren Fallon's strength has seen him win more than he should.

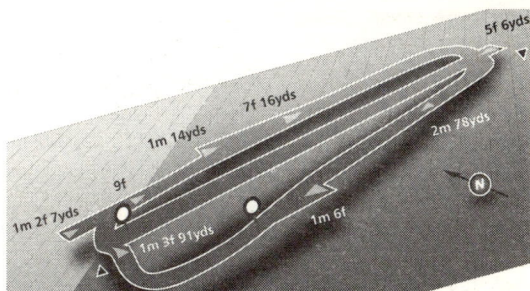

Time Test standard times

5f6yds	59.2	1m2f7yds	2min5
7f16yds	1min27	1m3f91yds	2min21.7
1m14yds	1min40	1m6f	2min57
1m1f	1min52	2m78yds	3min30.4

Favourites

2-y-o	39.1%	-£7.00
3-y-o+	30.0%	+£2.74
Overall	32.0%	-£4.26

Trainers	Wins-Runs	%	2yo	3yo+	£1 level stks
Sir M Prescott	4-8	50.0	1-2	3-6	+12.50
L Cumani	4-10	40.0	1-1	3-9	+20.00
N Callaghan	6-17	35.3	3-4	3-13	+21.00
H Candy	5-16	31.3	1-1	4-15	+9.83
S C Williams	4-13	30.8	0-0	4-13	+38.50
G Wragg	6-21	28.6	0-0	6-21	+5.08
D Loder	6-23	26.1	5-16	1-7	-2.72
H Cecil	4-16	25.0	0-3	4-13	-4.50
A Stewart	9-36	25.0	0-1	9-35	+19.29
D Nicholls	5-22	22.7	0-0	5-22	0.00
M Tregoning	8-39	20.5	2-11	6-28	-9.65
M Johnston	10-50	20.0	3-11	7-39	-0.51

Jockeys	Wins-Rides	%	£1 level stks	Best Trainer	W-R
K Dalgleish	3-12	25.0	-1.52	M Johnston	2-7
W Supple	8-33	24.2	+43.75	J Balding	1-1
R Miles	4-17	23.5	+46.00	T Mills	4-13
W Ryan	4-17	23.5	+9.50	I Balding	1-1
J Fanning	3-13	23.1	-0.09	M Johnston	2-10
L Dettori	18-78	23.1	+10.15	D Loder	4-14
R Hills	14-63	22.2	+7.83	J Gosden	4-6
D Holland	16-78	20.5	+17.75	G Wragg	5-16
R Thomas	3-16	18.8	+10.00	R J Price	2-3
K Fallon	24-128	18.8	-4.20	Sir M Stoute	8-33
B Doyle	4-24	16.7	+9.44	L Cottrell	1-1
T E Durcan	4-25	16.0	+11.00	M Tompkins	2-12

SOUTHWELL

Rolleston, Newark,
Notts, NG25 0TS.
Tel 01636 814 481

How to get there – Road: A1 to Newark, then A617 or M1 to Nottingham then A612
Rail: Rolleston
Features: LH fibresand, sharp
2004 Flat fixtures: Mar 30, Apr 2, 5 (turf), 15-16, 20 (turf), 27, 29, May 6, 15, 19, June 10, 16-17, July 26, Oct 7, 19, Nov 8-9, 17, 22-23, Dec 1, 7, 11-12, 14, 16, 21, 28

Pointers: David Barron sends many more runners here than anyone else, yet still makes a profit to level stakes. Hughie Morrison is rapidly making a name for himself and is clearly no time-waster.

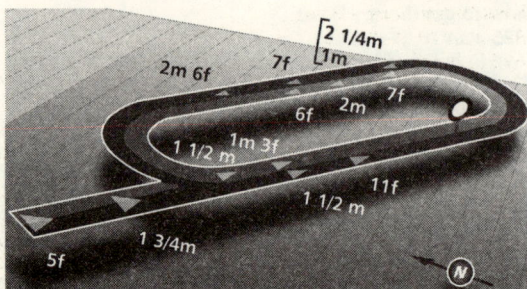

Time Test standard times

5f	57.7	1m4f	2min34
6f	1min13.5	1m5f	2min47.4
7f	1min27	1m6f	3min1.7
1m	1min40	2m	3min30
1m3f	2min21.6	2m2f	3min58

NB: Due to the shortage of meetings on the turf course, our trainer, jockey and favourite stats relate to AW racing only.

Favourites

2-y-o	37.2%	+£1.75
3-y-o+	29.5%	-£97.41
Overall	30.5%	-£95.66

Trainers	Wins-Runs	%	2yo	3yo+	£1 level stks
H. Morrison	15-39	38.5	2-4	13-35	+66.18
D. Cosgrove	4-11	36.4	0-2	4-9	+1.13
M. Bell	5-14	35.7	1-1	4-13	+4.75
M. Jarvis	6-17	35.3	1-1	5-16	+13.83
C. Wall	4-13	30.8	1-1	3-12	-5.57
Sir M. Prescott	21-79	26.6	5-26	16-53	-20.87
W. Haggas	11-45	24.4	2-16	9-29	+20.00
P. Cundell	7-31	22.6	0-4	7-27	+30.30
J.A. Gilbert	4-18	22.2	0-1	4-17	+37.33
B. Meehan	15-76	19.7	7-32	8-44	-5.97
P. Cole	11-56	19.6	4-14	7-42	+1.49
T D Barron	60-307	19.5	10-28	50-279	+61.87

Jockeys	Wins-Rides	%	£1 level stks	Best Trainer	W-R
L. Vickers	3-13	23.1	-0.25	D. Shaw	2-3
L. Treadwell	3-15	20.0	+19.00	D. Nicholls	2-6
D. Fox	14-81	17.3	+33.33	Miss A. Stokell	4-8
Paul Scallan	10-58	17.2	+18.43	B. Smart	7-33
D. Holland	15-88	17.0	-13.20	T.D. Barron	2-6
J-P. Guillambert	5-30	16.7	+13.05	N. Littmoden	3-10
P. Dobbs	6-37	16.2	-3.12	J. Balding	3-13
M. Worrell	5-31	16.1	+38.00	J. Balding	2-4
J. Egan	3-19	15.8	+10.00	Mrs H. Dalton	1-1
J. Weaver	12-76	15.8	-23.16	G. Bravery	2-7
G. Duffield	22-147	15.0	-42.87	Sir M. Prescott	9-31
J. Edmunds	10-67	14.9	+49.50	J. Balding	10-64

Station Road, Thirsk, N Yorkshire,
YO7 1QL. Tel 01845 522 276

THIRSK

How to get there – Road:
A61 from A1 in the west or
A19 in the east
Rail: Thirsk, 10 min walk
Features: LH, sharp, tight
turns, drains well
2004 Flat fixtures: Apr 16-
17, May 1, 8, 15, 24,
June 15, 24, July 23, 30-
31, Aug 9, 27, Sep 4, 14
Pointers: The first five in
the trainer's table grind
out a profit of sorts, Jamie
Osborne having a perfect
record with his two-year-
olds. Following Barry Hills
offers more excitement,
especially as he likes to
win the Classic Trial. Take note when Tim Easterby
books Kevin Darley.

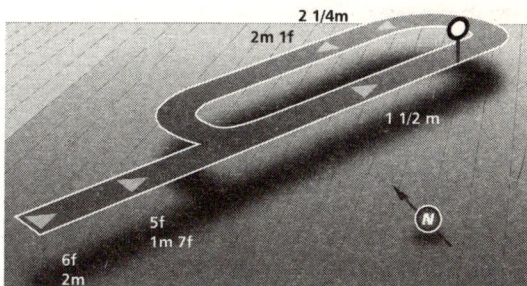

Time Test standard times

5f	57.4	1m	1min35.8
6f	1min9.5	1m4f	2min30
7f	1min23	2m	3min22.6

Favourites

2-y-o	41.2%	-£4.23
3-y-o+	34.4%	-£0.66
Overall	36.1%	-£4.89

Trainers	Wins-Runs	%	2yo	3yo+	£1 level stks
M.Tregoning	5-8	62.5	0-0	5-8	+0.81
J.Dunlop	8-13	61.5	0-1	8-12	+10.29
D.Loder	3-6	50.0	0-2	3-4	+1.98
H.Cecil	3-6	50.0	0-0	3-6	+2.91
J.A.Osborne	3-7	42.9	3-3	0-4	+8.50
E.Dunlop	3-9	33.3	0-1	3-8	-1.56
B.Hills	4-14	28.6	0-1	4-13	+3.08
W.Haggas	3-11	27.3	1-2	2-9	-2.15
W.G.M.Turner	4-16	25.0	4-15	0-1	-4.92
A.Turnell	3-14	21.4	0-1	3-13	+23.00
Sir.M.Stoute	4-20	20.0	0-1	4-19	-8.26
J.Glover	4-24	16.7	1-10	3-14	+6.75

Jockeys	Wins-Rides	%	£1 level stks	Best Trainer	W-R
D.Sweeney	3-4	75.0	+18.00	K.R.Burke	2-3
D.Holland	3-8	37.5	+6.63	G.Wragg	2-2
M.Henry	3-8	37.5	-0.70	J.Dunlop	2-2
B.Doyle	3-9	33.3	+3.63	B.Meehan	1-1
J.P.Spencer	5-18	27.8	+3.86	D.Loder	2-5
W.Ryan	3-12	25.0	+10.91	H.Cecil	2-3
R.Ffrench	7-32	21.9	+32.97	B.Smart	2-3
W.Supple	16-75	21.3	-23.92	M.Tregoning	5-7
K.Darley	13-70	18.6	-27.86	T.Easterby	3-9
T.E.Durcan	3-18	16.7	-6.81	M.Channon	1-3
T.Hamilton	6-36	16.7	+8.13	D.Nicholls	3-14
M.Tebbutt	3-20	15.0	+7.50	C.Dore	1-1

WARWICK

6 Hampton Street, Warwick
CV34 6HN. Tel 01926 491 553

How to get there – Road: M40 Jctn 14, A429
Rail: Warwick
Features: LH, sharp turns
2004 Flat fixtures: Apr 7, 12, 23, May 3, June 14, 19-20, July 2, 8, Aug 14, 30, Sep 6, 18, Oct 9
Pointers: Age has done nothing to wither John Dunlop's edge and it will always pay to side with him. Martin Pipe, who does well here over the sticks, is to be respected. Look out for anything ridden by young Ryan Moore.

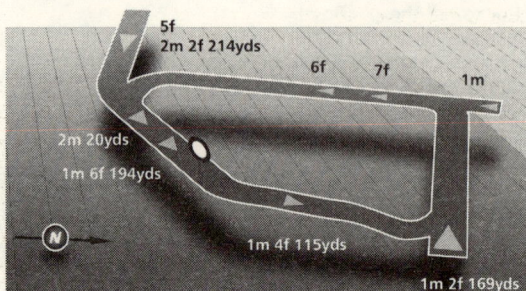

Time Test standard times

5f	58	1m4f115yds	2min34.6
5f110yds	1min4	1m6f194yds	3min6
6f	1min10.6	2m20yds	3min24
7f	1min22.2	2m2f214yds	3min58
1m	1min35.3	2m3f13yds	4min0
1m2f169yds	2min12		

Favourites

2-y-o	47.4%	+£6.25
3-y-o+	25.5%	-£54.99
Overall	30.4%	-£48.74

Trainers

Trainers	Wins-Runs	%	2yo	3yo+	£1 level stks
Sir M Stoute	9-19	47.4	1-5	8-14	+9.22
M Jarvis	4-12	33.3	1-2	3-10	+6.19
J Dunlop	7-21	33.3	3-8	4-13	-0.90
Mrs A J Bowlby	3-12	25.0	0-3	3-9	+13.00
A Reid	3-12	25.0	0-0	3-12	+14.00
M Johnston	4-17	23.5	1-6	3-11	-5.10
R Guest	3-13	23.1	1-6	2-7	+21.00
M Pipe	3-13	23.1	0-1	3-12	-2.90
H Morrison	3-15	20.0	0-4	3-11	+18.50
L Cumani	3-15	20.0	0-2	3-13	-2.50
R Johnson Houghton	3-15	20.0	1-3	2-12	-7.47
W Brisbourne	6-32	18.8	1-1	5-31	+3.50

Jockeys

Jockeys	Wins-Rides	%	£1 level stks	Best Trainer	W-R
J Reid	5-10	50.0	+8.15	R Johnson Houghton	3-3
R Miles	4-9	44.4	+27.50	A Newcombe	1-1
N Mackay	3-7	42.9	+6.00	L Cumani	2-3
K Fallon	3-11	27.3	+1.17	C Cyzer	1-1
K Darley	7-29	24.1	-4.54	M Johnston	2-2
R Hills	3-14	21.4	-3.46	Sir M Stoute	1-1
W Supple	7-34	20.6	-5.62	D Coakley	1-1
R Winston	4-21	19.0	+24.25	A Hales	1-1
J D Smith	3-16	18.8	+37.50	A Jarvis	1-1
M Hills	6-33	18.2	-12.01	B Hills	4-20
J Carroll	3-17	17.6	+4.38	A Berry	2-7
R L Moore	4-24	16.7	+6.00	I A Wood	2-3

Maidenhead Road, Windsor,
Berkshire SL4 5JJ.
Tel 01753 498 400

WINDSOR

How to get there – Road:
M4 Jctn 6, A355, A308
Rail: Windsor Central from
Paddington or Windsor
Riverside from Waterloo
Features: Figure of eight,
flat, easy turns, straight
almost 5f long
2004 Flat fixtures: Apr 5,
19, 26, May 10, 17, 24,
June 7, 14, 21, 26-28, July
5, 12, 19, 26, Aug 2, 8-9,
16, 23, 28, Sep 27, Oct 4,
11

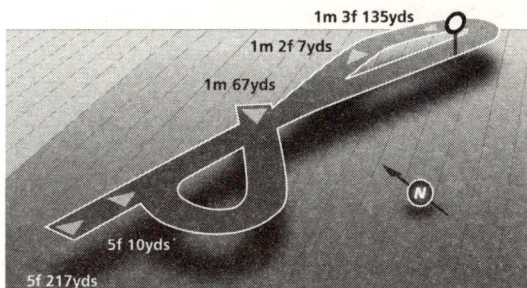

1m 3f 135yds
1m 2f 7yds
1m 67yds
5f 10yds
5f 217yds
N

Pointers: The further
south Mark Johnston's
horses travel, the better
they get. Joe Fanning can
be relied on to boot them home. Anything trained by a
'Sir' merits close perusal but it's new boy Dean Ivory's
record that catches the eye. A healthy strike-rate from a
meaningful number of runners.

Time Test standard times

5f10yds	59	1m2f7yds	2min3.6
5f217yds	1min10.2	1m3f135yds	2min22.6
1m67yds	1min41.6		

Favourites

2-y-o	36.4%	+£1.04
3-y-o+	26.7%	-£39.06
Overall	29.1%	-£38.03

Trainers

Trainers	Wins-Runs	%	2yo	3yo+	£1 level stks
S.Bin Suroor	3-6	50.0	0-0	3-6	+0.48
Sir M.Stoute	27-85	31.8	3-10	24-75	+3.17
Sir.M.Prescott	3-13	23.1	1-8	2-5	-3.45
M.Johnston	5-22	22.7	0-2	5-20	+21.25
J.Gosden	9-42	21.4	1-1	8-41	-6.70
T.Mills	8-41	19.5	0-4	8-37	+9.13
R.Charlton	8-42	19.0	2-14	6-28	-5.91
D.Ivory	6-32	18.8	2-10	4-22	+13.00
B.Hills	9-48	18.8	5-30	4-18	+8.00
M.Bosley	4-24	16.7	0-1	4-23	+57.00
Mrs.A.Perrett	11-68	16.2	1-7	10-61	-3.75
J.Noseda	5-31	16.1	2-9	3-22	-11.18

Jockeys

Jockeys	Wins-Rides	%	£1 level stks	Best Trainer	W-R
J.Fanning	5-14	35.7	+14.25	M.Johnston	3-6
K.Fallon	33-142	23.2	+2.43	Sir.M.Stoute	13-37
E.Creighton	3-14	21.4	+19.00	M.Channon	2-5
L.Dettori	3-16	18.8	-3.25	S.Bin Suroor	2-3
R.Miles	4-22	18.2	-1.25	T.Mills	4-13
R.Hughes	27-163	16.6	-41.34	R.Hannon	12-60
K.Darley	6-37	16.2	-11.06	I.Balding	2-3
Darren Williams	3-19	15.8	-3.00	H.Collingridge	1-1
T.Quinn	19-125	15.2	-33.00	P.Harris	3-13
R.Hills	4-29	13.8	+39.25	J.Hills	2-9
G.Gibbons	3-22	13.6	+13.00	J.R.Best	1-1
J.Fortune	15-112	13.4	-36.38	J.Gosden	5-15

WOLVES

Dunstall Park, Gorsebrook Road, Wolverhampton, West Midlands, WV6 0PE. Tel 08702 202 442

How to get there – Road: of A449, close to M6, M42 and M54
Rail: Wolverhampton, bus
Features: LH, fibresand, very sharp
2004 Flat fixtures:
Mar 27, 29, Apr 17, 19, 22-24, 26, May 5, 10, 11, 17, 28, June 4, 11, 25, 28, July 6, 9, 12, 23, Aug 9, 19-20, 23, Sep 4, 18, Oct 2, 18, 23, 25, 30, Nov 6, 8, 12-13, 15, 19-20, 26-27, 29, Dec 3-4, 6, 10-11, 13-14, 17, 20, 22, 27, 31

Pointers: Watch those two Newmarket operators, Michael Jarvis and Jeremy Noseda, carefully. They're always close to the mark. Gay Kelleway has a satellite yard here and Darryll Holland is a must-back booking for her.

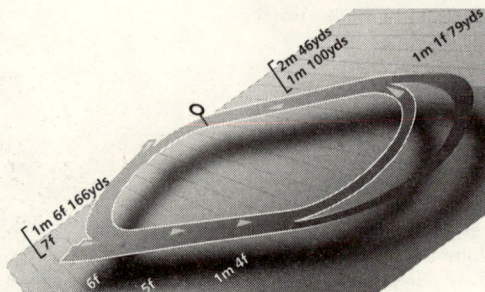

Time Test standard times

5f	1min0.3	1m1f79yds	1min57.6
6f	1min13.2	1m4f	2min35.3
7f	1min27	1m6f166yds	3min11.7
1m100yds	1min46.8	2m46yds	3min36.7

Favourites

2-y-o	32.0%	-£36.32
3-y-o+	29.3%	-£123.62
Overall	29.7%	-£159.94

Trainers

Trainers	Wins-Runs	%	2yo	3yo+	£1 level stks
D. Loder	10-17	58.8	5-6	5-11	+22.84
M. Pitman	3-6	50.0	0-0	3-6	+12.50
H. Cyzer	3-7	42.9	1-1	2-6	+9.00
R. Ingram	3-8	37.5	0-0	3-8	+8.13
J. Fanshawe	3-8	37.5	1-3	2-5	-1.01
J. Gosden	3-8	37.5	1-1	2-7	+9.71
J. Noseda	6-18	33.3	1-4	5-14	-6.30
M. Jarvis	13-43	30.2	2-7	11-36	+23.35
R. J. Smith	3-10	30.0	0-0	3-10	-0.90
M. Chapman	3-10	30.0	2-3	1-7	+6.25
R. Charlton	3-11	27.3	1-5	2-6	-3.27
Sir M Prescott	29-112	25.9	10-46	19-66	-15.83

Jockeys

Jockeys	Wins-Rides	%	£1 level stks	Best Trainer	W-R
Marie King	3-7	42.9	+13.50	P. Hiatt	3-7
P. Robinson	4-14	28.6	-3.88	M. Jarvis	3-8
J. P. Spencer	17-70	24.3	+10.28	D. Loder	6-8
S. Sanders	24-110	21.8	-0.27	Sir M. Prescott	13-28
Mark Flynn	4-19	21.1	+10.70	W. Brisbourne	4-12
D. Holland	26-125	20.8	+3.46	Miss G. Kelleway	3-5
R. Smith	6-32	18.8	+39.30	R Hannon	4-12
K. Darley	9-48	18.8	-3.10	N. Littmoden	3-12
J. Weaver	9-55	16.4	-6.42	Sir M. Prescott	2-3
J. Fortune	6-37	16.2	-13.74	C. Brittain	2-2
G. Duffield	19-119	16.0	-44.66	Sir M. Prescott	8-29
I. Mongan	63-393	16.0	+33.18	N. Littmoden	31-132

Jellicoe Road, North Denes,
Great Yarmouth, Norfolk,
NR30 4AU. Tel 01493 842 527

YARMOUTH

How to get there – Road:
A47 to end, A1064
Rail: Great Yarmouth, bus
Features: LH, flat, drains
well
2004 Flat fixtures: Apr 12,
May 14, June 2, 10, 30-
July 1, 22, 26, Aug 4-5, 11,
16, 24, 29, Sep 14-16,
Oct 16, 27, Nov 5,

Pointers: Paul Webber's
Flat runners are few and
far between but, for some
reason, he likes the
seaside gaff. David
Loder's two-year-olds are
always worth a look and, if
he has two in a race, the
value is with the longest-
priced.

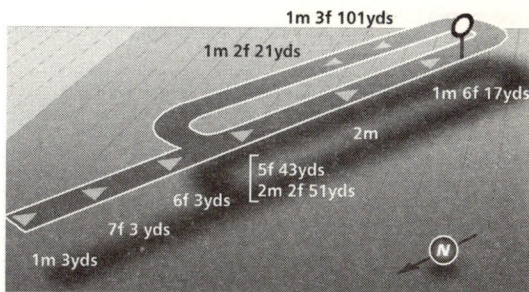

Time Test standard times

5f43yds	1min0.4	1m3f101yds	2min23
6f3yds	1min10.7	1m6f17yds	2min58
7f3yds	1min23	2m	3min25
1m3yds	1min35.5	2m1f170yds	3min48
1m2f21yds	2min3.3	2m2f51yds	3min54

Favourites

2-y-o	37.4%	-£18.16
3-y-o+	35.2%	-£4.82
Overall	35.8%	-£22.98

Trainers	Wins-Runs	%	2yo	3yo+	£1 level stks
P.R.Webber	5-8	62.5	0-0	5-8	+12.00
S.Bin Suroor	3-6	50.0	2-2	1-4	+14.79
D.Cantillon	5-13	38.5	0-0	5-13	+27.25
Sir M.Stoute	14-38	36.8	7-18	7-20	+11.87
D.Loder	5-14	35.7	4-12	1-2	+25.07
J.Gosden	8-26	30.8	2-11	6-15	+1.58
A.Stewart	7-23	30.4	0-2	7-21	+1.87
T.Mills	3-10	30.0	0-1	3-9	+12.00
Mrs.A.Perrett	5-19	26.3	0-4	5-15	-2.20
Sir.M.Prescott	6-24	25.0	3-12	3-12	+8.13
J.Noseda	5-22	22.7	3-9	2-13	-7.33
J.Fanshawe	10-44	22.7	2-11	8-33	+3.23

Jockeys	Wins-Rides	%	£1 level stks	Best Trainer	W-R
T.Quinn	18-61	29.5	+21.31	H.Cecil	4-13
J.Fortune	7-29	24.1	-6.88	J.Gosden	2-5
K.Fallon	21-87	24.1	-21.09	Sir.M.Stoute	7-20
B.Reilly	5-21	23.8	+48.00	H.Cyzer	1-1
L.Dettori	9-39	23.1	-0.45	D.Loder	3-9
J.P.Spencer	17-77	22.1	+37.34	L.Cumani	4-9
M.Dwyer	3-15	20.0	+13.20	R.Beckett	1-1
R.Hughes	10-52	19.2	-8.72	B.Hills	2-4
N.Mackay	6-34	17.6	+41.13	Miss.J.Feilden	2-3
D.McGaffin	3-18	16.7	+15.50	D.Morris	2-9
R.Hills	7-42	16.7	-11.46	J.Dunlop	2-4
O.Urbina	9-55	16.4	-10.49	J.Fanshawe	6-22

YORK

York, YO23 1EX.
Tel 01904 620 911

How to get there – Road: Course south of city on Knavesmire Road. From north, A1, A59 to York, northern bypass from A19 to A64. Otherwise, A64 Rail: York, bus

Features: LH, flat

2004 Flat fixtures: May 11-13, June 11-12, July 9-10, 24, Aug 17-19, Sep 1, 5, Oct 8-9

Pointers: Saeed Bin Suroor is an under-rated trainer. The quiet achiever has a brilliant strike-rate and, because of the competitive racing at York, a decent profit. Expect David Loder to make big waves now that he's not just training juveniles. Make both trainers the basis for a system. Pay close attention when David Nicholls puts his son Adrian in the driving seat.

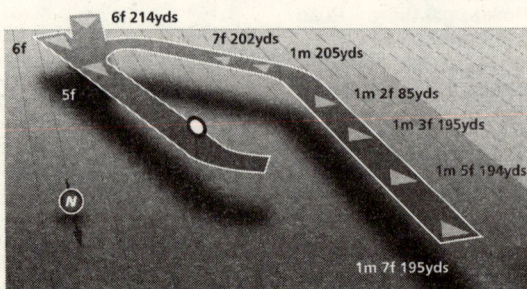

Time Test standard times

5f	56.6	1m2f85yds	2min7
6f	1min9.2	1m3f195yds	2min26.4
6f214yds	1min21.7	1m5f194yds	2min53
7f202yds	1min35.4	1m7f195yds	3min20
1m205yds	1min48		

Favourites

2-y-o	37.6%	-£1.91
3-y-o+	27.0%	-£12.49
Overall	29.8%	-£14.40

Trainers

Trainers	Wins-Runs	%	2yo	3yo+	£1 level stks
S. Bin Suroor	9-22	40.9	0-1	9-21	+17.66
Sir M Prescott	3-9	33.3	1-3	2-6	+2.75
D Loder	9-28	32.1	7-20	2-8	+6.58
A P O'Brien	6-23	26.1	2-7	4-16	+13.63
M Mullineaux	3-12	25.0	0-0	3-12	+6.50
R Charlton	6-26	23.1	4-6	2-20	-6.96
H Cecil	4-18	22.2	1-1	3-17	+41.20
Sir M Stoute	19-88	21.6	2-10	17-78	-14.15
J Noseda	6-33	18.2	5-12	1-21	+6.75
J Dunlop	6-38	15.8	2-6	4-32	-11.68
M Tregoning	3-20	15.0	2-4	1-16	-2.00
J Hills	3-21	14.3	0-4	3-17	-1.25

Jockeys

Jockeys	Wins-Rides	%	£1 level stks	Best Trainer	W-R
R L Moore	3-13	23.1	+14.75	S Dow	1-1
L Dettori	15-77	19.5	-6.78	S Bin Suroor	7-15
K Fallon	33-182	18.1	-14.82	Sir M Stoute	15-53
K Darley	27-166	16.3	+40.79	M Johnston	10-50
J P Spencer	12-75	16.0	+20.39	D Loder	4-8
E Ahern	4-26	15.4	+44.00	G A Butler	2-7
M Kinane	6-41	14.6	-1.81	A P O'Brien	5-16
S Sanders	5-37	13.5	+31.00	C G Cox	1-1
T Quinn	13-100	13.0	+22.03	H Cecil	4-16
G Duffield	9-78	11.5	-0.25	Sir M Prescott	3-8
R Hughes	9-80	11.3	-21.81	E Dunlop	2-4
S Hitchcott	3-27	11.1	-2.00	M Channon	2-3

Outlook

Sprintline
by Graham Wheldon

IT'S AMAZING to me how many otherwise-savvy punters and journalists still don't take the draw into account when sizing up a Flat race.

However sure you may be that you've found the best horse in a race, the simple truth is that, until you've considered the possibility of a draw bias, you won't be able to assess the chances of any runner with any accuracy.

It's fundamental. On some courses, a particular draw is almost impossible to overcome, while on others there are draws that confer a tremendous advantage – if you don't know which is which, you'd be as well finding your winners with a pin.

What follows is my outline of the factors you need to consider when betting at Britain's many Flat tracks. During the turf season, I'll be updating these thoughts every week in *Racing & Football Outlook*. I'll also be pointing out horses that have run well from poor draws, so you can back them next time out and turn these biases into profit.

COURSE BY COURSE: your guide to Britain's draw biases

ASCOT (right-handed)

Last year saw some pretty major biases appear (most notably at September's Festival Of Racing meeting, when runners were switching right over to the far side) but things were never consistent, with a lot down to watering.

Low numbers had appeared to hold the advantage during the first couple of days of the Royal meeting, but only once in the last ten years has the stands' rail ridden genuinely faster at this fixture; otherwise, those drawn very high in big fields have at least held their own.

That again proved the case later in the week, with Ratio (22 of 29) dead-heating in the Wokingham after wins for Attache (30 of 27) and New Seeker (27 of 29).

Over longer trips, runners tend to head wide down the side of the course on soft ground.

Stalls: almost always on the stands' side (low)

Biases: The far side (high) always rides quicker on soft or heavy ground. High numbers have an excellent record in the 2m4f Ascot Stakes.

Splits: Runners usually converge towards the stands' side, except in fields of 22+ or under exceptional circumstances (soft ground or when the far side is riding quicker).

AYR (left-handed)

As a rule, the draw only becomes a major issue in sprints at September's Western Meeting, with fields rarely big enough during the rest of the season for groups to form (high is almost always best in fields of 25 or fewer).

There was a turnaround in the Silver and Gold Cups last season, with the far side (low) coming out on top in both races. High numbers had dominated for many years.

This reverse was almost certainly down to a fresh (hardly watered) strip of ground down the far side – it will be interesting to see whether the management take the same approach this season.

The general view is that low numbers are best in big fields over 7f50y and 1m, but this rarely pans out, with fields often in single figures.

Stalls: Usually up the stands' side (high) in sprints, but occasionally on the other side (normally in the run-up to the Western Meeting, to preserve stands' side ground).

Biases: High numbers are usually best in sprints whatever the ground, apart from the odd occasion when the stalls are placed up the far side (low). A watching brief is advised on the Silver and Gold Cups this year.

Splits: Fields only usually split in the Silver and Gold Cups.

BATH (left)

The draw is basically of far less importance than the pace at which races are run.

In big fields, runners drawn low are often inclined to go off too fast to hold a rail position (the course turns left most of the way, including one major kink) and this can see hold-up horses drawn wide coming through late.

Conversely, in smaller fields containing little pace, up front and on the inside is often the place to be.

Stalls: Always go on the inside (low).

Splits: Fields usually stick together but soft ground (very rare) can see a split, with the outside rail (high) favoured.

BEVERLEY (right)

A high draw is essential on good to soft or faster ground over 5f and also on the round course, particularly in races of 7f100y and 1m100y.

In sprints, runners have to negotiate a right-handed jink not long after the start and it seems harder here than at any other course for runners drawn low to get over to the favoured rail (there's also a camber).

When conditions are genuinely testing, though, there's a strip of ground by the stands' rail that rides significantly quicker than the rest of the course, and under such conditions those drawn very low hold a decisive advantage.

The course management experimented with moving the stalls to the stands' side over 5f in 2002 (unsuccessfully, as it led to a huge low bias) and had planned to do so again last year, but were forced to abort after being unable to provide a level playing field (apparently the rail strip has become compressed thanks to the ambulance).

They will try it again this summer, but only in small fields. Major work is going to be carried out next winter in a bid to level the course out once and for all.

Stalls: On the inside (high) at all distances, but will be tried stands' side again over 5f at some point this summer.

Biases: High numbers are massively favoured at 5f on good to soft or faster ground, but very low draws take over on soft or heavy (hold-up horses are usually best avoided whatever the going). High numbers are also best on the round course.

Splits: Very rare, and only likely over 5f on soft ground.

BRIGHTON (left)

Much depends on the going and time of year.

On good to soft or slower ground, runners often head for the outside rail (high), while in late season it's often just a case of whichever jockey finds the least cut-up strip of ground.

Otherwise, low-drawn prominent-racers tend to hold sway in fast-ground sprints, with double-figures always facing an uphill task over 5f59y.

Stalls: Always on the inside (low) in sprints.

Splits: Occur frequently in the second half of the season, as jockeys look for a fresh strip on ground that churns up easily. George Duffield often takes an exploratory route.

CARLISLE (right)

For the past couple of seasons, runners racing with the pace and hardest against the inside rail (high) have done well in big fields early in the campaign.

This is entirely down to the fact that the Flat course and jumps course are one and the same, and that those racing nearest the fence are running where the hurdle wings were positioned, while those wider out are on the raced-on, carved-up surface.

Things have tended to level out as the year has progressed, though. On soft ground, the bias swings completely, favouring at all distances those runners racing widest (low) and grabbing the stands' rail in the straight.

Stalls: Normally on the inside (high) but can be down the middle in sprints (usually on slow ground).

Biases: High numbers are best in early-season sprints as long as the ground is no slower than good. Look to back low numbers on soft or heavy ground, although such going isn't often seen here, thanks to the course not racing after early September.

Splits: Rarely will two groups form in the straight but runners often spread out on easy ground.

CATTERICK (left)

When the ground is testing, the stands' rail is definitely the place to be, which suits high numbers in 5f races, and high-drawn prominent-racers at all other distances.

However, when the ground is good to firm or faster, horses drawn on the inside (low) often hold the edge, and there were several meetings last season when those racing prominently and hardest against the inside rail were able to dominate (over all trips, presumably as a result of watering).

Stalls: On the inside (low) at all distances these days (they often used to go on the outer over 5f212y).

Biases: Low numbers are best in sprints on fast ground (particularly watered firm going), but the stands' rail (high) rides faster under slower conditions.

Splits: Fields have usually stuck together in fast-ground 5f races in the past, but splits could become more common this term on genuine good ground.

CHEPSTOW (left)

High numbers enjoyed a massive advantage in straight-course races during 2000 and the course management duly took steps to eradicate the faster strip, using the same 'earthquake machine' as had been employed at Goodwood.

The bias then disappeared for the next two years, but it was back with a vengeance last term (it's presumably caused by compaction). Last year, the 18 straight-course races with 14 runners or more were won by horses drawn: 12/15, 17/19, 10/16, 12/20, 9/19, 16/17, 17/20, 16/20, 13/15, 8/15, 17/18, 16/16, 5/20 (far side), 13/18, 5/19 (far side), 16/16, 17/19 and 15/15.

Interestingly, the two winners who managed to score up the far side both contested 7f races (interesting because some believe the bias increases the longer the trip).

There were also numerous smaller-field winners who won thanks to grabbing the stands' rail in front, Material Witness and Benbaun being two that spring to mind.

Stalls: Always stands' side (high) on the straight course.

Biases: High numbers are massively favoured on the straight course (up to 1m14y) whatever the ground, and the good news with a view to this season is that the bias only increased as last year progressed.

Splits: Jockeys on low-drawn runners sussed out last year that they had more chance going to the far side than staying off the fence near side, so splits are again likely to be common in big-field straight-course races.

CHESTER (left)

It's well known that low numbers are favoured at all distances here, even in the 2m2f Chester Cup, and the bias is factored into the prices these days. That said, sprints (especially sprint handicaps) are still playable, with six of the eight events featuring ten runners or more being won by stalls 1, 2, 3 or 4 last year.

Stalls: On the inside (low) at all distances bar 1m2f75y and 2m2f117y (same starting point), when they go on the outside. Certain starters ask for the stalls to come off the inside rail slightly in sprints.

Biases: Low numbers are favoured at all distances. Soft ground seems to accentuate the bias until a few races have been staged, when a higher draw becomes less of a disadvantage as the ground on the inside becomes chewed up.

DONCASTER (left)

Draw biases here are usually as reliable as they come.

High numbers dominate in sprints, low numbers take over on the straight mile (as long as there are enough runners for a split) and either rail has the advantage over the middle at 7f.

Going into last September, the results from the previous two and a half seasons were spectacular, with 17 of the 25 sprints featuring 16 runners or more having been won by a horse in the top six stalls, and stall 1 having landed six of the 12 races run over the straight mile. **Stalls**: Always stands' side (high) on the straight course. **Biases**: High numbers are best in sprints, very high and very low numbers are favoured over 7f, while very low draws are best over the straight mile (as long as they're taken to the far side). The softer the ground becomes, the greater the biases.

Splits: Fields tend to stick together in sprints, apart from in fields of 20+, but it's not uncommon for a few to go far side at 7f and 1m.

EPSOM (left)

When the going is on the soft side, jockeys tack over to the stands' side for the better ground (this strip rides quicker in such conditions, as the course cambers away from the stands' rail towards the far side).

In 5f races, the stalls are invariably placed on the stands' side, so when the going is soft the majority of the runners are on the best ground from the outset. High numbers used to hold quite an advantage at this trip, regardless of the going, but the bias is not so great these days.

Prominent racers drawn low in round-course races are able to take the shortest route and on faster ground have a decisive edge over 6f, 7f and 1m114y.
Stalls: Always on the outside (high) over 5f and 6f (races over the latter trip start on a chute) and inside (low) at other distances, bar 1m4f10y (centre).
Biases: Low-drawn prominent-racers are favoured from 6f to 1m114y.
Splits: Good to soft ground often leads to a few trying the stands' side route.

FOLKESTONE (right)

The draw is often crucial on the straight course (up to 7f). Whatever the ground, the far rail (high) rides faster than the stands' rail, which in turn rides quicker than the middle of the track.

Last season, runners invariably went across to the far side over 6f and 7f (jockeyship often played a part, with several races going to whichever horse had secured the front up the rail, including Richard Hughes more than once).

However, over 5f, when the stalls were up the stands' rail, fields often split, with low numbers just about holding sway (it seems the ground lost by switching across over the minimum trip can't be regained from racing on the faster ground). Slow ground swings things even more in favour of high numbers.
Stalls: Usually go up the stands' side (low) on the straight track, but occasionally down the centre.
Biases: High numbers are favoured over 6f and 7f, and also over the minimum trip when 14 or more line up. However, very low numbers have a good record in smaller fields over 5f. Front-runners are well worth considering at all distances.
Splits: Fields only tend to divide over 5f these days.

GOODWOOD (right and left)

The course management took steps to end the major high bias seen in the Stewards' Cup throughout the late nineties by breaking up the ground with an 'earthquake machine' in 1998.

However, the inside strip has since become compressed again and the bias has returned with a vengeance (the first one home up the stands' side last year, the progressive Frizzante, was beaten around 4l).

All other sprints also tend to develop away from the stands' rail now, apart from on soft or heavy going (when low numbers continue to enjoy the edge), so it usually pays to concentrate on the top half of the draw in fields of 12+.

High numbers are favoured on the round course, particularly from 7f to 1m1f, except on good to soft or slower ground, when jockeys tend to tack over centre to stands' side in the straight.
Stalls: Invariably go on the stands' side (low).
Biases: High numbers are best from 7f to 1m1f, and the faster ground the more pronounced the bias (keep an eye out for the rail on the home turn being moved during Glorious week). High numbers are best in sprints of 12 runners or more, apart from on soft ground, when low draws take over.
Splits: Although fields tend not to break into groups in most sprints, runners often spread out to about two-thirds of the way across in fields of around 20.

HAMILTON (right)

Extensive drainage work was carried out in the winter of 2002 in a bid to level up the two sides of the track but, after encouraging early results, the natural bias in favour of high numbers (far side) kicked in again, particularly after the first soft-ground fixture.

Basically the course is stuck with this bias, which can only be altered by watering on faster going (be careful after a dry spell, as things can often swing in favour of low numbers). High numbers are also best over 1m65y, thanks to runners encountering a tight right-handed loop soon after the start.
Stalls: It's not uncommon for the ground to become too soft for the use of stalls, but otherwise they usually go on the stands' side (low).
Biases: High draws are best in soft or heavy-ground sprints, but the bias becomes middle to high otherwise (often switching to low on watered fast ground). Despite the stiffness of the course, front-runners do well at all distances.
Splits: High numbers will peel off in fields of 8+ when the stalls are stands' side, unless the ground is very fast.

HAYDOCK (left)

High numbers used to enjoy a major advantage in soft-ground sprints, but that seems to have been turned full circle by drainage work, with the far side (low) now best on very bad ground.

Otherwise, runners usually head for the centre these days, the draw rarely making much of a difference.
Stalls: Usually centre in the straight.

KEMPTON (right)

This has become one of the most complicated bias courses, with four factors to consider in every sprint: ground, watering, field size and stall positioning.

In midsummer, when fast ground and small fields usually prevail, the stalls are generally put down the centre and jockeys tend to stay there in one group.

However, when 10-16 line up, runners often split if the stalls are down the middle (no guaranteed bias), while they usually stick to either rail if the stalls are stands' side (low) or far side (high). When they stick to either rail, runners closest to that rail are favoured.

In fields of 17 to 20 runners (the course can take 24 but no more than 20 are allowed to run under new BHB rules), it's not uncommon for fields to split wherever the stalls are positioned, and much then comes down to watering. The judgement call continues to be low (definitely on soft ground), but the far side (high) has been known to dominate, particularly in early season.

High-drawn prominent-racers had an excellent record over 7f and 1m (Jubilee and round courses) last year.

Stalls: Can go anywhere, often down the centre in mid-summer.

Splits: Splits are common in sprints of ten runners or more.

LEICESTER (right)

There was a four-year spell between 1998 and 2001 when the centre-to-far-side strip (middle to high) enjoyed a decisive advantage over the stands' rail, jockeys eventually choosing to avoid the near side.

That changed last season, however, with very low numbers more than holding their own. Expect more of the same this year, and for the stands' rail to ride considerably quicker on slower ground.

Stalls: Invariably up the stands' side (low).

Splits: Given the switch in bias, fields are more likely to stick together in one group this year, although it's always worth looking for a 'draw jockey' drawn high in big fields.

LINGFIELD (left)
Turf

The draw advantage is nothing like as defined as in years past. In the first half of last year, the middle of the track (low) held its own with the stands' rail, and then completely took over around July, when high numbers may as well have stayed home. From the middle of August, though, that changed, with the stands' rail becoming dominant.

The one factor that can have a big effect on the draw is heavy rainfall onto firm ground. Presumably because of the undulating nature of the track (and the fact that the far rail on the straight course is towards the bottom of a slope where it joins the round course), rainfall seems to make the middle and far side ride a deal slower.

In these conditions, the top three or four stalls have a massive edge.

Stalls: Up the stands' side (high) from 5f to 7f, down the middle over 7f140y.

Biases: High numbers are massively favoured on fast ground after recent rain, but otherwise the most recent meeting is usually the best guide.

Splits: It's unusual to see two distinct groups, but runners often fan out centre-to-stands-side in big fields.

All-Weather

There's not much in the draw at longer distances but there certainly is over 5f, with stalls 1 to 5 enjoying a major advantage over boxes 6 to 10.

It's also best to be low-to-middle in 6f races and over 1m2f, where those drawn wider than 7 tend to struggle. That said, being drawn next to the inside rail can also be a disadvantage, with stalls 1 and 2 not performing well (boxes 3 to 7 are favoured).

MUSSELBURGH (right)

The bias in favour of low numbers at 5f looked greater than ever last season, even on fast ground.

That said, nobody tried going right to the far side from a very high draw (a tactic that had proved successful the previous summer), with most edging towards the main pack centre-to-stands-side.

The bias in favour of high numbers at 7f and 1m isn't as major as many believe.

Stalls: Usually up the stands' side (low) over 5f nowadays.

Splits: Look out for runners drawn very high in big-field 5f races on fast ground, as they occasionally go right to the far rail.

NEWBURY (left)

Prior to last season, it's hard to remember a race in which the far side (low) had come out on top in a straight-course race where the field had split. That changed in July's Weatherbys Super Sprint, with If Paradise ending the high-number dominance by scoring from the 1 box.

Ultimately, there's probably little between the two flanks these days, apart from on soft ground, in which case the stands' rail (high) is definitely the place to be.

When the ground is testing it's not uncommon to see runners race wide down the back straight and down the side at between 1m3f56y and 2m (particularly over 1m5f61y). In such circumstances, a high draw becomes a huge advantage.

Stalls: Can go anywhere for straight-course races.

Splits: Fields are not often big enough for a split.

NEWCASTLE (left)

On the straight course, it used to be a case of high numbers best on good or firmer, and low numbers having an advantage when the ground rode good to soft or softer.

That changed in 2001, when the far side proved best whatever the going, and again last year, when there was rarely much between the two sides on fast going.

There were four occasions last year when less than half a length separated the flanks; the races won by Karminskey Park (22/5), Strensall (26/7), Caribbean Coral (1/10) and If By Chance (22/10).

The far side (low) still rides considerably quicker on slow ground, though. Over the straight mile, the stands' rail (high) is the place to be, apart from on bad ground.

Stalls: Invariably on the stands' side (high), only being switched to the inside under exceptional circumstances.

Biases: Low numbers are best at up to 7f on good to soft or slower ground, but there's rarely much between the two sides on faster going. Very high numbers are best over the straight mile, apart from on very testing ground.

Splits: Two groups are usually formed when 14+ go to

248

post. The majority tend to go far side in sprints, but most stick stands' side over the straight mile.

NEWMARKET (right)
July Course

The major draw biases seen under former Clerks Of The Course have become a thing of the past since Michael Prosser took over, and now only the occasional meeting is affected. The course is permanently divided into two halves by a rail (the *Racing Post* now carry information regarding which side is to be used). As a rule of thumb, the two outside rails (stands' rail when they're on the stands' side half, far rail when they're on the far-side half) ride faster than the dividing rail.

Stands' side half: on fast ground (particularly watered), very high numbers are often favoured at up to 1m, when there's a narrow strip hard against the fence that rides quicker. However, on good to soft or slower ground, runners racing down the centre are favoured.

Far-side half: there's rarely much in the draw, except on slow ground, when the far side (low) rides much faster.

Stalls: Can go either side on either half of the track.

Splits: Runners just about form two groups in capacity fields, but are more likely to run to their draw here than at tracks such as Newcastle.

Rowley Mile

As with the July Course, the draw seems to have been evened out since Prosser took over. Occasionally a bias will appear, but they're hard to predict these days.

Stalls: Can go anywhere.

Biases: High numbers have dominated the 2m2f Cesarewitch in recent years, both the last two winners having come from 36 of 36. The logic here is that those on the inside can be switched off early, while low numbers have to work to get into position before the only right-handed turn.

Splits: It's not unusual for jockeys to come stands' side on slow ground in round-course races.

NOTTINGHAM (left)

On the straight course, it used to be a case of low numbers being favoured when the stalls were on the far rail and high numbers when they were stands' side, with low being best when the stalls spanned the entire course.

These days, though, it's less clear-cut and the feeling at the end of last season was that there's ultimately little between the two sides.

As in the previous year, the occasional meeting showed an advantage in favour of one side or the other, but even after the inside rail had been pulled in to unveil fresh ground in the autumn, there still wasn't much between the flanks. The bias in favour of low numbers at 1m54y is only slight.

Stalls: Tend to go on the stands' side (high) unless the ground is very soft.

Splits: Fields usually split in sprints when 14 or more start.

PONTEFRACT (left)

Low numbers have always been considered best here, but this is definitely not true. If anything, high numbers now have the edge in sprints, and massively so on soft or heavy.

Drainage work was carried out in the late nineties to try to eradicate the outside-rail bias on slow ground, and this worked immediately afterwards, but last season there

were definite signs that it's now riding much faster (doubters need only look back at L Dettori's riding of Rules For Jokers from stall 18 at the meeting on 6 October).

Of the nine sprint handicaps featuring 16 runners or more, six went to a runner drawn 15 or higher, including four from the 18 box – there's no way that's a fluke.

Stalls: On the inside (low) unless the ground is very soft, when they're switched to the outside rail.

Biases: Very high numbers did particularly well in big-field sprints last season and there's definite evidence that the outside rail now offers the advantage on any ground bar fast (runners sticking to the inner on soft or heavy may be worse off by as much as 20 lengths).

Splits: Although it's uncommon to see distinct groups, high numbers usually race wide these days on good to soft or slower ground. It's possible some will try going right to the outside rail this year.

REDCAR (left)

It's not unusual to see big fields throughout the season here, but the draw rarely plays a part, with runners inclined to converge towards the centre.

That said, there were a couple of breakaways last year who nearly carried the day, not least Local Poet, who finished second in the big sales race from stall 1 (raced with one other far side).

Stalls: Towards the stands' side (high).

Splits: Splits are unusual and of little consequence.

RIPON (right)

The draw is often the sole deciding factor in big-field sprints, but last year the picture became rather more clouded, presumably because of watering.

In the nine handicap sprints in which fields split, the far side only came out on top once, when Hidden Dragon won the Great St Wilfrid from 23 of 23 (all other winners coming from single figures) but there was a definite spell of far-rail (high) domination in midsummer.

Similarly, there was a period earlier in the season when the stands' rail enjoyed a massive advantage, highlighted by The Wizard Mul's race in late May, a race in which the near side was responsible for the first five home.

The best guide here these days, by some distance, is the most recent meeting.

Stalls: On the stands' side (low) except under exceptional circumstances.

Biases: Low numbers are best in sprints of 12 runners or fewer, but things can change in big fields. Front-runners (particularly from high draws over 1m) enjoyed a tremendous time of things on the round course last term, and any horse trying to make ground from behind and wide is always facing a tough task.

Splits: Fields tend to stay together in races of 12 or fewer, but a split is almost guaranteed when 15 or more line up. Look for 'draw' jockeys who might chance going far-side in fields of 13 or 14.

SALISBURY (right)

It's difficult to win from a single-figure draw in big-field fast-ground sprints, and also over 7f, but proven stamina and race suitability become the most important factors over the testing straight mile.

The far-side bias is at its greatest early and late season, before and after the erection of a temporary rail in July. The draw swings full circle on slower ground, as jockeys then invariably head towards the stands' rail.

Stalls: On the far side (high) unless the ground is soft, when they're often moved to the near side.

Biases: High numbers are best on the straight course on fast ground. There's not much in it on good to soft, while low draws take over on soft or heavy.

Splits: Fields only tend to divide on good to soft; otherwise they converge on either rail, depending on the going.

SANDOWN (right)

On the 5f chute, when the going is on the soft side and the stalls are on the far side (high), high numbers enjoy a decisive advantage. On the rare occasions that the stalls are placed on the stands' side, low numbers enjoy a slight advantage when all the runners stay towards the stands' rail, but when a few break off and go to the far side high numbers comfortably hold the upper hand again.

High numbers enjoy a decent advantage in double-figure fields over 7f and 1m on good going or faster, but jockeys invariably head for the stands' side on slow ground.

Stalls: Usually far side (high) over 5f, as the course is more level that side.

Splits: It's unusual for runners to split over 5f, with capacity fields rare and jockeys inclined to head far-side.

SOUTHWELL (right, All-Weather)

During last year, the bias over 5f seemed to swing back towards the stands' side (high) following a couple of years of far-side domination.

It's best to be drawn low over 6f, due to the start's proximity to the first bend, but over 7f and beyond it's generally preferable to be drawn middle-to-high, especially over those distances with a long run to the first bend.

THIRSK (left)

Sadly, biases here aren't as predictable as they were. Field sizes, watering and going always have to be taken into account in fields of 12 or more (if there are 11 runners or fewer, then it's unusual to see anything except one group on the stands' rail, with high numbers best).

Otherwise, low numbers are almost always favoured on good or softer ground, while either rail can enjoy the edge on watered fast ground. The one place not to be under any circumstances is down the middle.

Front-runners had a great time on fast ground on the round course last year, and low-drawn prominent-racers are well worth considering whatever the distance.

Stalls: Always up the stands' side (high).

Biases: High numbers are best in sprints when 11 or fewer line up, but it's hard to know which side is likely to do best in bigger fields on fast ground. The far (inside) rail is always best on good or slower going.

Splits: Runners invariably stay towards the stands' side in sprints of 12 or fewer runners (unless the ground is soft) and frequently when 13 or 14 line up. Any more and it becomes long odds-on that you'll see two groups.

WARWICK (left)

Low numbers are favoured in fast-ground sprints, but not

by as much as many believe. However, when the ground is genuinely soft, high numbers can enjoy a major advantage, as the outside rail then rides much faster.

Stalls: Always on the inside (low).

WINDSOR (figure of eight)

It's typical to see large fields all season, and the draw almost always plays a part. In sprints, high numbers are best on good or faster going (particularly watered fast ground). There's not much between the two sides on good to soft, while the far side (low) takes over on soft or heavy ground.

In longer races, high-drawn prominent-racers enjoyed a whale of a time on fast ground last year, and it again looked difficult for runners who were switched away from the stands' rail to make up the leeway. On slower ground, jockeys head centre-to-far side, and right over to the far rail on genuine soft or heavy (again, it's difficult to make ground from behind under such conditions).

Stalls: Can be positioned anywhere for sprints.

Biases: High-drawn prominent-racers are favoured in fast-ground sprints, and also over 1m67y. On good to soft going, there's rarely much between the two sides, but on bad ground it's a case of nearer to the far rail (low) the better.

Splits: Splits only tend to occur on good to soft ground, and even then it's rare to see two defined groups.

WOLVERHAMPTON (left, All-Weather)

At most meetings, the ground against the inside rail rides much deeper than the rest of the track, the exception being after very wet or very cold weather, when the track is usually deep-harrowed.

The bias is at its strongest over 5f, with stalls 1 and 2 having a poor record, although over 7f100y and 1m100y it's also a disadvantage to be drawn on the extreme outside, as both starts are very close to the first bend.

YARMOUTH (left)

High numbers enjoyed a major advantage for much of the nineties, but this was brought to an end when the course switched their watering system from pop-up sprinklers (affected by the off-shore breeze) to a Briggs Boom in 1999.

These days, a bias will appear occasionally – the far side (low) rode way faster in the summer of 2002 – but it's hard to predict, and runners often head for the centre whatever the going.

Stalls: One side or the other.

Splits: It's common to see groups form, often including one down the centre, in big fields.

YORK (left)

On good or faster ground, the fastest strip is centre-to-far side, somewhere between stalls 6 and 12, while those drawn low are favoured in fields of 12 to 14 runners.

On soft or heavy, the stands' side (high) becomes the place to be, and high numbers often get the rail to themselves, as this is not a bias well known among jockeys.

Low numbers are best on fast ground on the round course, although watering can reduce the bias.

Stalls: Can go anywhere.

Biases: Prominent-racers drawn down the centre are favoured in fast-ground sprints, but high numbers take over on genuine soft or heavy ground.

250

Win - free form!

THIS YEAR'S QUIZ could hardly be more simple, and the prize should prove invaluable to our lucky winner. We're offering a free subscription to Raceform, the BHB's official form book – every week from May to November, you could be getting the previous week's results in full, together with note-book comments highlighting future winners, adjusted Official Ratings and Raceform's *Performance* ratings. The winner will also get a copy of last year's complete form book.

All you have to do is this: study the picture below, which shows the finish to a Group 1 race last season. Then, decide the order in which you think these four horses finished – write their finishing positions next to their letters.

Send your answers along with your details on the entry form below, to:

**2004 Flat Annual Competition, Racing & Football Outlook,
Floor 23, 1 Canada Square, London, E14 5AP.**

Entries must reach us no later than first post on Monday April 26. The winner's name and the right answers will be printed in the RFO's 4 May edition. Six runners-up will each receive a copy of last year's form book.

Finishing positions:

A ☐ **B** ☐ **C** ☐ **D** ☐

Name

Address

Town

Postcode

In the event of more than one correct entry, the winner will be drawn at random from the correct entries. The Editor's decision is final and no correspondence will be entered into.

BETTING CHART

ON	ODDS	AGAINST
50	Evens	50
52.4	11-10	47.6
54.5	6-5	45.5
55.6	5-4	44.4
58	11-8	42
60	6-4	40
62	13-8	38
63.6	7-4	36.4
65.3	15-8	34.7
66.7	2-1	33.3
68	85-40	32
69.2	9-4	30.8
71.4	5-2	28.6
73.4	11-4	26.6
75	3-1	25
76.9	100-30	23.1
77.8	7-2	22.2
80	4-1	20
82	9-2	18
83.3	5-1	16.7
84.6	11-2	15.4
85.7	6-1	14.3
86.7	13-2	13.3
87.5	7-1	12.5
88.2	15-2	11.8
89	8-1	11
89.35	100-12	10.65
89.4	17-2	10.6
90	9-1	10
91	10-1	9
91.8	11-1	8.2
92.6	12-1	7.4
93.5	14-1	6.5
94.4	16-1	5.6
94.7	18-1	5.3
95.2	20-1	4.8
95.7	22-1	4.3
96.2	25-1	3.8
97.2	33-1	2.8
97.6	40-1	2.4
98.1	50-1	1.9
98.5	66-1	1.3
99.0	100-1	0.99

The table above (often known as the 'Field Money Table') shows both bookmakers' margins and how much a backer needs to invest to win £100. To calculate a bookmaker's margin, simply add up the percentages of all the odds on offer. The sum by which the total exceeds 100% gives the 'over-round' on the book. To determine what stake is required to win £100 (includes returned stake) at a particular price, just look at the relevant row, either odds-against or odds-on.

Sponsored by Stan James

RULE 4 DEDUCTIONS

When a horse is withdrawn before coming under starter's orders, but after a market has been formed, bookmakers are entitled to make the following deductions from win and place returns (excluding stakes) in accordance with Tattersalls' Rule 4(c).

Odds of withdrawn horse	Deduction from winnings
(1) ....3-10 or shorter	....75p in the £
(2) ....2-5 to 1-3	....70p in the £
(3) ....8-15 to 4-9	....65p in the £
(4) ....8-13 to 4-7	....60p in the £
(5) ....4-5 to 4-6	....55p in the £
(6) ....20-21 to 5-6	....50p in the £
(7) ....Evens to 6-5	....45p in the £
(8) ....5-4 to 6-4	....40p in the £
(9) ....13-8 to 7-4	....35p in the £
(10) ....15-8 to 9-4	....30p in the £
(11) ....5-2 to 3-1	....25p in the £
(12) ....100-30 to 4-1	....20p in the £
(13) ....9-2 to 11-2	....15p in the £
(14) ....6-1 to 9-1	....10p in the £
(15) ....10-1 to 14-1	....5p in the £
(16) ....longer than 14-1	....no deductions

(17) ....When more than one horse is withdrawn without coming under starter's orders, total deductions shall not exceed 75p in the £.

Starting-price bets are affected only when there was insufficient time to form a new market.

Feedback!

If you have any comments or criticism about this book, or suggestions for future editions, please tell us.

Write
Chris Cook,
2004 Racing Guide,
Racing & Football Outlook,
Floor 23,
1 Canada Square,
London E14 5AP

email
c.cook@mgn.co.uk

Fax
FAO Chris Cook, 0207 510 6457

Horse index

All horses discussed, with page numbers, except for references in the Group 1 and two-year-old form sections (page 80), which have their own indeces.